Co-Production and Co-Creation

Co-production and co-creation occur when citizens participate actively in delivering and designing the services they receive. It has come increasingly onto the agenda of policymakers, as interest in citizen participation has more generally soared. Expectations are high and it is regarded as a possible solution to the public sector's decreased legitimacy and dwindling resources, by accessing more of society's capacities. In addition, it is seen as part of a more general drive to reinvigorate voluntary participation and strengthen social cohesion in an increasingly fragmented and individualized society.

Co-Production and Co-Creation: Engaging Citizens in Public Services offers a systematic and comprehensive theoretical and empirical examination of the concepts of co-production and co-creation and their application in practice. It shows the latest state of knowledge on the topic and will be of interest to students at an advanced level, academics and reflective practitioners. It addresses the topics with regard to co-production and co-creation and will be of interest to researchers, academics, policymakers, and students in the fields of public administration, business administration, economics, political science, public management, political science, service management, sociology and voluntary sector studies.

Taco Brandsen is Professor of Comparative Public Administration at Radboud University, The Netherlands; secretary-general of the European Association for Public Administration Accreditation (EAPAA); co-chair of the EGPA Permanent Study Group on 'Civil Society, Citizens and Government'; and editor-in-chief of the journal *Voluntas*.

Trui Steen is Professor of Public Governance and Co-production of Public Services at KU Leuven Public Governance Institute, Belgium. She is co-chair of the IIAS Study Group on 'Co-production of Public Services'.

Bram Verschuere is Associate Professor in Public Management, Faculty of Economics and Business Administration, Ghent University, Belgium. He is co-chair of the EGPA Permanent Study Group on 'Civil Society, Citizens and Government'.

Routledge Critical Studies in Public Management
Edited by Stephen Osborne

The study and practice of public management has undergone profound changes across the world. Over the last quarter century, we have seen

- increasing criticism of public administration as the over-arching framework for the provision of public services,
- the rise (and critical appraisal) of the 'New Public Management' as an emergent paradigm for the provision of public services,
- the transformation of the 'public sector' into the cross-sectoral provision of public services, and
- the growth of the governance of inter-organizational relationships as an essential element in the provision of public services.

In reality these trends have not so much replaced each other as elided or co-existed together—the public policy process has not gone away as a legitimate topic of study, intra-organizational management continues to be essential to the efficient provision of public services, whilst the governance of inter-organizational and inter-sectoral relationships is now essential to the effective provision of these services.

Further, whilst the study of public management has been enriched by contribution of a range of insights from the 'mainstream' management literature, it has also contributed to this literature in such areas as networks and inter-organizational collaboration, innovation and stakeholder theory.

This series is dedicated to presenting and critiquing this important body of theory and empirical study. It will publish books that both explore and evaluate the emergent and developing nature of public administration, management and governance (in theory and practice) and examine the relationship with and contribution to the over-arching disciplines of management and organizational sociology.

Books in the series will be of interest to academics and researchers in this field, students undertaking advanced studies of it as part of their undergraduate or post-graduate degree and reflective policy makers and practitioners.

Co-Production and Co-Creation
Engaging Citizens in Public Services
Edited by Taco Brandsen, Trui Steen and Bram Verschuere

For a full list of titles in this series, please visit www.routledge.com

Co-Production and Co-Creation

Engaging Citizens in Public Services

Edited by Taco Brandsen,
Trui Steen and Bram Verschuere

Routledge
Taylor & Francis Group

LONDON AND NEW YORK

First published 2018 by Routledge

2 Park Square, Milton Park, Abingdon, Oxon, OX14 4RN

605 Third Avenue, New York, NY 10017

Routledge is an imprint of the Taylor & Francis Group, an informa business

First issued in paperback 2020

Library of Congress Cataloging-in-Publication Data
Names: Brandsen, Taco, editor. | Steen, Trui, editor. | Verschuere, Bram, 1977– editor.
Title: Co-production and co-creation : engaging citizens in public services / edited by Taco Brandsen, Trui Steen and Bram Verschuere.
Description: New York, NY : Routledge, 2018.
Identifiers: LCCN 2017059608 | ISBN 9781138700116 (hardback) | ISBN 9781351792578 (web pdf) | ISBN 9781351792561 (epub) | ISBN 9781351792554 (mobipocket)
Subjects: LCSH: Public administration—Citizen participation. | Political planning—Citizen participation. | Public administration—Public relations.
Classification: LCC JF1525.P6 C625 2018 | DDC 352.6/5—dc23
LC record available at https://lccn.loc.gov/2017059608

ISBN: 978-1-138-70011-6 (hbk)
ISBN: 978-0-367-73501-2 (pbk)

Typeset in Sabon
by Apex CoVantage, LLC

Contents

Figures and Tables

Contributors

John Alford is Professor of Public Sector Management at the Melbourne Business School in the University of Melbourne, and at the Australia and New Zealand School of Government.

Giuseppe Aquino collaborates with the Department of Economics, Management and Quantitative Methods, University of Milan (Italy) as an external expert.

Lehn M. Benjamin, Ph.D., is an associate professor at Indiana University's Lilly School of Philanthropy and the School of Public and Environmental Affairs.

Elena Bondarouk is Assistant Professor at the Institute of Public Administration, Leiden University.

Tony Bovaird is Emeritus Professor of Public Management and Policy at the University of Birmingham, UK, and a Director of Governance International.

Taco Brandsen is Professor of Comparative Public Administration at Radboud University, Nijmegen, The Netherlands.

Dr. Dirk Brand is an Extraordinary Senior Lecturer at the School of Public Leadership, Stellenbosch University, Bellville, South Africa.

Jeffrey L. Brudney, Ph.D., is the Betty and Dan Cameron Family Distinguished Professor of Innovation in the Nonprofit Sector, at the University of North Carolina Wilmington, in Wilmington, North Carolina, USA.

Michiel S. de Vries is a Professor of Public Administration at Radboud University, Nijmegen, Netherlands.

Johan A. M. de Kruijf is an Assistant Professor of Public Administration at Radboud University, Nijmegen, Netherlands.

Joost Fledderus, Ph.D., is an advisor at the department of Research and Statistics, municipality of Arnhem, the Netherlands.

Louise Freijser is a Ph.D. student in the Centre for Health Policy, University of Melbourne. Her research concentrates on co-production in health services.

Dr. András Gábor is an associate professor in the Department of Information Systems at the Corvinus University of Budapest and research director of Corvinno Technology Transfer Center.

Mila Gascó is the Associate Research Director of the Center of Technology in Government as well as a Research Associate Professor at the Rockefeller College of Public Affairs and Policy, both at the University at Albany–SUNY, USA.

Barbara Gausz is a consultant in Corvinno, Budapest.

JaiNiecya Harper is a recent Masters of Public Administration graduate from the University of Georgia.

Marlies Honingh is Assistant Professor at the Department of Public Administration, Radboud University, Nijmegen, The Netherlands.

Yassaman Imani is a principal lecturer at Herefordshire Business School and leads the Researcher Development Programme.

Sylke Jaspers is a Ph.D. Fellow at KU Leuven, Public Governance Institute, Leuven, Belgium.

Suyeon Jo is a doctoral candidate in public administration at the Syracuse University Maxwell School of Citizenship and Public Affairs.

Dr. Somya Joshi is a Senior Lecturer at eGovlab, Stockholm University.

Vasilis Koulolias is the Director at eGovlab, Stockholm University and advisor to the World Economic Forum.

Veiko Lember is Marie Skłodowska-Curie Research Fellow at KU Leuven, Belgium and Senior Research Fellow at Tallinn University of Technology, Estonia.

Elke Loeffler is Chief Executive of Governance International and Associate of the University of Birmingham, UK.

Mary S. Mangai is a Doctoral Researcher at the Department of Public Administration, Radboud University, Nijmegen, Netherlands.

Ntuthuko Mchunu is an Extraordinary Lecturer at Stellenbosch University, Cape Town, South Africa.

Caitlin McMullin is a Ph.D. Researcher in the Institute of Local Government Studies at the University of Birmingham.

Hannelore Mees is a researcher in Social Sciences at Antwerp University, Antwerp, Belgium.

Taina Meriluoto is a Doctoral Candidate in Political Science at the University of Jyväskylä, Finland.

Francisco Garcia Moran is Former Director General of IT at European Commission and EU Fellow at UC Berkeley.

Luisa Moretto is Professor at the Faculty of Architecture of the Université libre de Bruxelles (Belgium).

Tina Nabatchi is an Associate Professor of Public Administration and International Affairs at the Syracuse University Maxwell School of Citizenship and Public Affairs.

José Nederhand is a Ph.D. candidate at the Department of Public Administration and Sociology at Erasmus University Rotterdam, Rotterdam, the Netherlands.

Catherine Needham is Professor of Public Policy and Public Management at the Health Services Management Centre, University of Birmingham.

Hadley Nobles is a Doctoral Candidate in the Department of Public Administration & Policy at the University of Georgia.

Dr. Peter Ngala Ntumba is Researcher at Université officielle de Mbujimayi, Mbujimayi, RD. Congo.

Stephen P. Osborne is Professor of International Public Management and Director of the Centre for Service Excellence (CenSE) at the University of Edinburgh Business School.

Sunggeun (Ethan) Park is Doctoral Candidate at the University of Chicago, Chicago, USA.

Victor Pestoff is Professor at Ersta, Bräcke, Sköndal University College, Stockholm, Sweden.

Zoe Radnor is Dean of the University of Leicester Business School.

Marco Ranzato is Postdoctoral Researcher at the Faculty of Architecture of the Université libre de Bruxelles (Belgium) and co-director of Latitude Platform.

Mrs. Marleen Rolland is a Lecturer at the University of South Africa (UNISA), Pretoria, South Africa.

Hans Schlappa is Senior Lecturer at Hertfordshire Business School and leads the Masters in Leading and Managing Public Services.

Dan Silk is a Captain with the University of Georgia Police Department and also serves as an Instructor in the Criminal Justice Studies Program at the University of Georgia.

Maddalena Sorrentino is an Associate Professor in the Department of Economics, Management and Quantitative Methods, University of Milan (Italy).

Trui Steen is Professor Public Governance and Co-production of Public Services at KU Leuven, Public Governance Institute, Belgium.

Kirsty Strokosch is a Research Associate of the Centre for Service Excellence (CenSE) at the University of Edinburgh Business School.

Dawid Sześciło is a Head of Public Administration Research Unit at the Faculty of Law and Administration, University of Warsaw, Poland.

Francois Theron is a Senior Lecturer in the School of Public Leadership at Stellenbosch University, Stellenbosch, South Africa.

Anne Tortzen holds a Ph.D. from Roskilde University and is the Director of Center for Citizen Engagement, Copenhagen, Denmark.

Xuan Tu is Lecturer at Jiangsu Administration Institute, Nanjing, China.

Sanna Tuurnas is Postdoctoral Researcher at the Institute for Advanced Social Research, University of Tampere (UTA), Finland.

Charlotte van Dijck is a Ph.D. Candidate at KU Leuven, Public Governance Institute, Leuven, Belgium.

Carola van Eijk is a Researcher and a Lecturer at the Institute of Public Administration at Leiden University, the Netherlands.

Daphne Vanleene is a doctoral candidate at the Faculty of Economics and Business Administration, Ghent University, Belgium.

Ingmar van Meerkerk is Assistant Professor at the Department of Public Administration and Sociology at Erasmus University Rotterdam, Rotterdam, the Netherlands.

Bram Verschuere is Associate Professor in Public Management, Faculty of Economics and Business Administration, Ghent University, Belgium.

Brian N. Williams is an Associate Professor in the Department of Public Administration & Policy at the University of Georgia.

Part 1

Co-Production and Co-Creation

Definitions and Theoretical Perspectives

1 Co-Creation and Co-Production in Public Services

Urgent Issues in Practice and Research

Taco Brandsen, Trui Steen and Bram Verschuere

The Revival of Interest in Engaging Citizens

The involvement of citizens in the creation and production of public services is one of the major topics in current public administration and public management research. Academics from all over the globe seem to have joined forces in international scientific networks where citizen engagement in the public domain is the main focus of research. This should not come as a surprise, as also governments worldwide re-discovered the citizen as an important actor with a responsibility in the design and implementation of public policies and public services. To a certain extent, public administration and public management practice and research go hand in hand: (local) governments embrace citizen engagement, as they consider it as a valuable way to overcome some real or perceived challenges they are confronted with like the need to make public service delivery more efficient, effective and democratic, and to restore trust in and satisfaction with government and politics. Academics then have the responsibility to observe and evaluate this trend in a critical and scientific way. They focus on questions like: When citizens take a greater role in the design and implementation of public services, does this actually improve the services? Does co-production increase the democratic level of service delivery? Why would citizens want to make the effort of engaging in co-creation or co-production? And are public servants in turn interested in involving them? Answering these questions is not only relevant from a fundamental scientific point of view, but is potentially also helpful for practitioners that are in a constant need to improve the administrative practice of public policy making and public service delivery. Especially as citizen engagement gradually turns from marginal thoughts to mainstream practice, we need answers to these basic questions.

In this book, we explicitly focus on co-creation and co-production, roughly defined as a joint effort of citizens and public sector professionals in the initiation, planning, design and implementation of public services. For a more elaborate definition, we refer to chapter 2 by Brandsen and Honingh, in which also the conceptual distinction is made with classical types of citizen participation (in policy making, e.g.) and with partnerships between government and civil society organizations. Co-creation and co-production are different from classical citizen participation in policy making, as they focus on the output-side of the policy cycle: the provision of public services, with varying degrees of tangibility (services ranging from the creation of a public garden, to more abstract products like 'health' or 'safety'). The difference with government-civil society partnerships is that co-creation and co-production focus on the contribution of (groups of) individual citizens rather than organizations.

It is easy to forget, now that the participation of citizens is fashionable, that it was for long considered undesirable or unimportant; often, it still is. After Elinor Ostrom and her team published the first work on co-production in the 1970s, there was an initial surge of interest in the topic, which died down in the 1980s. It is clear to see why: it was simply not in tune with the times. Although there remained widespread support for more choice in public services, this took the shape of market-inspired reforms, in which citizens were cast as consumers. Although there is room for co-creation and co-production within such a perspective, it is different from one fostered in a paradigm of participation and collaboration (see chapter 4 by Victor Pestoff to this volume). After market-inspired reforms fell out of grace academically (although in practice they are still very much alive), interest in co-creation and co-production gradually revived. In public discourse, co-creation and co-production at the individual level still remain relatively less significant compared to classical types of individual participation and to partnerships between government and civil society. However, this may change as the former become more viable and the limits of the latter become more apparent.

Advances in technology and cultural changes have made co-production and co-creation far easier to implement now. In Elinor Ostrom's time, communication was a practical problem that made co-production time-intensive and costly. Simply getting people's personal contact details could require major effort. Now it is far easier for public employees to interact with citizens, both collectively and individually. As more sophisticated technologies become available, services that were hitherto dominated by professionals leave more room for individual input (see chapter 10 by Lember in this volume). For instance, it has become easier for people to assess their own health, to an extent that was until recently considered impossible. By implication, this changes patients' interactions with medical professionals.

Simultaneously, cultural shifts have created an environment in which co-creation and co-production have become more feasible and in which the potential of new technologies could be realized. Generally, individualization and the decline of traditional authority have changed the position of professionals in society (see chapter 8 by Steen and Tuurnas in this volume). It has become more accepted for citizens as non-experts (or, as others argue, experts on themselves) to take more responsibility for the services they or their dependents receive. Likewise, there is now more recognition among governments that citizens need to be involved in the design and implementation of policies. Co-creation especially has become a popular catch-phrase for all such efforts. However, the actual extent of citizen involvement still differs strongly between types of services, organizations and cultural contexts. If there is a movement towards a new type of service delivery, it is a slow and checkered one, even if the public discourse suggests a rapid transformation.

At the same time, it has become evident that participation is in itself not a panacea. It has been believed that new types of participation would help solve the so-called democratic deficit. Yet attempts by governments to engage citizens have often been dogged by disinterest, mutual frustration and limited representation. The reasons for this are various. The fact that policy makers and professionals are not prepared or able to follow up on the input of citizens certainly plays a part. Citizens may have unrealistic expectations of what governments can achieve. But the shape of participation also determines its effectiveness. If alternatives to representative democracy resemble the institutions of representative democracy, then they will also mirror its ills. Many types of participation copy the features of policy and politics: in their emphasis on certain (official) settings, a specialized discourse, the need for certain skills. Citizens without the necessary cultural capital are still likely to be excluded, even if the format is partially changed. This realization has encouraged the search for more radical alternatives, which include self-organization and co-production. Yet whether these alternatives function better, and under what conditions, still remains to be seen.

The State of the Research

Developments in research have reflected these broad trends in society. Following the first steps by Ostrom c.s., it consisted of early explorations of co-production in public services—particularly associated with the work of Brudney and England (1983), Pestoff (1998), Alford (2002) and Bovaird (2007). In subsequent years, these were accompanied by a number of mostly small and qualitative cases demonstrating the relevance and potential benefits of this type of participation (for instance, those bundled in Pestoff, Brandsen and Verschuere, 2008; 2012). More recently, there were efforts to make research in this area more systematic and rigorous. One of the explanations is that the research community has also become much more coherent, with the emergence of stable platforms for research on these topics (e.g. through the EGPA, IIAS, IRSPM networks). To a certain extent, research into co-creation and co-production has moved from agenda-setting to fact-finding. The data that are collected by researchers have improved in quality, and a number of methodologically more diverse and sceptical studies emerged examining specific aspects of co-production. This has begun to open up areas that were until recently black boxes. These include the motives for citizens to engage in co-production (for an overview see chapter 7 by van Eijk and Gasco) or its effects, for instance on trust (see chapter 19 by Fledderus) and inclusiveness (see chapter 18 by Verschuere, Brandsen and Steen). We now thus have more research that is providing first answers to the key questions of why, how, and with what effects co-creation and co-production take place (or not). But we also observe more attention for the uneasy and critical questions about the dark side of co-creation and co-production: although many practitioners still see participation as something that is mainly good practice, research also increasingly discusses and shows (potential) pitfalls and drawbacks in terms of unequal participation opportunities, quality of services and unequal benefits of co-produced public services (see chapter 21 by Steen, Brandsen and Verschuere on the dark side of co-creation and co-production).

The methods, traditionally single case studies, have further expanded to cross-national comparative case studies (e.g. Voorberg, Bekkers and Tummers, 2015; Bovaird et al., 2016; van Eijk, Steen and Verschuere, 2017), experiments (e.g. Jakobsen, 2013) and longitudinal studies (e.g., Fledderus, 2015). Although case study research with mainly qualitative data is still dominant in the field, we thus observe an increasing number of research that applies quantitative and even experimental methods.

Finally, given the potential of increased citizen participation to mitigate the effects of the big societal issues of our time (e.g. climate and environment, poverty, migration), researchers increasingly recognize that relying only on public administration paradigms and theories will not suffice to understand the benefits and risks of co-creation and co-production of public services for and with people that suffer from the effects of these issues. Multi- and inter-disciplinary approaches in which public administration scholars cooperate with scholars from other disciplines will need to be developed further (see chapter 14 by Moretto and Ranzato and the accompanying case studies by Mees and by Ranzato).

Despite these recent advancements in the field, there are still challenges to tackle as a research community. Most pressing, the diverse uses of the terms co-creation and co-production, combined with the prevalence of highly particular case studies, have hindered meaningful comparisons between different studies. In terms of scope and dynamics, individual participation in health care is quite different from the collaboration between local NGOs and municipalities, yet the co-production and co-creation labels have been used to cover all. Also, there were studies in which these terms have been stretched to cover any individual action directly or indirectly contributing to the effectiveness of public services. Anyone watching over their property might be regarded as co-producing public safety. Although individual contributions to the public good are undeniably essential, extending co-production to cover all of them brings us back to the weakness of functionalist theory: useful when carefully applied, but meaningless when stretched. Any phenomenon can be construed as having a function for society. Likewise, anything can be construed as public (to paraphrase Bozeman), which, as there is nearly always some connection to public services, implies that there would always be some element of co-production or co-creation. That makes the terms useless as academic concepts.

Various scholars have in recent years tried to tighten the definition of the co-production concept (Brandsen and Honingh, 2016; Osborne, Radnor and Strokosch, 2016; Nabatchi, Sancino and Sicilia, 2017), to strengthen the cumulative nature of studies. There have also been some efforts to link the previously separate concepts of co-production and co-creation (Voorberg, Bekkers and Tummers, 2015; chapter 2 by Brandsen and Honingh in this volume). It is unlikely that such initiatives will lead to a unified use of these terms. However, what can already be seen is that scholars are more explicitly positioning themselves among the different definitions, which will hugely benefit the comparability of empirical findings.

With this book, we have the ambition to present the advanced state-of-the-art in co-creation and co-production research by assembling chapters by leading scholars in the field. Though a successor to earlier collections (Pestoff and Brandsen, 2006; Pestoff, Brandsen and Verschuere, 2012), it is less a collection of separate cases and more a thematically structured overview. In this book, co-creation and co-production are examined along a number of important dimensions. By distinguishing between these dimensions, we recognize that:

- What we—as public administration scholars—call co-creation and co-production might be called something else in other disciplines although we are actually talking about the same phenomena. Therefore, in the first part of this book, we give an overview of different theoretical and conceptual foundations in different social science disciplines.
- Co-creation and co-production in the public spheres come with many issues that need to be taken into account: the relation between volunteers and professionals, leadership in co-production, the role of ICT and legal issues, only to name some. Therefore, in different chapters, we chose to discuss the state of the art in co-creation and co-production research with regards to these issues.
- The practice of co-creation and co-production might differ between different types of services (e.g. co-producing safety, health, communities, education, natural resources). It comes with different challenges, opportunities and practices, depending on the specificities of the service concerned. Therefore a set of thematic chapters are presented in the book to do justice to these differences.
- Co-creation and co-production of public services might come with positive and negative effects of various nature: trust in government, empowerment of citizens, service quality and effectiveness, access of vulnerable groups to the benefits of the service may all increase or decrease. Therefore a set of chapters is devoted to the potential effects of co-production,

including both anticipated but also unanticipated and potentially perverse effects.

Finally, with this book, we also want to inform practitioners on the state-of-the-art in co-production, and what they can learn from it. We do so by presenting real life cases of co-creative and co-productive practice throughout the book. For this purpose, we also assembled 'lessons for practice' from the different chapters. These lessons are presented at the end of the book.

References

Alford, J. (2002). Why Do Public Sector Clients Co-Produce? Towards a Contingency Theory. *Administration & Society*, (34, 1), 32–56.

Bovaird, T. (2007). Beyond Engagement & Participation: User & Community Co-Production of Public Services. *Public Administration Review*, 846–860.

Bovaird, T., Stoker, G., Loeffler, E., Jones, T. and Pinilla Roncancio, M. (2016). Activating Collective Coproduction for Public Services: Influencing Citizens' to Participate in Complex Governance Mechanisms. *International Review of Administrative Sciences*, (82, 1), 47–68.

Brandsen, T. and Honingh, M. (2016). Distinguishing Different Types of Co-Production: A Conceptual Analysis Based on the Classical Definitions. *Public Administration Review*, (76, 3), 427–435.

Brudney, J. and England, E. (1983). Toward a Definition of the Coproduction Concept. *Public Administration Review*, (43, 1), 59–65.

Fledderus, J. (2015). Building Trust Through Public Service Co-Production. *International Journal of Public Sector Management*, (28, 7), 550–565.

Jakobsen, M. (2013). Can Government Initiatives Increase Citizen Coproduction? Results of a Randomized Field Experiment. *Journal of Public Administration Research and Theory*, (23, 1), 27–54.

Nabatchi, T., Sancino, A. and Sicilia, M. (2017). Varieties of Participation in Public Services: The Who, When, and What of Coproduction. *Public Administration Review*, (77, 5), 766–776.

Osborne, S.P., Radnor, Z. and Strokosch, K. (2016). Co-Production and the Co-Creation of Value in Public Services: A suitable case for treatment? *Public Management Review*, (18, 5), 639–653.

Pestoff, V. (1998). *Beyond the Market and State. Civil Democracy & Social Enterprises in a Welfare Society*. Aldershot and Brookfield: Ashgate.

Pestoff, V. and Brandsen, T. (eds.). (2006). *Co-Production, the Third Sector and the Delivery of Public Services*. Routledge.

Pestoff, V., Brandsen, T. and Verschuere, B. (eds.). (2012). *New Public Governance, the Third Sector and Co-Production*. Routledge.

van Eijk, C., Steen, T. and Verschuere, B. (2017). Co-Producing Safety in the Local Community: A Q-Methodology Study on the Incentives of Belgian and Dutch Members of Neighbourhood Watch Schemes. *Local Government Studies*, (43, 3), 323–343.

Voorberg, W., Bekkers, V. and Tummers, L. (2015). A Systematic Review of Co-Creation and Co-Production: Embarking on the Social Innovation Journey. *Public Management Review*, (17, 9), 1333–1357.

2 Definitions of Co-Production and Co-Creation

Taco Brandsen and Marlies Honingh

Introduction[1]

In this chapter we discuss definitions of the two terms central to this book, co-production and co-creation. The term "co-production" finds its scholarly origins in the public sector, in the work of Ostrom and other economists who studied collaboration between public departments and citizens. "Co-creation", by contrast, is a term from commercial business that has only fairly recently become popular in the public sector. To confuse matters, these are only two of various terms that seem to denote similar practices, such as collaborative governance, community involvement, participation and civic engagement (Voorberg et al., 2015). Part of the practical appeal of such terms is of course exactly in their fuzziness, in innate goodness (who can be against any of it?) combined with a supple application to diverse phenomena. In practice, they are used to cover a wide variety of phenomena.

Yet for academic purposes, it is useful to try and arrive at something more precise. The main reason for this is comparability. The opening chapter of this book noted the swift advance of research in these areas. However, there are also grounds to be less optimistic about the linearity of progress (Verschuere, Brandsen and Pestoff., 2012; Alford, 2014). The cumulative effect of past research still remains relatively weak. Although scholars have inspired each other, they have not been able to link their findings systematically and contribute to theory-building as effectively as they otherwise might.

The confusion has been heightened by the increasing multi-disciplinarity of the discussion. The research community studying these phenomena has over time become larger and more multi-disciplinary. One can now see sociologists, economists, political scientists, public administration, marketing and management researchers engaged in a joint discussion, which is in itself good. However, it has also made the original definitions of the terms less suitable and on some points less clear. What is straightforward from one discipline's perspective is not so from another.

First, we will examine the commonalities and differences between co-creation and co-production. Next, we will demonstrate certain ambiguities, which point to underlying variation, which can be used to identify different types of co-production and co-creation. On this basis, we will then construct a basic typology of six categories of citizen input.

A Plea for Stricter Definitions

There are three ways of understanding the relationship between the two terms:

1   They mean roughly the same and refer to any kind of citizen input in public services.
2   Co-creation is the more encompassing term, referring to all kinds of citizen inputs in services, whereas co-production has a more specific meaning.
3   Co-creation and co-production have distinct meanings, referring to different kinds of citizen input.

There is something to be said for all these interpretations. In practice the terms are often used interchangeably, in various sorts of ways. However, in the context of public services at least, co-creation is the newer and more slippery term, whereas co-production already has a longer tradition, in which a more definite meaning is beginning to crystallize. This meaning usually relates to the later stages of the production cycle, the design and/or implementation of a service.

Voorberg et al. (2015) go a step further and define more specific meanings for the two terms:

> Some clarity can be provided by making a difference between three types of co-creation (. . .): (a) citizens as coimplementer: involvement in services which refer to the transfer of implementing activities in favour of citizens that in the past have been carried out by government, (b) citizens as co-designer: involvement regarding the content and process of service delivery and (c) citizens as initiator: citizens that take up the initiative to formulate specific services. Furthermore, based on this distinction, we would like to reserve the term 'co-creation' for involvement of citizens in the (co)-initiator or co-design level. Co-production is being considered as the involvement of citizens in the (co-)implementation of public services.
>
> (p. 15)

Although this is still fairly broad, such efforts to define tighter meanings are far preferable over letting it all hang out. One should distinguish between recognizing phenomena as important and accepting them as part of an academic definition. Of course, citizens deliver all sorts of inputs that impact upon the effectiveness of core services of an organization (Marschall, 2004). If people peep through their curtains at night and call the police when they see signs of trouble, or when they request government services electronically, are they not effectively helping to deliver public services (Clarke, Brudney and Jang, 2013)? Yet expanding concepts to cover all these inputs make them less distinct and makes systematic research much harder—whereas our starting-point was that we should be heading in the opposite direction, given the state of the art of the research.

As Agarwal (2013) has noted, "would my printing a boarding pass at an airline kiosk or using the Internet to buy an airline ticket make me a co-producer in the transportation business? I hardly think so. However, in public service, beginning in public safety in the 1970s, we have taken a rather expansive view of the term" (p. 702). Whether such activities from citizens matter is not at issue here. Daily teeth-brushing helps the dentist do his work and ultimately saves public money. Sucking a lollipop does the reverse. Whether it is useful to cover it all under the label of co-production is another matter.

The purpose of stricter definitions is not to exclude (as in: this does not fall into the scope of our definition, so it is irrelevant to society). The point is to avoid comparisons between activities that are entirely dissimilar. Distinguishing co-production and co-creation as distinct categories of activity will help in making cleaner comparisons, allowing a deeper understanding of the social mechanisms that shape their internal dynamics and outcomes. Distinguishing between subcategories will help even more. Even where scholars disagree on the definition, positioning themselves systematically in relation to one another will lead to greater clarity. Through the discussion of definitions, we hope to contribute to developing shared points of reference.

The Similarities Between Co-Creation and Co-Production

So what distinguishes co-production and co-creation from other, similar terms? We argue that they share a few commonalities.

The first is that they constitute a direct part of the production process. In other words, they do not include all inputs by citizens that in some way affect the overall planning, design and delivery of a service, but focus on the direct input of citizens during the production phase. "Direct" here means that the input by a citizen affects the service individually provided to her or him (as an individual, family or community). This need not be restricted to face-to-face contacts. Indeed, some interesting developments in this area are based on the Internet (for example, guided online self-treatment in mental health care).

Furthermore, they both refer to collaboration between professionalized service providers in public agencies and citizens. Whether this refers to citizens individually or individually as well as collectively remains open, but the definition clearly does not refer to organizations.

Finally, both terms refer to active input by citizens in shaping services. This distinguishes them from passive clientelism or consumerism: it is not enough simply to receive or use a product. The citizen can be a direct recipient of a service, but not necessarily so. For instance, the participation of family or community members on behalf of children or vulnerable people has been an oft-studied topic.

This excludes the research that focuses on inter-organizational collaboration, which Brandsen and Pestoff (2006) have referred to as "co-management" or "co-governance".[2] It also excludes input from citizens that, although they affect the outcome of the service, require only a passive role (as in the patient helping to produce his vasectomy by virtue of lying on the operating table).

An interesting issue is whether evaluation should be considered part of co-production and co-co-creation. There is a growing number of examples of users assessing public services jointly with providers. On the one hand, one could argue that evaluation is part of the production cycle and that this amounts to an ex-post type of co-creation or co-production. On the other hand, it may involve different kinds of skills and activities, which is an argument for keeping it separate. This is an issue that requires clarification in future scholarship.

The Differences Between Co-Creation and Co-Production

But what is distinct about co-production and co-creation? If our unit of analysis is the effort of (groups of) citizens, then the best way of setting them apart is by defining the types of input of citizens they refer to. These can vary drastically in nature.

Some authors have argued that co-production is an inherent part of the delivery of certain services and therefore not a question of choice. This is more than saying that co-production is necessary for effective service delivery because producer and citizen inputs are interdependent; rather, that it is impossible to have a situation without co-production (Osborne and Strokosch, 2013).

> From a service-dominant approach, there is no way to avoid the coproduction of public services because it is an inalienable element of such services. The question thus is not how to 'add-in' coproduction to public services but rather how to manage and work with its implications for effective public service delivery.
>
> (p. 146)

Yet even if co-production is inherent, citizens can design services with different degrees of active input (Porter, 2012).

If co-production is an inherent part of the production relationship, one could imagine situations where co-production is not freely given (Fledderus, Brandsen and Honingh, 2014). By extension, while co-production is to a large extent a subset of volunteering, it is not wholly so. It is possible to coerce citizens to co-produce, even if it is counterintuitive. Consider the example of a high school class: students may not have chosen to be physically present, but they determine the nature of the lessons nonetheless, even if they freely choose to withhold their attention. Although learning is essential to an effective lesson (Porter, 2012), it is possible to design lessons in any number of ways. Pupils can sit back and listen to a talk, with learning a one-way street; the teacher can prepare questions and exercises to encourage interaction; or can actively engage students in designing the lesson, jointly choosing what to address and how to shape the interaction. In other words, the lessons have both an inherent and a chosen element. One can have the former without the latter.

There is a further possibility, which is that students sit on representative councils and discuss the general design of lessons with staff and managers at the strategic level—indeed, this may be more common than input in the design of specific lessons.

In this way, the distinction between co-creation and co-production can be specified. Co-production is generally associated with services citizens receive during the implementation phase of the production cycle, whereas co-creation concerns services at a strategic level. In other words, when citizens are involved in the general planning of a service—perhaps even initiating it—then this is co-creation, whereas if they shape the service during later phases of the cycle it is co-production. Input in the design of a service can be both individual or collective, depending on the level at which a service is addressed.

Let us illustrate these choices using the example of housing cooperatives (Brandsen and Helderman, 2012):

- If tenants actively collaborate in the maintenance or design of the housing, it is co-production. If they only passively receive what they pay for, it is not.
- If tenants initiate the constructing of their housing, or deliberate in a representative council discussing issues of maintenance and design, it is co-creation.
- If the cooperative collaborates with a local council, it is neither co-production nor co-creation. This has elsewhere been referred to as "co-management" (Brandsen and Pestoff, 2006).
- If outsiders smash tenants' windows and cars, they are helping to shape the residential experience of the latter; but they are not co-producing or co-creating.

Core and Complementary Tasks

It is possible that the co-production in question does not directly produce public services, but does contribute inputs to an organization that supports the production process indirectly. This is more than a theoretical possibility, because various activities described in the co-production literature argu-ably do not relate directly to the organization's core services, even if they undoubtedly contribute to them. When university alumni give a guest lec-ture as part of a regular course, they directly contribute to the teaching process. When they speak at a publicity event for a university's programs, this ultimately contributes to the goals of the organization, but it is not a direct contribution to teaching. It does involve a joint process with the orga-nization's employees, but it is not part of the core (primary) process, which makes it co-production of a different sort.

Of course, the question what is the core process of an organization is open to different interpretations, which may shift over time. This cannot be determined a priori and should be defined on a case-by-case basis (and even where there is doubt, the discussion is in itself useful).

In other words, there is variation in the extent to which citizen inputs involve tasks that are part of the organization's core services. This is a basis for distinguishing different types of co-production and co-creation.

Varieties of Co-Creation and Co-Production

This means that we have now identified two key dimensions that help to distinguish citizen inputs:

- The extent to which citizens are involved, not only in the implementa-tion, but also in the design and initiation of a service. Co-production concerns the design and implementation of a service, whereas co-creation is about the initiation and/or strategic planning of a service.
- The proximity of the tasks that citizens perform to the core services of the organization. This cuts across both co-production and co-creation.

The combination of these dimensions then leads to six various potential types of co-creation/co-production, visualized in Table 2.1 below.

Table 2.1 Different Types of Co-Production and Co-Creation

	Planning	*Design and implementation*	*Implementation*
Complementary	Co-creation of a complementary service	Complementary co-production in service design and implementation	Complementary co-production in implementation
Core	Co-creation of a core service	Co-production in the design and implementation of core services	Co-production in the implementation of core services

Co-creation of a complementary service is a situation in which citizens are actively engaged in the strategic design and planning of a complementary task. Examples are parents taking the initiative to organize a sports competition between schools, or relatives suggesting excursions and Christmas entertainments for residents of elderly care homes. Again, these activities are undoubtedly necessary and important, but they do not directly contribute to the core activity of the organizations in question.

Co-creation of a core service occurs when citizens are actively engaged in the strategic design and planning of a core task. This happens, for instance when a depressed patient or group of patients are involved in the development of a coaching app or in defining a strategy to make better use of apps in treatments. Apps can be used as supportive devices in a treatment to report tasks and get some support with structuring daily life. If patients are involved in strategic choices about the use of apps, this is a clear example of co-creation of a core task, since apps support treatment and directly affect the work of the psychiatrist. Likewise, the general evaluation of such initiatives in service delivery could be seen as part of the co-creation process.

Complementary co-production in service design and implementation occurs when citizens are engaged in co-production, but in tasks that are complementary to the core process rather than part of it. This happens, for instance, when parents help plan and organize extra-curricular activities like school excursions or the design of a school garden. These activities are part of the professional organizations' mission, but they do not directly involve citizens in the core activities of teaching.

Complementary co-production in service implementation occurs when citizens are actively engaged in the implementation, but not the design, of a complementary task. Examples are students assisting the university in organizing welcome weeks or parents helping to prepare school plays: they are undoubtedly necessary and important, but they do not directly contribute to the core activity of teaching and they usually do not have the opportunity to design or redesign the events.

Co-production in the design and implementation of core services is a situation where citizens are directly involved in producing core services of an organization and are directly involved in both the design and implementation of the individual service provided to them. Examples are post-graduate training modules where entrants, together with instructors, define their own learning objectives and learning activities; participative building projects in which (future) tenants of a housing cooperative work with architects and builders in the design, construction and maintenance of their homes; or patients working with dietitians to modify their lifestyle.

Co-production in the implementation of core services occurs when citizens are actively engaged in the implementation, but not the design of an individual service that is at the core of the organization. For instance, as discussed earlier, co-production may be inherent to the production process ("inherent" meaning that active engagement by the client is essential to its successful implementation), but institutionally designed so that citizens do not have direct influence on how it is designed in their individual case. Examples are children's education during which students follow strictly defined lessons, yet their input is still crucial to effective learning; or enforced services, such as mandatory employment reintegration. Alternatively, co-production may not be inherent, but deliberately included as part of the design.

Using clearer definitions of co-creation and co-production will contribute to the comparability of different studies and allow a better understanding of the dynamics and outcomes of co-production. Recognizing variety within these broad concepts and working towards consistent typologies will enhance the cumulative value of research in this area and allow scholars to collaborate more effectively.

Notes

1 This chapter is partly based on Brandsen & Honingh (2016).
2 The term "co-production" with reference to inter-organizational links appears to have originated in a different tradition of research and the terminological similarity appears to be accidental. As Bovaird and Loeffler (2015) point out, some scholars have merged the different approaches and used co-production as a more encompassing label.

References

Agarwal, Pankaj K. (2013). Commentary: 311 Services: A Real-World Perspective. *Public Administration Review*, (73), 702–703.

Alford, J. (2014). The Multiple Facets of Co-Production: Building on the Work of Elinor Ostrom. *Public Management Review*, (16), 299–316.

Bovaird, T. and Loeffler, E. (2015). Co-Producing Public Services with Users, Communities, and the Third Sector. In James L. Perry and Robert K. Christensen (eds.), *Handbook of Public Administration*, 235–250. Third edition. San Francisco: Jossey-Bass.

Brandsen, T. and Helderman, J. (2012). The Trade-Off Between Capital and Community: The Conditions for Successful Co-Production in Housing. *Voluntas*, (23), 1139–1155.

Brandsen, T. and Pestoff, V. (2006). Co-Production, the Third Sector and the Delivery of Public Services: An Introduction. *Public Management Review*, (8), 493–501.

Clark, B., Brudney, J. and Jang, S. (2013). Coproduction of Government Services and the New Information Technology: Investigating the Distributional Biases. *Public Administration Review*, (73), 687–701.

Fledderus, J., Brandsen, T. and Honingh, M. (2014). Restoring Public Trust Through the Co-Production of Public Services: A Theoretical Elaboration. *Public Management Review*, (16), 424–443.

Marschall, M. (2004). Citizen Participation and the Neighborhood Context: A New Look at the Coproduction of Local Public Goods. *Political Research Quarterly*, (57), 231–244.

Osborne, S. and Strokosch, K. (2013). It Takes Two to Tango? Understanding the Co-Production of Public Services by Integrating the Services Management and Public Administration Perspectives. *British Journal of Management*, (24), 31–47.

Porter, D. (2012). Co-Production and Network Structures in Public Education. In Victor Pestoff, Taco Brandsen and Bram Verschuere (eds.), *New Public Governance, the Third Sector and Co-Production*, 145–168. London: Routledge.

Verschuere, B., Brandsen, T. and Pestoff, V. (2012). Co-Production: The State of the Art in Research and the Future Agenda. *Voluntas*, (23), 1083–1101.

Voorberg, W., Bekkers, V. and Tummers, L. (2015). A Systematic Review of Co-Creation and Co-Production: Embarking on the Social Innovation Journey. *Public Management Review*, (17), 1333–1357.

3 Co-Production and the Co-Creation of Value in Public Services

A Perspective from Service Management[1]

Stephen P. Osborne, Kirsty Strokosch and Zoe Radnor

Co-production is currently one of the cornerstones of public policy reform across the globe (e.g. OECD, 2011). *Inter alia*, it is articulated as a valuable route to public service reform (Nambisan and Nambisan, 2013) and to the planning and delivery of effective public services (Durose et al., 2013), a response to the democratic deficit (Pestoff, 2006) and a route to active citizenship and active communities (DoH, 2010), and as a means by which to lever in additional resources to public services delivery (Birmingham City Council, 2014). A significant body of public management research has also begun to mature (see also Verschuere, Brandsen and Pestoff (2012) and Alford (2014) for good summaries of this work). Despite this growing body of empirical research, though, co-production continues to be one of a series of 'woolly-words' in public policy.

From a service management perspective, co-production is intrinsic to any service experience. This contrasts to public management theory, where the exploration of co-production is almost exclusively on how to 'add-in' service user input into public services planning and delivery, on a voluntary basis. Co-production in this latter conceptualization thus does not challenge the basic premises of public management, because it can only occur at the behest of, and controlled by, service professionals (Brandsen and Pestoff, 2006).

From a service management perspective, however, the nature and role of co-production in public service delivery is somewhat different. Crucially, this literature is not concerned with how to 'enable' or 'build in' co-production to service delivery. *Its basic premise is that co-production is an essential and inalienable core component of service delivery: you cannot have service delivery without co-production.* Service users do not consciously choose to co-produce or otherwise—it occurs whether they choose to or not, whether they are aware of it or not, and whether the public service encounter is coerced or not. Indeed, resistance to service delivery, especially in the more coercive areas of public services such as the criminal justice system, is as much a form of co-production as a voluntary/conscious willingness to co-produce. *Co-production thus comprises the intrinsic process of interaction between any service organization and the service user at the point of delivery of a service—what Normann (1991) has termed 'the moment of truth' in service provision.*

Briefly, *traditional service management theory* stems from tripartite notions of intangibility, inseparability, and co-production (Gronroos, 2011): services comprise intangible processes not concrete products (even if they may utilize such concrete elements in their delivery); the production and consumption of such services are not separate processes but rather are inseparable and occur contemporaneously (you cannot 'store' a service for delivery at a later date—it is consumed at the point of its production; and the user/consumer is a (willing or unwilling, conscious or unconscious) participant in service production and enactment. The quality and performance of a service process is shaped primarily by the expectations of the user, their active or passive role in the service delivery, and their subsequent experience of the process. This is at the heart of co-production. Service organizations can only 'promise' a certain process or experience—the actuality is dependent upon service enactment, where user expectations of a service collide with their experience of it—and which determines both their satisfaction with the service experience and the performance and outcomes of this service encounter (Venetis and Ghauri, 2004). *Crucially, co-production is about the interaction between service users and service providers—it is not the same as 'consumerism' or even user empowerment.*

Service management theory has also evolved recently through the *service-dominant* perspective. Here, 'service' is not an industry description but is rather the process through which value is added to any service or product. Value is *co-created*[2] through the transformation of service components when a service is utilized at the point of co-production—termed 'value in use' (Lusch and Vargo, 2006). Thus a service does not have any intrinsic value to its users but is co-created through co-production (Prahalad and Ramaswamy, 2004; Vargo and Lusch, 2008; Gronroos, 2011; Edvardsson, Tronvoll and Gruber, 2011).[3] To take a simple example, the 'value' to a customer of a meal in a restaurant is not a simple financial transaction—it is not an aggregation of the cost of the ingredients of the meal and the wages of the restaurant staff. Rather, its value to the customer is co-created by that customer and the restaurant at the point of consumption and includes not only the quality of the meal itself but the ambience of the restaurant, the actions of the restaurant staff, and the impact of this upon the well-being of the customer. This latter point is directly related to the expectations of the customer of the meal and the extent to which they are met—is the meal meant to impress a potential business partner, for example, or to be a romantic episode or a celebration? The interaction of these expectations and the actual experience is where genuine value is co-created for the customer. This insight is fundamental to understanding the process and import of co-production for service delivery.

It is equally central to understanding the delivery and impact of public services (Osborne and Strokosch, 2013, Osborne, Radnor and Nasi, 2013). A classic public service example of such co-creation of value would be the experience of residential care for older people. The (conscious and unconscious) expectations and the personal characteristics and actions of the residents, and their significant others, of a residential home create the experience of that home as much as do the actions of its staff. The experience and performance ('value') of the residential home is continuously co-created by these interactions. One could have two identical residential homes which employed the same staff—but the experience and impact of each home would be different—because this would be co-created by the interactions with the residents of the home. Nor is such public service value co-creation dependent upon voluntary or conscious intent. Such residential homes can be a home to residents who resent being there but have no other option because of their own lack of self-care abilities (involuntary residence), or who may be suffering from conditions such as dementia and so are actually unaware of their residence (unconscious residence). Yet these individuals would still nonetheless co-produce both their own lived experience of the home and contribute to the quality of the experience of other residents.[4]

In reality, of course, such co-productive elements are more of a continuum than a steady state. Services such as residential care and education are instances where co-production and value co-creation are high, with iterative inter-personal contact between the service user and the service provider. By contrast, they are rather lower for electronic financial services, such as tax returns, because production and consumption occur through the medium of an electronic interface that does not have such inter-personal immediacy—here, the co-production of a financial service is essentially passive (the inputting financial data for their tax return by a citizen or choosing from a list of pre-set options, for example), mediated through a virtual interface.

Unlike much current public management literature, therefore, the service management literature emphasizes the iterative interactions between the service producer and the service user in the co-production of public services and the interdependency between these two at the operational level. The user's contribution as a co-producer during service production is not only unavoidable (and can be unconscious or coerced) but is also crucial to the performance of a service. *Such co-production leads to the co-creation of value for the service user, which we explore further below.*

If service theory has insights to offer to our understanding of co-production, it also has its limitations, however. It has no real understanding of the political and policy context of public services, for example, nor of service production in the context of unwilling or coerced service users (as in the case of the criminal justice system, for example) or where the desired outcomes of a service are multiple and/or contested—as can be the case in a range of child care services (e.g. child protection services). Further the concept of 'value in use' is limited in its understanding of public services both where there are contested outcomes expressed by different stakeholders and where 'repeat business' can be an admission of service failure rather than success (a patient returning to a doctor because their illness has not been resolved rather than for the positivity of the experience, for example). Nonetheless, service theory can contribute significant new insights to the understanding of public service delivery. This is already evolving—both in general terms through the positing of a *public service logic* (Osborne. 2018—previously 'public service-dominant logic' (Osborne, Radnor & Nasi 2013, 2015)) and through the use of this logic to explore co-production (Radnor et al., 2013). Crucially public service logic argues that it is public service users who create value through their interaction with public services—and it is public service organisations that co-produce this with them, not vice versa.

Conceptualizing Co-Production from a Service Management Perspective

Our approach, rooted in an understanding of the design and delivery of public services from a service management perspective (Osborne, Radnor and Nasi, 2013, 2015), links co-production directly to the co-creation of value in public service delivery. Central to this understanding, and to service management theory, is the premise that such service delivery does not occur within public service organizations (PSOs) alone, or even within networks of co-operating PSOs. Rather, public services are actually delivered within *holistic and dynamic public service systems* that include PSOs, service users and their significant others, the local community, hard and soft technology, and sometimes other significant stakeholders (Radnor et al., 2013).

This approach was first applied to co-production in Osborne and Strokosch (2013). Subsequently we refined this approach to produce a conceptual framework of co-production (Osborne et al., 2016). In this current chapter, this framework is developed to articulate the relationship between co-production and value creation in public services, focused upon *value creation in relation to individual services users or citizens and not society as a whole*.

In this context, we refer to three types of value which are co-created in public service delivery by the iterative interactions of service users and service professionals ('co-production') with public service delivery systems. These are value derived from

- the meeting of individual economic/welfare needs (enabling individuals with disabilities to enhance their lives),
- the generation of individual well-being as part of a service interaction (the well-being created for individuals as a result of helping them resolve the impact of a disability upon their life—or simply from their experiences within a public service),

- the creation of individual capacity to resolve problems in the future as a consequence of the above two value creation processes (the skills and/ or confidence created for individuals with disabilities that enable them to address and resolve other issues in the future).

Developed from Osborne et al. (2016), Figure 3.1 below conceptualizes four distinct processes through which co-production can lead to the co-creation of such value in public service delivery. It disaggregates these processes from an undifferentiated, and somewhat amorphous, cluster of concepts into a set of four differentiated processes that both are capable of proper research evaluation and are a usable framework to guide public policy creation and the delivery and management of public services.

The vertical dimension of the framework incorporates the perspectives of co-production as an inalienable and involuntary element of the public service delivery process and as voluntary action. The horizontal dimension incorporates an understanding of public services as individual services (a residential home or school) and as part of holistic service delivery systems (community care services or a local education system).

This produces a four quadrant typology of the processes of value co-creation. Quadrant I identifies value created by *'pure' co-production*, where the user (consciously or unconsciously) co-produces their service outcomes (public value) with public service staff (Etgar, 2008). As discussed previously, this process is not voluntary but rather is intrinsic to the nature of a public service as a 'service'—it is impossible to deliver any form of public service without at least some element of such technical co-production. Just because this process is unconscious, coerced, and/or unavoidable, however, does not mean that service users and staff cannot chose to actively engage with the

		Locus of co-production	
		Individual service	*Service system*
Nature of co-production	*Involuntary*	I: Co-production	II: Co-construction
	Voluntary	III: Co-management	IV: Co-design and Co-innovation

Figure 3.1 Conceptualizing Co-Production and the Co-Creation of Value in Public Services from a Service Management Perspective

process—indeed such active engagement is highly desirable in maximizing its role in co-creating value through public service delivery. Examples of such co-production would be elderly residents living within a residential home or students within a learning environment. Actively engaging with this pure co-production will maximize its potential to create value for service users.[5]

Quadrant II shifts the focus to the service system rather than the service in isolation. Here the wider life experiences and context of the individual service user experience of the service user interacts with their experiences within the service system as a whole to *co-construct* (Schembri, 2006) their 'lived experience' (Von Manen, 1990) of the service. This process creates value partly as a result of their satisfaction with their experience of the service, but also, more fundamentally, in how the service experience impacts upon their own life/well-being at an emotional and personal level. The personal life experience of the service user will affect how they engage with a service and what characteristics, expectations, or skills they bring to the service experience, whilst the lived experience of being within the service system will impact upon their life as a whole—the on-going service encounter within the service system will co-construct their life experience as it interacts with their holistic life experiences. Thus an adult with profound mental health problems will bring their disordered life experience to the process of service delivery, whilst the process of being within the broader mental health system will co-construct their own life experience as well through the relationships and occurrences within this system. Key here are the 'emotional touch-points' (Dewar et al., 2010) between the service system and the service users.

Quadrant III concerns co-production as a conscious and voluntary act and is concerned with how value is created for service users by their conscious *co-management* of their individual service experience. This will impact upon the extent to which it both meets their expressed needs and enhances their satisfaction (and well-being) with the service. Individual planning models for elderly people are a good example of this. The extent to which this genuinely creates value for the individual will be dependent upon the extent to which there is genuine co-production between service users and staff, rather than linear consultation. This form of value co-creation can fundamentally challenge existing power balances and relationships within public services.

Finally, Quadrant IV focuses upon the conscious and voluntary involvement of service users in the *co-design* (Lengnick-Hall, Manschot and De Koning, 2000; Steen et al., 2011) and improvement of existing public service systems (for themselves or as a whole) and the *co-innovation* of new forms of service delivery (Dinesen, Seemann and Gustafsson, 2011; Lee, Olson and Trimi, 2012). Service theory has long held that service users are the most significant source of innovation and change in service delivery, with over two-thirds of service innovations being derived directly from user involvement in the innovation process (Alam, 2006). This form of value co-creation is about the capacity to change both individual services and service systems. An example could be adults with physical disabilities working within the community care service system to generate new resources as alternatives to residential care.

This framework is a substantial step forward in enhancing our understanding of the relationship between co-production and value co-creation in public services. Further work is required to refine this framework further. We would highlight four issues here, but there are surely more. First this framework focuses primarily upon the role of service users. However, the role of service professionals is the other 'half' of the co-productive relationship and their role in value co-creation is significantly under-researched. Second, service theory makes explicit that co-production is not a normative good—it has the potential to lead to the *co-destruction* of value as much as to its co-creation (Ple and Cacares, 2010, Echieverri and Skalen 2011). This is true also for public services, though this insight has often been absent from much of the discourse about co-production. Failure to recognize the intrinsic co-productive activity comprised in Quadrant I, for example, could also lead to maladaptive behaviour by service staff or users that could lead to the destruction of value in the service encounter.

Third, the focus here has been primarily upon 'value' as welfare outcomes and personal well-being. The co-creation of value as capacity to change and develop has not been explored sufficiently. The framework provides a robust analytic structure for exploring and evaluating the impact of new developments upon both co-production and upon the co-creation of value in public services delivery.

Fourth, the delivery of public services also creates value for society as a whole and reflects what it values. The dynamics of this relationship require further exploration.

Notes

1 This chapter is an abridged and revised version of S. Osborne, Z. Radnor & K. Strokosch 2016 'Co-Production and the Co-Creation of Value in Public Services: A suitable case for treatment?' in *Public Management Review*, (18:5) pp. 639–653.
2 Co-creation in this context is conceptually different from its usage in relation to the co-design and co-creation of innovation in service delivery (e.g. Sanders and Stappers, 2008).
3 There is also a growing literature on service co-production in digital and virtual environments (e.g., Gummerus, 2010).
4 More broadly the provision of residential care also co-creates (social/public) value for society as a whole, through the extent to which it is seen as a normative social good, meeting societal objectives and needs, and/or enhancing social cohesion.
5 We know, for example, that the active involvement of oncology patients in the design and implementation of their care plan increases clinical outcomes, irrespective of any other clinical decision making or procedures (Katz et al., 2005).

References

Alam, I. (2006). Removing the Fuzziness from the Fuzzy Front-End of Service Innovations Through Consumer Interactions. *Industrial Marketing Management*, (35), 468–480.

Alford, J. (2014). The Multiple Facets of Co-Production: Building on the Work of Elinor Ostrom. *Public Management Review*, (16, 3), 299–316.

Birmingham City Council. (2014). *Responding to the challenge, Looking to the Future*. Birmingham: Birmingham City Council.

Brandsen, T. and Pestoff, V. (2006). Co-Production, the Third Sector and the Delivery of Public Services. *Public Management Review*, (8, 4), 493–501.

Dewar, B., Mackay, R., Smith, S., Pullin, S. and Tocher, R. (2010). Use of Emotional Touchpoints as a Method of Tapping into the Experience of Receiving Compassionate Care in a Hospital Setting. *Journal of Research in Nursing*, (15, 1), 29–41.

Dinesen, B., Seemann, J. and Gustafsson, J. (2011). Development of a Program for Tele-Rehabilitation of COPD Patients Across Sectors: Co-Innovation in a Network. *International Journal of Integrated Care*, (11, 1).

DoH (Department of Health). (2010). *Practical Approaches to Co-Production*. London: DoH.

Durose, C., Mangan, C., Needham, C. and Rees, J. (2013). *Transforming Local Public Services Through Co-Production*. Birmingham: University of Birmingham/ AHRC.

Echeverri, P. and Skalen, P. (2011). Co-Creation and Co-Destruction: A Practice-Theory Based Study of Interactive Value Formation. *Marketing Theory*, (11, 3), 351–373.

Edvardsson, B., Tronvoll, B. and Gruber, T. (2011). Expanding Understanding of Service Exchange and Value Co-Creation: A Social Construction Approach. *Journal of the Academy of Marketing Science*, (39, 2), 327–339.

Etgar, M. (2008). A Descriptive Model of the Consumer Co-Production Process. *Journal of the Academy of Marketing Science*, (36, 1), 97–108.

Gronroos, C. (2011). Value Co-Creation in Service Logic: A Critical Analysis. *Marketing Theory*, (11, 3), 279–301.

Gummerus, J. (2010). E-Services as Resources in Customer Value creation: A Service Logic Approach. *Managing Service Quality*, (20, 5), 425–439.

Katz, S., Lantz, P., Janz, N., Fagerlin, A., Schwartz, K., Liu, L., Deapen, D., Salem, B., Lakhani, I. and Morrow, M. (2005). Patient Involvement in Surgery Treatment Decisions for Breast Cancer. *Journal of Clinical Oncology*, (23, 24), 5526–5533.

Lee, S., Olson, D. and Trimi, S. (2012). Co-Innovation: Convergenomics, Collaboration, and Co-Creation for Organizational Values. *Management Decision*, (50, 5), 817–831.

Lengnick-Hall, C., Claycomb, V. and Inks, L. (2000). From Recipient to Contributor: Examining Customer Roles and Experienced Outcomes. *European Journal of Marketing*, (34, 3–4), 359–383.

Lusch, R. and Vargo, S. (eds.). (2006). *The Service Dominant Logic of Marketing*. New York: M E Sharpe.

Nambisan, S. and Nambisan, P. (2013). *Engaging Citizens in Co-Creation in Public Services: Lessons Learned and Best Practices*. Washington, DC: IBM Center for the Business of Government.

Normann, R. (1991). *Service Management: Strategy and Leadership in Service Business*. Chichester: John Wiley and Sons.

Organisation for Economic Cooperation and Development [OECD]. (2011). *Together for Better Public Services: Partnering with Citizens and Civil Society*. Paris: OECD.

Osborne, S. (2018). From Public Service-Dominant Logic to Public Service Logic: Are Public Service Organizations Capable of Co-Production and Value Co-Creation. *Public Management Review* (20, 2), pp. 225–231

Osborne, S., Radnor, Z., Kinder, T. and Vidal, I. (2015). The SERVICE Framework: A Public-Service-Dominant Approach to Sustainable Public Services. *British Journal of Management*, (26, 3), 424–438.

Osborne, S., Radnor, Z. and Nasi, G. (2013). A New Theory for Public Services Management? Towards a (Public) Service-Dominant Approach. *American Review of Public Administration*, (43, 2), 135–158.

Osborne, S.P., Radnor, Z. and Strokosch, K. (2016). Co-Production and the Co-Creation of Value in Public Services: A suitable case for treatment? *Public Management Review*, (18, 5), 639–653.

Osborne, S. and Strokosch, K. (2013). It Takes Two to Tango? Understanding the Co-Production of Public Services by Integrating the Services Management and Public Administration Perspectives. *British Journal of Management*, (24, S1), S31–S47.

Pestoff, V. (2006). Citizens as Co-producers of Welfare Services: Preschool Services in Eight European Countries. *Public Management Review*, (8, 5), 503–520.

Plé, L. and Chumpitaz Cáceres, R. (2010). Not Always Co-Creation: Introducing Interactional Co-Destruction of Value in Service-Dominant Logic. *Journal of Services Marketing*, (24, 6), 430–437.

Prahalad, C. and Ramaswamy, V. (2004). Co-Creating Unique Value with Customers. *Strategy & Leadership*, (32, 3), 4–9.

Radnor, Z., Osborne S., Kinder, T. and Mutton, J. (2013). Operationalizing Co-Production in Public Services Delivery: The Contribution of Service Blueprinting. *Public Management Review*, (16, 3), 402–423.

Sanders, E. and Stappers P. (2008). Co-Creation and the New Landscapes of Design in CoDesign. *International Journal of Co-Creation in Design and the Arts*, (4, 1), 5–18.

Schembri, S. (2006). Rationalizing Service Logic, or Understanding Services as Experience? *In Marketing Theory*, (6, 3), 381–392.

Steen, M., Manschot, M. and De Koning, N. (2011). Benefits of Co-Design in Service Design Projects. *International Journal of Design*, (5, 2), 53–60.

Van Manen, M. (1990). *Researching Lived Experience: Human Science for an Action Sensitive Pedagogy.* New York: SUNY.

Vargo, S. and Lusch, S. (2008). Service-Dominant Logic: Continuing the Evolution. *Journal of the Academy of Marketing Science*, (36, 1), 1–10.

Venetis, K. and Ghauri, P. (2004). Service Quality and Customer Retention. *European Journal of Marketing*, (38, 11/12), 1577–1598.

Verschuere, B., Brandsen, T. and Pestoff, V. (2012). Co-Production: The State of the Art in Research and the Future Research Agenda. *Voluntas*, (23).

4 Co-Production at the Crossroads of Public Administration Regimes

Victor Pestoff

Background

In the immediate post-WW II period citizens faced a rapidly expanding, yet basically traditional public administration, with its hierarchical chain of command, where they were primarily viewed as passive clients or beneficiaries of public services. Later, in the 1980s and 1990s, with the spread of New Public Management (NPM), they were expected to become consumers and exercise more choice between various providers of public financed services, either public, private, for-profit or nonprofit. Here the market replaced the state as the main mechanism for governing the expression of citizens' preferences. More recently, we find the spread of network society (Hartley, 2005) or New Public Governance (NPG) (Osborne, 2006, 2010). NPG implies a more plural and pluralist model of provision and governance of welfare services. It is based on public-private networks, where citizens are expected to play an active role as co-producers of some aspects of the services they demand and have come to depend upon in their daily life. A fourth alternative public administration regime (PAR) now appears on the horizon, called a Communitarian regime, for lack of a better term. We need, therefore, to inquire how changes in the public sector and differences between public administration regimes are reflected in their perspective on the role of service users and professional service providers.

Citizens and professionals are the two main actors in the classical definition of co-production by Ostrom and her colleagues in the early 1970s (Parks, et al., 1981, 1999; Ostrom, 1996). Yet, today co-production appears to be at the crossroads between different public administration regimes, each with a different focus on when, where, why and how citizens can and should participate in the design and delivery of public services. In particular, they have different ideas about the role of users and professionals in promoting service quality. Thus, co-production may mean something quite different in different public administration regimes, while scholars' perspective on and definition of co-production depend to a large extent on the context in which they study the phenomenon.

Four Public Administration Regimes

This section introduces the concept of public administration regimes and briefly presents four of them; i.e., traditional public administration, NPM, NPG and a Communitarian regime. Changes in public administration regimes can set limits for citizen participation and co-production of public services. Therefore, it is important to compare PARs and understand how they differ in terms of their values and focus.

Figure 4.1 briefly summarizes some of the main points about different public administration regimes, but does not attempt to cover all aspects, which would take us far beyond the scope and purpose of this chapter. Here we will briefly consider the theoretical roots, value base and some key concepts of each administrative regime. Taken together these elements comprise crucial aspects of different PARs, similar to the idea of welfare regimes (Esping-Andersen, 1990) and production regimes (Kitschelt et al., 1999). In particular, PARs attribute quite different weight to the role of citizens and professionals in public service delivery, and their perspective differs sharply on how to guarantee service quality (Vamstad, 2012).

From a historical perspective, we will begin with traditional public administration, as seen during most of the 20th Century; followed by NPM, starting in the 1980s; and more recently the newly emerging paradigm of NPG at the turn of the century, based on ideas of network governance. We conclude this brief overview with a potential new regime found in ideas of spontaneous community and voluntarism. While these four regimes differ in some important aspects, they also share some common features. Although each public administration regime may be linked to a particular ideology or historical

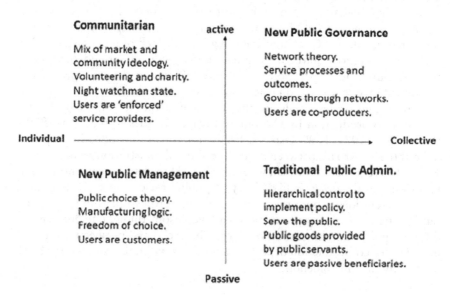

Figure 4.1 Public Administration Regimes: Citizen Participation and Responsibility

period, they can also be conceived as 'layered realities' that coexist with each other (Hartley, 2005; Osborne, 2010). Thus, more than one regime may be found in any given society at any given time, operating in different service sectors. One public administration regime may dominate in one public service sector, while another may do so in another. Moreover, they can shift over time, through the spread and ascent of a new public administration regime.

Two variables are employed herein to analyse the relations between and among public administration regimes: a) the degree of citizen activity in providing a public service and b) the institutional arrangement or degree of public responsibility for providing basic public services. The first variable is rather straightforward and ranges from low to high. The second is more complex, but reflects the degree of public vs. private responsibility for providing services to citizens. Health care or childcare can illustrate this. Is it a universal service provided to everyone in a given territory, or is it mainly dependent on individual initiative, where access to service often depends on controlling various private assets? In the former case there is a collective responsibility for providing a service, with certain limits or restrictions based on eligibility, while the responsibility is primarily individual in the latter case. This variable ranges from individual to collective. Figure 4.1 depicts these four PARs in terms of these two analytical dimensions.

Both a Communitarian regime and NPG require a high degree of citizen participation in the provision of social services, but they are found at opposite ends of a continuum ranging from individual to collective service provision. Similarly, neither traditional public administration nor NPM provide much room for citizens to participate actively in service design and delivery, and they also reflect different degrees of individual and collective responsibility for the provision of public services.

Traditional Public Administration

Traditional public administration has its theoretical roots in sociology, political science and public policy. It is based on a hierarchical model of command and control, stemming from ideas of Max Weber, with clear lines of vertical authority and responsibility. His ideas were later developed and expanded by U.S. President Woodrow Wilson (Ostrom and Ostrom, 1971). The value base of traditional public administration is found in public sector ethos or serving the public and its key concept is public goods that are provided by public or civil servants, who place a heavy emphasis on professional policy implementation and bureaucratic norms of equal treatment of all citizens.

New Public Management (NPM)

Its theoretical roots were found in growing criticism in the 1980s of the inefficiencies of traditional public administration, that were articulated in 'public choice' theory and management studies. It promoted ideas of the marketization and commercialization of public services in order to rectify these shortcomings and improve the efficiency and productivity of public sector services. Managerialism also plays a big role in this PAR. Its value base stems from industry and it promotes a manufacturing logic that emphasizes service inputs and outputs, rather than a service logic that focuses on outcomes (Osborne et al., 2013). Its key concepts are 'freedom of choice' for consumers and competition between various providers in order to promote service quality.

New Public Governance (NPG)

The theoretical roots of NPG stem from sociology and network theory and its value base is considered 'participatory democracy' by some (Pestoff, 2009) and 'neo-corporatist' by others (Osborne, 2010). NPG is based on a service logic of production that focuses on service processes and outcomes, where public value is a key concept. It governs through networks and partnerships, where the third sector and social enterprises can play an important role and citizens are active co-producers of public services.

Communitarian Regime

The following is an early approximation at best, although more clues are gleaned from Brudney and England (1983), Horne and Shirley (2009) and Bovaird and Löffler (2012). Several examples help illustrate a Communitarian type regime, although some may appear dated now. Nevertheless they provide historical examples of the development of Communitarian regimes. The Coalition Government in Great Britain after 2010 introduced a program called Big Society to promote community empowerment by reorganizing public services and facilitating social action (Slocock, 2015; Hudson, 2011). Its value base came from volunteering, philanthropy and charity, accompanied by massive budget cuts for public services, while encouraging families, communities and the third sector to fill the vacuum. Similar policies have surfaced elsewhere; in Japan, under the guise of 'Integrated Community Care' (Agenosono, 2014; Tsutsui, 2013; Tabata, 2014), NGOizaton in Thailand (Ungsuchaval, 2016) and in Europe, including Denmark (cf. Politiken) and the Netherlands (cf Nederhand and Van Meerkerk 2017), under the label of 'co-production and/or co-creation'. These diverse policy expressions are gathered herein under the heading of a 'Communitarian type of regime'. Government retains responsibility for design of service delivery, while citizens become 'enforced' co-producers (Fotaki, 2011), since they are now primarily responsible for implementing public services.

The Role of the Principal Actors in Determining Service Quality

Citizen/users and the professional staff are the two principal actors in classical definitions of co-production. We will, therefore, continue by briefly contrasting the role of each of them in the four public administration regimes.

The Role of Citizens and Users in Service Quality

The role of users in the provision of public financed services is central to this analysis. Following Figure 4.1, we can envision the role of users of public services either as beneficiaries, consumers, active co-producers or service providers, as depicted in Figure 4.2 below. It also indicates some important attributes of these different roles. They are related to the most important dimensions of our analysis, the level of activity by service users and the degree of individual or collective action necessary to avail themselves of such services.

Traditional public administration tends to be perceived as paternalistic by many since it is achieved through the 'professional gift' model of service provision. Here citizens are considered the beneficiaries of public services, but clearly with a passive role as recipients of services, without any meaningful exit or voice options available to them. Their only recourse or influence is found in the electoral system that at best can provide indirect, intermittent representation of their interest, depending on the outcome of an election.

NPM often attempts to achieve its goals by using a 'carrot and stick' approach to incentives, both for providers and users of services, which can either discourage or reward different kinds of behaviour. Here citizens are considered customers with some limited choice, but little voice and no

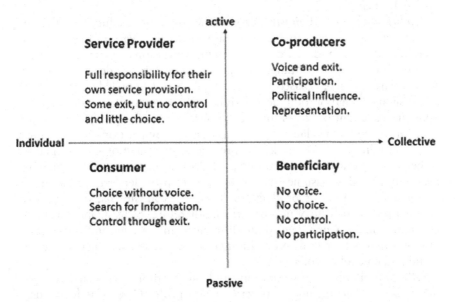

Figure 4.2 The Role of Citizens as Users of Public Services

representation. They can choose between pre-existing packages or 'offers', but they have little influence on the content or its features. Service quality is guaranteed through competition, where consumer choice determines the best quality.

NPG is based on ideas of establishing a partnership between citizens and the government, where citizens are considered co-producers of public services. This not only gives them both choice and voice in service provision, but in some cases, even representation that allows them greater direct influence than either traditional public administration or NPM. Here service quality is determined primarily by user participation, which allows service users to observe service delivery on a weekly or daily basis. This, in turn, promotes a dialog and mutual exchange between the professional providers and service users, among other things about service quality (Vidal, 2013).

In a *Communitarian regime* the role of service users is to provide many public services by and for themselves, with little or no public support, sometimes alongside, but often instead of the professionals. Here users and/or their loved-ones and neighbours become service providers, while professionals are transformed into 'back-up' agents who only intervene when the service provided proves insufficient. Determination of service quality becomes more patch-work, since access depends on the availability, willingness and capacity of service providers, which can vary considerably.

The Role of Professionals and Service Quality

The role of professionals in guaranteeing service quality is contrasted in Figure 4.3 below.

Traditional public administration relies heavily, if not exclusively, on training and professionalism to guarantee service quality (Vamstad, 2012). In a hierarchical command and control system, professionals guarantee service quality through their training. Thus, they alone can decide and prescribe appropriate measures, based on their professional knowledge, experience and insights. Collaboration, negotiations and competition are not normally taken into account in professional decisions.

NPM, by contrast, places heavy emphasis on competition and consumer choice, leaving it to the market to provide a guarantee of service quality, rather than the activities or training of professional service providers or negotiations. NPM assumes that better quality providers will attract more customers than inferior products or services. Professionals, regardless of whether public, private or non-profit, will, therefore, focus strongly on competition. Thus, it emphasizes quite different competencies and promotes a mind-set that is based on competition between providers, rather than command and control or collaboration.

NPG emphasizes collaboration and negotiation between partners, regardless of whether public, private or non-profit. Given this focus, user

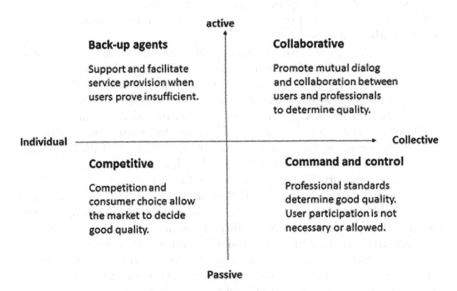

Figure 4.3 The Role of Professionals in Guaranteeing Service Quality

participation and mutual dialog between service users and the staff replaces professionalism or competition as the main guarantee of service quality (Vidal, 2013).

Finally, the perspective of a *Communitarian regime* remains largely undeveloped in this respect, but professionals can complement service provision by steering users to available resources in the community or to voluntary organizations. However, the consequence of this for service quality or availability for different groups of users remains to be seen.

Summary and Conclusions

The role of service users and professional service providers shows very clear contrasts in different PARs, especially in determining service quality. This analysis demonstrates that co-production appears very much at the crossroads today, with starkly different roles for its key actors, the users and professionals, and thus, it has a potential for developing in quite different directions. It will, therefore, take different meanings in different public administrative regimes. The role attributed to it will, however, depend in part on the level of activity ascribed to users and in part to the degree of individual or collective action necessary for providing the service. However, each direction not only implies different values, but also different roles for professionals and users/citizen participation. The way in which co-production develops depends, therefore, on the interplay of forces at the micro and macro levels of society that favour the development of a particular PAR rather than another.

Historically, co-production doesn't appear to be a highly relevant concept for either traditional public administration or NPM, since both rely mainly on passive clients/customers, although both may occasionally pay lip service to active clients for strategic considerations. By contrast, a Communitarian type of regime and NPG promote active users to a much greater extent, encouraging them to provide certain aspects of their own services, with or without public support and/or financing. In an NPG type of PAR, promotion of co-production will go hand in hand with a greater emphasis on citizens, democratic participation and the revitalization of democracy (Pestoff, 2009). In a communitarian type of PAR, by contrast, efficiency and cutback in public spending will provide the main motive for promoting greater community and volunteer responsibility for service provision. It is natural, therefore, to expect that co-production will develop both in an individual or collective fashion and that it will involve more or less citizen participation, depending on the public administration regime. However, the mix of these two variables will be regime specific and service specific.

Thus, co-production is currently at the crossroads of major economic, social and political developments. The public debate is particularly lively in terms of the future of the public sector and the delivery of public services, as seen in several European and Asian countries. So co-production will probably develop along different trajectories under different circumstances. If governments want to enlist more user/citizen participation in public service provision, it is important to recognize the variation in the roles associated with different public administration regimes and to calibrate policy expectations of user and professional behaviour. Careful calibration of policy expectations will help avoid unrealistic or unattainable goals in public policy and will, therefore, result in greater goal achievement. By contrast, less consideration of the fundamental differences in user and professional behaviour in different public administration regimes will often result in failure to enlist sufficient user/citizen participation. Thus, having the right policy tool for the appropriate public administration regime will prove essential for achieving basic policy goals and promoting user/citizen participation in public service design and delivery.

References

Agenosono, Y., Kamazawa, S. and Hori, T. (2014). *Japan's Next Care System: How Do Communities Participate*. London: 3rd International Conference on Evidence-Based Policy in Long-Term Care.

Bovaird, T. and Loeffler, E. (2012). From Engagement to Co-Production: How Users and Communities Contribute to Public Services. Ch. 2 in V. Pestoff, T. Brandsen and B. Verschuere (eds.), *New Public Governance, the Third Sector and Co-Production*. London and New York: Routledge.

Brudney, J. and England, R. (1983). Towards a Definition of the Coproduction Concept. *Public Administration Review*, 59–65.

Esping-Andersen, G. (1990). *The Three Worlds of Welfare Capitalism*. Cambridge, UK: B. Blackwell, Polity Press.

Fotaki, M. (2011). Towards Developing New Partnerships in Public Services: Users as Consumers, Citizens and/or Co-Producers Driving Improvements in Health and Social Care in the UK and Sweden. *Public Administration*, (89, 3), 933–995.

Hartley, J. (2005). Innovation in Governance and Public Services: Past and Present. *Public Money & Management*, 27–34.

Horne, M. and Shirley, T. (2009). *Co-Production in Public Services: A New Partnership with Citizens; Cabinet Office, the Strategy Unit*. London: HM Government.

Hudson, B. (2011). Big Society: A Concept in Pursuit of a Definition. *Journal of Integrated Care*, (19, 8), 17–24.

Kitschelt, H., Lange, P., Marks, G. and Stephens, J. D. (eds.). (1999). *Continuity and Change in Contemporary Capitalism*. Cambridge and New York: Cambridge University Press.

Nederhand, M. J. and Van Meerkerk, I. F. (2017). Activating Citizens in Dutch Welfare Reforms: Framing New Co-production Roles and Competences for Citizens and Professionals. Policy & Politics. https://doi.org/10.1332/030557317X1503569 7297906

Osborne, S. P. (2006). Editorial on 'The New Public Governance'. *Public Management Review*, (8, 3), 377–387.

Osborne, S. P. (2010). The (New) Public Governance: A Suitable Case for Treatment? In S. P. Osborne (ed.), *The New Public Governance? Emerging Perspectives on the Theory and Practice of Public Governance*. London and New York: Routledge.

Osborne, S. P., Radnor, Z. and Nasi, G. (2013). A new theory for public service management? Towards a (public) service dominant approach. *American Review of Public Administration Review*, (43, 2), 135–158.

Ostrom, E. (1996). Crossing the Great Divide: Coproduction, Synergy, and Development. *World Development*, (24, 6), 1073–1087. Reprinted in 1999 as Ch. 15, Polycentric Governance and Development. In Michael D McGinnis (ed.), *Readings from the Workshop in Political Theory and Policy Analysis*. Ann Arbor, MI: University of Michigan Press.

Ostrom, E. and Ostrom, V. (1971). Public Choice: A Different Approach to the Study of Public Administration. *Public Admin. Review*, (March/April), 203–216. Reprinted in 1999 as Ch. 1. In M. McGinnis (ed.), *Polycentric Games and Institutions*. Ann Arbor: University of Michigan Press.

Parks, R. B., Baker, P. C., Kiser, L., Oakerson, R., Ostrom, E., Ostrom, V., Perry, S. L., Vandivort, M. B. and Whitaker, G. P. (eds.). (1981). Consumers as Co-Producers of Public Services: Some Economic and Institutional Considerations. *Policy Studies Journal* 9, 1001–1011. Reprinted in 1999 as Ch. 17. In Michael D. McGinnis (ed.), *Local Public Economies. Readings from the Workshop in Political Theory and Policy Analysis*. Ann Arbor, MI: University of Michigan Press.

Pestoff, V. (2009). Towards a Paradigm of Democratic Governance: Citizen Participation and Co-Production of Personal Social Services in Sweden. *Annals of Public and Cooperative Economy*, (80, 2), 197–224.

Politiken (s.d.). https://politiken.dk

Slocock, C. (2015). *Whose Society? The Final Big Society Audit.* London: Civil Change.

Tabata, K. (2014). *Health and Welfare Policy in Japan. Toward the Establishment of Integrated Community Care System.* Paper presented at the CIREC 30th Congress, Buenos Aires.

Tsutsui, T. (2013). Implementation Process and Challenges for the Community-Based Integrated Care System in Japan. *International Journal of Integrated Care.*

Ungsuchaval, T. (2016). *NGOization of Civil Society as Unintended Consequence? Premises on the Thai Health Promotion Foundation and Its Pressures Toward NGOs in Thailand.* Stockholm: ISTR Conference.

Vamstad, J. (2012 & 2015). Co-Production and Service Quality: A New Perspective for the Swedish Welfare State. Ch. 16 in V. Pestoff, T. Brandsen and B. Verschuere (eds.), *New Public Governance, the Third Sector and Co-Production.* London and New York: Routledge.

Vidal, I. (2013). Governance of Social Enterprises as Producers of Public Services. Ch. 10 in P. Valkama, S. Bailey and A-V. Anttiroiko (eds.), *Organisational Innovation in Public Services. Forms and Governance.* New York and London: Palgrave Macmillan.

4.1 Case Study—Co-Production of Care Services

Co-opting Citizens in the Reform Agenda

José Nederhand and Ingmar van Meerkerk

Introduction

The idea of co-producing and self-organizing public services has penetrated the discourse of politicians and civil servants in all kinds of policy areas, such as energy, urban development and care. The reforms that have taken place in the Dutch care regime during the past four years provide an exemplary case to empirically examine how these discourses are shaped in the Netherlands, as this policy area is traditionally characterized by a strong presence of government. Due to an ageing population, the demand for care services is rising and the preservation of the welfare state in its current form is under pressure. In order to keep the system future proof and affordable, the national government has introduced a revision of the Social Support Act in 2015. In this reform national government emphasizes the shifting 'back' of responsibilities towards society. Governments want to utilize society's resources more fully. By transferring a part of former public service delivery to citizens, welfare delivery should become a more explicit and stronger form of co-production of care professionals and citizens.

Background

The Dutch welfare system is traditionally characterized by significant governmental expenditures. In fact, the Netherlands has long been ranked among the top spending countries on welfare policies. After years of rising government expenditures, professionalization and (later) privatization, increasing attention is being paid to codifying and institutionalizing the role of citizens in the care process. The welfare system is gradually shifting from an orientation on collective solidarity towards one that is predominantly based on individual responsibility (SCP, 2005; Van Oorschot, 2006). In this shift an increasingly important role is assigned to informal carers such as family members, volunteers and/or people from the social network of people with limitations. Whilst informal care has always been there, the current reform explicitly frames informal carers as being partners in the production of welfare services.

From a content analysis of 37 national governmental policy letters in the period 2012–2015, we observed the strong sense of urgency government creates for reorganizing the welfare system and the role of citizens in this reform (see Nederhand and Van Meerkerk, 2017). This 'change necessity' frame contains different reasons and narratives: to keep care provision payable, accessible and in line with changing societal demands. The growth of demand (a growing population of elderly people), but also changing demands to care (people want more customized care) are mentioned as reasons for reforming the system. Making the welfare system financially sustainable is one of the most mentioned reasons for the reform, together with maintaining or even improving the quality and continuity of care. The most important way government wants to simultaneously realize these two ambitions is by making more use of resources of citizens. Interesting to note here is that citizen involvement is predominantly seen as a means to enhance the efficiency and effectiveness of public governance, and not so much to enhance citizens' democratic influence. The background of this reform lies for an important part in cutting back expenditures and keeping the system financially sustainable in relation to a growing population of elderly people.

Experiences

In the case of the Dutch welfare state reform, we observe a strong attention for citizens as co-producers.

With the adoption of the 2015 revision of the Act, a major decentralization in welfare competences has occurred. Welfare tasks are now the responsibility of municipalities. With the adoption of care plans, municipalities define together with the involved persons what people with limitations should do for themselves and codify how informal carers and professionals will help. In this way, informal carers are involved in the design of the service (care plan) as well as in the implementation of a service (the actual welfare provision). Hence, in the care sector co-production in both the design and implementation of services has become an increasingly important theme.

Government frames citizens as partners in the delivery of welfare services and frames the role of regular care providers as complementary and supportive to the role of citizens. They should equip and enable people to bear responsibility. The documents stress that while people can still rely on professional care, this type of care is provided in collaboration with the people themselves and their environments. In this process, regular care providers should have an eye for the needs of informal carers and support them in delivering care. Identifying needs of and supporting informal carers have become part of the new competencies of professionals. Professionals could for instance capacitate informal carers in taking specific care measures. As the resources of citizens are framed as being an inextricable part of the care system, of which local governments eventually remain responsible, the documents clearly emphasize the importance of activating citizens in a process of co-production. The total amount of care is co- produced by regular and citizen providers.

Overall, we can distinguish three different narratives to describe the role of regular care providers when it comes to co-producing public services with citizens: an activation, supportive and partnership role. These narratives strongly connect to and complement one another. By incorporating multiple roles, regular care providers have a central role in guiding this process of co-production. In this way, the national government places the efforts of citizens under a shadow of hierarchy.

How the multitude of narratives function in practice has to be established. Whereas in discursive practices all types of narratives can peacefully coexist, it might well be that, in policy practice, various conflicts and tensions arise as a result of incomprehensible roles. The practical implications of this hybridization of roles thus have to be established.

References

Nederhand, M. J. and Van Meerkerk, I. F. (2017). Activating Citizens in Dutch Welfare Reforms: Framing New Co-production Roles and Competences for Citizens and Professionals. Policy & Politics. https://doi.org/10.1332/030557317X150356 97297906

Oorschot, W. (2006). The Dutch Welfare State: Recent Trends and Challenges in Historical Perspective. *European Journal of Social Security*, (8, 1), 57–76.

SCP. (2005). *Societalization of Care. [Vermaatschappelijking in de zorg]*. The Hague: Social Cultural Planning Bureau.

5   Public Management and Co-Production

John Alford and Louise Freijser

Introduction

Like non-identical twins separated at birth, co-production and public management have been connected with but distanced from each other since the 1970s. Until the turn of the century, co-production had not prospered as well as public management, and like those twins, their fates have also followed different paths, as the relationship between them has gone through stages. At first co-production was seen (and often misinterpreted) by government reformers as similar to or part of the idea of public participation in decision-making—both seen as interesting ideas but with slightly naïve advocates. Meanwhile, public management had become the dominant construct in the public sector, spreading across the world under labels such as the New Public Management (NPM), corporate management or managerialism (Pollitt and Bouckaert, 2000). It appealed to management reformers with its emphasis on performance, control and incentives.

But as the 21st century progressed, officials were realising that the characteristic instruments of public management were problematic in various ways. Most significant was that they discouraged co-ordination between organisational units inside and outside departments. Reformers began to turn to collaborative or networked organisational forms, which would foster better co-operation between them. One of these forms was co-production (Parks et al., 1981; Brudney and England, 1983; Whitaker, 1980).

Meanwhile, the literature that had grown up around public management was starting to surrender ground to a burgeoning body of work on co-production. This chapter considers co-production and public management and the relationship between them. It shows how NPM or managerialism (or other similar term) is largely derived from and similar to corporate management. On that basis, we look at whether the two approaches are compatible. Specifically, to what extent are the characteristic devices of public management barriers or facilitators to co-production?

Defining Co-Production and Co-Creation

As Brandsen and Honingh point out (chapter 2 this volume), the host of definitions of co-production and co-creation can be categorised along many dimensions, which overlap in some respects but also differ from each other. Consequently, distilling a definition is difficult if not impossible. Instead of the *correct* definition, we say what *we* mean when we use these terms. We share the general consensus in the literature that co-production and co-creation are essentially about the participation in or contribution of citizens and/or clients in the work of *producing* public services. These terms have no significance without an element of clients contributing work to service delivery. Specifically, co-production refers solely to doing the work of service delivery, whereas co-creation includes that but also includes deciding about what is to be done, and/or how. This means that terms like co-planning, co-design or co-evaluation do not in themselves refer to doing the work, but they can be added to co-production to broaden its meaning to something approaching co-creation.

More expansively, co-creation goes beyond co-production because the act of creation can entail other activities or skills which are not well described as 'production'. In particular, creating value can sometimes be the result of imagination, in which opportunities are discerned by managers, clients or citizens who together fashion different configurations of resources.

Moreover, public management is both a generic term and a label for a particular model. Generically, it is sometimes assumed to be interchangeable with public administration, in the sense that it is generally about what *public servants* do, as opposed to corporate executives or NFP leaders. Some public administration scholars react adversely to this usage, typically regarding public management as inappropriately paying homage to what they see as a private sector construct. But here we use the term pragmatically as a shorthand for particular phenomena as the circumstances dictate. We will adopt the more specific usages, stating what *we* mean by them in this chapter, while occasionally referring to generic terms for simplicity's sake.

But the key features can be identified from the various accounts, most notably by Hood (1991), Hughes (2003) and Pollitt (1990), from which we distil what follows. The essence of public management involves focusing on results rather than processes, giving managers the autonomy, means and incentives to achieve those results (Pollitt and Bouckaert, 2000). It evolved over time, from the 1980s to more sophisticated forms from the late 1990s. Initially it was sometimes referred to as 'managerialism' and entailed reform within the public sector. Its key elements, drawn from Hood (1991) were:

- establishing goals or purposes at a corporate level, with a strategy aimed at achieving those goals,
- disaggregation of organisational units within the public sector, each responsible for a particular set of logically connected outputs or outcomes groups,
- explicit standards and measures of performance,
- applying the performance measures in the disaggregated agencies to incentivise managers to perform well,

- codifying these understandings as contracts comprising specifications, carrots and sticks,
- scaffolding this with a set of HR practices, such as incentive pay and recruiting or promoting generalist management talent.

There was also the beginning of some experimentation with privatising, usually in the form of selling off government assets.

From the 1990s this approach was elaborated into a more encompassing one, the watchword of which was 'competition', not only between public and private organisations but also among public ones. It decoupled service delivery functions from core policy departments, as exemplified by the UK's 'Next Steps' agencies (Jenkins et al., 1988) and New Zealand's Crown Entities (Shick, 1996), and increased the 'contestability' of public outputs with respect to non-government providers. The slogan was that senior managers would be 'steerers, not rowers' (Osborne and Gaebler, 1992). The pace of public assets sales stepped up, as did outsourcing of increasing numbers of previously public functions. By the end of the century, the public sector in at least the Anglo-American countries looked quite different from twenty years earlier, although it still had the residual underlays of the previous stages.

These reforms tended to be reactions to the shortcomings of whatever preceded them—in this case what we will call 'traditional public administration', which was focused on processes and hence a myriad of rules, which limited managers' flexibility. Moreover, the reforms tended to be promulgated for whole governments rather than individual programs or organisations. Public management as a whole model took shape initially in New Zealand, Britain and Australia and some Australian states. There were also significant reforms in other countries such as the Scandinavians, and also the United States, albeit more patchily because they emerged in individual departments rather than whole governments. Also noteworthy was the considerable inter-jurisdictional borrowing (Boston, 1996; St Martin, 2004)—in particular via management consultants, who had long embraced the corporate model as the norm for Fortune 500 companies, and tended to apply it to governments they advised.

Whatever the causes, the public management model spread rapidly through the advanced industrial world, and held sway for a couple of decades, until some of its shortcomings began to crystallise. These problems were exacerbated by the expressed need for governments to tackle complex problems in a more resilient manner, calling for 'joined-up government', more use of external providers, especially in the non-profit sector, and project working. In the early 2000s, networked governance and its many cousins were the central preoccupations of senior managers and other reformers. Just as public management was a response to the problems of traditional public administration, so collaborative working came into being as a 'solution' to public management's difficulties. In each stage, the later model didn't so much displace its predecessor but rather became an overlay to what had gone before. Thus public management has continued to have an impact on the progress of co-production, notably because it was not the model of choice for public management reformers during the high point of NPM in the last two decades of the century.

Public Management and Co-Production

But it never quite went away. One reason was that in a considerable proportion of services, such as programs for the unemployed, education or health, public sector organisations simply cannot do their work without time and effort from their clients. Regardless of whether an organisation wanted to adopt co-production, in many cases it was already engaged in it (Alford, 2009), nor could it function without it. For other services, co-production is an 'optional extra': in the sense that the organisation can still deliver services without it. But even in some of those cases, it may be that even if the organisation can get by without co-production, it may be a little cheaper or more effective in cost-benefit terms than in-house production by public service professionals. However, more than a few organisations are caught in sub-optimal performance because a requirement to co-produce is inherent in their particular service but is not recognised as such.

For example, in order to do its work, a fire brigade relies on property owners and occupants to perform key tasks such as to eliminate fire hazards or install smoke alarms. These tasks can only really be done by the owners/occupants, since they are structurally situated in the position where they can and must take action. Thus many fire brigades devote some time to encouraging fire safety measures by members of the community, in addition to delivering services themselves. By contrast, a public housing authority might find that physical maintenance work in housing estates could either be done by the tenants themselves—with encouragement in the form of tools and training—or done by the agency's own staff, or for that matter by hired contractors. The choice would rest on the type of cost-benefit analysis that informs private companies' decisions to 'make or buy'.

But whether it is unavoidable or not, or in the latter case beneficial or not, the nature and extent of co-production is affected by the degree to which public management is predominant in the public service landscape. What follows draws on Hood's list of features of NPM to explore the ways in which the public management model might be positive or problematic for co-production.

Disaggregation of Organisational Units

The first of the pathologies prompted by NPM was the predilection for the horizontal disaggregation of organisational units into groups, known as 'silos' or 'stovepipes', with each unit autonomous and responsible for a particular set of logically connected outputs or outcome groups. These groups were not the same as those used in traditional public administration, which corresponded more with inputs (such as line-item expenditure categories) and processes (such as processing payments). By contrast, each of the NPM-inspired stovepipes was organised in alignment with the outputs and outcomes. For instance, an environmental protection agency might previously have been organised into functions such as policy, standards, operations, and finance and administration—each function including different types of environmental degradation such as air pollution, water pollution or solid waste. But under NPM the overarching organisational units are the types of pollution, with functions structured as sub-sets within each pollution-oriented unit. These arrangements had the potential to better concentrate the operations of each unit on its ultimate purposes—the production of outputs and outcomes—rather than its inputs and processes. Not only would this enhance intra-unit co-ordination, but also it would orient staff to focus on results—and therefore, it was argued, to greater efficiency.

But whether or not NPM facilitated better performance by public sector organisations overall, there are question marks about its impact on *co-production* by clients. On the one hand, the focus on results held out the likelihood that the organisation's work was more likely to connect with external parties such as clients, who would be closer in the service chain to its outputs and outcomes than to its inputs. However, fragmentation in services can lead to low trust between front-line workers and clients, as Needham (2008) found in her research on public housing (for example, officers expected to act as 'gatekeepers' for a rationed key service did not have access to information desired by the clients); this in turn impedes co-production.

Other features of 'silos' made it more difficult to engage in co-production. First, it had a tendency to foster turf wars, in which each silo fights to secure some of the territory occupied by others, or to defend it against others. Closely related are contests for resources, which of course also occur in other processes such as traditional line-item budgeting, but can aggravate ongoing conflicts, which are hardly conducive to co-production. Second these tendencies can resonate with organisational cultures in a way that reinforces their intensity in conflict situations. Tuurnas (2015) found that NPM-based silos hamper the innovativeness of professionals; cross-sectoral cooperation was so low that professionals in her study concentrated on increasing that rather than looking out for co-production opportunities with non-public actors. In short, silos and their manifestations of conflict can be undesirable not only for the functioning of the organisation, but also for its amenability to client co-production.

These problems could be overcome to a degree, but they are often structurally embedded into the situation. The metaphor of the silo signifies this structural inherency: it is very hard to shift the grain in a wheat storage tower sideways into the other towers.

Steering not Rowing

Whereas silos entail horizontal separation, the notion of 'steering, not rowing' refers to a divide between entities arranged vertically. It originated in

the UK in the late 1980s, with the government's Next Steps initiative—
in which the functions of policy development, strategizing or purchasing
(decision roles) were assigned to a core department of state, while those
of production or implementation ('doing' roles) were assigned to another
entity known as an 'Executive Agency'. It therefore embodied the 'principal-
agent' (or 'purchaser-provider') model proposed in the public choice literature, which sought to increase the influence of the politician and reduce that
of the agent. At a strategic level, through the application of tightly drawn
contracts, the former would oversee the latter, who would nevertheless have
more operational autonomy.

This vertical separation poses two problems for co-production. First, the
tight specifications of the contract could undermine the kind of flexibility
and mutual adjustment that sustain the voluntary impulse so necessary to
co-production, by 'crowding out' prosocial motivations (see Frey, 1997).
But at the same time, as Stewart (1996) points out, such precision in defining policy in advance of action hinders flexibility in the not uncommon
circumstances where things are turbulent.

Second, one of the risks of the separation of the principal from the agent
is that it makes it harder for the principal to garner information about how
the agent is performing and what might be done to improve that (Dubnick and Frederickson, 2009). This is especially knotty where the agent
relies to a large degree on the contributions of co-producers, who usually
require another link in the chain of communication between decision and
implementation.

Thus both the horizontal and vertical dimensions of structuring organisations tend to hamper the agility required to work towards defined purposes
with co-producers while maintaining trust and commitment.

Performance Measurement

Performance measurement is a central feature of public management. It
informs the articulation of objectives, the assignment of responsibilities and
the allocation of rewards. In its standard model, performance measurement
in an organisation appears to be straightforward. There is a clearly specified
task, which the public servant is able to do. There is a 'line of sight' between
the outcome and/or output required by the organisation and metrics that
permit task achievement to be monitored, whether as a simple 'Yes/No' or a
calibrated scale (Score = 7 out of 10). But these conditions do not hold uni-
versally, primarily because the challenges of gleaning and interpreting information lend a degree of indeterminacy. This becomes even trickier when
there is an element of co-production. The reason is that the co-production is
to some degree out of the organisation's control, and the outcomes less easy
to define, let alone measure (Tuurnas, 2015; Bovaird and Loeffler, 2012).
Also, as Bovaird and Loeffler (2013) point out, co-produced services often
incur costs in one service but benefits in another, with long-term and complex effects (see also Boyle and Harris, 2009). It is therefore difficult to

ascertain whether the blame for a poor performance or the credit for a good one is due to public servants or client co-producers—an even trickier problem if there is a degree of interdependence between them. For instance, a psychiatric service faces a difficult task in measuring progress (e.g. number of patients 'cured'), because the truly relevant information resides in the heads of the patients, and it is hard to elicit it without time and cost.

Monetary and Non-monetary Incentives and Motivation

The motivation issue is important to co-production because it usually involves prompting people who are not subject to one's hierarchical command and therefore cannot really be compelled to co-produce. Eliciting their willingness to co-produce calls for more subtle tools than rewards or punishments. But applying those tools is itself prone to complexities.

This chapter has already alluded to the fact that people co-produce for more than material self-interest. This position is clearly divergent from that attributed to the rational utility-maximising individual sometimes known as *homo economicus*. Four arguments can be mounted against that position.

First, there is abundant evidence that we are motivated by a variety of factors, some of which resonate with our self-interest—such as material gain and fear of sanctions—others appealing to non-material motivations, such as intrinsic reward, social affiliation or adherence to moral purposes (Hackman and Lawler, 1971; Kahnemann and Tversky, 1979; Fehr and Gintis, 2007). Second, and related, is that we each hold to different mixes of these motivations. Third, to the extent that utilisation of material self-interest requires a means of setting and measuring performance, it is prone to the difficulties of that method, as discussed above, since specification and measurement are complex arts, especially in the public sector. Finally, material self-interest can have perverse results (Frey, 1997). If one party offers another a financial reward to perform an urgent task, then the next time the issue comes around, the payee will insist on the same payment. They may previously have been motivated to do the work by more pro-social concern, but the monetary payment will have 'crowded out' the original moral basis of their contribution. This is especially likely to be a problem where incentive-oriented public managers encounter volunteers who are contributing because they have a moral commitment to the cause in question (Alford and O'Flynn, 2012).

What makes this especially important is not only that public managers lack hierarchical control over co-producers, which mitigates the impact of traditional carrots and sticks such as money or sanctions. It is also that combining wider sets of motivators, while potentially very effective, needs to be carried out gradually and interactively.

Despite the difficulties, there are means of ameliorating them to some extent. Two techniques can go some way to mitigating the problems without abrogating the public management model's need for a focus on results.

Both involve acknowledging the place of co-producers not only in delivering outputs but also in helping shape and even governing the process.

One concerns the interdependency problem: that it can be hard to distinguish the contributions of internal and external processes which are intertwined with each other. The reason is often that managers have neglected to take account of the external co-producers' roles *ex ante*. They may have well-framed, sophisticated measures of outcomes or quality, and indeed of some processes, but they tend not to devote as much consideration to what might be called 'co-producer outputs or outcomes', which could thereby become useful markers of what is happening at different stages of the production process. More generally, both co-production and public management could be enhanced if the internal and external producers could together engage in deliberation about the design, delivery and evaluation of services.

Conclusion

Co-production is a concept and a set of practices which is affected in various ways when it is immersed in the framework of public management and its characteristic form of NPM, as the experience since they first emerged in the 1970s has shown. As a result, co-production and public management have been related but somewhat estranged. Some of their artefacts sit awkwardly together; these mainly relate to the orientation of public management towards precision, incentives and delineating responsibilities. Others can function as bridges between the two ways of looking at the world, for example by facilitating the shared ownership of framing indicators.

References

Alford, J. (2009). *Engaging Public Sector Clients: From Service Delivery to Co-Production*. Basingstoke: Palgrave Macmillan.

Alford, J. and O'Flynn, J. (2012). *Rethinking Public Service Delivery: Managing with External Providers*. Basingstoke: Palgrave Macmillan.

Boston, J. (1996). Origins and Destinations: New Zealand's Model of Public Management and the International Transfer of Ideas. In P. Weller and G. Davis (eds.), *New Ideas, Better Government*. St Leonards, NSW: Allen and Unwin.

Bovaird, T. and Loeffler, E. (2013). From Engagement to Co-Production. In *New Public Governance, the Third Sector, and Co-Production*, 35–60. London: Routledge.

Boyle, D. and Harris, M. (2009). *The Challenge of Co-Production*. London: New Economics Foundation.

Brudney, J. L. and England, R. E. (1983). Toward a Definition of the Coproduction Concept. *Public Administration Review*, (43, 1).

Dubnick, M. J. and Frederickson, H. G. (2009). Accountable Agents: Federal Performance Measurement and Third-Party Government. *Journal of Public Administration Research and Theory*, (39).

Fehr, E. and Gintis, H. (2007). Human Motivation and Social Co-Operation. *Annual Review of Sociology*, (33), 43–64.

Frey, B. (1997). *Not Just for the Money: An Economic Theory of Personal Motivation*. Cheltenham: Edward Elgar.

Hackman, J. and Lawler, E. (1971). Employee Reaction to Job Characteristics. *Journal of Applied Psychology*, (55), 259–286.

Hood, C. (1991). A Public Management for All Seasons? *Public Administration*, (69). Spring.

Hughes, O.E. (2003). *Public Management and Administration: An Introduction*. Third edition. New York: Palgrave.

Kahneman, D. and Tversky, A. (1979). Prospect Theory: An Analysis of Decisions Under Risk. *Econometrica*, (47), 313–327.

Needham, C. (2008). Realising the Potential of Co-Production: Negotiating Improvements in Public Services. *Social Policy and Society*, (7, 02), 221–231.

Osborne, D. and Gaebler, T. (1992). *Reinventing Government: How the Entrepreneurial Spirit Is Transforming the Public Sector*. New York: Addison-Wesley Publishing Company.

Parks, R. B., Baker, P. C., Kiser, L., Oakerson, Ostrom, E., Ostron, V., Percy, S. L., Vandivort, M. B., Whitaker, G. P. and Wilson, R. (1981). Consumers as Co-Producers of Public Services: Some Economic and Institutional Considerations. *Policy Studies Journal*, (9, 7), 1001–1011.

Pollitt, C. (1990). *Managerialism and the Public Services: The Anglo-American Experience*. Oxford: Basil Blackwell.

Pollitt, C. and Bouckaert, G. (2000). *Public Management Reform: An International Comparison*. Oxford: Oxford University Press.

Schick, A. (1996). *The Spirit of Reform: Managing the New Zealand State Sector in a Time of Change*. Report for State Services Commission. < http://www.ssc.govt.nz/display/document.asp?docid=2845>. (November 2009).

St Martin, D. (2004). *Building the New Managerialist State: Consultants and the Politics of Public Sector Reform*. Oxford: Oxford University Press.

Stewart, J. (1996). A Dogma of Our Times: The Separation of Policy-Making and Implementation. *Public Money & Management*, (16, 3).

Tuurnas, S. (2015). Learning to Co-Produce? The Perspective of Public Service Professionals. *International Journal of Public Sector Management*, (28, 7), 583–598.

Whitaker, G. (1980). Co-Production: Citizen Participation in Service Delivery. *Public Administration Review*, (40), May/June.

6 What Do Voluntary Sector Studies Offer Research on Co-Production?

Lehn M. Benjamin and
Jeffrey L. Brudney

Introduction

Co-production was introduced in the United States during the 1970s and early 1980s to describe the active involvement of service recipients in the service delivery process (e.g., Brown, 1978; Brudney and England, 1983; Gersuny and Rosengren, 1973; Ostrom et al., 1973; Parks et al., 1981; Whitaker, 1980). Although research on the topic seemed to languish in the late 1980s to the early 2000s, the concept of co-production has found new currency among researchers in public administration, particularly in the United Kingdom and Europe (Alford, 2009; Pestoff, Brandsen and Vesrchuere, 2013). This research has considered questions such as, what are the costs and benefits of supplementing employees' service-delivery activity with citizen effort, what types of co-production lead to better outcomes, and what motivates citizens to co-produce?

More recently researchers have turned their attention to voluntary sector organizations to consider how service users in these settings actively participate in the service delivery process (e.g., Benjamin and Campbell, 2015; Pestoff and Brandsen, 2008; Prentice, 2006; Vamstad, 2012). This literature has examined such questions as: Are voluntary sector organizations more able than government agencies to support citizen co-production? What are the risks of relying more extensively on the voluntary participation of service users to deliver services in these settings? What does co-production require of paid staff in voluntary organizations? With these organizations playing an increasingly central role in delivering public services, a treatment of co-production in the context of voluntary sector organizations is timely.

Accordingly, this chapter considers how the research from voluntary sector studies, which at this writing spans nearly half a century, can inform our understanding of co-production. We define co-production as the active role that service users can play in the service delivery process. This definition follows Brandsen and Honingh's definition of co-production in this volume (chapter 2), as they state that co-production is citizens' direct input into the production process that affects the services individually provided to them. We use the terms voluntary sector and voluntary sector studies to refer to research about organizations that are neither for-profit nor public (government) agencies, including professional social service nonprofits and grassroots organizations with no paid staff. We reserve the term volunteer for individuals who are not direct service recipients or "co-producers" but who may assist in service delivery nonetheless.

We organize our discussion around three primary themes: motivation for co-production, capacity for co-production, and organizational conditions supporting co-production. Throughout our discussion we integrate recent research on co-production in the voluntary sector, and where appropriate reference other literature. We conclude with suggestions for further research.

Volunteer Motivation and Co-Production

Securing the voluntary participation of individuals to address common problems is a principal concern of nonprofit organizations. Without the benefit of funding through either taxation (government) or conventional market transactions (business), nonprofit organizations find themselves perpetually in need of generating resources to pursue their missions. One of these resources is voluntary labor contributed by citizens. In addition to the "time, talent, and treasure" people devote to participating on boards of directors of nonprofit organizations, often called "policy volunteering," citizens volunteer their time to help nonprofits carry out their missions on the ground, through "service volunteering" activities, such as assisting clients or paid staff (Connors, 2012).

The largest repository of data on volunteering is the United States. According to the U.S. Bureau of Labor Statistics (2017), one-quarter of the U.S. civilian non-institutional population age 16 and over (24.9 percent) volunteered in the year ending in September 2015 (the most recent year for which data are available): About 62.6 million people did unpaid work (except for expenses) through or for an organization at least once between September 2014 and September 2015. Bruddney (1990) estimates that between 70 and 80 percent of all volunteer effort goes to nonprofit organizations, and Hager and Brudney (2004a, 2004b) find through a survey of a nationally representative sample of charities that four in five nonprofit organizations use service volunteers. Although no one country can be representative of the volume and diversity of volunteering worldwide, the level of volunteering both in the United States and cross-nationally is substantial (United Nations Volunteers, 2015).

Given this large endowment of unpaid labor, the motivations of people to donate their time are a central issue and concern for practitioners and scholars in nonprofit organizations. How might these motivations relate to the willingness of those receiving services to take on greater responsibility voluntarily in producing the services they receive, or co-production? Empirical and conceptual research provide useful clues.

Seven surveys based on a nationally representative sample have been conducted on the motivations of volunteers in the United States (Brudney, 2016). Although, lamentably, the surveys may have become dated, the consistency of the responses of the volunteers across the surveys suggest that these motivations are enduring. Because an activity as complex as giving time may have many roots or motivations, volunteers could select multiple reasons for this activity; thus, the percentages in any one survey sum to more than 100 percent.

By far, the survey responses given most frequently by U.S. volunteers expressing their reasons for volunteering are: "doing something useful" and to "help other people," stated by as many as 60–70 percent of volunteers, especially in the more recent national surveys. The next most common motivation of the volunteers pertains more centrally to the benefits that volunteers may receive through this activity: "enjoy doing volunteer work" or "interest in the activity or work," stated by about 35–40 percent of volunteers. A sense of obligation is also present among a sizable group of volunteers: "Religious concerns" or a "sense of duty" command around 30 percent of volunteers. Similarly, having a "friend or relative who received service," which may engender a sense of obligation, was a reason stated by 17 percent.

Although these surveys may activate biases in response, for example, toward social desirability and against revealing self-serving reasons for volunteering, relatively few of the volunteers across the seven surveys professed self-interested motivations that might be most germane to engaging citizens receiving services in co-production, such as "volunteer received service" (9–17%) and volunteering is a "learning experience" (8–16%).

On the conceptual level, Clary and colleagues (Clary and Snyder, 1991; Clary et al., 1998) have proposed the Volunteer Functions Inventory (VFI) to capture the motivations that may animate volunteers into action. Voluminous research has used or discussed the VFI (for a recent review see Ashhar, 2015). The VFI consists of six dimensions: The *Values* function expresses that the person is volunteering in order to express or act on important values, such as humanitarianism and helping the less fortunate. The *Understanding* function expresses that the volunteer is seeking to learn more about the world and/or exercise skills that are often unused. The *Enhancement* function provides that the individual is seeking to grow and develop psychologically through involvement in volunteering. The *Career* function proposes that the volunteer has the goal of gaining career-related experience through volunteering. The *Social* function conceives that volunteering can allow a person to strengthen social relationships. Finally, the *Protective* function recognizes that the individual may use volunteering to reduce negative feelings, such as guilt, or to address personal problems.

Contemporary research adds nuance to these earlier findings. Hustinx and Lammertyn (2003) propose that volunteering is undergoing a major change in style from "collective" to "reflexive." Yet, scholars continue to accept and use the Volunteer Functions Inventory to comprehend and assess volunteer motivations, although they find that these functions are related differentially to such factors as individual well-being, satisfaction with volunteering, and intention to continue volunteering (for example, Stukas *et al.* 2016). Again using the VFI to understand and classify volunteer motivations, Dunn, Chambers, and Hyde (2016) investigated the motivations for episodic volunteering across sectors (sport, tourism, events, health, and social welfare) and found a more complex set of functions served in this type of volunteering (more than 80 percent of the motives were classified according to the VFI functions, particularly enhancement, values, and social functions). Other research examines volunteering formally (through an organization) versus informally (alone); based on representative national samples of the Japanese public, Mitani (2014) found that while socioeconomic resources (education) were more strongly related to formal than to informal volunteering, subjective dispositions such as empathy and religious mind were essential facilitators of both kinds of volunteering. Research has also addressed the differences between volunteering on-line through electronic media versus offline in more traditional organizational settings in which the volunteer is physically present; Ihm (2017) reports that volunteering in one sphere can complement volunteering in the other sphere.

Research on co-production has also revealed diverse motivations for participation, although we should not expect these motivations to be identical to those of volunteers since co-producers benefit directly from the services they help to provide. According to van Eijk and Steen (2016, 29), "Despite many studies in the field, we know little about what drives individuals to engage in co-production." They propose an integrative model to account for the willingness to engage in co-production consisting of three sets of factors: perceptions of the co-production task and the competency to contribute to the public service delivery process, individual characteristics, and self-interested and community-focused motivations. In earlier research to provide an understanding of "Why People Co-Produce," these authors draw on the literatures of citizen participation, political efficacy, volunteerism, public service motivation, customer engagement, as well as co-production (van Eijk and Steen, 2014). Their review indicates that "while specific insights in citizens' motivations for co-production is still limited" (p. 362), individual capacity, including human capital and social capital, and willingness, comprising both self-centered (egoistic) and community-oriented (pro-social) motivations, might help to explain citizens' decisions to participate in co-production. Fledderus and Honingh (2016) found that participants in activation services are more motivated in general and have higher levels of trust and control, a finding they relate to the possibility of "creaming," i.e., the selective participation of clients in co-production according to the strength of their intrinsic motivations.

Like van Eijk and Steen (2014, 2016), Alford (2002) conceives of eliciting co-production as a function of increasing citizens' willingness and ability to contribute; he identifies the key motivators for co-production as sanctions, material rewards, intrinsic rewards, solidary incentives, and normative appeals. In one study Alford (2002) observed that citizens receiving services are motivated by material, solidarity, and expressive incentives, a result confirmed by Pestoff (2008). But Alford also found that low-income service recipients in workforce development programs negotiate complex feelings of hopelessness and lack of confidence, which complicate their motivation. This finding is substantiated in a broad body of research in social psychology, anthropology, and sociology (e.g., Mauss, 1990/1950; Gouldner, 1960). Coupled with the literature on volunteer motivation, the co-production literature suggests that scholars might consider a more diverse mix of motivations for co-production, and how these motivations may vary depending on the extent to which service recipients volunteer and feel confident about their ability to engage in co-production.

Capacity for Co-Production

Dating back to the writings of de Tocqueville in the 1830s, observers of voluntary organizations have pointed out that citizens do not simply help solve common problems, but as Clemens (2006, 207) points out, in working to solve these problems individuals "become citizens": they conceive of themselves in public ways and they learn skills needed to participate more effectively in public life. What does this understanding suggest for scholars of co-production? Although the voluntary sector literature has primarily focused on developing the citizenship capacity of volunteers, we extend this logic here to suggest that *how* direct service recipients are asked to co-produce has consequences not only for service outcomes but also for their capacity as citizens.

For example, nonprofit mental health clubhouses are organizations where individuals with mental illness work side by side, with paid staff to run the organization. The first clubhouse was started in the late 1940s and grew out of an effort by individuals with mental illness to provide a place of mutual support and an alternative to institutionalization. As these members work with staff to run the house (e.g., answer telephones, perform administrative tasks, help prepare meals, etc.), they also learn to develop common agendas, work through conflict, consider another's viewpoints, deal with other people, and lead. This experience can in turn foster solidarity among a larger community and realization of a common cause. Such development can also help support norms of reciprocity that make future collective action possible and lead to greater engagement in political life, for example, voting (Putnam, 1993). In this respect voluntary organizations are not only alternative sites for co-producing publicly financed services, but also they function as "schools of co-production," to adapt a phrase from de Tocqueville.

For their part, co-production scholars have called attention to the fact that citizens must learn to co-produce, and that not all citizens are equally equipped or prepared to do so (see Jacobsen and Eriksen, 2013 and Prentice, 2006). These researchers have also pointed to the importance of co-production for revitalizing democracy, but to our knowledge this research has not considered the development of service users as citizens, as a separate and important result, alongside desired policy outcomes. The voluntary sector literature suggests that citizenship development is an important outcome for those participating in these not for profit, non-governmental organizations. Although most attention by voluntary sector scholars has been given to the citizenship development of volunteers, some recent literature considers the citizenship outcome for those participating in services (see Karriem and Benjamin, 2016; Small, 2009). Examining these two distinct outcomes is also consistent with research on policy feedback, which has found a direct relationship between policy design and civic and political engagement by service recipients (see Bruch, Ferree and Soss, 2010; Mettler and Soss, 2004; Soss, 1996).

But the voluntary sector literature also suggests that enhanced capacity of citizens is not a foregone conclusion of participation. Three observations may be of particular interest for scholars of co-production. First, this literature indicates that voluntary organizations are more likely to cultivate these citizenship skills and attitudes when these organizations are less professionalized and less bureaucratic. In other words, voluntary organizations are more likely to cultivate these skills and attitudes when they provide more opportunities for participation, and when that participation comes with greater authority to make decisions (Clemens, 2006, 210). Second, this literature suggests that we cannot assume that more participation is better, that it leads to better outcomes, democratic values, and enhanced citizenship capacity. The literature contains numerous examples of voluntary organizations which have enhanced solidarity among citizens but used exclusionary practices that resulted in uncivil behavior (Berman, 1997). Finally, the voluntary sector literature shows that although participation can lead to the development of civic skills, individuals do not necessarily use the skills they have developed to participate in public life. For example, Eliasoph (1998) found that individuals participating in voluntary organizations avoided talking about politics, which led to more apathetic behavior. Brandsen and Helderman (2012) reported similar results in their study of housing cooperatives.

Because much of this discussion in voluntary sector studies has focused on volunteers, not necessarily on service users, the question for researchers of co-production is what kinds of lessons do service users learn in the service delivery process? What do they learn about their capacity and role not only as co-producers but also as citizens? And how does this learning change when service users participate to a greater or lesser degree or engage in some types of service related activities rather than others?

Conditions for Co-Production

The question of what conditions might support greater and more effective co-production on the part of those receiving services has been a central concern for scholars of co-production since the 1970s. In early research Ostrom and her colleagues found that decentralized service provision provided more opportunities for citizens to engage with municipal police, which resulted in enhanced neighborhood safety (Ostrom et al., 1973). In addition to this service arrangement, researchers have identified several other conditions that can affect co-production, including the attitudes and skills of professional staff, the size of the organization, and the accessibility of services (Bovaird and Loffler, 2012; Pestoff, 2012).

The voluntary sector literature also considers how organizational form/ structure can constrain and/or facilitate participation among volunteers, members, and clients. As noted in the previous section, one of the principal findings of this literature is that the more professionalized and bureaucratic the organization, the less likely that the organization will engage in participatory practices with clients and the broader community. This literature identifies a number of reasons consistent with the findings in the co-production research, including staff resistance, lack of dedicated resources to support such efforts, and professional jargon (Benjamin in press).

Yet this literature also shows that even voluntary sector organizations that start out using participatory practices may eventually abandon them. In fields as diverse as domestic violence, community development, and community health care, studies have shown how difficult it is to maintain participatory practices in these organizations (e.g., see Hwang and Powell, 2009; Stoecker, 1997; Wies, 2008). Although several factors may lead to voluntary organizations abandoning more participatory practices, including Michels' "iron law of oligarchy," of particular interest to co-production scholars is the impact of government funding. If we are interested in the co-production of publicly financed services, which are increasingly delivered by voluntary organizations, how does such financing affect co-production in these organizations?

When nonprofits receive funding, particularly government funding, the organization must meet the attached accountability requirements. Studies have found that these requirements lead to organizational formalization and a reduction in responsiveness to service recipients and the community more broadly. For example, researchers have noted that client and community engagement becomes limited to advisory groups or boards of directors, which often have little influence on organizational decision making (Smith, 2012); other studies corroborate this finding (e.g., Hwang and Powell, 2006; Smith and Lipsky, 1993). Recent co-production research likewise supports these findings. For example, Vamstad (2012) found that in municipal agencies providing childcare, staff saw themselves as professional experts, and consequently engaged parents less in service delivery. In contrast, in cooperatives providing the same service, the staff and parents worked side-by side to deliver childcare.

We cannot take this conclusion for granted, however. Other research suggests that receipt of government funding does not inherently preclude more participatory practices in voluntary sector organizations. For example, Ospina and her colleagues (2002) found that despite funding requirements, nonprofits do find ways to engage clients and remain responsive to them. LeRoux (2009) determined that government funding was associated with more participatory practices in nonprofit human service organizations; more specifically, she reports that nonprofits receiving government funding were more likely to have clients participate in work groups compared to nonprofits that did not receive government funding. In her in-depth study of twelve human service organizations, eleven of which received government funding, Benjamin (in press) found that these organizations used a wide variety of strategies to reduce bureaucratic and professional authority and increase client participation in the service delivery process. These strategies included reducing rules, allowing clients to choose the staff person they worked with, using peer based learning strategies, and supporting staff to build more mutual relationships with participants.

For co-production researchers, this literature leads to the conclusion that we cannot paint government funding of voluntary organizations with a broad brush. For example, government contracts come with more specific requirements than grants, which may make it more difficult for voluntary organizations to have the flexibility they need to engage program and service participants (Salamon, 2002). Some government financing comes with explicit requirements that voluntary organizations demonstrate responsiveness and accountability to service recipients. At the same time, we need to understand government funding of these services in the larger nonprofit revenue context. For example, organizations that match public funds with private donations may find it easier to sustain greater service user engagement, compared to nonprofits that receive a majority of government funding. In part this is because individual donors usually do not require specific reports or requirements.

Conclusion

The literature on voluntary sector studies is extensive, and a chapter of this length cannot do justice to this work or to the burgeoning research on co-production. Instead, we focused on three themes from the voluntary sector literature of interest to co-production scholars. First, we suggested that motivations for co-production may vary depending on the extent to which the citizen receiving services also volunteers. Second, we suggested that the form and type of participation that services require of recipients have consequences not only for policy outcomes but also for citizenship outcomes. Finally, in reviewing the conditions that support co-production, we focused on whether government funding, and the resulting requirements attached to this funding, support or constrain co-production in voluntary sector organizations; the results to date are mixed.

As research and practice on co-production continue to cross disciplinary boundaries, policy domains, and organization types, we see many areas that could benefit from further inquiry. We suggest four broad questions that might inform the contribution of voluntary sector studies to research on co-production: First, to what extent, and in what ways, might co-production differ in voluntary organizations versus government agencies? Second, and relatedly, can we view co-production through these organizations as "laboratories" not only of service outcomes but also of citizenship development? Third, how might government funding, regulation, and evaluation of voluntary, nonprofit organizations affect co-production processes? Will such extrinsic interest by government in co-production mediated through these organizations distract or even displace them from their presumably intrinsic interest in and commitment to client participation? Finally, if nonprofit sector service-delivery organizations are to support the co-production of programs and service participants, do staff possess the appropriate background and training? What curricular changes might be needed in nonprofit management (and related) education programs to support or equip staff members for this responsibility?

In this chapter we considered how the research on voluntary sector organizations not only furthers our understanding of service users' motivation to co-produce, their capacity to co-produce, and the conditions that support their co-production, but we also suggest that this research raises new questions for co-production scholars. As we rely on many voluntary sector organizations to help achieve public outcomes regardless of whether they are delivering publicly financed services, we anticipate that the research on these organizations will become even more useful for public management scholars interested in co-production. In the end we see far more generative research possibilities from fully integrating the research on voluntary sector organizations and co-production in public management.

References

Alford, J. (2002). Why Do Public-Sector Clients Coproduce? Toward a Contingency Theory. *Administration & Society*, (34, 1), 32–56.

Alford, J. (2009). *Engaging Public Sector Clients: From Service Delivery to Coproduction*. London: Palgrave Macmillan.

Ashhar, H. (2015). The Volunteer Functions Inventory: Examination of Dimension, Scale Reliability and Correlates. *International Journal of Innovative and Applied Research*, (3, 4), 52–64.

Benjamin, L. M. (In press). Client Authority in Nonprofit Human Service Organizations. In Ram Cnaan and Carl Milofsky (eds.), *Handbook of Community Movements and Local Organizations*, 2nd ed. New York: Springer Publishing.

Benjamin, L. M. and Campbell, D. C. (2015). Nonprofit Performance: Accounting for the Agency of Clients. *Nonprofit and Voluntary Sector Quarterly*, (44, 5), 988–1006.

Berman, S. (1997). Civil Society and the Collapse of the Weimar Republic. *World Politics*, (49, 3), 401–429.

Bovaird, T. and Loeffler, E. (2012). From Engagement to Co-Production: The Contribution of Users and Communities to Outcomes and Public Value. *Voluntas*, (23, 4), 1119–1138.

Brandsen, T. and Helderman, J. (2012). The Trade-Off Between Capital and Community: The Conditions for Successful Coproduction in Housing. *Voluntas*, (23, 4), 1139–1155.

Brown, M. K. (1978). The Impact of Alternative Forms of Citizen Control on Police Organization and Police Discretion. *Nonprofit and Voluntary Sector Quarterly/ Journal of Voluntary Action Research*, (7, 1–2), 85–101.

Bruch, S. K., Ferree, M. M. and Soss, J. (2010). From Policy to Polity: Democracy, Paternalism, and the Incorporation of Disadvantaged Citizens. *American Sociological Review*, (75, 2), 205–226.

Brudney, J. L. (1990). *Fostering Volunteer Programs in the Public Sector: Planning, Initiating, and Managing Voluntary Activities.* San Francisco: Jossey-Bass.

Brudney, J. L. (2016). Designing and Managing Volunteer Programs. In D. O. Renz (ed.), *The Jossey-Bass Handbook of Nonprofit Leadership and Management*, 4th ed., 688–733. Hoboken, NJ: John Wiley and Sons.

Brudney, J. L. and England R. E. (1983). Toward a Definition of the Coproduction Concept. *Public Administration Review*, (43, 1), 59–65.

Clary, E. G., and Snyder, M. (1991). A Functional Analysis of Altruism and Pro-Social Behavior: The Case of Volunteerism. *Review of Personality and Social Psychology*, (12), 119–148.

Clary, E. G., Snyder, M., Ridge, R. D., Copeland, J., Stukas, A. A., Haugen, J. and Miene, P. (1998). Understanding and Assessing the Motivations of Volunteers: A Functional Approach. *Journal of Personality and Social Psychology*, (74, 6), 1516–1530.

Clemens, E. (2006). The Constitution of Citizens: Political Theories of Nonprofit Organizations. Ch. 9 in W. W. Powell and R. Steinberg (eds.), *The Nonprofit Sector: A Research Handbook*, 2nd ed. New Haven, CT: Yale University Press.

Connors, T. D. (ed.). (2012). *The Volunteer Management Handbook: Leadership Strategies for Success; Second Edition.* Hoboken, NJ: John Wiley and Sons.

Dunn, J., Chambers, S. K. and Hyde, M. K. (2016). Systematic Review of Motives for Episodic Volunteering. *Voluntas*, (27, 1), 425.

Eliasoph, N. (1998). *Avoiding Politics: How Americans Produce Apathy in Everyday Life.* Cambridge: Cambridge University Press.

Fledderus, J. and Honingh, M. (2016). Why People Co-Produce Within Activation Services: The Necessity of Motivation and Trust—an Investigation of Selection Biases in a Municipal Activation Programme in the Netherlands. *International Review of Administrative Sciences*, (82, 1), 69–87.

Gersuny, W.R. and Rosengren, C. (1973). *The Service Society.* Schenkman Publishing Co.

Gouldner, A. (1960). The Norm of Reciprocity: A Preliminary Statement. *American Sociological Review*, (25, 2).

Hager, M. A. and Brudney, J. L. (2004a). *Balancing Act: The Challenges and Benefits of Volunteers.* Washington, DC: Urban Institute, December.

Hager, M. A. and Brudney, J. L. (2004b). *Volunteer Management Practices and Retention of Volunteers.* Washington, DC: Urban Institute, June.

Hustinx, L. and Lammertyn, F. (2003). Collective and Reflexive Styles of Volunteering: A Sociological Modernization Perspective. *Voluntas*, (14, 2), 167–187.

Hwang, H. and Powell, W. W. (2009). The Rationalization of Charity: The Influences of Professionalism in the Nonprofit Sector. *Administrative Science Quarterly*, (54), 268–298.

Ihm, J. (2017). Classifying and Relating Different Types of Online and Offline Volunteering. *Voluntas*, (28), 400–419.

Jakobsen, M. (2013). Can Government Initiatives Increase Citizen Co-Production? Results of a Randomized Field Experiment. *Journal of Public Administration Research and Theory*, (23, 1), 27–54.

Karriem, A. and Benjamin, L. M. (2016). How Civil Society Organizations Foster Insurgent Citizenship: Lessons from the Brazilian Landless Movement. *Voluntas* (27, 1), 19–36.

LeRoux, K. (2009). Paternalistic or Participatory Governance? Examining Opportunities for Client Participation in Nonprofit Social Service Organizations. *Public Administration Review*, (69, 3), 504–517.

Mauss, M. (1990/1950). The Exchange of Gifts and the Obligation to Reciprocate. Ch. 1 in *The Gift: The Form and Reason for Exchange in Archaic Societies*. London: Routledge.

Mettler, S. and Soss, J. (2004). The Consequences of Public Policy for Democratic Citizenship: Bridging Policy Studies and Mass Politics. *Perspectives on Politics*, (2, 1), 56.

Mitani, H. (2014). Influences of Resources and Subjective Dispositions on Formal and Informal Volunteering. *Voluntas*, (25), 1022–1040.

Ospina, S., Diaz, W. and O'Sullivan, J. F. (2002). Negotiating Accountability: Managerial Lessons from Identity-Based Nonprofit Organizations. *Nonprofit and Voluntary Sector Quarterly*, (31, 1), 5–31.

Ostrom, E., Baugh, W. H., Guarasci, R., Parks, R. B., and Whitaker, G. P. (1973). Community Organization and the Provision of Police Services. *Administrative & Policy Studies* Series.

Ostrom, E. and Whitaker, G. (1973). Does Local Community Control of Police Make a Difference? Some Preliminary Findings. *American Journal of Political Science*, (17, 1), 48–76.

Parks, R. B., Baker, P. C., Kiser, L., Oakerson, R., Ostrom, E., Ostron, V., Percy, S. L., Vandivort, M. B., Whitaker, G. P. and Wilson, R. (1981). Consumers as Co-Producers of Public Services: Some Economic and Institutional Considerations. *Policy Studies Journal*, (9, 7), 1001–1011.

Pestoff, V. (2012). Co-Production and Third Sector Social Services in Europe. In V. Pestoff, T. Brandsen, and B. Verschuere (eds.), *New Public Governance, the Third Sector and Co-Production*, 13–34. London, UK: Routledge.

Pestoff, V. and Brandsen, T. (eds.). (2008). *Co-Production: The Third Sector and the Delivery of Public Services*. London: Routledge.

Pestoff, V., Brandsen, T. and Verschuere, B. (eds.). (2013). *New Public Governance: The Third Sector and Coproduction*. London: Routledge.

Prentice, S. (2006). Childcare, Coproduction and the Third Sector in Canada. *Public Management Review*, (8, 4), 521–536.

Putnam, R. D. (1993). *Making Democracy Work. Civic Traditions in Modern Italy*. Princeton: Princeton University Press.

Small, M. L. (2009). *Unanticipated Gains: Origins of Network Inequality in Everyday Life*. New York: Oxford University Press.

Smith, S. R. and Lipsky, M. (1993). *Nonprofits for Hire: The Welfare State in the Age of Contracting*. Cambridge, MA: Harvard University Press.

Soss, J. (1996). *Unwanted Claims: The Politics of Participation in the U.S. Welfare System*. Ann Arbor: University of Michigan Press.

Stocker, R. (1997). The Community Development Corporation Model of Urban Redevelopment: A Critique and an Alternative. *Journal of Urban Affairs*, (19, 1), 1–23.

Stukas, A. A., Hoye, R., Nicholson, M., Brown, K. M. and Aisbett, L. (2016). Motivations to Volunteer and Their Associations with Volunteers' Well-Being. *Voluntas*, (45, 1), 112–132.

United Nations Volunteers. (2015). *State of the World's Volunteerism Report 2015: Transforming Governance*. United Nations.

Vamstad, J. (2012). Coproduction and Service Quality: The Case of Cooperative Childcare in Sweden. *Voluntas*, (23, 4), 1173–1188.

van Eijk, C. J. A. and Steen, T. P. S. (2014). Why People Co-Produce: Analysing Citizens' Perceptions on Co-Planning Engagement in Health Care Services. *Public Management Review*, (16, 3), 358–382.

van Eijk, C. J. A. and Steen, T. P. S. (2016). Why Engage in Co-Production of Public Services? Mixing Theory and Empirical Evidence. *International Review of Administrative Sciences*, (82, 1), 28–46.

Whitaker, G. (1980). Coproduction: Citizen Participation in Service Delivery. *Public Administration Review*, (40, 3), 240–246.

Wies, J. R. (2008). Professionalizing Human Services: A Case of Domestic Violence Shelter Advocates. *Human Organization*, (67, 2), 221–233.

Part 2

Influences on the Process of Co-Production and Co-Creation

7   Unravelling the Co-Producers

Who are They and What Motivations do They Have?

Carola van Eijk and Mila Gascó

Introduction

All over the world new initiatives emerge in which citizens play an active role in public service delivery processes. Sometimes governments create opportunities for citizens to take up responsibilities; in other instances, citizens themselves request a more active role. But regardless of who the initiator is, for public service employees it means they collaborate with these citizens: the so-called "co-producers". As a result, they need to share tasks, power, and responsibilities. In this chapter, we focus on the *co-production* of public services: the process in which citizens and public employees collaborate to, among other things, secure the quality and continuity of public services (Ewert and Evers, 2012; Brandsen, Pestoff and Verschuere, 2012; Brandsen and Honingh, 2016).

In co-production, co-producers co-design, co-prioritize, co-finance, co-deliver, and/or co-assess public services alongside public employees (Bovaird and Loffler, 2012). But who are these co-producers? The co-production literature presents a wide range of engaged co-producers, including local community members participating in neighbourhood watch schemes (van Eijk, Steen and Verschuere, 2017), vulnerable people taking part in activation programs (Fledderus and Honingh, 2016), parents involved in childcare services (Pestoff, 2008; Thomsen and Jakobsen, 2015), social housing residents discussing improvement of service delivery with frontline housing officers (Needham, 2008), voluntary caregivers involved in elderly care (Wilson, 1994), and citizens involved in participatory budgeting with their local government (Barbera, Sicilia and Steccolini, 2016). These examples show that co-producers can have different relations with the services produced: in some cases they are the direct service recipients (like the mentioned activation programs) while in other cases the co-producers' efforts are directed at the production of social benefits (like the example on participatory budgeting).

In order to optimize co-production processes, it is important that the public employees have an idea of who the co-producers are, what expectations of the collaboration they have, and what motivates them to engage (cf. OECD 2001). Insight about the co-producers' motivations may also help to better understand the barriers and opportunities hindering or stimulating potential co-producers from engaging. The goal of our chapter is thus to review the current co-production literature in order to answer the following two questions about co-producers: *Who are the co-producers? And what different motivations do co-producers have?* In the following sections we address these two questions in this specific order and finish with concluding remarks that include implications for practitioners and suggestions for further research.

On Co-Producers

Over time, scholars have approached co-production in various ways (see also chapters 1 and 2 in this volume). One of them is related to who the co-producer is, resulting in several definitions that range from "people or organizations other than the producing unit" (as such even including other public sector organizations; Alford, 1993) to "(groups of) individual citizens" (Brandsen and Honingh, 2016). Although for the co-production process, it certainly makes a difference whether lay citizens or highly professionalized organizations are involved, in this chapter we focus on individual *citizen* co-producers, that is, lay actors who are members of the public serving voluntarily as citizens, clients, and/or customers (Nabatchi, Sancino and Sicilia, 2017). We therefore exclude third sector organizations (cf. Pestoff's (2012) distinction between co-production, co-management and co-governance). But even when we narrow down our focus to citizen co-production, actual co-production processes vary widely as does the "position" of co-producers herein (cf. Voorberg, Bekkers and Tummers, 2015; Nabatchi et al., 2017; Alford and Yates, 2016). We identify three important elements, namely different co-producers' roles, the level of co-production, and the activities performed. Below we give further detail of each of these elements.

Co-Producers' Role

According to Voorberg, Bekkers and Tummers (2015), co-producers can be co-implementers, co-designers, and initiators. The authors show that most co-producers are involved as *co-implementers* of public services: the co-production process is initiated and designed by the public organizations, and citizens' input is restricted to certain specific tasks. An example is the collaboration between patients, their families, and healthcare professionals: the families rely on professionals' accurate information on what activities to perform to ensure seamless care at home and in clinical settings (Sabadosa and Batalden, 2014).

Co-designers can also be frequently found. In these cases, the initiative for co-production is taken by the public organizations, but citizens have an important say in how the service will be delivered. An example is the initiative of an English regional transportation department to collaborate with disabled people to better understand the barriers they face in their everyday lives, with the ultimate aim to improve current service delivery (Copestake, Sheikh, Johnston and Bollen, 2014). Finally, the less frequent role is that of the *initiator*: citizens initiate the service being delivered and governments become actors that follow. Examples include picking up litter from an adjacent street (Brudney and England, 1983) or a residents' project in a Flemish neighbourhood with the aim to cancel a planned parking space and improve the green area (Vanleene, Verschuere and Voets, 2016).

Back in 2002, Alford (2002) took a different approach and distinguished among three types of co-producers: clients, citizens, and volunteers. Clients are service-recipient individuals or service users, with a direct, individual, and private interest in the services produced. Volunteers provide input to the organization, but do not individually consume the services. With their efforts they contribute to the production of services (which is of public value), but they do not directly benefit from them. Citizens do receive value, but collectively instead of individually. As such, there is no direct nexus between their co-production efforts and the values received from the regular service provider (Alford, 2002, 33–34). Alford and Yates (2016) refine this distinction and refer to citizens as collective consumers of public value and service users (or clients) as individual consumers of private value. They further differentiate between clients and volunteers and state that the latter contribute to co-production but do not receive any service from the public organization. More recently, Nabatchi et al. (2017) have adopted similar terms and distinguish among citizens, clients, and customers. Citizens are members of a specific geographic or political community. Clients are recipients of public services to which they are legally entitled and for which they are not required to directly pay the providing organization. Finally, customers are recipients of public services for which they must directly pay the providing organization. The authors state that the roles of citizen and client are more common than those of customer, and that actors may simultaneously serve in multiple roles.

Level of Co-Production

Another element that provides more insight into who the co-producers are has to do with the level of co-production, referring to whether activities are performed by a group of citizens or rather on an individual basis. The literature distinguishes among co-production at the individual level, co-production in groups, and co-production at a collective level (cf. Brudney and England, 1983). In *individual co-production*, co-producers and regular producers work directly with each other. Often, co-producers are the clients or consumers of the service being produced, or they produce the service for a loved-one who directly and on a personal basis benefits. An example are voluntary caregivers (Wilson, 1994).

In *group co-production*, the regular producer works "directly and simultaneously with a specific cluster or category of lay actors who share common characteristics or interests" (Nabatchi et al., 2017, 5). The group members benefit from the services produced themselves, while spillover effects are beneficial to society at large; although equal distribution might be problematic (Brudney and England, 1983). Examples studied include different types of patient fora in health and social care (Allen et al., 2010; Fotaki, 2011) and parents' involvement in childcare (Prentice, 2006).

Finally, *collective co-production* is about the collaboration between public organizations and citizens with the aim to produce services that are beneficial to society at large. So, the ultimate goal is the production of social benefits rather than personal benefits. A classic example is neighbourhood watch, aimed at the improvement of safety and livability (van Eijk et al. 2017).

Activities Performed

Among the different cases that have been studied, a wide variety of activities performed by the co-producers can be identified. Brandsen and Honingh (2016), for instance, divide among complementary and non-complementary tasks. With non-complementary tasks they refer to citizens providing input to the core (primary) process of the organization and the service delivery process. Citizens' complementary tasks, on the contrary, do have an impact on the effectiveness of the delivery process, yet citizens do not come inside the organizational context (Brandsen and Honingh, 2016). The case of co-production of community safety is useful to understand both types of activities (cf. Renauer, Duffee and Scott, 2003): witness assistance or participation in "learning how not to be victimized" educational programs (Layne, 1989, 16) can be perceived as complementary tasks, while neighbourhood watch police programs are non-complementary.

An alternative way to look at co-producers' activities is to analyze the extent to which co-producers are able to produce the service themselves, without the regular producers' input. Consider parents' contributions to Christmas celebrations or school gardens at primary schools; the parents are able to organize similar activities on their own. Yet, the added value of co-production is in the "legitimization" of the activities conducted and the input provided by the professionals (e.g., money, knowledge) (Van Kleef and van Eijk, 2016). In contrast, citizens' co-producing probation services can only do so effectively and safely when professionals are also highly involved in prisoners' return to society (Surva, Tõnurist and Lember, 2016).

Co-Producers' Motivations

During the 1980s, both scholars and governments made popular the idea of co-production (cf. Parks et al. 1981; Osborne, 2010; Osborne and Gaebler, 1992), therefore, starting to wonder about the motivations of citizens to contribute efforts to the co-production of public services. Stemming from the dominant economic approach on the concept of co-production (particularly in the 1980s), it was just commonly assumed that citizens co-produce because of the direct benefits they acquire. As co-production was defined as the collaboration between regular service providers and those members of the public who directly benefit from these services (Parks et al., 1981; Whitaker, 1980), the argument was that citizens are willing to co-produce because of the opportunity to increase the amount and/or quality of services they enjoy (Kiser and Percy, 1980, as referred to by Brudney and England, 1983, 60). This approach started to change after Alford's 2002 article in which the author, following a contingency theory, shows that citizens are not simple utility maximizers but are also motivated by a complex mixture of nonmaterial incentives. In this section we address this transition in the literature.

The Early 2000s: The Contribution of Different Disciplines

Alford's (2002) contribution to understanding co-producers' motivations originates in the distinction among clients, citizens, and volunteers and the expectations regarding each of these roles. In general, all types of co-producers are expected to ensure the service is produced, and that this is done as efficiently as possible and with the highest quality (cf. definitions and aims of co-production provided by Parks et al. 1981; Brandsen et al. 2012; Brandsen and Honingh, 2016). Yet, specific roles entail specific expectations. Clients' connection is expected to be primarily based on material interests, because of the private value they receive. They feel responsible for the services they consume themselves and are less concerned with the public value of these services. Volunteers do not receive services in exchange, and so they are assumed to feel responsible for others (similar to other voluntary activities like being active in the local football club). Citizens do receive public value on a collective basis, causing them to feel responsible for both the service itself and their fellow citizens (cf. Alford, 2002).

If co-producers are not necessarily the direct consumers of the services produced, maximizing benefits may not be their sole motivation. In addition, citizens may be willing to co-produce because they simply perceive co-production as an interesting, enjoyable, or worthwhile activity (Pestoff, 2006). Thus, motivations may be the result of both material and nonmaterial incentives (Alford, 2002), of both extrinsic and intrinsic rewards (Deci, 1972). Co-producers may also be driven by other values, such as altruism or sociality (Verschuere, Brandsen and Pestoff, 2012), following the literature on volunteering and citizen participation (cf. Alford, 2002; Pestoff, 2012).

Integrating the insights of additional fields of research, such as volunteering and political participation, resulted in the identification of a wide variety of factors that might have an impact on co-producers' decision to engage in the co-production of public services. The literature on volunteering, for example, supports the view that people might want to take responsibility for their community (Reed and Selbee, 2003). As "active citizens", people do not only stress their rights but also the responsibilities they have for society (Clarke et al., 2007). Such altruistic motivations stem from fellow-feeling with other citizens or identification with public purposes (Alford, 2014), while willingness to initiate reciprocity is stimulated by social norms and feelings of trust (Ostrom, 2009). Additionally, literature on volunteering mentions the importance of social interaction—people volunteer for enjoyment purposes or to meet new people (Dunn, Chambers and Hyde, 2016)—and status—the possibility to prove their capabilities to oneself and others (Taylor and Shanka, 2008).

The literature on political participation also adds to the understanding of co-producers' motivation. Salience, for example, can be taken as a determinant of motivation. It refers to the importance of the issue at hand for a citizen: only when the issue is perceived as relevant enough, participation is considered (Pestoff, 2012). Perceptions on one's competencies also result in increasing motivations to participate. The literature on political participation refers to this factor as "efficacy", and distinguishes between internal and external efficacy. The former refers to "beliefs about one's own competence to understand and to participate effectively in politics", while the latter can be defined as "beliefs about the responsiveness of governmental authorities and institutions to citizen demands" (Craig, Niemi and Silver, 1990, 290). In co-production, we might expect that co-producers only decide to co-produce if they perceive themselves capable to do so and when they consider the public organization provides enough room for their interaction (so, they are convinced their interaction will matter in the service delivery process) (van Eijk and Steen, 2016).

The literature on political participation also stresses the importance of networks and the social capital stemming from these networks—for instance church attendance, group membership, and marital status impact on citizens' decisions (Amnå, 2010; Putnam, 1993; Svendsen and Svendsen, 2000). Finally, according to the literature on both political participation (Timpone, 1998) and volunteering (Dekker and Halman, 2003), socio-economic variables like education, income, and jobs are found to have an impact on citizens' decision to participate/volunteer. Table 7.1 summarizes the above contributions.

The 2010s: Co-Production from a Public Administration/Public Management Perspective

Although scholars' broader perspective provided useful additional insights, substantive progress in answering the question why people co-produce was limited, as the question was only answered by putting forward theoretical assumptions (cf. Verschuere et al., 2012) and during the 2000s even faded to the background. Moreover, ascribing motivations derived from the

Table 7.1 Summary of the Contribution of Different Fields to the Study of Co-Producers' Motivation

Stream of research	Citizens' motivations to co-produce
Economics	Extrinsic motivations: material self-interest, maximizing benefit (quantity and/or quality of public services)
Public management	Both extrinsic and intrinsic motivations: dependent on the specific role (i.e., clients, citizens, volunteers) in the co-production process and the expectations regarding each of these roles
Volunteerism	Intrinsic motivations: taking responsibility for the community, altruism, social interaction, status
Political participation	Both extrinsic and intrinsic motivations: salience, internal and external efficacy, networks and social capital, socioeconomic variables

volunteering and citizen participation literature leaves the question aside of whether the *context* of political participation and volunteering is comparable to that of co-production. That is, co-producing public services might be a process that is distinct from taking part in political processes or volunteering; just like one can hardly compare participation in a political process such as commenting on a zoning plan with volunteering activities in a sport club. Another difference concerns the interaction (or lack thereof) with public employees: the interaction between co-producers and public employees is inherent to co-production, while volunteering often does not take place in a professionalized service delivery process (Verschuere et al., 2012). Thus, although a multidisciplinary approach is helpful to develop new theories explaining co-producers' engagement, it can only be so when the insights are tested in or added with insight from the specific co-production context (van Eijk, 2017).

A renewed interest for what motivates the individual co-producer to co-produce public services and the acknowledgement of the need for empirical knowledge resulted in a new wave of studies during the 2010s. Pestoff (2012) put the issue of co-producers' motivations on the research agenda again. He argued that citizens' involvement is the result of two elements. First, the regular service provider (i.e., the public organization involved) needs to encourage citizens by making co-production easier for them; for instance by reducing transaction costs and by removing obstacles. Second, there is the individual motivation necessary to let someone decide s/he wants to become active as a co-producer. According to Pestoff (2012, 24–25), this is linked with the idea of *salience*: the more important the service provided is for the individual, his/her family, loved ones, or friends, the more likely (s)he will participate.

Although useful, Pestoff's work still does not address what specific motivations these individuals have, as the range of motivations probably includes more than the salience of the service provided alone. In their study, van Eijk and Steen (2014) take a different approach to answer this question. While Alford (2002) argued that when co-producers are involved as citizens or volunteers their motivations might be similar to those identified for citizen participation or volunteering respectively, van Eijk and Steen (2014) take one step back by questioning whether citizen participation and volunteering can indeed be perceived as similar to co-production. They investigate what self-reported motivations can be identified in a particular co-production process (i.e., client councils at health care organizations) and conclude that different viewpoints can be identified, each reflecting a different set of motivations. For example, some co-producers hold a more professionalized viewpoint: they are motivated out of desire to contribute something to the health care organization and feel capable to do so because of the competencies they have. Other co-producers value the idea of doing good for the benefits of all users in general (instead of contributing to the organization) or contrarily are motivated to take part because this allows them the opportunity to build "cozy" relationships with other co-producers (van Eijk and Steen, 2014).

Following van Eijk and Steen (2014), different scholars have become interested in the issue of co-producers' motivations. Yet, studies have been conducted in a limited number of countries and policy domains, the latter including health care (e.g., Bovaird, Stoker, Jones, Loeffler and Roncancio, 2016), community safety (van Eijk et al., 2017), care of the local environment (Vanleene, Voets and Verschuere, 2017), and activation programs for unemployed people (Fledderus and Honingh, 2016). Based on the different studies, three conclusions can be drawn.

First, co-producers' motivations turn out to be rather nuanced, complex, and sometimes even inconsistent (cf. van Eijk and Steen, 2014; Blakely and Evans, 2009). The empirical studies list a number of factors that explain co-producers' engagement, and these factors prove to different extents the theoretical assumptions mentioned above; we will elaborate on this further below. Moreover, research findings indicate that it is hard to develop just one theory explaining the engagement of *all* co-producers, as it seems that (even within one co-production initiative) different groups of co-producers are differently motivated (cf. van Eijk et al. 2017). Some co-producers might be more driven by altruistic motivations, while others get motivated by the opportunity to master new competencies.

Second, co-producers' engagement can partly be explained by factors at the individual level. Vanleene et al. (2017) refer to this as "personal motivations". A factor that is often mentioned is internal efficacy. In line with the theoretical assumptions derived from the literature on political participation, a number of studies conclude that co-producers' perceptions on their capabilities to engage in co-production are an important motivating factor (e.g., Bovaird, Van Ryzin, Loeffler and Parrado, 2015; Thomsen, 2015; Thomsen and Jakobsen, 2015). Thus, the belief that one can actually make a difference increases the likelihood of co-producers' willingness to engage

(Bovaird et al., 2016; Parrado, Van Ryzin, Bovaird and Löffler, 2013). This relation between internal efficacy and engagement might be mediated, however, by age: younger people often report lower levels of efficacy, negatively influencing their decision to engage (Thijssen and Van Dooren, 2016).

Empirical studies, furthermore, prove Pestoff's (2012) arguments on the importance of ease and salience for co-producers' decision to engage in co-production of public services (e.g., Vanleene et al. 2017; van Eijk, 2017). Further, empirical results show that personal (material) incentives or self-interest are far less relevant for many co-producers (Vanleene et al. 2017; van Eijk et al. 2017): in line with the literature on the motivations of volunteers (cf. Perry, Brudney, Coursey and Littlepage, 2008; Clerkin, Paynter and Taylor, 2009), co-producers seem to be motivated by a drive to take responsibility for society and fellow citizens (Vanleene et al., 2017).

Third, and finally, co-producers' engagement may be explained by additional factors. Socio-demographic variables have been studied by Bovaird et al. (2015), who show that older citizens, women, and higher educated citizens engage more often in individual forms of co-production compared to younger citizens, men, or lower educated citizens. Also, contextual factors, such as the level of social capital, seem to have an impact on co-production: according to Thijssen and Van Dooren (2016), living in a specific neighbourhood impacts co-producers' engagement because of the social capital present in the neighbourhood.[1] Thus, social capital can be understood as an important accelerator of co-production processes (Bovaird et al., 2016; Voorberg et al., 2015; Ostrom, 1996): it is easier to mobilize people when they are involved in neighbourhood associations that are directly involved with the neighbourhood or when they have a large stockpile of other contacts (Thijssen and Van Dooren, 2016). When social ties are strong, people are more willing to share their resources and abilities in favour of the community (Voorberg et al. 2015).

However, the literature shows mixed results when it comes to the effects of encouragement by public employees. Theoretically, it is often assumed that they should encourage citizens to co-produce, for instance by providing the necessary information and advice via booklets and training programs (e.g., Alford, 2002; Percy, 1984). Some empirical studies support the idea that public employees can encourage citizens to co-produce by offering training programs (van Eijk and Steen, 2013) and by providing the necessary resources (defined in terms of knowledge and basic tools) for the co-production process to happen (Jakobsen, 2013). However, there are also contradictory results. For example, Thomsen and Jakobsen's (2015) study on parents' involvement in the development of their children's reading skills showed that distributing information material did not affect parents' level of contribution. Finally, the literature makes reference to public employees' attitude and how this is perceived by the co-producers: public employees' signs of appreciation are found to positively impact co-producers' motivations (van Eijk, 2017), and when (potential) co-producers trust public employees, this increases their willingness to participate in co-production processes (Fledderus and Honingh, 2016).

Some Concluding Thoughts

In this chapter, we summarized what is known about co-producers and their motivations. The review shows that there are different perspectives to understanding the *role of co-producers* (e.g., co-implementer/co-designer/ initiator vs client/volunteer/citizen), that there are different *levels of co-production* (individual, group, and collective co-production), and that there is a wide range of *co-production activities* (dividing among complementary/non-complementary tasks and the extent to which co-producers are able to produce the services themselves). Regarding co-producers' motivations, our review shows that in the early years of co-production literature, co-producers' motivations were mostly addressed from an economic point of view, and therefore only considering extrinsic motivations. Over time, this perspective has changed, and has incorporated new insights from other disciplines, such as volunteerism, political participation, and even public management, showing that co-producers' motivations are both extrinsic and intrinsic and that context matters. In sum, our review shows that different groups of co-producers can be differently motivated, even within one co-production process.

Based on the insights gathered in this literature review, we conclude that the context of the specific co-production process (including among others the cultural setting of the country, the particular policy domain, the public organization involved, and the type of services produced) has a major impact on co-producers' motivations. Although the relevance of context could explain why current co-production literature is dominated by single case studies (cf. Voorberg et al., 2015), it also exposes a need for more comparative studies to better explain the role of context. This is an important avenue for further research. Another suggestion for further research concerns public organizations' role in encouraging citizens to co-produce. Given the importance of individual motivation factors, public organizations' efforts should be better directed at influencing citizens' *ability* to co-produce, providing them with relevant resources and/or training programs. Further, public organizations should invest more in understanding citizens' expectations and, particularly, managing external efficacy. New research is therefore needed to further investigate the theoretical and practical implications of public organizations' role in motivating citizens.

Note

1 Social capital is about the social networks and connections among individuals, and includes norms of reciprocity and trustworthiness (Putnam, 1993).

References

Alford, J. (1993). Towards a New Public Management Model: Beyond 'Managerialism' and Its Critics. *Australian Journal of Public Administration*, (52, 2), 135–148.

Alford, J. (2002). Why Do Public Sector Clients Co-Produce? Towards a Contingency Theory. *Administration & Society*, 34 (1), 32–56.

Alford, J. (2014). The Multiple Facets of Co-Production: Building on the work of Elinor Ostrom. *Public Management Review*, (16, 3), 299–316.

Alford, J. and Yates, S. (2016). Co-Production of Public Services in Australia: The Roles of Government Organisations and Co-Producers. *Australian Journal of Public Administration*, (75, 2), 159–175.

Allen, P., Wright, J., Keen, J., Dempster, P. G., Hutchings, A., Townsend, J., Street, A. and Verzulli, R. (2010). *Investigating the Governance of NHS Foundation Trusts*. Final report. NIHR Service Delivery and Organisation Programme.

Amnå, E. (2010). Active, Passive, or Stand-By Citizens? Latent and Manifest Political Participation. In E. Amnå (eds.), *New Forms of Citizen Participation: Normative Implications*, 191–203. Nomos: Baden-Baden.

Barbera, C., Sicilia, M. and Steccolini, I. (2016). What Mr. Rossi Wants in Participatory Budgeting: Two R's (Responsiveness and Representation) and Two I's (Inclusiveness and Interaction). *International Journal of Public Administration*.

Bovaird, T. and Loeffler, E. (2012). From Engagement to Co-Production. How Users and Communities Contribute to Public Services. In V. Pestoff, T. Brandsen and B. Verschuere (eds.), *New Public Governance, the Third Sector and Coproduction*, 35–60. New York and London: Routledge.

Bovaird, T., Stoker, G., Jones, T., Loeffler, E. and Roncancio, M. P. (2016). Activating Collective Co-Production of Public Services: Influencing Citizens to Participate in Complex Governance Mechanisms in the UK. *International Review of Administrative Sciences*, (82, 1), 47–68.

Bovaird, T., Van Ryzin, G. G., Loeffler, E. and Parrado, S. (2015). Activating Citizens to Participate in Collective Co-Production of Public Services. *Journal of Social Policy*, (44, 1), 1–23.

Brandsen, T. and Honingh, M. (2016). Distinguishing Different Types of Coproduction: A Conceptual Analysis Based on the Classical Definitions. *Public Administration Review*, (76, 3), 427–435.

Brandsen, T., Pestoff, V. and Verschuere, B. (2012). Co-Production as a Maturing Concept. In V. Pestoff, T. Brandsen, and B. Verschuere (eds.), *New Public Governance, the Third Sector and Co-Production*, 1–9. London, UK: Routledge.

Brudney, J. L. and England, R. E. (1983). Toward a Definition of the Coproduction Concept. *Public Administration Review*, (43, 1), 59–65.

Clarke, J., Newman, J., Smith, N., Vidler, E. and Westmarland, L. (2007). *Creating Citizen-Consumers: Changing Publics & Changing Public Services*. London: Sage.

Clerkin, R. M., Paynter, S. R. and Taylor, J. K. (2009). Public Service Motivation in Undergraduate Giving and Volunteering Decisions. *The American Review of Public Administration*, (39, 6), 675–698.

Copestake, P., Sheikh, S., Johnston, S. and Bollen, A. (2014). *Removing Barriers, Raising Disabled People's Living Standards*. London: OPM.

Craig, S. C., Niemi, R. G. and Silver, G. E. (1990). Political Efficacy and Trust: A Report on the NES Pilot Study Items. *Political Behavior*, (12, 3), 289–314.

Deci, E. L. (1972). Intrinsic Motivation, Extrinsic Reinforcement, and Inequity. *Journal of Personality and Social Psychology*, (22, 1), 113–120.

Dekker, P. and Halman, L. (2003). Volunteering and Values: An Introduction. In P. Dekker and L. Halman (eds.), *The Values of Volunteering. Cross-Cultural Perspectives*, 1–17. New York: Kluwer Academic/Plenum Publishers.

Dunn, J., Chambers, S. K. and Hyde, M. K. (2016). Systematic Review of Motives for Episodic Volunteering. *Voluntas*, (27, 1), 425–464.

Ewert, B. and Evers, A. (2012). Co-Production: Contested Meanings and Challenges for User Organizations. In V. Pestoff, T. Brandsen, and B. Verschuere (eds.), *New Public Governance, the Third Sector and Coproduction*, 61–78. New York and London: Routledge.

Fledderus, J. and Honingh, M. (2016). Why People Co-Produce Within Activation Services: The Necessity of Motivation and Trust—an Investigation of Selection Biases in a Municipal Activation Programme in the Netherlands. *International Review of Administrative Sciences*, (82, 1), 69–87.

Fotaki, M. (2011). Towards Developing New Partnerships in Public Services: Users as Consumers, Citizens and/or Co-Producers in Health and Social Care in England and Sweden. *Public Administration*, (89, 3), 933–955.

Jakobsen, M. (2013). Can Government Initiatives Increase Citizen Coproduction? Results of a Randomized Field Experiment. *Journal of Public Administration Research and Theory*, (23, 1), 27–54.

Kiser, L. and Percy, S. L. (1980). *The Concept of Coproduction and Its Implications for Public Service Delivery*. Paper presented at the Annual Meeting of the American Society for Public Administration, San Francisco, 13–16 April 1980.

Layne, K. (1989). *Perfect Partners: Co-Production and Crime Prevention*. Las Vegas: Las Vegas Metropolitan Police Department.

Nabatchi, T., Sancino, A. and Sicilia, M. (2017). Varieties of Participation in Public Services: The Who, When, and What of Coproduction. *Public Administration Review*, online-first publication.

Needham, C. (2008). Realising the Potential of Coproduction: Negotiating Improvements in Public Services. *Social Policy and Society*, (7, 2), 221–231.

OECD. (2001). *Citizens as Partners. OECD Handbook on Information, Consultation and Public Participation in Policy-Making*. Paris: OECD.

Osborne, D. and Gaebler, T. (1992). *Reinventing Government: How the Entrepreneurial Spirit Is Transforming the Public Sector*. New York: Plume.

Osborne, S. P. (2010). Delivering Public Services: Time for a New Theory? *Public Management Review*, (12, 1), 1–10.

Ostrom, E. (1996). Crossing the Great Divide: Co-Production, Synergy, and Development. *World Development*, (24, 6), 1073–1087.

Ostrom, E. (2009). *Beyond Markets and States: Polycentric Governance of Complex Economic Systems*. Nobel Prize Lecture, Oslo.

Parks, R. B., Baker, P. C., Kiser, L., Oakerson, R., Ostrom, E., Ostron, V., Percy, S. L., Vandivort, M. B., Whitaker, G. P. and Wilson, R. (1981). Consumers as Coproducers of Public Services: Some Economic and Institutional Considerations. *Policy Studies Journal*, (9, 7), 1001–1011.

Parrado, S., Van Ryzin, G. G., Bovaird, T. and Loeffler, E. (2013). Correlates of Co-Production: Evidence from a Five-Nation Survey of Citizens. *International Public Management Journal*, (16, 1), 85–112.

Percy, S. L. (1984). Citizen Participation in the Coproduction of Urban Services. *Urban Affairs Review*, (19, 4), 431–446.

Perry, J. L., Brudney, J. L., Coursey, D. and Littlepage, L. (2008). What Drives Morally Committed Citizens? A Study of the Antecedents of Public Service Motivation. *Public Administration Review*, (68, 3), 445–458.

Pestoff, V. (2006). Citizens and Co-Production of Welfare Services. *Public Management Review*, (8, 4), 503–519.

Pestoff, V. (2008). Citizens and Co-Production of Welfare Services. Childcare in Eight European Countries. In V. Pestoff and T. Brandsen (eds.), *Co-Production. The Third Sector and the Delivery of Public Services*, 11–28. New York: Routledge.

Pestoff, V. (2012). Co-Production and Third Sector Social Services in Europe. In V. Pestoff, T. Brandsen, and B. Verschuere (eds.), *New Public Governance, the Third Sector and Co-Production*, 13–34. London, UK: Routledge.

Prentice, S. (2006). Childcare, Co-Production and the Third Sector in Canada. *Public Management Review*, (8, 4), 521–536.

Putnam, R. D. (1993). *Making Democracy Work. Civic Traditions in Modern Italy*. Princeton: Princeton University Press.

Reed, P. and Selbee, L. K. (2003). Do People Who Volunteer Have a Distinctive Ethos? A Canadian Study. In P. Dekker and L. Halman (eds.), *The Values of Volunteering. Cross-Cultural Perspectives*, 91–109. New York: Kluwer Academic/ Plenum Publishers.

Renauer, B. C., Duffee, D. E. and Scott, J. D. (2003). Measuring Police-Community Co-Production. Trade-Offs in Two Observational Approaches. *Policing: An International Journal of Police Strategies & Management*, (26, 1), 9–28.

Sabadosa, K. A. and Batalden, P. B. (2014). The Interdependent Roles of Patients, Families and Professionals in Cystic Fibrosis: A System for the Coproduction of Healthcare and Its Improvement. *BMJ Quality and Safety*, (23, 1), 90–94.

Surva, L., Tõnurist, P. and Lember, V. (2016). Co-Production in a Network Setting: Providing an Alternative to the National Probation Service. *International Journal of Public Administration*, (39, 13), 1031–1043.

Svendsen, G. L. H. and Svendsen, G. T. (2000). Measuring Social Capital: The Danish Co-Operative Dairy Movement. *Sociologia Ruralis*, (40, 1), 72–86.

Taylor, R. and Shanka, T. (2008). Cause for Event: Not-for-Profit Marketing Through Participant Sports Events. *Journal of Marketing Management*, (24, 9–10), 945–958.

Thijssen, P. and Van Dooren, W. (2016). Who You Are/Where You Live: Do Neighbourhood Characteristics Explain Co-Production? *International Review of Administrative Sciences*, (82, 1), 88–109.

Thomsen, M. K. (2015). Citizen Coproduction: The Influence of Self-Efficacy Perception and Knowledge of How to Coproduce. *American Review of Public Administration*, (47, 3), 340–353.

Thomsen, M. K. and Jakobsen, M. (2015). Influencing Citizen Coproduction by Sending Encouragement and Advice: A Field Experiment. *International Public Management Journal*, (18, 2), 286–303.

Timpone, R. J. (1998). Structure, Behavior, and Voter Turnout in the United States. *American Political Science Review*, (92, 1), 145–158.

van Eijk, C. J. A. (2017). *Engagement of Citizens and Public Professionals in the Co-Production of Public Services*. Leiden: Leiden University, dissertation.

van Eijk, C. J. A. (2017). Helping Dutch Neighborhood Watch Schemes to Survive the Rainy Season: Studying Mutual Perceptions on Citizens' and Professionals' Engagement in the Co-Production of Community Safety. *VOLUNTAS*, on-line first publication.

van Eijk, C. J. A. and Steen, T. P. S. (2013). Waarom burgers coproducent willen zijn. Een theoretisch model om de motivaties van coproducerende burgers te verklaren. *Bestuurskunde*, (22, 4), 72–81.

van Eijk, C. J. A. and Steen, T. P. S. (2014). Why People Co-Produce: Analysing Citizens' Perceptions on Co-Planning Engagement in Health Care Services. *Public Management Review*, (16, 3), 358–382.

van Eijk, C. J. A. and Steen, T. P. S. (2016). Why Engage in Co-Production of Public Services? Mixing Theory and Empirical Evidence. *International Review of Administrative Sciences*, (82, 1), 28–46.

van Eijk, C. J. A., Steen, T. P. S. and Verschuere, B. (2017). Co-Producing Safety in the Local Community: A Q-Methodology Study on the Incentives of Belgian and Dutch Members of Neighbourhood Watch Schemes. *Local Government Studies*, (43, 3), 323–343.

Van Kleef, D. D. and van Eijk, C. J. A. (2016). In or Out: Developing a Categorization of Different Types of Co-Production by Using the Critical Case of Dutch Food Safety Services. *International Journal of Public Administration*, 39 (13), 1044–1055.

Vanleene, D., Verschuere, B. and Voets, J. (2016). The Democratic Quality of Co-Production in Community Development: A Pilot Study in the Rabot Neighbourhood in Ghent, Belgium. *EGPA Conference, Proceedings*. Presented at the EGPA Permanent Study Group VIII: Civil Society, Citizens and Government.

Vanleene, D., Voets, J. and Verschuere, B. (2017). Co-Producing a Nicer Neighbourhood: Why Do People Participate in Local Community Development Projects? *Lex Localis*, (15, 1), 111–132.

Verschuere, B., Brandsen, T. and Pestoff, V. (2012). Co-Production: State of the Art in Research and the Future Agenda. *Voluntas*, (23, 4), 1083–1101.

Voorberg, W., Bekkers, V. and Tummers, L. (2015). A Systematic Review of Co-Creation and Coproduction. *Public Management Review*, (17, 9), 1333–1357.

Voorberg, W., Tummers, L., Bekkers, V., et al. (2015). *Cocreation and Citizen Involvement in Social Innovation: A Comparative Case Study Across 7 EU countries*. LIPSE, Rotterdam.

Whitaker, G. P. (1980). Coproduction: Citizen Participation in Service Delivery. *Public Administration Review*, (40), 240–246. May/June.

Wilson, G. (1994). *Co-Production and Self-Care: New Approaches to Managing Community Care Services for Older People*. London: LSE Research Online.

7.1 Case Study—The Spanish Project Pla BUITS

Mila Gascó and Carola van Eijk

Introduction

How can new public spaces be created out of derelict urban spaces in times of austerity? The city of Barcelona, in Spain, faced the challenges of urban planning at a time of economic crisis. Following the trend in other countries, in 2012 a new project focused on citizen participation started, called Pla BUITS (*Buits Urbans amb Implicació Territorial i Social*—Empty Urban Spaces with Social and Territorial Involvement). Pla BUITS aimed at re-using empty spaces throughout the city, in order to improve citizens' quality of life. Public and private non-profit organizations (varying from charities to residents' associations and parents' organizations) but, also, individuals were encouraged to propose a use or activity and temporary management for the period of one year (extendible to three). Examples were community gardens, art installations, community dining rooms, and bikes garages. In other words, Pla BUITS invited neighborhood entities to co-manage abandoned parcels, and as such is a way to make citizens co-responsible for the public environment they are living in.

Background

The Barcelona urban model has evolved over the years, from a local political agenda, driven by a desire for redistribution at the neighborhood level in the 1980s, to a model focused on international renown and economic development, based on large-scale transformations in the 1990s. In the last few years, and as a result of the economic recession that negatively hit Spain in 2009 and after, the latter model was called into question, having an important impact on the design of new public spaces and on the maintenance of the ones already in use. The stagnation of the real-estate market and the dearth of available public funding gave rise to vacant spaces throughout the city that quickly became a nest for bad/anti-social practices and behaviors as well as serious situations of social exclusion.

Interestingly enough, in the wake of the political, social, and economic unrest in Spain, grassroots entities and horizontal collaborative practices started to emerge, some out of anger, some out of necessity. The Barcelona City Council identified an opportunity and recognized the need to collaborate with them instead of keeping traditional urban policy making practices and conceiving participation as just city meetings or voting. That is how Pla BUITS was born.

Different types of local organizations and some individual citizens actively engage in the project. They have a role in both the design and implementation phase, making it a clear example of co-production. Thus, in this case local government, local (non-profit) organizations, and citizens collaborate to produce a public service (i.e., reuse of empty spaces). Under the leadership of the Department of Urban Planning, the city ceded 19 parcels throughout the city to local non-profit entities for them to use and manage provisionally. The recipients were selected through a competition. At the time of writing, this process has already taken place twice, once in 2013 and once in 2015 (Pla BUITS, 2017).

Experiences

The local organizations and individual citizens (the co-producers in this case) are totally responsible for the empty spaces they are managing and, therefore, are in charge of implementing the proposed project, be it an urban garden or a bikes garage. Yet, not all entities have the same tasks and responsibilities. Here we can distinguish between co-called 'promoting organizations' and 'non-promoting organizations'.

- Promoting organizations are the local organizations or citizens who proposed the project. They are the ones in charge of the management of the overall project, and act as the contact organization to both the Department of Urban Planning and the district. Different actors play this promoting role. Some of them have protest roots (such as the 15-M movement); for these organizations, occupying these empty spaces is an old claim. Some other organizations are charity entities, usually with links to the Catholic Church and with a long tradition of social work. Others are residents' associations, deeply rooted in the neighborhood and with a strong interest in seeing an increase of its quality of life. Also a few individuals have volunteered to join promoting organizations in the competition for a vacant space. They have done so because of their personal interest in improving the conditions of the neighborhoods they live in.
- Non-promoting organizations are mainly supporters of the initiative and play specific roles at different times. It is the case of residents' associations, parents' associations, handicapped foundations, schools, libraries, small companies, and universities. They have found the projects to be particularly interesting for their mission and goals. They also believe they can make a difference in the projects due to the knowledge of the field they have.

Regardless of the specific role as (non-)promoting organizations, all co-producers developed important feelings of ownership. They expressed a willingness to take responsibility for the empty space. And although networking was not always smooth (for instance due to disagreement among different actors on what to do or how to do it), the collaborative spirit and commitment of different citizens and associations rooted in the neighborhood were highly valued (Voorberg et al., 2015, 129).

Several factors influence the co-producers' engagement (Voorberg et al., 2015; Gascó, 2015). Some stimulating factors include: 1) a vibrant civil society with a strong associational network, 2) an easy methodology to co-produce, 3) the city government's will and commitment, at both the political and the executive level, and 4) the individuals' motivation to co-produce (that is, organizations' will to participate in the co-production process was the result of their representatives' motivations to collaborate). On the contrary, among the barriers hindering participation, one can find: 1) a lack of resources (which conditions the entities' ability to co-produce or their internal efficacy), 2) the city council's bureaucratic structure, which slows down the co-production process and, therefore, its outputs/outcomes, 3) the high number of co-producers and the, sometimes, difficult relationships among them, which makes management of the empty spaces more challenging than desired, and 4) the low level of individual citizen involvement (there seems to be a need for individual co-producers who combine roles as clients and volunteers and who go beyond being mere recipients of the services being offered at the empty spaces).

References

Gascó, M. (2015). *A Tale of Two Cities. Co-Production and Social Innovation in Urban Environments.* Paper presented at the 2015 Public Management Research Association Conference. Minneapolis MN, 11–13 June.

Pla BUITS. (2017). *Pla BUITS.* Published at <http://ajuntament.barcelona.cat/ecolo giaurbana/ca/pla-buits>. Accessed May 2017.

Voorberg, W., Tummers, L., Bekkers, V., Torfing, J., Tonurist, P., Kattel, R., Lember, V., Timeus, K., Nemec, J., Svidronova, M., Mikusova Merickova, B., Gasco, M., Flemig, S. and Osborne, S. (2015). *Cocreation and Citizen Involvement in Social Innovation: A Comparative Case Study Across 7 EU Countries.* LIPSE, Rotterdam.

8 The Roles of the Professional in Co-Production and Co-Creation Processes

Trui Steen and Sanna Tuurnas

Introduction

In co-production actors "who are not in the same organization" (Ostrom, 1996, 1073) contribute their input for the production of a good or a service. This involves, on one side of the process, a citizen or group of citizens and, on the other side, a "regular producer" as representative of a public organisation (Ostrom, 1996). In this chapter we focus on the professional side of co-production and co-creation, that is, the regular producer who can be a single professional or, in a networked environment, a group of professionals (Tuurnas, Stenvall, Rannisto, Harisalo and Hakari, 2015). We use the term "professional" to address the public sector employee as a "regular producer" in a broad sense. A wide group of professionals are involved in co-production and co-creation, from health care workers co-producing a treatment strategy with their patients, to police officers co-producing safety with the local community, to community development workers assisting citizens in increasing the livability of their neighbourhood. Thus, we not only include what is seen as "true" or "classic" professionals such as medical doctors or university lecturers; yet at the same time we acknowledge that characteristics such as holding specific knowledge and expertise, and having a certain degree of autonomy (cf. Freidson, 1994; Evetts, 2003; Ferlie and Geraghty, 2005) are relevant for these actors concerned with providing public services.

Co-production and co-creation are based on relations between professional staff and service users. How these relations evolve is dependent on all the co-producing parties. Here, education can be seen as a classic example. Teacher and the pupil both play an important role for gaining effective learning results—learning being the task of the teacher nor the pupil alone (see also Honingh, Bondarouk and Brandsen in this volume, chapter 13). Citizen involvement thus not only concerns questions regarding citizens but also regarding how public professionals "view themselves and their responsibilities relative to citizens" (Thomas, 1999, p. 83). For instance, supervision by professional health staff is found to be vital to support success of community health programmes in developing countries where community health workers are used to render basic health services to their communities (Lehmann and Sanders, 2007). Public service professionals are seen as most relevant in studying co-creation and co-production processes. They have a role as coordinators, facilitators and enablers (cf. Bovaird and Löffler, 2012; Boyle and Harris, 2009; Ryan, 2012; Moynihan and Thomas, 2013; Tuurnas, 2016; Verschuere, Brandsen and Pestoff, 2012). Moreover, professionals' willingness to co-produce is seen as essential for the implementation of co-production (Ostrom, 1996; Vamstad, 2012). Literature also acknowledges that new skills are needed on both sides of the co-production process (Porter, 2012; Verschuere, Brandsen and Pestoff, 2012; Wagenaar, 2007), not the least by "professionals working on the micro-level of service production" (Tuurnas, 2016, 53). Yet despite this, empirical studies of public professionals' roles and attitudes towards co-production and co-creation are still rare.

The Changing Role of the Professional in Public Service Delivery

Different authors try to capture the changing role of professionals in public service delivery along the lines of the dominant modes of public administration, referring to Osborne's (2006) ideal-type distinction between Traditional Public Administration, New Public Management and New Public Governance. These public administration regimes each imply different perspectives on the role of professionals in guaranteeing service quality (Noordegraaf, 2007; Vamstad, 2012; Brandsen and Honingh, 2013; Fledderus, 2016; Pestoff in chapter 4 in this volume). Traditional Public Administration focuses on public services being provided by public servants working in a hierarchical and bureaucratic system (Sehested, 2002). In this model, providing service quality is based on the regular providers' professional knowledge, experience and insights; leaving little room for collaboration with or input from service-users. Here, the professional-client relationship refers to "the former defining need and the latter as the passive and grateful recipient" (Houligan, 2001, 8). In the regime of New Public Management, the focus has shifted towards issues such as controls of service outputs, competition between providers and consumer choice, and professionals' orientation has changed from professional standards and control mechanisms to managerial control and customers' wishes (Brandsen and Honingh, 2013). Sehested (2002, 1519) recognises changes in the monopoly of the professionals' working arenas through the emergence of new administrative units as well as changes in their ideological controls through citizen-user influence. In literature, co-production and co-creation are generally linked with a third regime, that of New Public Governance, where interdependencies and collaboration between public, private and non-profit actors are emphasised (Osborne, 2010). Service users change from being regarded as passive consumers, over rational customers, to being seen as an inevitable part of the service process and interacting with professional staff as active co-producers (Fledderus, 2016, 12).

Moreover, co-production and co-creation occur not only with individual service users but with a wider community. To demonstrate, Taylor and Kelly (2006) emphasise that localism and other forms of community governance affect professionals' work—especially their discretion—in various ways, forcing them to position themselves into new structures and processes. Finally, Pestoff (chapter 4 in this volume) adds to these three commonly defined regimes, the perspective of Communitarianism, in which "professionals complement informal care provision, mainly by steering users/caregivers to available resources in the community or voluntary organizations."

All in all, the different public administration regimes provide an interesting window to the changing professional-citizen relations. The position of expert knowledge, possessed by professionals, is changed in these regimes. Professional bases of legitimacy no longer are professional standards only but also organizational output and collaboration skills, while users voice their opinion based on user-experience—such as for example a patient questioning the doctor's opinion (Brandsen and Honingh, 2013; Sullivan, 2000; Taylor and Kelly, 2006). The professional-client relation changes from a top-down, one-directional relationship to a collaborative relationship based on user empowerment and interdependence (Ewert and Evers, 2012; Bovaird, 2007; Bovaird, Löffler and Hine-Hughes, 2011; Moynihan and Thomas, 2013). This makes professionals key actors for achieving effective and successful co-production with citizen-clients (cf. Tuurnas, 2016). Therefore it is essential to ask, how professionals are influenced by co-production and co-creation but also what is required from the professionals to foster effective co-production?

Professionals Role in Shaping the Institutional Context for Co-Production and Co-Creation of Public Services

According to Cepiku and Giodano (2014), "information asymmetry in highly professionalized services makes evident the need for training citizens to become co-producers; however, the skills required by civil servants involved in co-production—thus, as advisers rather than as producers— are seldom questioned". Yet, literature does recognize that if citizen-professional collaboration alters the way in which professionals perform, this calls for developing new professional competencies. Emphasized in this context are *enabling skills:* "the skills required to engage partners arrayed horizontally in networks, to bring multiple stakeholders together for a common end in a situation of interdependence" (Salamon, 2002, 16). Literature on collaborative governance refers to civil servants needing to possess individual attributes such as open-mindedness and empathy, interpersonal skills such as being both good communicators and excellent listeners, and group process skills (for an overview and discussion of collaborative skills as presented in literature, see O'Leary, Choi and Gerard, 2012). Relating to co-production specifically, Alford and O'Flynn (2012, 242–243) refer to the need for understanding client needs, holding a client focus in managing relations with co-producers and being able to segment between client groups. Additionally, literature points at the importance of *increasing the ease of co-producing for citizens*, to improve the ability of citizens to co-produce and ensure that they possess the resources needed (e.g., Houligan, 2001, 10; Moynihan and Thomas, 2013). Professionals might do so, for example, by simplifying co-production tasks, or by providing language support to an immigrant population (Moynihan and Thomas, 2013, 791). For teachers, for example, this implies having responsibility not only to educate students in a specific discipline, but to educate future citizens for engagement with the real world (Kennedy, 2005). Likewise, in a context of community policing (cf. Scheider, Chapman and Schapiro, 2009), a policeman not only has to solve crimes but also has a major role in observing what is going on in the community; and in building a "sense of community" by stimulating contact, respect and cohesion among the different members of the neighbourhood. In this task, the professionals can also be considered as bridging and bonding forces between different individuals and communities (Jones and Ormston, 2013; Kearns and Parkinson, 2001; Lowndes and Sullivan, 2008; Marschall, 2004; Scott, 2002; Tuurnas, 2016). Overall, competences required from the professionals are relational, focussing on the ability to facilitate and mobilise others, rather than technical skills or substantive knowledge of the subject at hand (cf. Kreber, 2016; Needham, Mangan and Dickinson, 2014; Sullivan, 2000).

Different authors specifically point out the need for professionals to be knowledgeable of citizens' motivations to co-produce, and to stimulate potential co-producers. This is the case for instance when co-creating service processes to better meet the needs of the clients, or developing cosier and safer neighbourhoods for its residents. In both examples, it is essential to motivate the citizens to take part in the development to gain effective results. Providing a number of guidelines to professionals on how to effectively work with citizens as co-producers, Moynihan and Thomas (2013, 791–72) suggest to retain the options of providing material and financial incentives, or even applying sanctions, yet they believe activating social norms and social networks to be more effective for professionals who seek assistance for the public. A challenge in motivating citizen-users to co-produce, they detect, is that citizens may (accurately) feel that government is dumping responsibilities (Moynihan and Thomas, 2013, 791). In line with this, Houligan (2001, 10) points at the need for professionals to produce demonstrable outcomes in co-producing with citizens. Tuurnas (2015) suggests that motivating citizens to co-produce is a key point of learning for professionals, as for some of them it may imply a totally new task to perform.

Public professionals have a responsibility that extends beyond the professional-client relationship focussing on individual clients' problems

(Flynn, 1999). Yet, at the same time professional standards typically acknowledge the limits that exist to standardization of professional work and the need to treat individual clients as unique individuals (cf. Bransden and Honing, 2013, 878). In co-production and co-creation, the professionals hold a task not only in motivating and enabling individual co-producers to help plan, design and deliver services, but also in *ensuring that potentially diverging interests are coordinated and that value is attained* not only by these individual co-producers. Indeed, citizens who engage as co-producers influence not only the private value they receive from service delivery, but also the public value as it is delivered to other clients or stakeholders who do not necessarily engage in the co-production process (Alford, 2002; Bovaird and Löffler, 2012).

Thus, there is a need for professionals not only to mobilise and activate citizens as potential partners, but also *to support and "orchestrate" the collaboration*, yet taking into account the expectations of the public organization in terms of whether, what and with whom to co-produce (cf. Alford and O'Flynn, 2012) and ensuring accountability of co-production efforts. In a rather top-down view on co-production (which provides less attention to the possibility of citizen activism and bottom-up co-creation and co-production initiatives), this entails professionals analysing the co-production process and identifying what are key points where co-producers are involved or where their involvement is desired for services to be effective (cf. Verschuere, Brandsen and Pestoff, 2012; Cepiku and Giordano, 2014; Moynihan and Thomas, 2013, 791). For example, in the co-production of public safety, it is vital that professionals as public authorities set the framework for co-production activities to prevent excesses on the usage of the authority by the citizen-volunteers, working by the side of the police (cf. Verschuere, Brandsen and Pestoff, 2012, 6). Another example is environmental protection, where different groups of citizens may value the problem, and see the solutions in a different way. This may create conflicts. Here, the professionals as public authorities may act as nodes between the different groups, providing opportunities for co-production of solutions (Maiello, Viegas, Frey and Ribeiro, 2013). As such, professionals are ascribed a specific role in supporting co-creation and co-production through shaping the institutional context in which co-production happens, creating conditions for better interaction with individual co-producers, but also keeping an eye on creating public value going beyond individual interactions.

A Motivated Motivator? Professionals' Attitudes Towards Involvement of Citizen-User

Eventually, in keeping citizens motivated to co-produce, research points out the need for professionals to demonstrate an open attitude towards collaboration (Ostrom, 1996; Vamstad, 2012). Van Eijk and Steen (2016) discuss how citizens' motivation as co-producers is influenced by their perception of professionals to be willing to listen to their ideas and inclined to actively share information. Studying the interaction between professionals in a work corporation and participants involved in a program aimed at helping them return to the regular labour market, Fledderus (2015, 561) hints at a similar role, since professionals "who are personally involved with users' activities, who are being helpful and whose leadership style is less hierarchical, are more likely able to create a feeling of reciprocity among the group of participants". When citizen-users feel mistrusted by professionals, their attitudes towards co-production and co-creation become more negative. When, in contrast, public professionals show "credible leadership", this positively affects co-producers' efforts and ultimately influences the program's effectiveness. While professionals' attitudes towards co-production and co-creation are thus acknowledged as essential for successful co-production of public services, far less scholarly attention is directed to empirically studying what motives professionals compared to the study of motivations of citizens to co-produce (for the latter, see Alford, 2002; van Eijk and Steen, 2014, 2016; van Eijk, Steen and Verschuere, 2017). Studies tend to analyse public administrators' perspectives towards citizen participation in decision making (e.g. Moynihan, 2003; Yang and Callahan, 2007; Coursey, Yang and Pandey, 2012; Huang and Feeney, 2016) rather than in designing or producing services. However, we assume that insights from this research may contribute also to understanding (the effects of) professionals' attitudes towards citizen co-production.

Expertise has been seen as a way to separate professionals from other kinds of workers and laymen (Brandsen and Honingh, 2013). Finding a balance between professional expertise and democratic governance, according to Fisher (1993, p. ix), is "an important political dimension of our time". Moynihan and Thomas (2013, 790) point at the challenge that professionals see themselves mainly as service providers or experts, while they "would do better to view themselves as the lead partners in service development and delivery, where effectiveness requires that the public also contribute".). Bovaird's (2007) study of co-production cases shows initial professional resistance to co-production eventually shifting to a willingness by professionals to work in partnership. Different studies relate differences in professionals' attitudes to individual characteristics. Fledderus (2015), for example, argues that professionals will cede power to citizens only when they trust users to be able to take over tasks. This is supported by Yang (2005), who finds that professionals' attitude towards citizen participation is influenced by their trust in citizens (Yang, 2005). Both Coursey, Yang and Pandey (2012), and Huang and Feeney (2016) study the effect of public service motivation on encouraging civic participation. Since public service motivation relates to a propensity to pursue the public interest, they expect that professionals with higher public service motivation will be more supportive of citizen participation in order to ensure government activities correspond to citizen demands, even when encouraging citizen participation may be time-consuming and increase administrative costs and burden. Both studies indeed find a positive relationship between professionals' intrinsic motivation for serving the public interest and encouragement of citizen participation.

Professionals in Co-Production and Co-Creation: Connecting Between Citizens and Management

In order to deal with—sometimes contradictious—targets and values in co-production and co-creation, managerial support within the organization is needed. Indeed, the professional side of co-production and co-creation includes not just the interaction with the citizen-users; the professionals are embedded also in institutional structures of their working organization that may be hindering or supporting towards co-production (Tuurnas, 2016b) and might influence their personal stances. Managers play a vital role as *collaborative capacity-builders* (Weber and Khamedian, 2008). Bussu and Bartels (2014) highlight the *facilitative leadership* as a success factor "making things happen". Specifically, managers formulate co-production strategies and bring together relevant stakeholders to achieve those strategies (Feldman and Khademian, 2007; Thomas, 2013; Verschuere et al., 2012). Creation of arenas or platforms for interaction with the citizens is a fundamental element to support professionals in co-production and co-creation. Here, the role of managers is to lead the process, for instance by identifying the policy objectives and organizational strategies to accomplish those objectives in the top-management level (Maiello et al. 2013; Thomas, 2013; Tuurnas, 2016). Managerial support is also needed to define the "limits" of co-production. A case study of neighbourhood community development (Tuurnas, 2015) suggests that the management can encourage professionals to utilise non-professional knowledge and partnerships in new ways by organizing negotiations on the accepted levels of risks, included in experiments and pilots (cf. Brown and Osborne, 2013).

The scholars also study the effect of performance-based rewards, and of value congruence between the professionals and the public organizations for which they work. Huang and Feeney (2016) find that the impact of local government professionals' public service motivation on levels of citizen participation is contingent on the extent to which they feel alignment between their personal and the organization's values and goals. Then again, Coursey et al. (2012) do not find such a mediating effect. Coursey et al. (2012) do find, however, that the effect of public service motivation on professionals' evaluation of citizen participation is moderated by the perceived importance the organization they work for places on citizen participation. Additionally, Huang and Feeney (2016) find that output-oriented performance management has negative effects on citizen participation. This might be explained by performance measurements reducing "the focus on other, harder-to-measure outcomes such as the inclusion of citizen input in decision-making activities (. . . and) drawbacks associated with citizen participation such as time-consuming decision-making processes or difficulty coordinating various demands may further make it difficult to report 'measureable performance' thus discouraging investment of manager time and resources into citizen participation efforts" (2016, 191). Tuurnas (2015) points out that co-production can be encouraged or hindered by the organization's management through developing suitable performance management tools for co-production. For instance, the increased sense of community because a performance is difficult to illustrate as a numeral value. Here, the saying "you get what you measure" may lead to a lack of innovativeness and willingness to create new solutions for community building, as it does not fit the evaluation framework.

Zhang and Yang (2009) study the impact of professionalism on the level of citizen participation in the budget process adopted in the organization. They find that professionals' attitudes towards citizen participation, their professional education and their participation in professional associations positively relate to citizen participation; in contrast with professional experience and institutional authority (autonomy) which negatively relate with citizen participation. Additionally, Zhang and Yang (2009) find that a healthy and stable political environment encourages professionals to consider citizen participation. Similarly, Yang and Callahan (2007) find that the level of citizen involvement efforts in local governments is influenced by pressures from (external) stakeholders and administrative practicalities such as availability of time, yet greatest explanatory power is attributed to the attitudes of the professionals in the organization. Interestingly, while professionals' lack of time was found to lead to weaker efforts to involve citizens, resource shortages showed a positive impact on the use of citizen involvement mechanisms, leading the researchers to conclude that "it is also likely that resource scarcity forces government to rely more on citizen participation through volunteering, advisement, and co-production" (Yang and Callahan, 2007, 258). Moreover, van Eijk, Steen and Torenvlied (2017) likewise find that professionals' engagement in co-planning is influenced by their work environment, including their perceptions of professional autonomy and organizational support for co-production and co-creation. Additionally, the study finds that professionals' perceptions of red tape associated with co-production activities negatively influences their perceptions of the importance and impact of co-production, as well as their personal involvement therein. This suggests that professionals may be concerned that red tape originates as the result of interaction with stakeholders.

Overall, literature suggests the importance of public professionals working in an organization that places a strategic focus on citizen participation, develops an organizational culture open towards citizens involvement and demonstrates credible commitment, for example, by adjusting structures and procedures—such as for example incentive structures—in order to encourage professionals to include citizens as partners. Supporting organizational culture has therefore an essential role for institutionalising co-production in service organizations (Tuurnas, 2015; Verschuere et al., 2012; Voorberg et al., 2015).

Conclusion

In co-production research, a debate has started on the new role co-production and co-creation define for the professional vis-à-vis citizens. Different authors refer to the transition from traditional public administration, over New Public Management, to New Public Governance to theoretically discuss the evolving role of public service professionals. Literature explains how through co-production and co-creation, the responsibility of professional actors to provide services is shared with citizen-users, and what implications this implies for professionals in terms of competencies and autonomy. Research on the challenges co-creation or co-production bring about for the regular provider of public services focuses on the regular producers' need to strategize how to gain citizens' collaboration, e.g., by considering what kind of incentives to apply, and on the extent to which professionals show an openness to allow user involvement. In general, however, empirical research on the topic is rare, leaving plenty room for future research on the evolving role of the professional.

An important avenue for future research would be to examine the various co-production tasks given to professionals. As it has been demonstrated in this chapter, professionals are key actors in the realisation of co-production, whilst they also shape the broader institutional context for co-production. Therefore it would be interesting to empirically analyse how the different tasks together shape the new role of professionals in public service delivery. Knowledge about the different co-producing tasks could also help to understand the multiplicity of the components affecting the co-production and co-creation processes. As for the literature that examines the motivational side of professionals, it would be critical to study how different professions cope with co-production, and whether there are some crucially different understandings about co-production and co-creation between different professions. Finally, a fundamental question is also the changing legitimacy of professionalism in an environment where knowledge structures become ever more dispersed.

References

Alford, J. (2002). Why Do Public-Sector Clients Coproduce? Towards a Contingency Theory. *Administration and Society*, (34, 1), 32–56.

Alford, J. and O'Flynn, J. (2012). *Rethinking Public Service Delivery. Managing with External Providers*. Houndmills: Palgrave Macmillan.

Bovaird, T. (2007). Beyond Engagement and Participation: User and Community Coproduction of Public Services. *Public Administration Review*, (67, 5), 846–860.

Bovaird, T. and Löffler, E. (2012). From Engagement to Co-Production. How Users and Communities Contribute to Public Services. In V. Pestoff, T. Brandsen and B. Verschuere (eds.), *New Public Governance, the Third Sector and Coproduction*, 35–60. New York and London: Routledge.

Bovaird, T., Löffler, E. and Hine-Hughes, F. (2011). *From Passive Customers to Active Co-Producers: The Role of Co-Production in Public Services*. Governance International, Birmingham.

Boyle, D. and Harris, M. (2009). *The Challenge of Co-Production. How Equal Partnerships Between Professionals and the Public Are Crucial to Improving Public Services*. Discussion paper. London: NESTA.

Brandsen, T. and Honingh, M. (2013). Professionals and Shifts in Governance. *International Journal of Public Administration*, (36, 12), 876–883.

Brown, L. and Osborne, S. (2013). Innovation in Public Services: Old and New Directions for Knowledge. In S. Osborne and L. Brown (eds.), *Handbook of Innovation in Public Services*, 563–566. Cheltenham: Edward Elgar Publishing Limited.

Bussu, S. and Bartels, K. P. (2014). Facilitative Leadership and the Challenge of Renewing Local Democracy in Italy. *International Journal of Urban and Regional Research*, (38, 6), 2256–2273.

Cepiku, D. and Giordano, F. (2014). Co-Production in Developing Countries: Insights from the Community Health Workers Experience. *Public Management Review*, (16, 3), 317–340.

Coursey, D., Yang, K. and Pandey, S. (2012). Public Service Motivation and Support for Citizen Participation. *Public Administration Review*, (72, 4), 572–582.

Evetts, J. (2003). The Sociological Analysis of Professionalism. *International Sociology*, (18, 2), 396–415.

Ewert, B. and Evers, A. (2012). Co-Production. Contested Meanings and Challenges for User Organizations. In Pestoff, V., T. Brandsen and B. Verschuere (eds.), *New Public Governance, the Third Sector and Co-Production*, 61–78. New York and London: Routledge.

Feldman, M. S. and Khademian, A. M. (2007). The Role of Public Manager in Inclusion: Creating Communities of Participation. *An International Journal of Policy, Administration and Institutions*, (20), 305–324.

Ferlie, E. and Geraghty, K. J. (2005). Professionals in Public Service Organizations: Implication for Public Sector "reforming". In E. Ferlie, L. E. Lynn, and C. Pollitt (eds.), *The Oxford handbook of public management*, 422–445. New York: Oxford University Press.

Fisher, F. (1993). Citizen Participation and the Democratization of Policy Expertise: From Theoretical Inquiry to Practical Cases. *Policy Science*, (26), 165–187.

Fledderus, J. (2015a). Building Trust Through Public Service Co-Production. *International Journal of Public Sector Management*, (28, 7), 550–565.

Fledderus, J. (2016). *User Co-Production of Public Service Delivery: Effects on Trust*. Nijmegen: Radboud Universiteit Nijmegen, dissertation.

Flynn, R. (1999). Managerialism, Professionalism and Quasi-Markets. In M. Exworthy and S. Halford (eds.), *Professionals and the New Managerialism in the Public Sector*, 18–36. Buckingham: Open University Press.

Freidson, E. (1994). *Professionalism Reborn: Theory, Prophecy, and Policy*. Cambridge: Polity Press.

Houlihan, B. (2001). Citizenship, Civil Society and the Sport and Recreation Professions. *Managing Leisure*, (6), 1–14.

Huang, W.-L. and Feeney, M. F. (2016). Citizen Participation in Local Government Decision Making: The Role of Manager Motivation. *Review of Public Personnel Administration*, (36, 2), 188–209.

Jones, T. and Ormston, C. (2013). Localism and Accountability in a Post-Collaborative Era: Where Does It Leave the Community Right to Challenge? *Local Government Studies*, (40, 1), 141–161.

Kearns, A. and Parkinson, M. (2001). The Significance of Neighborhood. *Urban Studies*, (38, 12), 2103–2110.

Kennedy, K. J. (2005). Rethinking Teachers' Professional Responsibilities: Towards a Civic Professionalism. *International Journal of Citizenship and Teacher Education*, (1, 1), 3–15.

Kreber, C. (2016). The 'Civic-minded' Professional? An Exploration Through Hannah Arendt's 'vita activa'. *Educational Philosophy and Theory*, (48, 2), 123–137.

Lehmann, U. and Sanders, D. (2007). *Community Health Workers: What Do We Know About Them?* Policy Brief. Geneva: Department of Human Resources for Health, WHO.

Lowndes, V. and Sullivan, H. (2008). How Low Can You Go? Rationales and Challenges for Neighborhood Governance. *Public Administration*, (86, 1), 53–57.

Maiello, A., Viegas, C. V., Frey, M. and Ribeiro, J. L. (2013). Public Managers as Catalysts of Knowledge Co-Production? Investigating Knowledge Dynamics in Local Environmental Policy. *Environmental Science & Policy*, 141–150.

Marschall, M. (2004). Citizen Participation and the Neighborhood Context: A New Look at the Coproduction of Local Public Goods. *Political Research Quarterly*, (57, 2), 231–244.

Moynihan, D. P. (2003). Normative and Instrumental Perspectives on Public Participation: Citizen Summits in Washington, D.C. *The American Review of Public Administration*, (33, 2), 164–188.

Moynihan, D. P. and Thomas, J. C. (2013). Citizen, Customer, Partner: Rethinking the Place of the Public in Public Management. *Public Administration Review*, (73, 6), 786–796.

Needham, C., Mangan, C. and Dickinson, H. (2014). *The Twentieth Century Public Service Workforce: Eight Lessons from the Literature*. Birmingham: University of Birmingham.

Noordegraaf, M. (2007). From 'pure' to 'hybrid' Professionalism: Present-Day Professionalism in Ambiguous Policy Domains. *Administration & Society*, (39, 6), 761–785.

O'Leary, R., Choi, Y. and Gerard, C. M. (2012). The Skill Set of the Successful Collaborator. *Public Administration Review*, (72, 1), 70–83.

Osborne, S. (2006). The New Public Governance? *Public Management Review*, (8, 3), 377–387.

Osborne, S. (2010). Delivering Public Services: Time for a New Theory? *Public Management Review*, (12, 1), 1–10.

Ostrom, E. (1996). Crossing the Great Divide: Coproduction, Synergy, and Development. *World Development*, (24, 6), 1073–1087.

Porter, D. (2012). Coproduction and Network Structures in Public Education. In V. Pestoff, T. Brandsen, and B. Verschuere (eds.), *New Public Governance, the Third Sector and Co-Production*. London: Routledge.

Ryan, B. (2012). Co-Production: Option or Obligation? *Australian Journal of Public Administration*, (71, 3), 314–324.

Salamon, L. M. (2002). The New Governance and the Tools of Public Action: An Introduction. In L. M. Salamon (ed.), *The Tools of Government. A Guide to the New Governance*, 1–47. Oxford and New York: Oxford University Press.

Scheider, M. C., Chapman, R. and Schapiro, A. (2009). Towards the Unification of Policing Innovations Under Community Policing. *Policing: An International Journal of Police Strategies and Management*, (32, 4), 694–718.

Scott, J. D. (2002). Assessing the Relationship Between Police-Community Coproduction and Neighborhood-Level Social Capital. *Journal of Contemporary Criminal Justice*, (18, 2), 147–166.

Sehested, K. (2002). How New Public Management Reforms Challenge the Roles of Professionals. *International Journal of Public Administration*, (25, 12), 1513–1537.

Sullivan, M. V. (2000). Medicine Under Threat: Professionalism and Professional Identity. *CJMI*, (162, 5), 673–675.

Taylor, I. and Kelly, J. (2006). Professionals, Discretion and Public Sector Reform in the UK: Re-Visiting Lipsky. *International Journal of Public Sector Management*, (19, 7), 629–642.

Thomas, J. C. (1999). Bringing the Public into Public Administration: The Struggle Continues. *Public Administration Review*, (59, 1), 83–88.

Thomas, J. C. (2013). Citizen, Customer, Partner: Rethinking the Place of the Public in Public Management. *Public Administration Review*, (73, 6), 786–796.

Tuurnas, S. (2015). Learning to Co-Produce? The Perspective of Public Service Professionals. *International Journal of Public Sector Management*, (28, 7), 583–598.

Tuurnas, S. (2016). Looking Beyond the Simplistic Ideals of Participatory Projects: Fostering Effective Co-Production. *International Journal of Public Administration*, (39, 13), 1077–1087.

Tuurnas, S. (2016b). *The Professional Side of Co-Production*. Academic dissertation. Acta Universitatis Tamperensis 2163. Tampere: Tampere University Press.

Tuurnas, S. P., Stenvall, J., Rannisto, P.-H., Harisalo, R. and Hakari, K. (2015). Coordinating Co-Production in Complex Network Settings. *European Journal of Social Work*, (18, 3), 370–382.

Vamstad, J. (2012). Co-Production and Service Quality: A New Perspective for the Swedish Welfare State. In V. Pestoff, T. Brandsen, and B. Verschuere (eds.), *New Public Governance, the Third Sector and Coproduction*, 297–316. New York and London: Routledge.

van Eijk, C. J. A. and Steen, T. P. S. (2014). Why People Co-Produce: Analysing Citizens' Perceptions on Co-Planning Engagement in Health Care Services. *Public Management Review*, (16, 3), 358–382.

van Eijk, C. J. A. and Steen, T. P. S. (2016). Why Engage in Co-Production of Public Services? Mixing Theory and Empirical Evidence. *International Review of Administrative Sciences*, (82, 1), 28–46.

van Eijk, C. J. A., Steen, T. P. S. and Torenvlied, R. (2017). Public Professionals' Engagement in Co-Production: Dutch Elderly Care Managers' Perceptions on Collaboration with Client Councils. Working paper, Leiden University.

van Eijk, C. J. A., Steen, T. P. S. and Verschuere, B. (2017). Co-Producing Safety in the Local Community: A Q-Methodology Study on the Incentives of Belgian and Dutch Members of Neighbourhood Watch Schemes. *Local Government Studies*, (43, 3), 323–343.

Verschuere, B., Brandsen, T. and Pestoff, V. (2012). Co-Production: The State of the Art in Research and the Future Agenda. *VOLUNTAS: International Journal of Voluntary and Nonprofit Organizations*, (23, 4), 1083–1101.

Voorberg, W. H., Bekkers, V. J. and Tummers, L. G. (2015). A Systematic Review of Co-Creation and Co-Production: Embarking on the Social Innovation Journey. *Public Management Review*, (17, 9), 1333–1357.

Wagenaar, H. (2007). Governance, Complexity and Democratic Participation: How Citizens and Public Officials Harness the Complexities of Neighbourhood Decline. *American Review of Political Science*, (37), 17–50.

Weber, E. P. and Khademian, A. M. (2008). Wicked Problems, Knowledge Challenges, and Collaborative Capacity Builders in Network Settings. *Public Administration Review*, (68), 334–349.

Yang, K. (2005). Public Administrators' Trust in Citizens: A Missing Link in Citizen Involvement Efforts. *Public Administration Review*, (65, 3), 262–275.

Yang, K. and Callahan, K. (2007). Citizen Involvement Efforts and Bureaucratic Responsiveness: Participatory Values, Stakeholder Pressures, and Administrative Practicality. *Public Administration Review*, (67, 2), 249–264.

Zhang, Y. and Yang, K. (2009). Citizen Participation in the Budget Process: The Effect of City Managers. *Journal of Public Budgeting, Accounting & Financial Management*, (21, 2), 289–317.

8.1 Case Study—Mediation Service

Crossing the Line Between the Roles of Traditional Welfare State Professionals and Citizens as Voluntary Mediators

Sanna Tuurnas

Introduction

Mediation service is offered in criminal and certain civil cases, offering an opportunity to seek conciliation between the offender and victim of the crime. Mediation gives a chance to 'discuss the mental and material harm caused to the victim by the crime and to agree on measures to redress the harm' (National Institute for Health and Welfare, 2016).

Mediation can be described as a unique public service in the Finnish welfare state model that substantially relies on trained professionals. In this context, the mediation service makes an exception: the service relies on the efforts of citizen-volunteers as mediators. Being a service based on citizen co-production, mediation is also intriguing in a sense that it is a legally regulated public service that is obligatory to organize. Therefore, municipalities across Finland are required to offer mediation services for their resident-citizens. For the citizens as parties of mediation (the victim and the offender), the mediation is a voluntary and free service. Rather than obliging, the service creates a chance for the parties to reconcile the occurred offence in the presence of non-party mediators (National Institute for Health and Welfare, 2016.)

The mediation service is aimed especially at preventing reoffending of young people, and it has in fact proved to be an effective way to stop the undesired path of criminal activity among the young. Especially in the case of young offenders, the idea is to give them a chance to face the consequences of their actions, and thus to understand the harm caused to the other party. Therefore the function of mediation is also social and educative. Finally, the underlying idea is to speed up criminal and civil proceedings (National Institute for Health and Welfare, 2016.)

Background

To give an overview of the service, mediation service is supervised and guided by regional state authorities. A regional mediation office organizes mediation activities; they train and coordinate the volunteers for their assignment as mediators. Mediation service is also based on inter-sectoral cooperation: the mediation office staff work together with, among others, the local police authorities, prosecuting authorities and social welfare authorities. As for the process, the initiative for mediation may come from the police, the prosecution, social workers or even from the parties to mediation, the offender or the victim. Finally, the court decides whether a mediation process should be started. After the decision is made, the mediation office staff contacts the volunteers, who, for their part, contact the parties to the mediation. The professional staff of the mediation office also take part in the mediation process with the volunteering mediators. After the mediation process is completed in the mediation office, the case returns to the district court for final resolution (National Institute for Health and Welfare, 2016.)

Mediation illustrates co-production between civil society and traditional welfare state professionals. The National Institute for Health and Welfare (2016) describes the role of the volunteering mediators in the following way: 'trained, impartial volunteer mediators, bound by professional confidentiality, help the parties of mediation to negotiate and resolve the offence.' Here, the role of the professional social workers working in the mediation office is rather to coordinate the process in the background, whereas the volunteering mediators are the ones who encounter the clients.

Reflecting the case to the conceptualization provided by Brandsen and Honingh in this book, the case illustrates *co-production in the design and implementation of core services*, as the voluntary citizens as mediators manage the service processes. They organize the meetings with the parties of mediation, but they also use discretion to create solutions for the mediation. By acting as mediators in the actual mediation process, they provide substantial input for the implementation of the service, as well.

Experiences

The case of mediation is especially interesting from the viewpoint of accountability relations and the emerging roles of citizen-volunteers and trained professionals. At first sight, the accountability relations seem quite straightforward by the definition of the National Institute for Health and Welfare (2016): 'The mediators act in the mediation offices under the control and supervision of the professional staff.' Yet in reality, the accountability relations can become 'messy' in service arrangements where actors with different backgrounds cooperate. In these kinds of arrangements, the basis of accountability is not simply legal compliance or professional expertise, but rather the shared process where each actor has his/her own part to play. From the point of view of the management, this notion brings out the significance of the careful planning of a co-production process. It is important for all the parties to understand that they are a part of the wider process, and that they understand their role as accountees (Tuurnas, Stenvall and Rannisto, 2016).

In mediation service, the process is coordinated by professional social workers, but the relations with the volunteers are based on partnership rather than manager-subordinate relations. This composition requires new skills from the professionals, as well. They have to learn to operate with volunteers and respect their expertise that differs from their professional expertise. This way, the mediation service model brings 'experiential expertise,' gained through life experience of the volunteers alongside the professional expertise, gained through professional training. This diversity of expertise can be used to solve the complex problems that often arise in mediation.

Finally, the volunteers, as opposed to public service professionals, can be more approachable for the parties of mediation (especially the offenders), who might distrust authorities. This in an essential point also for wider debates about the role of citizen-volunteers in public welfare services. Especially in highly professionalized public service systems, such as in Finland, the new solutions of human-to-human service solutions may complement and enrich the welfare services provided by officials and professionals. In fact, this is already a growing trend in Finland: the newspaper *Aamulehti* (Ahonen, 2016) reported that already a majority of social services are being completed by services provided by citizen-volunteers.

References

Ahonen, H-M. (2016). Vapaaehtoisten rooli kasvaa SOTE-palveluissa [The role of volunteers is growing in social and health care services]. *Aamulehti*, A18–A19. December 16.

National Institute for Health and Welfare. (2016). *Rikos- ja riita-asioiden sovittelu* [Mediation in Criminal and Civil Cases]. THL, Helsinki.

Tuurnas, S., Stenvall, J. and Rannisto, P-H. (2016). The Impact of Co-Production on Frontline Accountability: The Case of the Conciliation Service. *International Review of Administrative Sciences*, (28, 1), 131–149.

8.2 Case Study—The Role of Staff with Lived Experience in the Co-Production of Substance Use Disorder Treatment Services

Sunggeun (Ethan) Park

Introduction

In many social and health service fields working with marginalized and stigmatized populations, there are growing expectations for providing person-centered services (i.e., psychosocial care) through collaborative provider-user processes. However, diverse factors (e.g., mutual mistrust and power imbalances) often hinder such efforts. The substance use disorder (SUD) treatment service field in the U.S. provides a unique opportunity to understand how staff members with addiction histories facilitate co-production processes by bridging SUD service users and professional clinicians without addiction history.

Background

Collaborative service production appeals to both SUD treatment service users and providers. Service users desire responsive services to satisfy multifaceted and complex SUD treatment and other service needs. Many individuals with SUD have co-occurring issues, such as homelessness and mental illness, and can benefit from coordinated access to clinical treatment, housing and transportation support, and care management. Likewise, service providers and clinicians recognize the need to involve SUD patients in care decisions. Because diverse sociopolitical and environmental factors influence users' recovery processes, multiple stakeholders (e.g., funders and consumers) pressure clinicians to provide more relevant and cost effective services by incorporating users' contextual and private information.

Unfortunately, building a collaborative relationship can be a challenging task for both SUD treatment service users and providers. Based on their prior experiences of directive service processes, users may have low expectations of having any real control over service decisions. Some users may be hesitant to cooperate with providers because they receive SUD services involuntarily, following court orders or employee mandates. For providers, collaborating with SUD patients—often perceived as untrustworthy and manipulative individuals with limited capacity to contribute—or incorporating users' accounts into the clinical decision-making process can be challenging and sometimes perceived as "unprofessional" conduct.

Experiences

In such situations, staff members with SUD histories—regardless of their formal training backgrounds—are often uniquely situated to mediate the perspectives, knowledge, and preferences of service users and staff members without addiction experience by leveraging their dual identity as formal employees of clinics and previous (and potential) service users. From the perspective of service users, staff members with SUD histories are relatively trustworthy collaboration partners, who can connect to their struggles and provide diverse non-clinical social and emotional supports. For instance, in many SUD clinics, staff with lived experience conduct intake interviews. Although it is a necessary procedure for assessing patients' baseline status and needs, reviewing addiction history and taking monitored urine tests can be a potentially embarrassing process that patients may refuse to cooperate with (Integrated Behavioral Health Project, 2014). Compared to staff members without a first-hand experience of addiction, staff members who have "been there" are better positioned to facilitate such procedures, as they share the experience of addiction and stigma. Recovering staff are able to empathize with the pain that users experience when they detoxify, and understand more intimately the difficulties in reestablishing trust with family and community members. Staff with first-hand experience can also share tips that they have learned along the way and function as living confirmation that life can get better.

From the perspective of professional clinicians, staff with addiction histories can be more reliable and trustworthy information sources than current users, and can be engaged with lower organizational cost. For instance, in many SUD clinics, patients are not invited to participate in discussions of their treatment plans. Instead, medical professionals and clinicians often ask staff with lived experience to offer opinions on the status and service needs of patients (Brasher and Rossi, 2014). While research has shown that recovering staff deliver clinical services that are just as effective as professional counselors without addiction histories, it is recovering staffs' first-hand experience and knowledge of the physiology, psychology, and culture of addiction that are particularly valued assets, granting them authority as *subject matter experts*. As patients disclose detailed and accurate information on current situations and needs through relatively "trustworthy" staff members, SUD treatment clinics can use appropriate resources to promote patients' long-term recoveries.

Contributions of staff with addiction experience to collaborative and responsive service production in the SUD treatment field come with some limitations. Because these staff members are commonly hired as frontline clinicians, their efforts may have bounded efficacy and limited influence over organization-level changes. Furthermore, staff with SUD histories may reinterpret patients' original narratives based on their own personal experiences. The dual identity of staff with SUD histories may also harm their trustworthiness, positioning them as co-opted agents from users' perspectives and/or as biased staff from other professionals' standpoints. Depending on the environmental context and nature of interactions, these limitations may hinder the role of staff with lived experience in easing co-production at SUD treatment centers.

Despite the potential limitations, staff with lived experiences provide valuable opportunities for vulnerable and often stigmatized SUD service users to influence clinical experience and decisions. Staff with addiction histories facilitate co-production by leveraging their dual identities when there is mutual distrust and power imbalances between service providers and users. By mediating dialogues and power relationships between professional clinicians and service users, staff with lived experience contribute to providing person-centered services in the SUD treatment field.

References

Brasher, D. and Rossi, L. D. (2014). *Meaningful Roles for Peer Providers in Integrated Healthcare: A Guide.* California Association of Social Rehabilitation Agencies, Martinez CA.

Integrated Behavioral Health Project. (2014). Community Clinic and Health Center Case Study Highlights: Integrating Substance Abuse Treatment Staff and Reducing Stigma in Community Clinics and Health Centers. Integrated Behavioral Health Partners, Los Angeles CA.

9 Who Is in the Lead? New Perspectives on Leading Service Co-Production

Hans Schlappa and Yassaman Imani

Introduction

Co-production theory implies that citizens and regular producers have to negotiate with, and adapt to, each other's ideas on what should be done and how the skills and resources each brings to the process can best be utilised. If, as established theory implies, co-production is more than telling citizens what to do and expecting co-producers to follow established procedures and protocols, then regular and citizen co-producers have to make sense of what they are trying to achieve, negotiate potentially conflicting ideas on desired outcomes and how to achieve them, and then engage in the practical delivery of a co-produced service. The question of "who is in the lead?" when professionals and citizens come together to co-create and co-deliver a service goes to the heart of the analysis of the co-production process because leadership is about power to set and influence direction and to determine the way success and failure are assessed. Leadership is also about rationales and motivations for action and the context in which such actions happen. Hence leadership theory offers an insightful perspective on the actual mechanisms through which co-production is enacted.

Transactional and Transformational Leadership

Within the mainstream public leadership literature, leadership is considered to occur between independent actors of whom the leader is positioned hierarchically above others in the team or organisation. Here we find that two concepts dominate the theory in use by public administration scholars, namely transactional and transformational concepts of leading (Van Wart, 2003; Van Wart, 2013). The transactional perspective on leading gained popularity with the advent of the New Public Management paradigm where the logic of hierarchy and economic rationality prioritised leadership models that focused on issues concerned with efficiency, effectiveness and economy. This put an emphasis on performance management based on rewards that are contingent on the efforts made to achieve defined goals and resulted in giving preference to leadership styles that promised the achievement of pre-defined outcomes (Bass, 1990; Moynihan and Thomas, 2013). Such a perspective on leading seems to have only limited application to co-production, not just because the instrumental-rational approach that is implied belies the active, process shaping role citizen co-producers can be expected to play, but also because the notion of citizens as passive consumers of services has been discredited as being based on the Fordist model of production where the complexities of human abilities, needs and desires are subordinated to management principles rooted in the logics of linear and mechanistic manufacturing processes (Osborne, 2010). Much of the criticism levelled at contemporary co-production practice found in this volume and elsewhere reflects a critique of rational-instrumental approaches to service provision and points to the tensions between the interest of professional regular producers intent on ensuring stability, avoiding risks, meeting commitments to cost, efficiency and quality standards versus the potential or actual contribution of the citizen co-producer in terms of ideas, expertise, knowledge and resources.

Transformational leadership theory, on the other hand, emphasises the values individuals in leadership positions hold and their ability to set out a vision that inspires followers to perform beyond expectation. It is a popular concept in contemporary management studies due to its largely unproven promise to bring about radical yet innovative and performance enhancing change in public as well as private sector organisations (Andrews and Boyne, 2010). Edwards and Turnbull (2013) contrast the transactional leader as someone working within a given culture to achieve pre-determined goals, with the transformational leader who changes culture and sets new directions. However, at its core transformational leadership is concerned with organisational change that is grounded in networks of leadership relations which cross organisational and professional boundaries (Currie and Lockett, 2007). Both the transactional and transformational perspective on leadership remain relevant for the study as well as the practice of leading public services in that they provide some explanatory frameworks for contemporary challenges the leaders of public service organisations encounter as well as influencing most leadership development programmes in both private and public sectors. Leadership of the co-production process, however, is not primarily concerned with the management of organisations; it is about the interactions that occur between regular and citizen co-producers. To surface and better understand the dynamics at work in co-production practice and to distinguish between effective and less effective practices, we require a critical relational perspective which draws on distributed leadership theory.

Distributed Leadership

Leadership of the co-production process is about meaning making, persuasion and negotiation between regular and citizen co-producers in a context of unequal power relationships. Leading co-production is therefore a shared responsibility where citizens and paid staff aim to combine the skills, resources and authority of one another to accomplish a particular task. Such a relational perspective on leadership suggests that regular producers do not hold a privileged position in relation to citizens, casting them into the role of followers of an appointed, or self-appointed, leader with power to reward or punish. Theory of distributed leadership builds on a perspective which perceives leading as an activity which is shared and dispersed throughout teams and organisations. Bolden et al.(2008) define distributed leadership as:

> . . . a less formalized model of leadership where leadership responsibility is dissociated from the organizational hierarchy. It is proposed that individuals at all levels in the organization and in all roles can exert leadership influence over their colleagues and thus influence the overall direction of the organization.
>
> (ibid, p. 11)

Of the abundance of terms used to describe this phenomenon, shared and distributed leadership are the most common (for a review, see Bolden, 2011). Despite the variety of perspectives they represent, both terms build on the notion that leadership is an emergent property of interacting individuals and that expertise is distributed across the actors, not controlled by a few individuals in privileged positions (Bennett et al., 2003). A distributed leadership perspective offers insights into the mechanisms through which leadership functions might be shared. For example, MacBeath et al. (2004) identify that distributed leadership can have its roots in formal distribution (i.e. through its delegation), pragmatic distribution (i.e. through negotiation and division between actors), strategic distribution (i.e. shaped by the inclusion of people with specific skills or knowledge), incremental (i.e. where leadership is progressively enacted against experience), opportunistic (i.e. the ad hoc acceptance of responsibility) or cultural (the natural and organic assumption and sharing of responsibility). Similarly, Spillane (2006) points to differences in distribution of leadership functions, such as between collaborated distribution (individuals work together in time and place to execute leadership routines), collective distribution (individuals work separately but interdependently to enact leadership routines) or coordinated distribution (individuals work in sequence in order to complete leadership routines). Leithwood et al. (2006) consider how leadership is distributed in such ways that can either lead to "alignment" or "misalignment" based upon the extent to which the resulting formations of responsibilities within groups of actors achieve shared group purposes, and do so efficaciously.

While distributed leadership resonates with the principles of co-production, the conceptual frames it relates to require an extension because theory is premised on the principle that leading is shared among regular producers of an organisation—the notion that citizens are among those who enact leadership within the organisation is not acknowledged in the distributed leadership literature. This points to a significant gap in the explanatory frameworks we have to hand when it comes to service co-production. For example, citizen co-producers are not professionals, yet according to distributed leadership theory professionals would need to share leadership functions with citizens. Furthermore, citizen co-producers are likely to have superior knowledge of problems and access to skills and resources which enhance the capabilities of service organisations to address them, but citizens are not bound by organisational controls in the same way as regular producers. Bolden (2011) acknowledges that the tendency to confine leadership studies within organisational boundaries with a sole focus on staff to the exclusion of external stakeholders represents a significant gap in research and weakens the explanatory power of the theory on distributed leadership. He calls for: ". . . a more critical perspective which facilitates reflection on the purpose(s) and discursive mechanisms of leadership and an awareness of the dynamics of power and influence in shaping what happens within and outside organizations" (Bolden, 2011, 263). In the remainder of this chapter we present a new way to conceptualise leadership in the context of the co-production process that is based on critical relational leadership theory.

A Critical Relational Perspective on Leading Co-Production

The emphasis that the concept of co-production places on collaboration between professionals and citizens suggests that leading co-production should be seen as a relational and interdependent process, in contrast to assuming that services are led through hierarchical and rational relationships between independent individuals. Yet, constructing a new perspective on leadership in the context of service co-production faces a number of conceptual as well as practical challenges: First, actors who intend to co-produce services cannot be considered independent from each other because their interdependence shapes the contexts as well as the process through which service outputs and outcomes are produced. Hence any exploration of the co-production process needs to acknowledge that two very different types of actors who have different, perhaps conflicting, motivations and expectations need to make sense of the purpose, means and outcomes of their collaboration. Second, citizen co-producers are not bound by organisational controls in the same way that regular producers are, i.e. they cannot easily be made to perform the role of co-producer if they do not feel able or reluctant to do so; neither is their contribution easily regulated or likely to fit into particular procedures and performance measures public service organisations maintain to manage and support their professional staff. Hence leading co-production requires an approach that is different to leading professionals, teams, organisations and networks if the motivations, expertise, knowledge and resources of citizen co-producers are to be harnessed. Third, questions about leadership are not confined to managerial and organisational issues. Where co-production is the declared aim, the exploration of how regular and citizen co-producers lead the process goes to the heart of questions aimed at understanding how co-production mechanisms work. By asking "who is in the lead" we are more likely to surface collaborative practices, evaluate them and develop guidance on effective practices that foster co-production than by applying normative frameworks on leadership which do not seem to reflect the relational nature of the co-production process.

We suggest that leadership in co-production is best explored from a critical relational perspective (Hosking et al., 2012b) on leadership, which draws on distributed leadership theory (Gronn, 2002; Gronn, 2009; Thorpe et al., 2011). Such a perspective focuses on interactions through which realities are co-constructed and provides the conceptual tools to explore issues such as motivations, structure and power, which are central to understanding collaborations between actors who aim to accomplish something together (Uhl-Bien, 2006; Hosking et al., 2012a; Ospina et al., 2012; Shamir, 2012). A critical relational perspective on leading co-production encourages us to focus on actions and power dynamics among professional and citizen co-producers in the context in which they occur. From this perspective, leading co-production poses distinctive challenges that those involved need to mediate. We put forward here suggestions as to how regular and citizen-co-producers might approach and make sense of leading service co-production. These include:

- Deliberately exploring the often conflicting goals and motivations co-producers bring to the process. A growing body of literature points to the complex range of motivations which citizens and officials bring to co-producing relationships and that are open to influence and change according to context and purpose of the co-production process (van Eijk and Steen, 2014; Vanleene et al., 2015). It is essential, therefore, that leading co-production includes a focus on nurturing opportunities for dialogue about the content and purpose of co-production, as well as challenging assumptions and expectations that are rooted in different knowledge and expertise professional and citizen co-producers bring to the co-production situation.
- Where possible, minimising the restrictions and rules which constrain discussions and actions between co-producers. Government together with other external and internal stakeholders will continue to impose constraints which make collaborations between officials and citizens difficult, but research presented in this volume shows that public organisations can create spaces that minimise such constraints and are "lightly structured" (Hosking et al., 2012b). Citizen co-producers need to have opportunities to shape a context conducive to participating in the provision of services, regardless of whether they are core or complementary to the functions of the organisation (Brandsen and Honingh, 2016).

- Understanding and accepting that power is relational and negotiated (Stacey, 2007; van Der Haar and Hosking, 2004) between people who co-produce a service. Although citizen co-producers are often portrayed as being "un-empowered" (van Eijk and Steen, 2015; van Eijk and Steen, 2014), there are also arguments which show that power shifts between official and citizen co-producers according to their expertise, knowledge, resources, position and other contextual factors (Tuurnas, 2016). This changes perceptions of the co-producer relationship from one where the official "is in the lead" to one where leadership and associated expressions of power are negotiated and dynamic.

Adopting a critical relational perspective reveals co-production as an emergent and negotiated process where institutional structure, motivations and power dynamics between professionals and citizens are of central importance. Such a perspective might sensitise both the regular co-producers, who tend to perceive themselves as having to maintain standards, as well as the citizen co-producers, who often feel unempowered to change the service system, to their interdependencies and the power each holds over the process.

Challenges of Leading Co-production

A clear focus on power, motivations and context when regular and citizen co-producers interact encourages both scholars and practitioners to ask questions about the contingent and dynamic aspects of public administration systems and complements the more normative analytical frameworks on leadership in use. However, leading co-production is a contested process, not only because citizens and officials bring values, attitudes and beliefs to co-production efforts which are not necessarily in tune with each other, but also because they are also hard to change. The critical relational approach towards leading advocated here challenges many assumptions inherent in professional practice about control, accountability and standards (Tuurnas, 2015). Resistance to sharing leadership is not only rooted in the comfort and certainty that traditional models of leading service provision bring to regular producers, but there is a clear threat that lack of formal authority in co-ordinating work activities is likely to give rise for increased power struggles and conflicts between those involved. In the absence of traditional approaches to leading, deadlines might not be kept and lack of clearly defined roles and responsibilities might result in slower decision making processes. Furthermore, misunderstandings between actors might increase, resulting in reduced cohesion, which would make it more difficult to establish consensus, thus making those involved in co-production less effective and productive.

However, the literature on leadership development in public service organisations points to a number of practices that facilitate sharing leadership functions. In particular reflective practices, such as reflecting on leading the self, growth in connection with others and soft relational skills associated with coaching and mentoring have been found effective in fostering relational perspectives on leading and sharing leadership functions in practice (Woods, 2015; Woods, 2004). The table below attempts to capture behaviours that are likely to foster or lead to resistance in adopting shared leadership practices. The idea here is that not all co-production situations can be led by adopting a relational approach; at times it might be necessary for either party to tell and explain in no uncertain terms what needs to happen, in the case of facing a medical emergency for example. Hence the columns here do not present binary choices, but should be seen as a heuristic to the range of actions and responses possible and as a framework for assessing the extent to which observed behaviours support or hinder co-production efforts.

Co-production theory implies that citizen and regular producers have to negotiate with, and adapt to, each other's ideas on what should be co-produced and how the skills and resources each brings to the process can best be utilised. The process of co-producing therefore cannot be conceived as being primarily top-down, where organisational priorities or professional judgements determine what happens. Neither can it be primarily a bottom-up process where citizens take control. In regard to co-production research and practice we need to challenge assumptions that the power and ability to determine processes and outcomes reside within independent individuals. Instead we need to recognise that co-producers are interdependent and rely on each other to achieve the outcomes each is aiming for.

Table 9.1 Behaviours that are Likely to Foster or Lead to Resistance in Adopting Shared Leadership Practices

Leading one another based on a relational perspective would entail:	*Leading the other based on a hierarchical perspective would entail:*
Asking	Telling
Conversations	Explanations
Trusting	Transacting
Reflective practice	Evidence based practice
Belief in collectivity	Belief in hierarchy
Shared responsibility	Self interest
Shared sense of purpose	Personal vision
Adaptive process	Rigid process
Emergent outcomes	Pre-defined outcomes

Conclusion

Exploring how co-production works requires attention to interdependencies between individuals, organisations, service systems and networks. While the growing body of literature on co-production is advancing our understanding of these interdependencies, leadership is one factor that is often overlooked yet offers a valuable perspective on the actual mechanisms through which co-production is enacted. A critical relational perspective encourages us to perceive leadership as distributed and collective, rather than residing with individuals, shaping and being shaped by context and having shared sense of purpose and respect for desired outcomes. Such a lens fits well with contemporary notions of "public leadership" whereby authority and responsibility associated with leading communities, public policy and organisations is distributed horizontally across and vertically within organisations (Brookes and Grint, 2010). However, this marks a distinct departure from established perspectives on leadership found in public administration research which are rooted in assumptions that control and power resides with independent individuals or groups where one has power and control over the other.

References

Andrews, R. and Boyne, G. A. (2010). Capacity, Leadership and Organisational Performance: Testing the Black Box Model of Public Management. *Public Administration Review*, (70), 443–454.

Bass, B. M. (1990). From Transactional to Transformational Leadership: Learning to Share the Vision. *Organizational Dynamics*, (18), 19–32.

Bennet, N., Wise, C., Woods, P. A. and Harvey, J. A. (2003). *Distributed Leadership*. Nottingham: National College of School Leadership.

Bolden, R. (2011). Distributed Leadership in Organizations: A Review of Theory and Research. *International Journal of Management Reviews*, (13), 251–269.

Bolden, R., Petrov, G. and Gosling, J. (2008). *Developing Collective Leadership in Higher Education*. London: Leadership Foundation for Higher Education.

Brandsen, T. and Honingh, M. (2016). Distinguishing Different Types of Co-Production: A Conceptual Analysis Based on the Classical Definitions. *Public Administration Review*, (76), 427–435.

Brookes, S. and Grint, K. (2010). A New Public Leadership Challenge? In S. Brookes and K. Grint (eds.), *The New Public Leadership Challenge*. Basingstoke: Palgrave Macmillan.

Currie, G. and Locket, A. (2007). A Critique of Transformational Leadership: Moral, Professional and Contingent Dimensions of Leadership Within Public Services. *Human Relations*, (60), 341–370.

Edwards, G. P. and Turnbull, S. (2013). A Cultural Approach to Leadership Development Evaluation. *Advances in Developing Human Resources*, (15), 46–60.

Gronn, P. (2002). Distributed Leadership as a Unit of Analysis. *Leadership Quarterly*, (13), 423–451.

Gronn, P. (2009). Leadership Configurations. *Leadership Quarterly*, (5), 381–394.

Hosking, D. M., Shamir, B., Ospina, S. and Uhl-Bien, M. (2012a). Exploring the Prospects for Dialogue Across Perspectives. In M. Uhl-Bien and S. Ospina (eds.), *Advancing Relational Leadership Research: A Dialogue Among Perspectives*. New York: New Information Age Publishing.

Hosking, D. M., Shamir, B., Ospina, S. M. and Uhl-Bien, M. (2012b). Exploring the Prospects for Dialogue Across Perspectives:. In: M. Uhl-Bien, M., and S. M.

Ospina, S, M. (ed.), *Advancing Relational Leadership Research: A Dialogue Among Perspectives*. Charlotte, NC: New Information Age Publishing Inc.

Leithwood, K., Day, C., Sammons, P., Harris, A. and Hopkins, D. (2006). *Successful School Leadership: What It Is and How It Influences Pupil Learning*. Nottingham: DfES Publications.

Macbeath, J., Oduro, G. K. T. and Waterhouse, J. (2004). *Distributed Leadership in Action: A Study of Current Practice in Schools*. Nottingham: National College for School Leadership.

Moynihan, D. P. and Thomas, J. C. (2013). Citizen, Customer, Partner: Rethinking the Place of the Public in Public Management. *Public Administration Review*, (73), 786–796.

Osborne, S. (2010). Delivering Public Services: Time for a New Theory? *Public Management Review*, (12), 1–10.

Ospina, S., Foldy, E. G., Hadidy, W. E., Dodge, J., Hofman-Pinilla, A. and Su, C. (2012). Social Change Leadership as Relational Leadership. In M. Uhl-Bien and S. Ospina (eds.), *Advancing Relational Leadership Research: A Dialogue Among Perspectives*. New York: Information Age Publishing.

Shamir, B. (2012). Leadership Research or Post-Research? Advancing Leadership Theory Versus Throwing the Baby Out with the Bath Water. In M. Uhl-Bien and S. Ospina (eds.), *Advancing Relational Leadership Research: A Dialogue Among Perspectives*. New York: Information Age Publishing.

Spillane, J. P. (2006). *Distributed Leadership*. San Francisco: Jossey-Bass.

Stacey, R. D. (2007). *Strategic Management and Organisational Dynamics: The Challenge of Complexity to Ways of Thinking About Organisations*. London: Pearson Education.

Thorpe, R., Gold, J. and Lawler, J. (2011). Locating Distributed Leadership. *International Journal of Management Reviews*, (13), 239–250.

Tuurnas, S. (2015). Learning to Co-Produce? The Perspective of Public Service Professionals. *International Journal of Public Sector Management*, (20), 583–598.

Tuurnas, S. (2016). *The Professional Side of Co-Production*. University of Tampere, Doctor of Philosophy.

Uhl-Bien, M. (2006). Relational Leadership Theory: Exploring the Social Processes of Leadership and Organizing. *Leadership Quarterly*, (17), 654–676.

Van Der Haar, D. and Hosking, D. M. (2004). Evaluating Appreciative Inquiry: A Relational Constructionist Perspective. *Human Relations*, (57), 1017–1036.

van Eijck, C. and Steen, T. (2014). Why People Co-Produce: Analysing Citizens' Perceptions on Co-Planning Engagement in Health Care Services. *Public Management Review*, (16), 358–382.

van Eijck, C. and Steen, T. (2015). *Why Is This Citizen Layman Entering My Domain? The Effect of Autonomy, Organizational Support, and Red Tape on Public Professionals' Openness Towards Co-Production*. IIAS Conference on Co-Production, Nijmegen.

Van Wart, M. (2003). Public Sector Leadership Theory: An Assessment. *Public Administration Review*, (63), 214–228.

Van Wart, M. (2013). Administrative Leadership Theory: A Reassessment After 10 Years. *Public Administration*, (91), 521–543.

Vanleene, D., Verschuere, B. and Voets, J. (2015). *Co-Producing a Nicer Neighbourhood: Why Do People Participate in Community Development Projects?* Paper presented at the IIAS Study Group on Co-Production, Nijmegen.

Woods, P. A. (2004). Democratic Leadership: Drawing Distinctions with Distributed Leadership. *International Journal of Leadership in Education*, (7), 3–26.

Woods, P. A. (2015). What Is Democratic Leadership? In D. Griffiths and J. Portelli (eds.), *Key Questions for Educational Leaders*. Burlington, Ontario: Word and Deed Publishing.

9.1 Case Study—Leading Co-Production

The Case of Hertfordshire Fire and Rescue Service's Community Volunteer Scheme

Yassaman Imani and Hans Schlappa

Introduction

This case study illustrates the shifting leadership and control in co-production of preventative services by a voluntary scheme in HFRS (Hertfordshire Fire and Rescue Services). More specifically, it demonstrates how citizen co-producers can exercise some control and lead initiatives despite HFRS's rigid structure and its command and control culture.

The UK fire and rescue services have become a victim of their own success in achieving their core organizational goals, namely reducing fires. This success together with two other factors, namely, a vision of a fire service that is more closely integrated with other emergency services (e.g., ambulance, police, health and social care services) and the UK government's harsh austerity measures after the 2008 global financial crisis imposed an average budget reduction of 28% on the fire and rescue services between 2010 and 2015 (National Audit Office, 2014). The case of HFRS's pioneering CVS (Community Volunteer Scheme) illustrates leadership in co-production practice, as a long-term budgetary austerity turned a small complementary service into a core service provided and co-produced by volunteers.

How the Scheme is Organized

The CVS was launched in January 2008, initially in response to the then UK's Labour Government policy of promoting social inclusion because volunteers were expected to enhance engagement with difficult to reach communities, especially concerning fire prevention initiatives. From 2010 onwards, the purpose of the scheme changed as a result of the austerity measures by the UK government that cut the budget for preventative services by 47.1% in real terms. This inadvertently created a strategic role for the scheme to deliver a core service.

Volunteers receive extensive training to undertake home safety checks and other specialized training (Hertfordshire County Council s.d). Currently the scheme has 105 regular volunteers who dedicate at least 6 hours of their time each month and deliver a wide range of *preventative* services such as home fire safety checks, arson patrols, attending school fairs, working alongside trading standards officers from the municipality and other specialized services (Hertfordshire County Council s.d). In 2014/15 the CVS provided 31,000 hours of volunteer working time, providing a range of services of which home safety visits and street patrols feature most highly. Their work also interlinks with trading standards inspections, public events and educational campaigns, which means that the scheme has grown into a core service on which the HFRS heavily relies.

Leading Co-Production in Practice

The first challenge managers faced was how to set up a volunteering scheme on which they could not impose the control mechanisms used for regular employees of their hierarchical force. Eventually, they decided that it should be largely independent from the mainstream service with one officer (the scheme manager) providing the link between paid staff and volunteers. The lists of required jobs come down from the scheme manager, who collects them from local fire stations from across the county, but how and when they are carried out is organized locally and facilitated by an experienced volunteer with no formal authority other than a nominal title. This structure effectively enabled some distribution of leadership within the co-production process. Both the scheme manager and volunteers perceived that the delivery process was controlled by fire service protocols, rules and structures, so when we asked the volunteers who was leading, they all named the scheme manager. Interestingly, the scheme manager said he could only exercise his positional power over the paid staff but relied heavily on soft skills, which he said were "basically the opposite of all I had learnt in leadership development courses". Volunteers also felt they just carried out orders because preventative services are pre-designed and controlled by detailed protocols, but in fact they took leading roles in some situations. The volunteers had joined the scheme "to give something back to the society" but all were surprised by the scale and scope of the unexpected physical and mental health problems, isolation and other problems they came across. A volunteer told us: "No matter what you're doing your knowledge and your sensibility tell you there's something else here. So you address that issue as well. . . . We do use our initiatives". Some volunteers felt that they worked as "operating in a bubble", a reflection of both their limited interactions with the mainstream service provided by paid staff and the inherent tension between a hierarchical structure where the professional retains control over the design and delivery of the service, and a semi self-organizing "light" structure which facilitated the sharing of leadership roles between regular and citizen co-producers. To deliver a core fire prevention service, volunteers would follow the rigid protocol designed by professionals but in the "light structured" part of their work when they entered people's homes they would change the nature of the service significantly if they came across unexpected issues. In these unpredictable situations, volunteers take the lead using their own judgments and "making a difference". This was the unpredictable, uncategorized dimension of a pre-designed core service that enabled volunteers to lead a particular part of the service process, which in practice required a flexible approach to leadership. However, both regular and citizen co-producers underplayed how leadership would shift between them depending on situations. Volunteers tended to downplay their considerable influence on the co-production process and put it down to their "spirit of limitless time", which they felt the regular firefighters did not have. In practice, this meant that citizen-led co-production could provide a holistic approach which necessitated and put in effect a more distributed leadership.

Conclusion

This case study highlights the dynamic nature of co-production where both regular and citizen co-producers take the lead, even if citizen co-producers do not acknowledge their leading roles. The CVS has effectively and successfully co-produced a core service and in the process both regular and citizen co-producers have taken leading roles and developed unique understating of the needs of their communities. Yet, despite its obvious potential benefits to a cash strapped public service provider, the scheme's future remains uncertain and might even get closed down despite governments' new integrated service policy, which would benefit highly from it.

References

Hertfordshire County Council. (s.d.). *Fire Service Volunteers Make a Real Difference* (online).

National Audit Office. (2014). *Local Government: The Impact of Funding Reductions on Local Authorities*. London: National Audit Office.

9.2 Case Study—Enhancing Co-Creation Through Linking Leadership

The Danish 'Zebra City' Project

Anne Tortzen

Introduction

Co-production and co-creation are currently high on the strategic agenda of Danish municipalities and a range of initiatives are launched by public managers to enhance collaboration with citizens and public service users. This case study describes a community development initiative in the Danish municipality of Roskilde labelled 'The Zebra City project'. The project is a case of complementary co-creation, where the municipality set out to facilitate a range of citizen-driven collaborative activities with the aim of strengthening social capital in a 'vulnerable' local community. Through a 'linking'-type of leadership, the 'Zebra City' initiative succeeded in linking a variety of actors, goals and interests, thereby enhancing the co-creation process.

The 'Zebra City' project has been initiated, framed and facilitated by civil servants from the municipality of Roskilde, categorizing it as a 'top-down' co-creation initiative. The case study explores how the hands-off (governing) and hands-on (facilitating) leadership interventions enacted by the public administrators influenced the co-creation initiative, illustrating some general conclusions in terms of the link between leadership and co-creation (Tortzen, 2016). Firstly, the hands-off leadership interventions exercised by the public agencies are central to top-down co-creation processes. Secondly, top-down co-creation processes tend to take place within a cross pressure of governance logics. In the case of 'Zebra City', a 'linking' strategy was applied that reflexively coped with this pressure by linking interests, actors and governance logics, thereby enhancing the co-creation process.

Background

The 'Zebra City' initiative took place in a 'vulnerable' public housing community in Roskilde characterized by social problems and a relatively high proportion of immigrant inhabitants. The initiative was part of the municipality's strategic ambition to innovate public welfare and solve complex problems by mobilizing local resources (Roskilde Kommune, 2012). It was aimed at empowering the local citizens and strengthening the social networks between local actors in the area by bringing them together in a range of activities.

The hands-off leadership of the 'Zebra City' was characterized by a tension between governance regimes expressed in terms of two conflicting framings of the initiative. On the one hand, the initiative was framed by the top managers according to a New Public Governance understanding, i.e. awarding the municipality a role of facilitating 'network- and community-building' and the 'creation of synergy among local resources'. The designation 'Zebra City' also draws on this understanding, as the zebra is described as a particularly social animal that tends to protect the weakest individuals of the community.

On the other hand, however, the top management of the municipality framed the 'Zebra City' project in terms of a number of performance targets derived from a New Public Management understanding. Project targets were set in terms of a certain number of activities initiated locally, a certain number of citizens engaged in these activities and a wish to increase the number of citizens participating in existing local voluntary organizations. At the same time the politicians wanted the 'Zebra City' project to serve as a platform for their personal meetings with local citizens. Conclusively, the initiative was characterized by governance tensions and a complexity of goals and interests (Tortzen, 2016).

This tension was handled through the hands-on leadership of the 'Zebra City' project in terms of facilitating collaboration between a variety of local actors. The hands-on leadership was mainly exercised by the project manager, who was well aware of the tensions and different interests to be handled in the process. Drawing on her anthropological background, she applied a 'linking strategy' aiming at linking citizens and public administrators from different sectors with different interests, goals and resources through collaboration.

Experiences

The 'linking leadership' interventions performed by the project manager turned out to enhance the co-creation process. A so called 'Zebra Day' was arranged early in the process inviting all local citizens to attend and opening the doors of the local public institutions such as the school and kindergarten, the health center and nursing home.

Furthermore, the project manager facilitated a range of activities driven by local citizens and organizations, and the 'Zebra Day' was attended by the mayor and other local politicians. Thereby the 'Zebra Day' served both as a visible event, network building activity and a platform for the politicians to meet local citizens.

Other 'linking leadership' interventions consisted in actively including marginalized groups in the project by reaching out to immigrant citizens and the inhabitants of a local social psychiatric institution, who were invited to participate by cooking meals for other Zebra participants. Furthermore, the 'linking leadership' performed by the project manager resulted in a number of local activities, i.e. setting up a local choir, establishing an urban garden and a 'flea market for nerds'. Notably, some of these activities were citizen-initiated and -driven, facilitated by the 'Zebra City' project. The urban garden is an example of a citizen-initiated and -driven project which, according to one of the initiators, a woman with a severe stress diagnosis, would not have been realized without the 'Zebra City' initiative: "I would not have been able to do this on my own. Many of us have scratches, cracks and dents, but we give what we have" (Tortzen, 2016).

The 'Zebra City' co-creation initiative has been evaluated mainly positively by the participants, stressing the development of stronger relations among the inhabitants across ethnic groups as well as among the public servants working in the local area. By facilitating collaborative activities among local citizens, voluntary organizations and public administrators, this initiative succeeded in linking different actors, goals and interests. Thereby simultaneously the project succeeded in meeting the municipal performance targets and contributing to the strengthening of local networks and of individual citizens. It served as an opportunity for vulnerable citizens to take the role as co-initiators and co-designers supported and facilitated by the municipality.

References

Roskilde Kommune. (2012). *ZebraByer i Roskilde Kommune.*
Tortzen, A. (2016). *Samskabelse i kommunale rammer-hvordan kan ledelse understøtte samskabelse?* Roskilde: Roskilde Universitet.

10   The Increasing Role of Digital Technologies in Co-Production and Co-Creation

Veiko Lember

Introduction[1]

As the success of contemporary tech giants demonstrates, not only can modern ICT (information and communication technologies) provide ample new solutions and services with a high value to society, but the very basis of the success of the contemporary technology and other industries is fundamentally based on user co-production. Technologies and institutions that make it possible to transform the vast user-generated input into socially and economically valuable products and services have become the key ingredient of the economic and social change (Von Hippel, 2016).[2]

It follows then almost naturally that in the light of the rapid digitization of everyday life, coupled with increasing computational power and ongoing austerity policies, modern ICT is expected to change the way citizens are engaged with and provide input for public services, too (Noveck, 2015; Clark et al., 2013; Linders, 2012). Indeed, a new wave of technology-induced co-production practices has recently emerged around the globe. In Mexico City, which has one of the largest public-transportation systems in the world with 14 million rides per day, the citizens were able to co-produce the city's first ever public transportation map within just two weeks by sharing their travel data through a mobile app (OECD, 2017). In Oxford, UK, citizens launched a flood detection network using water-level monitoring sensors and the Internet of Things to establish real-time monitoring and an advanced alert system that would complement the existing public service (www.oxfordsmartcity.uk/cgi-bin/oxfloodnet.pl). Applications like Firedepartment (http://firedepartment.mobi/) and PulsePoint (www.pulsepoint.org/) empower individuals to be part of the rescue operations, cooperating actively with paramedics when, for example, registered and competent users are alerted if someone nearby has a heart attack or needs medical assistance (Paletti, 2016). In Japan, citizens use their mobile phones as sensors to track litter in cities and enable local governments, using a mix of artificial intelligence, video and GPS technologies, to automatically design quick and measured responses (OECD, 2017). These and numerous other examples imply that technology can indeed change the way citizens contribute to public services, trigger entirely novel services and involvement, and even replace the traditional human-centric co-production with fully automated processes. As such, modern technologies can empower millions of citizens around the world and help them to enjoy a better quality of life (Noveck, 2015).

Yet, technological change never automatically creates "better life"—it is an open-ended process riddled with value and other conflicts that may create severe unintended and negative consequences (Jasanoff, 2016; Morozov, 2013). Next to all the visible success stories, new technologies increasingly structure how and what citizens can co-produce, often diminishing their choices to actively participate in public-service provision (Kitchin, 2016; Ashton et al., 2017). And sometimes digital technologies may not only disempower citizens, but as "weapons of mass destruction" amplify the real-world biases and discriminatory practices and thus directly harm them (O'Neil, 2016).

This chapter takes stock on the existing evidence and revisits the key technological issues relevant for public service co-production and co-creation. The chapter will focus on ICT—the dominant technology of the current techno-economic paradigm (Perez, 2002)—which has arguably also had the strongest impact.[3] It will discuss what kind of impacts emerge from introducing new digital technologies into this context and what are the open issues.

Main Technological Developments Influencing Co-production

Today there is an entire cluster of digitally enabled technologies emerging that potentially have a deep impact on how citizens contribute to public-service delivery. The majority of existing studies observing this relationship have so far focused on social media (Meijer, 2011; Linders, 2012; Nam, 2012; Mergel, 2016; Noveck, 2015; Paletti, 2016). In addition, the various technologies associated with the "smart city", such as electronic sensors or urban control rooms (Townsend, 2013; Cardullo and Kitchin, 2016), as well as emerging technologies, such as blockchain, that enable peer-to-peer service delivery (Pazaitis et al., 2017a) are becoming more central to the ways citizens engage with public-service delivery.

Some of the new technologies affect co-production *indirectly*. Digital technologies can simply be useful for coordinating co-production and co-creation, by allowing for more efficient information flows and providing support functions (e.g. stakeholders can have real-time access to and exchange of information or use various digital products from digital signatures to electronic databases). Real-time data collection and provision can provide the governments with an opportunity to nudge how citizens contribute to public-service delivery (e.g. users can be notified of how their real-time energy consumption compares to their neighbours', consequently nudging them to change their behaviour and thus how they co-produce environmental protection, see Linders, 2012).

There is also a wide array of new technologies that potentially *transform* what we know as traditional co-production. Some of these technologies create entirely new practices, while some just add a digital layer on top of the traditional human-centred processes. For example, assisted living technologies such as telecare (remote monitoring of emergencies through sensor devices and personal alarms) and telehealth (transmission of medical information over telecommunication) provide opportunities for elders to live independently at homes, while assuming a significant shift in co-production practices (Wherton et al., 2015). Hackathons and living labs can be considered to be closest to the idea of co-creation of new technologies (Cardullo and Kitchin, 2017a). Hackathons represent both a new method of co-creation (e.g. government-sponsored weekend-long prototyping/coding events for citizens, often based on government-provided open data) and a source for new co-creation initiatives (e.g. apps and other technical solutions enabling further co-creation). Living labs are a bottom-up approach to test digital technologies with their users "in-vivo settings" and to solve local issues through community-focused civic hacking, various kinds of workshops and engaging with local citizens to co-create digital interventions and apps (Cardullo and Kitchin, 2017b). A similar idea is behind technology co-design workshops, where in the format of participatory design users and designers express and exchange ideas to develop technology-intensive services (Wherton et al., 2015).

In addition, through various digital crowdsourcing platforms, governments can tap into the collective wisdom of the crowds by systematically collecting ideas, opinions, solutions and data from service users and citizens (Noveck, 2015).[4] Here the examples include not only social media harvesting (e.g. using Twitter for sentiment analysis for getting real-time feedback for implemented initiatives) or data-collecting through "fix-my-street" and 311-type solutions, but also engaging citizens to voluntarily contribute their personal data for developing new public services (see e.g. www. decodeproject.eu/). As a paradoxical twist, the widely spread crowdfunding platforms have made it also possible for government organizations to raise money directly from citizens to implement public projects such as acquiring school equipment or building public walkways (The Economist, 2013; Davis, 2015).

Crowdsourcing and other digital co-production and co-creation attempts are increasingly facilitated by gamification strategies, that is, by using game-thinking or game mechanisms in non-game contexts to incentivize citizens to participate and provide input for public service delivery (Mergel, 2016). For example, when co-creating the city's first ever public transportation map, the citizens of Mexico City were allocated points based on their inputs, whereas the highest earners were given cash prizes and electronic devices as incentive to participate (OECD, 2017).

In addition, much of the latest thinking about digitally enabled co-production is related to the idea of government as platforms (Linders, 2012). Fundamentally, platforms are "frameworks that permit collaborators—users, peers, providers—to undertake a range of activities, often creating de facto standards, forming entire ecosystems for value creation and capture" (Kenney and Zyzman, 2015). As platforms bring together different services, applications and technologies, as well as all types of stakeholders (Janssen and Estevez, 2013), they are believed to reorganize how value is created in society, who captures the value and control (Kenney and Zyzman, 2015). For example, in China, the WeChat platform, with 806,000,000 individual and 20 million company users, combines multiple platforms into one app with multiple social media functions, big data maps and integration of public service provision, investment services and mobile payment functions. These functions provide also many new co-production opportunities, from the ability to make doctors' appointments to on-line reporting or paying a traffic fine online (OECD, 2017).

The development of platforms has evolved hand-in-hand with the advancements in the so-called big, open and linked data (Janssen and van den Hoven, 2015; Toots et al., 2017). This constitutes a new approach to every-day generated data, including on a meta-level, which should be made generally available (opened up) and linked in order to generate the full potential of the data. Using web-based interfaces, open-government data enables citizens and other interested parties to design and implement services based on data owned and stored by the government (Kornberger et al., 2017). This would not be possible without the user-generation of data, whether or not this happens knowingly (Janssen and van den Hoven, 2015). Platforms can also mash up different data sources, such as social media, sensors or geo-informational data. For instance, in Greater Jakarta, a tool called PetaBencana.id was created that combines data from hydraulic sensors with citizen reports over social media and civic applications and that allowed for the creation of real-time flood maps (OECD, 2017).

Finally, there are the new technologies that have the potential to *substitute* traditional practices. This means, on the one hand, that thanks to the digital technologies, the co-production process can be fully or partly automated, changing the role of citizens from active to passive. Increasing use of remote health-monitoring sensors that can provide 24/7 real-time and automated feedback about the health conditions of the patient is one of the examples here. Another emerging trend is the use of algorithm-based decision-making models and the Internet of Things to monitor the behaviour of crowds and service performance. Here the mere presence and action of citizens in public spaces provides the governments potentially valuable feedback (Cardullo and Kitchin, 2017a) and makes it possible to build predictive governance models based on the actual behaviour of citizens without actively engaging them (Athey, 2017). This includes initiatives as varied as the management of public spaces (e.g. mega-stadiums; see, e.g., https://dcu.asu.edu/content/

smart-stadium), predictive policing (algorithms predict, based on citizens' past behaviour, where the next crime will take place and correspondingly trigger the preventive actions by the police, see e.g., Hunt et al., 2014) and corruption surveillance (e.g. a recent study claimed that based on citizens-created social-media data it is possible to predict up to one year before the fact which specific politicians in China will later be charged with corruption, see Qin et al., 2017).

Simultaneously, there is also an increasing presence of technologies that give the full control of service provision to citizens without the need for direct or even indirect government participation. Here the citizens own and decide on the initiatives, choose the design and implementation methods, co-create the technologies and coordinate the activities from start to finish (Pazaitis et al., 2017b). The key here is the use of (open-source) digital technologies that enable the citizens to coordinate and deliver the peer-to-peer initiatives on a much larger scale than was possible before and without the presence of the central coordinating authority (e.g. the government). So, instead of top-down government or private-sector-coordinated initiatives, we now have not only highly influential peer-to-peer produced solutions, such as Wikipedia or community-owned public taxi services such as in Austin (US), but entire eco-systems of user-driven innovators which are increasingly capable of coming up with bottom-up solutions for their communities (see also von Hippel, 2016). In other words, digital technologies may effectively substitute traditional service provision models with models of self-organization.

Preliminary Evidence and Open Questions

In spite of the rapid technological change in recent years, the knowledge of how digital technologies actually impact the very nature of citizen engagement and co-production is still limited (Meijer, 2012; Clark et al., 2013; Noveck, 2015). While the overall mood is highly optimistic and the preliminary evidence demonstrating the positive influence is seemingly stockpiling, one should be aware that the technological change can influence co-production and co-creation in many different ways. While some of the gains are often quickly visible and easy to understand (e.g. reporting apps provide citizens with a convenient and effective means to contribute to safety and environmental protection), many of the drawbacks tend to have long-term impacts and take years to become visible (e.g. disempowerment of citizens as digital platforms re-allocate control in society). As digital technologies are never neutral to social acts (Jasanoff, 2016), new technologies may significantly change the very nature and meaning of what and how citizens co-produce with the public sector (Meijer, 2012). In other words, while technologies can seemingly give citizens more opportunities to contribute to public service delivery, they simultaneously structure for good or ill how and when they provide input (see e.g. Kitchin, 2016). What follows is a short overview on the impact the digital technologies have had on co-production, co-creation and related open issues.

Empowerment

The central argument for using digital solutions in co-production is that these technologies can considerably *empower citizens* as they enable shared sovereignty and responsibilities (Noveck, 2015). Consequently, the digital technologies can create new social interactions and practices (Townsend, 2013), where citizens not only contribute to public service delivery in novel ways, but can do it more collectively (Bovaird and Löffler, 2010). Although many of the examples outlined in this chapter and elsewhere (see e.g. Gov-Lab, 2013; OECD, 2017) seem to indicate that this has indeed been the case, there is yet no systemic evidence available about the impact of digital technologies on citizen empowerment.

Moreover, the increasing reliance on digital governance may paradoxically marginalize the role of citizens as co-creators of public services. When observing the recent developments in the context of smart cities, Kitchin (2016) has stated that:

> Such automated management facilitates and produces instrumental and technocratic forms of governance and government. That is, rote, procedural, rule-driven, top-down, autocratic means of managing how a system functions and how it processes and treats individuals within those systems. Algorithmic governance is the technical means to manage a city understood in technical terms: wherein there is a belief that the city can be steered and controlled through algorithmic levers.

The code underlining digital solutions for co-production and co-creation always entails normative assumptions and values that in the end structure how citizens can provide input; yet the normative assumptions of digital solutions are seldom debated openly, especially when proprietary technologies and commercial secrecy are applied (O'Neil, 2016). If to delineate between communication, consultation and co-production as the main citizen-engagement and -participation forms (Martin, 2005), it seems that the emerging technological advancements mostly cluster around communication, consultation and minimal co-production practices, and far less around what Bovaird (2007) has labelled full co-production. This tendency is visible, for example, in the so-called global smart-city movement, where the recent advancements cluster predominantly around top-down technologies, such as dashboards, smart meters, sensor networks, centralized control rooms and various applications that foremost cater to the needs of governments and provide opportunities for markets rather than enabling truly co-creative practices (Cardullo and Kitchin, 2017a). In other words, growing digitalization and a related engineering mentality increasingly structure how citizens provide input, without citizens being always able to influence how this is structured and to hold the technology provider accountable.

Participation and Inclusiveness

It is also expected that digital technologies lead to higher-level *citizen participation* and engagement and thus contribute to more inclusive policy-making as well as create more trust in society and towards the government (Meijer, 2012). Indeed, in many ways the ability to contribute to public-service delivery has never been easier—mobile apps provide opportunities to co-produce 24/7 and no matter your location, reporting a problem can take just a few seconds, and finding the right citizen expert to solve a policy challenge can be swiftly done by algorithms. Many studies have confirmed these expectations, demonstrating that new media and online networks can boost co-production and information exchange between citizens and their government (Meijer, 2011) and without necessarily neglecting vulnerable social groups (Clark et al., 2013).

Still, many other studies have argued that technology does not make co-production or participation in general more representative or inclusive (Smith et al. 2009; Clark et al., 2013). Digital technologies provide governments with opportunities to simply load off their functions and leave the costs to be borne by the most vulnerable people (Townsend, 2013). Accessibility to new technologies is unevenly distributed in society, where the educated professionals have more skills and time to engage with technology-induced co-production and co-creation than many other social groups (ibid.; Mergel, 2016). The regressive nature of digital participation is especially strong when citizens are expected to co-create digital public services, while technologies such as crowdfunding provide opportunities for re-privatizing many traditional public services. Preliminary empirical evidence shows also that often the citizens co-producing or co-creating via digital means remain not only a small group but also an anonymous one (Kornberger et al., 2017).

Efficiency and Effectiveness

The attempts to overcome the *fiscal pressure* in public service delivery are arguably the most powerful drivers behind co-production (Nabatchi et al., 2017). The potential of technology-enabled co-production to substitute public service delivery is appealing to many, especially under the current austerity paradigm (see e.g. Wherton et al., 2015). Also, digital technologies can be the catalyst that enables participatory user engagement leading to inclusive and user-driven innovation processes and providing *better products and services* (Townsend, 2013). Both markets and governments have considerable limits in understanding the emerging needs of citizens, which are often too scattered and latent to be noticed (von Hippel, 2016). By designing new social technologies (apps most notably), citizens are not only best positioned to use the existing knowledge on articulating specific needs and novel ideas, but also to provide quickly effective solutions through either individual initiatives or collective ones (e.g. hackathons, app contests, crowdsourcing) (Townsend, 2013). By adopting digital collaborative problem-solving strategies, "government agencies can crowd-source their way out of problems" (Nam, 2012).

Indeed, as shown in the case of Mexico City's public transportations system above, digital technologies can provide both extremely efficient as well as effective tools to co-produce public services. Also, studies have shown that new digital technologies can sharply decrease the costs of "old" practices (e.g. citizens' reporting systems that are based on internet or smartphone apps can cost as much as 80–90% less than phone-based systems, see Clark et al., 2013). Do-it-yourself services that became possible because of digital technologies (e.g. changing one's driving licenses online) have significantly reduced costs for public service providers and saved a considerable amount of time for service users (see also Linders, 2012).

Nevertheless, the existing evidence also points towards important limitations. Sometimes technology-mediated solutions designed to increase efficiency can undermine service effectiveness or just fail to produce expected impact. For example, meetings with relatives over on-line video as opposed to on-spot meetings is a great way to increase service efficiency in prisons, yet over a longer time period, video chats weaken the social ties compared to face-to-face meetings and thus increase the likelihood for re-offending or misconduct (Smith, 2016). In several recent studies on England, it was found that in spite of increasing policy focus and investments into assisted living technologies for the elderly, these technologies are seldom co-created, rarely fit for purpose, fail to trigger new co-production practices and have no significant effect on care efficacy or cost reduction (Wherton et al., 2015). Another issue is that the spontaneous and organic bottom-up technology-induced co-production and co-creation have proved difficult to sustain over a longer period of time, either because initiators just lose their interest or because micro-solutions are often difficult to up-scale (Townsend, 2013). For example, an app was launched in Chicago that enabled citizens to register and adopt fire-pumps in order to keep them clean from snow (storms), and although many registered and adopted one, most fire-pumps were quickly abandoned (ibid.). Thus, although promising, the existing evidence on the impact of digital technologies on the efficiency and effectiveness of co-production still seems to be mixed.

New Tasks and Capabilities

It has been argued that technology-facilitated co-production and co-creation leads to a *change in government tasks*. Rather than being a service provider (traditional public-administration paradigm) or purchaser (New Public

Management paradigm), the government's core tasks would include those closer to a mediator (New Public Governance): it becomes a framer, sponsor, mobilizer, monitorer and provider of the last resort (Linders, 2012, see also Townsend, 2013). The idea of government as a platform best epitomizes this claim, where government is expected to be mainly responsible for developing and providing access to its e-infrastructure and data, and where the role of citizens is to develop services based on this infrastructure (e.g. by developing community maps or apps for public transportation time-tables).

However, so far the systemic impact of digital technologies on the task reallocation within the public sector and between citizens and government has been limited. As it became evident in a recent case study on Vienna, if there is a strong resistance to co-production or limited capacity to engage with citizens, technology is likely to lead to a selective behaviour and reproduce the existing routines rather than facilitate substantive participation and co-production (Kornberger et al., 2017). Mergel (2016) has noted that the use of social media has not brought about radical changes in public organizations, rather, "overall, the traditional information paradigm is replicated on social media". Similarly, Clarke and Margetts (2014) have observed that so far the open and big data movements have largely failed to deliver more citizen-centric governments. Also, the global quest for smart cities is yet to produce examples of truly co-creative initiatives (Cardullo and Kitchin, 2017a). Therefore, technology is sometimes applied by governments in co-production just to look cool rather than with the aim to radically change the task allocation (Nam, 2012; Townsend, 2013).

It is still very much open in which directions the digital technologies will push the evolution of co-production and co-creation, and thus the reallocation of tasks between the government and citizens. In some areas the significance of citizens as co-producers of public services is likely to increase (e.g. assisted living or health-care). In many other instances, such as sharing personal data with the government, claiming documents and benefits, filling in tax declarations or providing feedback—all of which traditionally involve active co-production elements—it is the machine-to-machine interactions that increasingly take over the roles of citizens as active service co-producers and even make co-production redundant in many fields. Yet in other cases, it is the role of the government that is being substituted, as citizens are increasingly able to organize and coordinate services on their own.

New technologies for co-production and co-creation are proposed, justified and introduced with many competing or hidden goals. When adopting new technologies, governments need to strike a balance, for example, between economic development, citizen empowerment and political and administrative control goals as well as related interests (Kornberger, 2017), and these interests and goals are not always mutually reinforcing (Townsend, 2013). In fact, technological or not, innovation by its very meaning always creates winners and losers, thus also political opposition and lobbying (Taylor, 2016). In this inherently political process, stakeholders such as technology companies or bureaucrats often possess better information as well as technological, political and organizational capabilities than citizens. As such, the digital discourse often hides the inherently political nature of organizing societal processes in a narrative of innovation and progress and thus puts those questioning the digital advancements in the laggard or anti-progress categories. Consequently, the use of technological applications may also reallocate control and power towards specific groups in society.

Digital technologies do not only challenge the existing authority relationships and governance models, but also government capabilities (Ashton et al., 2017). Instead of simply reacting to external technological changes, the public sector needs to proactively develop a new set of technological capacities to explore, develop and/or adapt new technological solutions in (co-)producing and (co-)creating public services (Lember et al., 2018). This still seems not to be the case today (Kronberger et al, 2017; Mergel, 2016; Noveck, 2015). As a response, many governments around the globe have not only started to experiment with different services, but have launched dedicated innovation, technology and living labs to accelerate technological innovations in the public sector (Tõnurist et al., 2017; Cardullo and Kitchin, 2017b). All these approaches aim at putting user experience at the centre of the public sector innovation processes; however, these experimental units and methods are still far from becoming an organic part of the public sector and its change. Thus, understanding the institutional and organizational mechanisms behind the public-sector technological capacities remains one of the central questions to be tackled by both practitioners and the research community.

Conclusion

What the previous short overview emphasizes is that technology clearly plays an increasingly central role in co-production and co-creation. To summarize, we can see at least three trends emerging: first, technology as changing traditional co-production and co-creation; second, technology as enabling new forms; and third, technology as replacing traditional (human-centric) processes with automated and self-organizing ones. These trends create new opportunities for co-production while potentially empowering citizens, reallocating tasks between citizens and professionals, increasing the participation of citizens and increasing the efficiency and effectiveness of public-service delivery.

But there is also a great deal of ambiguity involved in how digital technologies shape co-production and co-creation, as they also frame it and at times reduce it, thereby diminishing the bottom-up potential. In spite of great expectations and promising preliminary evidence, it may be the case that open data, crowdsourcing and other technologies may not be capable of providing deep understanding on real-life developments and citizens' needs (see also Fountain, 2014). The current state-of-affairs seems to indicate that in many fields the direct interactions between professionals and service users as well as the use of "good old" methodologies, such as observatory participations, are to remain integral parts of co-production. In order to understand better the potential as well as the limits of digital technologies with respect to co-production and co-creation, we need not only theoretically more critical thinking and long-term empirical investigations on the issue, but also quite different technological capabilities in the public sector to facilitate the process. Meanwhile, co-creating the technologies underpinning co-production as much as possible may be a useful suggestion to follow (Kitchin, 2016).

Notes

1 The project leading to the paper has received funding from the European Union's Horizon 2020 research and innovation programme under the Marie Skłodowska-Curie grant agreement No 750378. I am thankful to the editors and especially Robert Krimmer, Taco Brandsen, Piret Tõnurist and Laidi Surva for their comments and suggestions, and Keegan McBride for his research assistance.
2 According to McKinsey (2016), today the value of globally traded data exceeds the one of physical commodities.
3 The influence of technologies on co-production cannot be, of course, limited to digital technologies only. For example, as Ostrom and others (1973) have demonstrated, the emergence of patrol cars had a direct and significant impact on the ability of police to form productive relationships with the community. As another example, in many countries citizens do not sort household plastic waste anymore, as due to changes in energy production technologies, plastic waste is now simply burned together with other domestic waste.
4 In comparison, when Elinor Ostrom and colleagues founded the co-production research in 1970s, a lot of effort was put on simply getting addresses and contacting people. This is immeasurably easier today.

References

Ashton, P., Weber, R. and Zook, M. (2017). The Cloud, the Crowd, and the City: How New Data Practices Reconfigure Urban Governance. *Big Data & Society*, (4, 1).

Athey, S. (2017). Beyond Prediction: Using Big Data for Policy Problems. *Science*, (355, 6324), 483–485.

Bovaird, T. (2007). Beyond Engagement and Participation: User and Community Coproduction of Public Services. *Public Administration Review*, (67, 5), 846–860.

Bovaird, T. and Loeffler, E. (2010). User and Community Co-Production of Public Services and Public Policies Through Collective Decision-Making: The Role of Emerging Technologies. In J. Gotze and C. B. Pederson (eds.), *State of the eUnion: Government 2.0 and Onwards*, 257–274. 21Gov.net.

Cardullo, P. and Kitchin, R. (2017a). *Being a 'citizen' in the smart city: Up and Down the Scaffold of Smart Citizen Participation*. Programmable City Working Paper, 30.

Cardullo, P. and Kitchin, R. (2017b). *Living Labs, Vacancy, and Gentrification*. Programmable City Working Paper, 28.

Clark, B., Brudney, J. and Jang, S.-G. (2013). Coproduction of Government Services and the New Information Technology: Investigating the Distributional Biases. *Public Administration Review*, (73, 5), 687–701.

Clarke, A. and Margetts, H. (2014). Governments and Citizens Getting to Know Each Other? Open, Closed, and Big Data in Public Management Reform. *Policy and Internet*, (6, 4), 393–417.

The Economist. (2013). Civic Crowdfunding. Breaking Ground. *The Economist*.

GovLab. (2013). Towards Reimagining Governance. Mapping the Pathway Towards More Effective and Engaged Governance. *GovLab*.

Janssen, M. and Estevez, E. (2013). Lean Government and Platform-Based Governance—Doing More with Less. *Government Information Quarterly*, (30), S1–S8.

Janssen, M. and van den Hoven, J. (2015). Big and Open Linked Data (BOLD) in Government: A Challenge to Transparency and Privacy? *Government Information Quarterly*, (32, 4), 363–368.

Jasanoff, S. (2016). *The Ethics of Invention*. New York and London: W.W. Norton & Company.

Kenney, M. and Zysman, J. (2015). *Choosing a Future in the Platform Economy: The Implications and Consequences of Digital Platforms*. Draft paper presented at Kauffman Foundation New Entrepreneurial Growth Conference, 18–19 June.

Kitchin, R. (2016). *Reframing, Reimagining and Remaking Smart Cities*. Programmable City Working Paper, 20.

Kornberger, M., Meyer, R. E., Brandtner, C. and Höllerer, M. A. (2017). When Bureaucracy Meets the Crowd: Studying 'Open Government' in the Vienna City Administration. *Organization Studies*, (38, 2), 179–200.

Lember, V., Kattel, R. and Tõnurist, P. (2018). Technological Capacity in the Public Sector: The Case of Estonia. *International Review of Administrative Sciences*, DOI: 10.1177/0020852317735164.

Linders, D. (2012). From E-Government to We-Government: Defining a Typology for Citizen Coproduction in the Age of Social Media. *Government Information Quarterly*, (29, 4), 446–454.

Martin, S. (2005). Engaging with Citizens and Other Stakeholders. In T. Bovaird and E. Löffler (eds.), *Public Management and Governance*. First edition, 189–202. London and New York: Routledge.

McKinsey. (2016). Digital Globalization: The New Era of Global Flows. New York: McKinsey Global Institute.

Meijer, A. (2012). Co-Production in an Information Age: Individual and Community Engagement Supported by New Media. *Voluntas*, (23, 4), 1156–1172.

Meijer, A. J. (2011). Networked Coproduction of Public Services in Virtual Communities: From a Government-Centric to a Community Approach to Public Service Support. *Public Administration Review*, (71, 4), 598–607.

Mergel, I. (2016). Social Media in the Public Sector. In D. Bearfield and M. Dubnick (eds.), *Encyclopedia of Public Administration and Public Policy*, 3, 3018–3021. Abingdon: Taylor & Frances.

Morozov, E. (2013). *To Save Everything, Click Here*. London: Penguin Group.

Nabatchi, T., Sancino, A. and Sicilia, M. (2017). Varieties of Participation in Public Services: The Who, When, and What of Coproduction. *Public Administration Review*, published online on 30 March 2017.

Nam, T. (2012). Suggesting Frameworks of Citizen-Sourcing via Government 2.0. *Government Information Quarterly*, (29, 1), 12–20.

Noveck, B. S. (2015). *Smart Citizens, Smarter State. The Technologies of Expertise and the Future of Governing.* Cambridge, MA and London, UK: Harvard University Press.

OECD. (2017). *Observatory of Public Sector Innovation.* Paris: OECD.

O'Neil, C. (2016). *Weapons of Math Destruction. How Big Data Increases Inequality and Threatens Democracy.* Bristol, UK: Allen Lane.

Paletti, A. (2016). Co-Production Through ICT in the Public Sector: When Citizens Reframe the Production of Public Services. In L. Caporarello, F. Cesaroni, R. Giesecke, and M. Missikoff, (ed.), *Digitally Supported Innovation,* 141–152. First edition. Springer International Publishing.

Pazaitis, A., De Filippi, P. and Kostakis, V. (2017a). *Blockchain and Value Systems in the Sharing Economy: The Illustrative Case of Backfeed.* Working Papers in Technology Governance and Economic Dynamics, 73, Ioannina.

Pazaitis, A., Kostakis, V. and Bauwens, M. (2017b). Digital Economy and the Rise of Open Cooperativism: The Case of the Enspiral Network. *Transfer: European Review of Labour and Research,* (23, 2), 177–192.

Perez, C. (2002). *Technological Revolutions and Financial Capital.* Cheltenham: Edward Elgar Publishing.

Qin, B., Strömberg, D. and Wu, Y. (2017). Why Does China Allow Freer Social Media? Protests Versus Surveillance and Propaganda. *The Journal of Economic Perspectives,* (31, 1), 117–140.

Smith, A., Schlozman, K., Verba, S. and Brady, H. (2009). *The Internet and Civic Engagement.* Washington DC: Pew Internet.

Smith, J. (2016). The End of Prison Visitation. *Mic.*

Taylor, M. Z. (2016). *The Politics of Innovation: Why Some Countries Are Better Than Others at Science and Technology.* Oxford: Oxford University Press.

Tõnurist, P., Kattel, R. and Lember, V. (2017). Innovation Labs in the Public Sector: What They Are and What They Do? *Public Management Review,* (19, 10), 1455–1479.

Toots, M., McBride, K., Kalvet, T. and Krimmer, R. (2017). Open Data as Enabler of Public Service Co-creation: Exploring the Drivers and Barriers. In *Proceedings of the 2017 International Conference for E-Democracy and Open Government (CeDEM 2017).* Krems, Austria: IEEE Computer Society, in press.

Townsend, A. M. (2013). *Smart Cities: Big Data, Civic Hackers, and the Quest for a New Utopia.* New York: W. W. Norton & Company.

Von Hippel, E. (2016). *Free Innovation.* Cambridge, MA: MIT Press.

Wherton, J., Sugarhood, P., Procter, R., Hinder, S. and Greenhalgh, T. (2015). Co-Production in Practice: How People with Assisted Living Needs Can Help Design and Evolve Technologies and Services. *Implementation Science,* (10, 75), 1–10.

10.1 Case Study—How Public Services in Sweden Help Newcomers to Integrate in the Labour Market and Society Through the Digital Platform Mobilearn

Somya Joshi, Vasilis Koulolias, Francisco Garcia Moran and Elke Loeffler

Introduction

This case study illustrates how migrants in Sweden were involved in the development of a new online platform Mobilearn (Mobilearn, n.d.). In particular, it shows how migrants have shaped the design of a new digital tool in collaboration with service providers from a range of public agencies. The resulting digital tool, Mobilearn, provides a number of key services tailored to the needs of migrants and helps to make public services provided to migrants more efficient. It is therefore a case study of the co-creation of a core service. Mobilearn has received multiple awards and is now being disseminated in other countries.

Background

Mobilearn was developed through a bespoke social innovation methodology, using an inter-disciplinary approach and engaging with migrants and other key partners from an early stage.

Claes Persson and Ernest Radal, himself the son of immigrants who arrived in Sweden in the 1970s and struggled for years with language barriers and administrative hurdles, started to co-create a digital tool in 2010, working closely with a focus group of approximately 30 newcomers and consulting with a wider group of stakeholders, using an eight-step approach:

• *Identification of the migration challenge*: This involved a bi-weekly one-day workshop for the duration of one year with representatives of different migrant communities and experts in digital technologies. The focus group was recruited from migrants seeking services from the Municipality of Gothenburg.

- *Multi-stakeholder consultations*: The results of the migration challenge were presented to public servants of the Municipality of Gothenburg to obtain their views. This phase also involved weekly meetings with migrant communities.
- *Development* of a business case and technological specification of the new online platform.
- *Prototyping and further multi-stakeholder consultations*: A basic version of the platform was tested in the Municipality of Gothenburg.
- *Pilot project*: In 2011 the municipality launched a pilot project to test the platform with the migrant community and public officials.
- *Validation*: After approximately six months of testing, the online platform was approved as fully developed.
- *Launch of Mobilearn* in mid-2011 in Gothenburg.
- *Feedback loop*: The consultations with the stakeholders were undertaken off-line as the migrants were mainly refugees and anonymity was important to them.

All in all, this co-design process took 18 months. The online platform continues to be developed, based on the input of the migrant user groups.

Experiences with Mobilearn

Mobilearn provides timely information about public services and available support for newcomers to help them learn the Swedish language, find a new home, integrate in their neighbourhood and find jobs or training opportunities. It gathers relevant information from government agencies and other public service providers into a single database and makes this information accessible in a user-friendly way. In particular, Mobilearn uses open data from local and regional authorities, the Police, the Tax Agency, the Swedish Migration Board (Migrationsverket) as well as the Social Insurance Agency, the Employment Service (Arbetsförmedlingen).

Mobilearn is not an app. This means that newcomers do not need a smartphone but can access the information through any internet browser, including their mobile phone. The information in Swedish is translated in four languages (English, Arabic, Persian and Somali) with Swedish subtitles. This helps newcomers to learn Swedish.

However, Mobilearn is more than just a 'digital one-stop shop' tailored to the needs of newcomers. It helps users to do things for themselves, such as writing CVs, and acquire services that help to speed up their integration into the Swedish labour market and society as a whole. In particular:

> Mobilearn enables newcomers to self-assess their hard and soft skills, so that they can improve their CV and also identify development needs. Users are also provided with information on job offers suitable

for their skills profile. By adding some of their personal details to Mobilearn, migrants can create CVs and apply for jobs online. The platform is certified by the Swedish Data Protection Authority, which ensures that Mobilearn meets data privacy standards in accordance with EU laws. The end-users are in complete control and have to approve any requests to access their data.

Mobilearn also provides information on the private housing market and, when possible, suggests accommodation in areas where there is work that matches the skills of the end-user.

Mobilearn also enables newcomers to learn the Swedish language by enrolling in online training. Depending on their language skills, they can access different levels of language training. Typically, the courses last one year. The newcomers who complete the training receive a certificate from the Swedish Employment Agency.

The University of Stockholm undertook a combined network and cost-benefit analysis to identify how the costs and benefits generated by Mobilearn are distributed between key stakeholders. This research revealed that migrant women, in particular, benefit from the services offered by Mobilearn, since they often face difficulties in accessing local public services in person. The digital service enables them to access relevant information from home and to improve their language skills.

The total benefit of the open data solutions offered by Mobilearn to public services in Sweden has been calculated to be approximately 150,000 SEK (approximately 15,000 euro) per year (Henkel, Perjons and Drougge, 2016). By the end of 2016, about half of all local authorities, counties and regional governments in Sweden and the Swedish Migration and Labour Office had purchased a license to use Mobilearn, which has now had approximately 40,000 migrant users.

References

Henkel, M., Perjons, E. and Drougge, U. (2016). *Using Open Data to Support Case Management*, Conference Paper, IEEE 20th International Enterprise Distributed Object Computing Workshop (EDOCW).

Mobilearn. (n.d.). Mobilearn website [online].

10.2 Case Study—ICT and Empowerment of Frail Elderly in Flemish Municipalities

Sylke Jaspers

Introduction

Service providers are searching for a variety of ways to improve social care by making use of technological innovations and including specific user groups in co-designing them. Including user groups should help overcome the possible neglect of these groups' needs and capabilities. The municipal welfare departments of two Belgian cities, Bruges and Ostend, experiment with a digital platform 'Cubigo', through which users co-create and co-produce (in)formal care enabling qualitative living at home for elderly.[1]

Background

Core partners of the project 'Online Buurten' ('Neighbouring online') are the municipal welfare departments of Bruges and Ostend, the company Aristoco (developer of the Cubigo platform), a third sector organisation BlueAssist (www.blueassist.eu) and two university colleges (HoWest and VIVES). Professionals provide tablets and co-produce the process (designing applications) together with the target group, frail elderly persons. After contacting, selecting and motivating potential users of the service, the public service providers coach the elderly in using the tablet. The user co-producer's role is to participate in the design, learn how to use the devices, attend workshops and focus groups, and eventually use the device to keep in contact with other participants. The first goal of the device is to increase empowerment and decrease social isolation of the frail elderly (Online buurten n.d.). The project aims at de-isolating frail elderly by making it easier for them to get in touch with their family, friends, neighbours, caretakers and others. The project coordinator of Online buurten, a civil servant, described this as:

> By digitally unlocking a target group, you give tools to that group by which they can maintain a network, search for activities in the neighbourhood. [Additionally] we want to apply a peer-to-peer based sharing (or a sharing economy) to a group of frail elderly by making use of the [Cubigo] platform. (ZORG Magazine, 2016, 10)

A second aim is to achieve more social participation among the target group. The digital tool enables communication, which results in elderly now being better informed about local activities and participating more in those activities (Online buurten n.d.). A final goal of the project is cost-reduction in service provision.

Experiences

Real measurement of the project's impact are absent, yet actors perceive that social relations have indeed improved in the neighbourhood and thus that the frail elderly became less isolated: "In some neighbourhoods a good network is lacking and for many the tablet works as a reinforcement" (ZORG Magazine, 2016, 8; translation by author). The time and place independency of using the platform, and its user-friendliness, are seen as assets. However, while peer-to-peer care seems evident, participants are shy or (think) they are not able to provide reciprocity. In focus groups the initiators try to find ways to address this demand and overcome shyness.

The project coordinator experiences some weaknesses of the project, which relate to tablets being lent for one year only, after which participants are expected to purchase their own tablet, and the tablet's use depending on availability of WIFI. Furthermore, the project shows to be a costly investment for local government, which invests in tablets and professional support. New services were designed and new positions were created in order to support the project. Professionals come to the homes of elderly to lower digital barriers, or public professionals and community workers recruit the elderly, teach them how to use the app, assist them with problems and connect demand with supply. Eventually, however, it is hoped that tackling isolation of elderly will help reduce health costs.

The project coordinator also reveals some opportunities and risks of using ICT in service delivery. Developing the platform offers opportunities for designing many other applications. Once the platform exists, other service providers and service co-productions may be connected to or initiated through it. Secondly, it provides opportunity to assure communication. Connecting service providers, care partners and users may result in:

> a close relationship with the partners. One is establishing a cooperation, it can thus be a tool to organise [connected] neighbourhood care. [. . .] Users may send a request to their whole network. It offers an opportunity to tackle the discontinuity and increase the continuity of communication on care by developing a participatory model in which informal and formal (commercial) organisations and people are involved. (Interview)

A risk is that simplifying the platform is an added value for new users but not for those who already master the internet. According to the project manager: "how can you connect your platform with the world wide web and make sure that your target group keeps using the platform? And how can we guard the identity of the platform?" Secondly, membership entails the risk of exclusion. When communicating solely through the platform, some residents will not be reached, which makes it necessary to keep communicating also through other channels. Thirdly, there is uncertainty about accessibility and costs of the project after its test-period. Fourthly, a technological application might not be desirable in every neighbourhood. A similar project started in another city, yet it was quickly realised that frail elderly in this neighbourhood desired regular meetings rather than being provided tablets. A final threat of the technological application, which is pointed out, is that professionals in the health sector might not be interested in using it, as it might be unclear what is in it for them.

Note

1 For this pilot case study, I make use of the online published documents on the websites of the project (www.onlinebuurten.be and www.zorgproeftuinen.be/nl/nl/platforms/online-buurten). The quotes presented in this document are quoting the online documents and websites, or are secondary quotes from interviews already conducted for the publication of those documents. Secondly, I conducted an interview with the project coordinator of Online buurten, employed by the municipal welfare department in Bruges.

References

Online buurten. (n.d.). Projecten in de kijker: iPad: da's straffe koffie (online).

ZORG Magazine. (2016). Iedereen digitaal met een tablet . . . of toch maar niet? *ZORG Magazine: ICT & Zorgtechnologie*, mei 2016, 8–11.

10.3 Case Study—Remote Health Monitoring with Wearable Sensors and Smartphones

András Gábor and Barbara Gausz

Introduction

The health care sector, especially in Central and Eastern European countries, is facing several challenges, including the outbound mobility of skilled professionals, financing problems and a fast aging population. Additionally, chronic diseases and missed or delayed diagnoses remain a heavy economic burden for hospitals. Effective home care supported by remote health monitoring can contribute to the stability of the progressive health care system by shifting from clinic-centric services to home care and patient-centric services. Patients' health data transmission to the concerned specialists in hospitals can reduce doctors' visit time, increase the time between two visits and may help to maintain good drug compliance.

We present a case in which low-power and low-bandwidth sensor devices are applied to Hungarian patients with chronic cardiac diseases. The PISCES (Promoting future Internet Solutions in health Environments) EUREKA project's goal was to develop a remote health monitoring system which helps to detect health problems and shorten the necessary treatment periods and the time spent in hospital. There were two institutions involved in the project, a private outpatient clinic and a cardiology department of a state-owned hospital. PISCES' solution facilitates people getting the best possible health care even when patients are living in an area with a relatively low doctor-to-patient ratio. The case shows that integrating health care technologies for prevention and monitoring not only facilitates efficient allocation of health care resources but also contributes to a better quality of life for patients.

Background

Health care can be considered a service rather than a product manufactured by the health care system. Medical teams work together with patients in order to restore or maintain an optimal health level (Batalden et al., 2015). In cases where treatment is needed urgently, there's no room left for co-design or co-production. Unlike emergency medical situations, however, health care provided for chronically ill people is largely dependent on the cooperation between physician and patient. One of the internationally accepted indicators of the success of the cooperation is (drug) compliance, which describes the degree to which a patient correctly follows medical advice. Compliance can be supported by new technologies like health monitoring systems. Based on the extent to which citizens are involved in the process and the proximity of the tasks that citizens perform to the core services of the organization, the PISCES solution can be considered as co-production in the design and implementation of core services. Contribution from patients means provision of health state data and support in the design process of the user interface.

PISCES' responsive health monitoring system represents a complex information system that facilitates remote monitoring of patients' health-related data and health status under given environmental conditions (Kő et al., 2015). Wearable sensors used in the experiment are able to track patients' geographical location and record primary vital signs (respiration, heart rate, etc.). The data is interpreted and evaluated by the system, providing real-time feedback for patients about their health state and keeping doctors, paramedics and care-givers informed for support and interaction. Speed of data processing in remote health monitoring is of crucial importance (World Health Organization, 2011). Processing sensors' data in one step is impracticable due to bandwidth requirements and high costs of transmission (for example, an electrocardiogram produces 40MB per minute). PISCES' solution's most important innovative feature is the division of the time-critical processing in two parts: the first part takes place on the smartphone, the second part on the server.

PISCES' solution is designed not only to monitor the health status of the participants, but to react in any case of irregularity. In the experiment, two levels of critical values had been determined: "yellow" alert means that patients get a notification, while in the case of "red" alert, health care personnel will be informed immediately. After the initial data collection phase, it is possible to set personalized alarm values as well.

Experiences

Statistical results show that data was collected reliably through the *sensor-smartphone-mobile data transfer-server* route. Regarding patients' actual health status, heart rate, respiration and meteorological data had been analysed using statistical methods, but no significant correlation was found.

After the testing period, participants were asked to provide feedback about their experiences. Patients proposed to include a panic button in case of emergency. Fortunately, no local alarms were reported (later data analysis proved that there was no need for local alarms). Participants also reported that wearing sensors did not cause major inconveniences, but increased their sense of security. Based on the feedback provided, it was concluded that the simpler the user interface, the more accepted the application is by the patients. The portal interface available for doctors was also redesigned in order to achieve better searchability, as patients could mark the period in the flow of data when they were not feeling well. By improving searchability, doctors could detect rarely occurring cardiac arrhythmias.

The system can successfully collect real-time physiological parameter values, and these data can be connected with other parameters such as movement and meteorological information, provided automatically by the system. Besides improving patients' quality of life, this practice helps to reduce the number of doctor-patient encounters and of hospital admissions, cutting down the costs and lightening the load on the already overburdened health care system.

Home care supported by remote health monitoring helped patients to maintain good drug compliance, reduced doctors' visit time and increased the time between two visits. Patients not only received home care but felt safer, as they were informed about their health state in real-time. Last but not least, life quality of caregivers has been improved by getting an invisible hand.

References

Batalden, M., Batalden, P., Margolis, P., Seid, M., Armstrong, G., Opipari-Arrigan, L. and Hartung, H. (2015). Coproduction of Healthcare Service. *BMJ Quality & Safety*, (25, 7), 509–517.

Kő A., Gábor, A. and Szabó, Z. (2015). Innovative eHealth Services—PISCES Solution. In A. Kő and E. Francesconi (eds.), *Electronic Government and the Information Systems Perspective. EGOVIS 2015. Lecture Notes in Computer Science*, vol 9265. Springer, Heidelberg/New York.

World Health Organization. (2011). *mHealth. New Horizons for Health Through Mobile Technologies: Second Global Survey on eHealth*. Geneva: World Health Organization.

11   Legal Dilemmas of Co-Production and Co-Creation

Dawid Sześciło

Introduction[1]

Public services systems of the European welfare states have been characterized by their legalistic and bureaucratic nature (Mejier, 2012; Hemerijck, 2013), i.e. a state's responsibility for providing services and its focus on adherence to legal procedures in the process. The period of emergence and the golden era of the welfare state (1950s and 1960s of the 20th century) was also the time of Juristenmonopol, i.e. the dominance of juridical thinking in public administration and the key role of statutory regulations in shaping public services systems (Kickert, 2005).

The welfare state crisis that led to expansion of new public management methods marked the end of this era and opened debate about the need for revision of the role of law (especially administrative law) in public administration. It is now clear that legal norms create a platform for administrative actions, but they are not sufficient to ensure the effective and efficient operations of public administration (Vigoda, 2002). While much has been written already about the alleged tension between law and new public management (Bertelli, 2007; Ziller, 2009), little attention has been paid so far to the relationship between law and other new phenomena in public governance, such as co-production and co-creation.

This chapter aims to fill in the gap by providing an overview of key legal dilemmas associated with co-production and co-creation. It focuses on the role of law, both "law in books" and "law in action," in improving outcomes of co-productive arrangements in public services systems. The potential benefits, but also the "dark side of co-production," have been recognized in the literature already, so from a legal perspective, the major question is whether the law and its application could contribute to maximizing the benefits of co-production and mitigating potential risks and challenges associated with it. It appears clear that because of the nature of co-production as a rather voluntary and bottom-up undertaking, legislation is not the key trigger of co-production. However, the law still may serve as a useful instrument for promotion of co-production and dissemination of it, as well as a tool for mitigating its adverse effects. The conclusion of this chapter is a proposal for a set of regulatory strategy measures for co-production and co-creation.

Regulatory Strategies for Co-Production and Co-Creation: General Observations

The question about the role of law in delivering change in public administration is not the central dilemma in public management discourse of recent decades. Legal research remains outside the main thread of the debate about evolving paradigms of public administration. Some authors still believe that the law in public management is like the hands of an artist who transforms abstract ideas into tangible reality (Moe, 1997).

Taking into account this reservation, we strive to position the law correctly in the debate on co-production and co-creation. For this purpose, we start from the concept proposed by Christensen, Goerdel and Nicholson-Crotty (2011), who claimed that with regard to public management reforms, the *law not only constrains but also enables*. In other words, a regulatory framework fulfills two major functions in public management—providing the mandate to act and, at the same time, limiting the autonomy of the regulator and setting boundaries for administrative actions in order to prevent violation of public values or individual rights and freedoms of citizens. This concept applies to introduction of all innovations to a public administration system, including co-production and co-creation. Therefore, this chapter focuses on exploring the potential of law as an enabler, but also constrainer (preventer of values and rights violations) of co-production and co-creation.

Law as an Enabler

Co-production relies on joint activities in the course of regular service procedures, primarily by public agencies and customers. From the customers' perspective, participation in co-production generally does not require any special legal mandate. "What is not prohibited is permitted" remains the key principle governing citizens' roles within the legal system. However, with regard to citizens' participation in the production of public services, this rule clashes with the defining principle of a public services system, i.e. the state's responsibility for provision of services. Co-producing citizens enter the domain of public administration. Thus, specific "competence injunction" may arise when citizens want to perform activities that are assigned by legislation to public bodies. This situation creates a need for legal provisions enabling the transfer of some powers and responsibilities to citizens for the public service delivery process.

For instance, introduction of participatory budgeting as a form of co-creation relating to planning the allocation of a local budget usually requires modifications of budgetary procedures established by relevant laws, especially when the citizens' rights in the process are not limited to consultation. Providing citizens with direct co-decision rights leads to interference with statutory competencies of relevant bodies in the budgetary process, and therefore requires adjustments to the regulatory framework.

Another example is the case of a public institution's involvement in co-production, when the situation becomes even more complex. Regardless of legal tradition, continental *Rechtstaat* tradition or the Anglo-Saxon model of more flexible public interest administration, the operations of public administration remain determined to significant extent by (administrative) law. Administrative law is a constraint that operates on the set of actions, or policy choices, that a bureau or individual bureaucrat may take (Bertelli, 2007). Specifically, in the legal tradition of continental European countries, administrative actions are organized by the concept of competence—formal, statutory power assigned to an administrative body and enabling it to take actions, dispose public funds, grant individual entitlements or impose binding obligations on citizens (Ziller, 2009). However, competence does not have to be formulated as detailed instruction for all administrative actions. The scope of regulation has to be proportional to its impact on the legal position of citizens. The norms regulating administrative actions must be more detailed and precise if they provide ground for interference with the rights and obligations of individuals. They could be more general if there is no direct impact of the regulation on the legal status of the citizens involved.

From this perspective, it is clear that the participation of public agencies (administrative bodies) in co-production requires some, at least general, legal basis. Co-production cannot involve public bodies, public funds and assets if there is no clear legal mandate for it. Although the law does not have to (and should not) serve as a complete framework for co-productive arrangements, lack of legally-defined competence is an entry barrier for any substantial engagement by public institutions into co-production.

Some of the most relevant elements of the regulatory framework for co-production might be distinguished. Firstly, the law should distinguish general distribution of powers and responsibilities in the public service delivery process between regular producers (public agencies) and customers (citizens). It is necessary to clarify to what extent the responsibility for service provision might be divided between public providers and co-producing citizens. The law should provide guidance for administrative bodies on how to proceed when citizens engage or want to engage into service provision.

Secondly, there is a need for a clear legal mandate for public bodies to commit public funds and assets (e.g. public infrastructure) to projects co-implemented and co-created with citizens. This stems from rigorous principles of public finance and public assets management that require legal authorization for transferring public funds or assets to non-public bodies. Co-production and co-creation in many cases involve mixing up private and public resources, including the use of public infrastructure by citizens or transferring some public funds to citizens. Such operations cannot be performed without clear legal authorization.

Law as a Preventer

Another element of regulatory strategy for co-production and co-creation is utilizing the law as an instrument for safeguarding key values of the public services systems. Provision of public services is governed by key public values—universal and equal access to services. Universality requires all human beings to be equally entitled to human rights (Ramcharan, 2015) and civil rights. Thus, equality could be perceived as an underlying principle of universality (Spring, 2000) or an essential tool to guarantee universality (Brems, 2001). The law and procedural mechanisms established in legislation serve as a guardian of public values. While there is no inherent conflict between co-production or co-creation and principles of equality and universality, several potential challenges to those values have been already identified in the literature.

It has been noted that participants in co-production primarily come from wealthy communities (Clark, Brudney and Jang, 2013). Wealthier, better educated and non-minority groups of citizens are in a better position to take control over decisions made in a participatory manner or services requiring more users' involvement (Verschuere, Brandsen and Pestoff, 2012; Poocharoen and Ting, 2015). For example, better educated parents with higher socio-economic status are more willing to engage in their children's education. Wealthier parents are also able to provide their children with extra private lessons, which can be seen as a form of co-production of education, leading to increases in the gap in educational attainment between richer and poorer populations (Andrews, Boyne and Enticott, 2006). Medical patients with higher socio-economic status have more capacity to self-manage their condition by adjusting their lifestyle, diet and habits to the requirements of treatment. Also, long-term economic problems generally weaken the motivation for social engagement, which is a kind of luxury good, available in the first place to those whose basic needs are secured. Participation itself is not an antidote to the structural inequalities and power imbalances in society (Entwistle, 2010).

Therefore, in legal terms, co-production may be considered as a factor potentially triggering discrimination in access to public services. Discrimination in this context does not have direct and explicit form, i.e. the access to specific services is not formally excluded for any group, but an indirect discriminatory effect might result from specific arrangements relating to service delivery. While it is clear that discrimination against less affluent and less educated groups of service users is not an inherent feature of co-production, the risk of discrimination based on socio-economic status of service users' needs to be addressed in the legislative framework for co-production.

Discriminatory effects of co-production might be associated not only with the dominance of wealthier and better educated groups. The same problem may emerge if the co-production leads to capture of control over public services by groups of one specific ideological or political orientation. Control such as this may subsequently result in de facto restriction of access to services for others. Education seems to be particularly vulnerable to this risk. Co-production in education is primarily represented by the concept of charter (voucher) schools, i.e. freedom of establishing schools by private entities (parental groups, religious groups, not for profit organizations, companies) combined with unrestricted parental rights to choose schools according to their own preferences. In the United States in 2013 there were over 5,600 charter schools (Knaak and Knaak, 2013). For Saiger (2013) in the specific American context, charter schools foster gradual desecularization of school systems and strengthening capacity of religious organizations. Black (2013) adds that because of expansion of charter schools, public education can no longer provide universal common experiences or disseminate values contributing to social cohesion. This is a valuable reminder that the mission of public education is not limited to providing knowledge, but also involves promoting values of democratic societies. Charter schools promote greater diversity, individualization and autonomy in terms of methods, but also the content of education. With limited state control over schools, this may lead to emergence of numerous parallel school systems, including religious and sectarian schools.

Law remains one of the main instruments at the disposal of the state to counter threats to universality and equality that are associated with some forms of co-production. What regulatory tools can be used for this purpose? First of all, standards of availability and quality of public services should be defined in the law. The law might specify which public services and at what standard of quality are available to everyone, regardless of personal involvement or lack of involvement in the service production process. The minimum standard of accessibility laid down by law must be broad enough to avoid making co-production a *de facto* condition for obtaining a public service. At the same time, material regulation should be accompanied by a procedure allowing for the protection of these standards in individual cases, including the judicial path for pursuing the right of access to public services.

Furthermore, the potential for discriminatory effects of co-production needs to be tackled by providing relevant public institutions with a clear and specific mandate for scrutiny over the accessibility of co-produced services. For example, there should be a legal mechanism enabling and requiring state response if a school run by a parent cooperative provides a curriculum contradictory to the state of scientific knowledge or violating constitutional values of the state. The state reaction in such cases should be based on the proportionality principle, i.e. ensuring fair balance between restrictions or other measures imposed and the severity of the activities sanctioned.

The last piece of a legislative framework protecting key public values in the context of co-produced public services systems is the liability regime. How does the co-production pose a challenge to liability mechanisms?

For Joshi and Moore (2004) it is clear that co-production blurs accountability schemes based on precise boundaries between private and public. Verschuere, Brandsen and Pestoff (2012) put this problem into the simple question: "(. . .) who can the users hold accountable when the users themselves are part of the production process?" Co-production cannot repeal state liability for provision of public services and cannot serve as an exculpatory defense for public bodies in case of failure in provision of services meeting the standards set in the legislation. It is a role of laws regulating delivery of services in co-productive formula to prevent the blame game between public agencies and citizens that might otherwise nullify any effective liability scheme.

Co-production in healthcare is a good illustration of particularly serious liability issues arising from diluted accountability. Introduction of shared decision-making may hamper investigation in clinical malpractice cases, if it is not accompanied by clear regulation specifying distribution of decision-making powers (and accountability) between the patient and the clinician. "Regulatory vacuum" in this matter might have a particularly detrimental effect on patients' rights, as it may encourage some clinicians to mitigate liability risk by getting patients involved in taking responsibility for medical decisions (Sześciło, 2016).

There is no uniform strategy for regulating liability issues in all areas and forms of co-production. However, a set of general guidelines may be proposed. First of all, the law should clearly specify who makes each decision (choice) relevant for the final outcome of the service delivery process, or require such specification to be made through binding agreement among all parties involved in co-production. The latter approach seems to be more adjusted to the nature of co-production, as it provides for flexibility and tailor-made arrangements. A detailed regulatory framework, in the form of a binding "user manual," would undermine the innovative potential of co-production. On the other hand, the legislation should be detailed enough to effectively protect the position of the weaker or more vulnerable groups participating in co-production (e.g. patients).

Addressing the challenges for universality and equality principles should be an important element of the law-making process in the area of public services. Regulatory impact assessments accompanying the policy and legal proposals introducing (enabling) co-production in public services systems should identify potential threats to universality and equality as key risks to be mitigated by adequate regulatory intervention.

Concluding Remarks

As Ziller (2009, 174) noted: "(. . .) law as such is not an obstacle to administrative reform, nor to the introduction of management: it is a set of tools which can be used well or badly according to the quality of legal education of those who have to set up and implement new modes of management". This statement fully applies to the role of law in introducing and managing co-production and co-creation of public services. The regulatory framework is a necessary element of the strategy for implementation and dissemination of co-production and co-creation and may considerably improve the overall outcome of both approaches. The key task for both legal research and non-legal scholarship dealing with co-production and co-creation is to establish a platform for communication and common understanding of key terms and concepts. From the perspective of legal scholars and practitioners, entering the world of co-production and co-creation is challenging due to the complexity and ambiguity of both concepts. However, there is no alternative to involving lawyers in the planning, programming and implementation of co-production.

Note

1 This chapter was prepared within the framework of the research project funded by the National Centre of Science under contract no. UMO-2013/11/B/HS5/03896.

References

Andrews, R., Boyne, G. and Enticott, G. (2006). Performance Failure in the Public Sector: Misfortune or Mismanagement? *Public Management Review*, (8), 273–296.

Bertelli, A. M. (2007). Law and Public Administration. In Ewan Ferlie, Laurence E. Lynn Jr. and Christopher Pollitt (eds.), *Oxford Handbook of Public Management*, 133–155. Oxford: Oxford University Press.

Black, D. W. (2013). Charter Schools, Vouchers, and the Public Good. *Wake Forest Law Review*, (48), 101–143.

Brems, E. (2001). *Human Rights: Universality and Diversity*. The Hague: Martinus Nijhoff Publishers.

Christensen, R. K., Goerdel, H. and Nicholson-Crotty, S. (2011). Management, Law, and the Pursuit of the Public Good in Public Administration. *Journal of Public Administration Research and Theory*, 1 (supplement), i125–i140.

Clark, B.Y., Brudney, J.L. and Jang, S.G. (2013). Coproduction of Government Services and the New Information Technology: Investigating the Distributional Biases. *Public Administration Review*, (73, 5), 687–701.

Entwistle, T. (2010). Collaboration. In R. Ashworth, G. Boyne, and T. Entwistle (eds.), *Public Service Improvement*. Oxford: Oxford University Press.

Hemerijck, A. (2013). *Changing Welfare States*. Oxford: Oxford University Press.

Joshi, A. and Moore, M. (2004). Institutionalised Co-Production: Unorthodox Public Service Delivery in Challenging Environments. *Journal of Development Studies*, (40), 31–49.

Kickert, W. (2005). Distinctiveness in the Study of Public Management in Europe. A Historical-Institutional Analysis of France, Germany and Italy. *Public Management Review*, (4), 537–563.

Knaak, W. and Knaak, J. (2013). Charter Schools: Educational Reform or Failed Initiative. *The Delta Kappa Gamma Bulletin*, (4), 45–53.

Meijer, A. (2012). Co-Production in an Information Age. In V. Pestoff, T. Brandsen and B. Verschuere (eds.), *New Public Governance, the Third Sector, and Co-Production*, 192–210. London: Routledge.

Moe, R. (1997). The Importance of Public Law: New and Old Paradigms of Government Management. In Philip J. Cooper and Chester A. Newland (eds.), *Handbook of Public Law and Administration*. San Francisco: Wiley.

Poocharoen, O. and Ting, B. (2015). Collaboration, Co-Production, Networks: Convergence of Theories. *Public Management Review*, (17), 587–614.

Ramrachan, B. G. (2015). *Contemporary Human Rights Ideas: Rethinking Theory and Practice*. London: Routledge.

Saiger, A. (2013). Charter Schools, the Establishment Clause, and the Neoliberal Turn in Public Education. *Cardozo Law Review*, (34), 1163–1225.

Spring, J. (2000). *The Universal Right to Education: Justification, Definition, and Guidelines*. Mahwah: Lawrence Erlbaum Associates.

Sześciło, D. (2016). Emergence of Coproduction and Participatory Care in European Clinical Practice. *International Journal of Person Centered Medicine*, (6, 3), 155–161.

Verschuere, B., Brandsen, T. and Pestoff, V. (2012). Co-Production: The State of the Art in Research and the Future Agenda. *Voluntas*, (23), 1083–1101.

Vigoda, E. (2002). The Legacy of Public Administration: Background and Review. In Eran Vigoda (ed.), *Public Administration. An Interdisciplinary Critical Analysis*, 1–15. New York: Marcel Dekker.

Ziller, J. (2009). The Continental System of Administrative Legality. In Jon Pierre and B. Guy Peters (eds.), *The Handbook of Public Administration*, 260–268. London: SAGE.

11.1 Case Study—The European Disability Card

Charlotte van Dijck

Introduction

The EU disability card, a project launched in February 2016, aims to bring the Member States closer together regarding the rights of people that have a disability. By setting up a system of mutual recognition, the EU Disability Card will ensure equal access to specific benefits, mainly in the areas of culture, leisure, sports and transport (European Commission, 2010, n.d.; Service Public Fédéral, n.d).

The project was kick-started in a first group of eight EU countries on a voluntary basis. In every pilot country the European Disability Card is a co-production with many different actors. The federal and regional public institutions that work on social inclusion of people with a disability work together closely with people with a disability who are engaged through NGOs as experts by experience. Additionally, the project involves many partners who, on a voluntary basis, agree to provide benefits to people with the European Disability Card. These partners include a variety of cultural entities (museum, festivals), businesses (hotels), sports clubs and transport agencies among many others. By participating the partners agree that they will (1) recognize everyone with a European Disability Card as someone with a disability—whether the disability is visible or not, (2) take actions to improve the accessibility for these people and (3) provide them with some benefits to improve their sports/transport/leisure experience and independence.

Background

One in six people in the EU (European Union) have a disability that ranges from mild to severe. For taking part fully in society, they frequently need to overcome different environmental and attitudinal barriers. In order to do so they are dependent on others (cultural organisers, transport companies, . . .) who are rarely equipped to correctly judge the full effects of one's disability and the appropriate benefits. Co-production could change that.

The involvement of experts by experience first of all helps countries to better identify appropriate eligibility criteria for distributing the EU Disability

Card. The experts can point out issues faced by people with less common and less visible disabilities who might otherwise have not been included in the initiative. Secondly the citizens with first-hand experience with disabilities are highly instrumental in setting up the list of potential benefits that partners can offer when taking part in the project. These include potential benefits such as free and easy access to bathrooms, or seats close to the escape route in case of an emergency. The co-producers' contribution to this list of potential benefits is vital since they are best equipped to point out the problems persons with a disability face and the actions they could benefit from.

Still this project could do more than make benefits better adapted and more accessible at the national level. This is where the EU legal framework comes into play. In the European Union there are currently still 28 different national sets of laws governing the rights of citizens who have a disability. Not only is there no mutual recognition of disability status between EU Member States, the benefits given to people with a disability also differ strongly among the 28 EU countries. In Member States like Germany, France and Denmark, there is a well-established system of national Disability Cards, while in Sweden, Italy or Greece such cards do not exist. This means national disability cards are not recognised in all EU countries at the moment and there is no equal access to certain specific benefits, creating uncertainty for people with a disability when traveling within the EU. The creation of social legislation in the EU is a sensitive issue for many EU member states and mostly requires unanimity. This is why there is little EU-wide social legislation and very little hard law in that respect. It makes it difficult for the EU to reach its goals of promoting active inclusion and full participation of disabled people in society in line with the EU human rights approach to disability issues. Co-producing active inclusion, however, can circumvent some of the issues social rights encounter at the technical legal level through the connections in this project on a more practical level. While top-down legislation may be hard to create, bottom-up change in practise can be easier to bring about in this case. The mechanism behind this is elaborated on in the next paragraph.

Experiences

The card lacks the legal framework to change national eligibility criteria or rules. In accordance with EU law, Member States retain their discretion to decide who is eligible to receive the Card, using the national definition of disability, and to determine the issuing procedure. Yet the system of mutual recognition between participating states indirectly causes countries to recognise the disability status of EU citizens with a European Disability Card, even if such citizens would not be eligible for the card everywhere in the EU. In terms of equal rights, this does not ensure that a citizen who would be eligible for the card in country A is eligible for the card in country B, but it does guarantee that everyone eligible for the card in their own country can enjoy all benefits connected to it in all countries that signed the protocol for the European Disability Card. Compared to the current situation, this co-production increases the EU-wide benefits for a large portion of EU citizens with a disability, yet not for all. In time this project could open the door for a mutual baseline in terms of eligibility criteria in practice, bypassing the difficulties of creating legislation to make that happen.

In practice, these benefits, advised by experts by experience and granted by the different partners involved at the national level, can be many things. In a museum or landmark, the benefit could be a free audio guide or a reduced fee for a guided tour. At a concert of festival, the card could give access to a reserved area where people in a wheelchair could have a better view. Apart from providing reserved parking spots, partners can also provide special discounts.

Although partners still suggest these benefits on a voluntary basis in this stage of the project, they are encouraged to do so in different ways. By being mentioned in the European Disability card data base they can increase their social image and have some free publicity. Apart from that they can contribute to a more inclusive society. Working via a co-production initiative thus allows an increase in services for persons with disabilities, without the difficulty of creating or changing social legislation in the EU. In time, if the project is successful and the number of partners grows, recognising equal rights and providing benefits may become standard, regardless of the existence of social laws to that effect. The rapidly growing co-production surrounding the European Disability Card could increase the EU-wide standards for benefits to people with disabilities thereby creating a practise of inclusion. If so, the co-production project would do what is legally and politically very difficult to achieve: creating mutual rights and benefits for people with a disability across the EU.

References

European Commission. (2010). *European Disability Strategy 2010–2020: A Renewed Commitment to a Barrier-Free Europe*. Brussels: European Commission.

European Commission. Employment, Social Affairs & Inclusion (n.d.). *EU Disability Card* (online).

Service Public Fédéral. Sécurité Social. Direction générale Personnes handicapées. (n.d.). *European Disability Card* (online).

Part 3

Co-Production and Co-Creation in Different Domains

12 Co-Production in Healthcare

Caitlin McMullin and
Catherine Needham

Co-production has been promoted as a way of organising services and restructuring relationships between service users and professionals in a range of different public services. We understand co-production to refer to the direct contribution of patients, service users and/or family members to the health or wellbeing service from which they (or their family members) benefit (Brandsen and Honingh, this volume). Healthcare is a service sector in which there is a particular impetus for co-productive approaches, as responsive and inclusive services can enhance individual and collective wellbeing, but it is also a setting in which the barriers to co-production may be particularly prohibitive. In this chapter, we will discuss the distinctive context of co-production in healthcare and the particular obstacles that this approach creates in the health sector.

Healthcare Reform

Co-production is suggested as a way to combat many of the problems facing contemporary welfare states—such as stretched public finances, an increasing demand for more personalised services, technological advances, ageing populations and other demographic changes (Pestoff, 2008; Dunston et al., 2009; NESTA, 2013; Slay and Stephens, 2013). Whilst these challenges are often discussed in the literature about public services in general, health services are acutely impacted by these issues as countries are driven to develop more innovative configurations of health services to deal with the strain of austerity measures and demographic change (World Health Organization, 2015).

Many countries since the 1980s have taken an approach of introducing market reforms into the health sector (Christensen and Laegreid, 2007). This impetus to take a more market-oriented approach to service commissioning and delivery has arguably changed the policy focus of healthcare from seeing patients as recipients of health services to becoming consumers, with a greater focus on providing choice of providers and services (Thomson and Dixon, 2006). This change in focus has been accompanied by a range of measures to increase the influence of patients over their care and treatment, such as the move towards narratives of 'patient centred care' and person-alised health (Hyde and Davies, 2004; Needham, 2009). However, accord-ing to Dunston et al. (2009), measures to increase the options and outcomes available to patients through market choice or 'voice' via consultation pro-vided disappointing results. Co-production has thus been suggested as a more effective means to improve the service offer within health, produce better outcomes for patients and save money (Needham, 2008; NESTA, 2013; Dunston, 2014). The increased attention to co-production has also been recognition of the bottom-up initiatives through which citizens have increasingly pressed to have more influence over their own health and well-being. For example, survivor groups within mental health services in the USA (Mclean, 1995), and campaigns for improved reproductive rights for women around the world (Doyal, 1996) have been high profile examples of citizen actors demanding more say in key aspects of their lives.

Co-Production and Healthcare

As we saw in the chapter by Brandsen and Honingh in this volume (chap-ter 2), some definitions of co-production suggest that the types of service that comprise healthcare necessarily involve a degree of co-production—in the sense that medical professionals and patients must work together to ensure the best health outcomes (Alford, 2009). Patients must, for exam-ple, take medication and follow medical advice themselves if health inter-ventions are to be effective. Beyond this notion of co-production as being inherent to healthcare services, there are several typologies of co-production activities that have been studied in recent literature which we will discuss in this section.

Co-Production Typologies and Healthcare

Brandsen and Honingh (this volume) suggest that co-production can be sub-defined to differentiate between the contribution to *core services* as well as *complementary tasks*, meaning the activities that support the service process indirectly. In this model, the contribution of service users or patients is not necessarily limited to the involvement in the design and direct delivery of the main aspects of the service, but extended to include involvement in planning of both core services and complementary tasks (or co-creation). This pro-vides a useful typology for co-production of healthcare, where co-delivery of certain medical services is impossible due to the medical expertise needed, but where patients' lived experiences can be valuable additions to other stages of the service process (Batalden et al., 2015; Dunston, 2014). Thus whereas patients cannot co-produce their surgery, or their emergency room treatment, they can be actively involved in decisions about where emer-gency provision is located within a region, or can shape the prioritisation of forms of surgery—e.g. access to bariatric surgery for people who are obese

(Daniels, 2000). The movement towards user involvement in healthcare has gathered momentum during the 21st century, building on the work of pioneers such as Kate Lorig, a nurse who developed the Stanford model to support patient involvement in the USA (Department of Health, 2005). This builds on both a normative account of the legitimacy of patient voice, and also on the recognised service benefits of designing interventions that meet patient needs (Greenhalgh et al, 2011).

An alternative typology of co-production distinguishes between individual activities, group co-production and collective co-production—where activities benefit the community rather than a particular group (Brudney and England, 1983). Within healthcare, this distinction helps us to better understand the activities that take place. On one end of the spectrum, patients and practitioners can co-produce an individual's medical intervention, in activities that blur the edges between co-production and related policy drivers such as personalisation and person-centred care (Needham, 2011). Group co-production encompasses activities such as mutual support groups for long-term health conditions or group appointments where clinicians and patients work together towards the shared goal of better outcomes (Batalden et al., 2015). Finally, several examples have been described of patient involvement in governing councils of hospitals or other organisations where their expertise is used to inform broader strategic decisions of the health service provider (van Eijk and Steen, 2014).

Patient Motivations to Co-Produce

The process of co-production and role of various participants are also of particular interest in studying healthcare services. Several recent studies have investigated the motivations for participants (patients or service users, as well as medical professionals) for taking part in co-production. van Eijk and Steen (2014) found that service users who participated in co-planning 'client councils' chose to take part for a range of reasons, ranging from personal social drivers to those who aim to take part to improve health systems for the population at large.

The issue of motivations for patients to co-produce is particularly relevant in health, where there are incentives but also barriers and challenges that may not exist in other sectors. Encountering ill-health may be a strong incentive to be actively involved in health service design and delivery, although it also creates barriers to people's capacity to be involved. Health inequalities mean that these barriers may be particularly intensely experienced by people from lower socio-economic groups (Marmot, 2010). There is also a concern that framing co-production in terms of reciprocity puts pressure on participants to 'pay back' in the future (Boyle et al., 2006, 45). As Taylor puts it, 'Excluded communities should not have to "participate" in order to have the same claim on service quality and provision as other members of society' (2003, 165, in Bovaird, 2007, 856). Thus, co-production must not just target poor people or be 'government attempting to dump its difficult problems on users and communities' (Bovaird, 2007, 855).

People with long-term health conditions are likely to be involved in a fuller range of co-productive activities, as the knowledge they build up through living with a condition for a long time leads them to become 'expert patients' (Alakeson, 2011; Slay and Stephens, 2013). The Department of Health in the UK, for example, has acknowledged that patients with chronic conditions such as diabetes and HIV may well have a better knowledge of their own case histories, symptoms and care management needs than medical staff (DH, 2006). Co-production becomes a key aspect of management of these conditions, as medical staff offer diagnosis and support patients in self-care, as well as facilitating access to peer support networks. Within mental health services, for example, peer support workers have been used effectively alongside patients in acute and community settings, helping to co-design appropriate support (Social Care Institute for Excellence, 2013). In several countries, people with long-term conditions have also been given access to individualised budgets to enable them to have more control over treatment choices, in dialogue with clinicians (Grit and De Bont, 2010; Alakeson, 2014).

Professional Motivations to Co-Produce

Building on motivations to co-produce, Vennik et al. (2015) explored the reasons that professionals decide to take part in co-production, studying hospitals in the Netherlands who introduced structured, intensive patient and staff involvement exercises. They found that hospitals were driven to co-produce by the belief that increasing and improving patient participation would improve the quality of care that patients received. In addition, it was felt that these interventions would help maintain the hospital's position in an increasingly competitive healthcare market, and finally, that prioritising patient participation was important in order to adhere to the hospitals' goals and ethos as organisations. These motivations are by no means unique to healthcare, but they do illustrate the ways in which the wider policy environment and driving logics and motivations of health services shape co-production behaviours. On the one hand, co-production maintains a normative appeal in healthcare, where there is a widespread belief that greater participation is beneficial for both healthcare professionals and patients. On the other hand, participation is viewed pragmatically as a way to increase service efficiency and improve a provider's competitive edge.

Challenges to Co-Producing Healthcare

Healthcare is a sector where the benefits of co-production have been strongly advocated as part of reform programmes in many countries, despite the particular challenges that may be encountered with this approach. There are two primary areas of contention to be considered for policy-makers, practitioners and researchers interested in co-production in health. First is the definitional boundary between 'personalisation' and 'co-production', and the extent to which over-emphasis on individual co-production may limit the scope for collective approaches to improve health and mitigate health inequalities at a population level. Second is the issue of expertise and, in particular, the ways in which patients' and service users' lived experience intersect with professional knowledge. Third is the issue of legal liability in a co-productive setting. These are discussed in turn.

Co-Production and Personalisation

What becomes clear in studying co-production in health is that much of the debate appears to be around individual co-production—such as self-management of long-term conditions—and that the difference between what constitutes co-production and what is defined as personalisation of healthcare is unclear. Personalisation is typically linked with more consumerist reforms to public services, highlighting a service user's right to more choice of provider and choice of types of service (Leadbeater, 2004). This approach puts more emphasis on the pragmatic benefits of involvement in decision-making to the individual patient, as opposed to the democratic and societal benefits that are advocated by proponents of more systematic group and collective co-production efforts. 'Personalisation', 'co-production' and even 'patient involvement' are frequently used interchangeably in grey literature and some academic publications about healthcare, bringing into question the distinctiveness of the terms and the extent to which there is scope for collective approaches to improving health at a population level. Gofen and Needham's (2015) work on non-vaccination in Israel indicates that personalised approaches can empower people as self-managers of their health and welfare, cutting costs and improving outcomes; yet they also have the potential to generate forms of behaviour that can be characterised as anti-public. They conclude, 'The claims of personalization—the primacy of individual sovereignty, the distinctiveness and expertise of the citizen— undermine the very legitimacy of standardized public health approaches' (Gofen and Needham, 2015, 280).

Despite the normative appeal of co-production, it may not be the most appropriate or desirable model for improving service quality in a way that assures equity. There are many health services where the patient may be incapable or unwilling to participate in co-production with professionals, particularly patients who are from potentially marginalised groups such as people with low levels of education or recent immigrants with limited language skills (Cornwall, 2008). This may be particularly the case in interventions that are ad hoc or one-off participation exercises. Co-production of healthcare necessitates a degree of widespread, top to bottom culture change throughout health systems to make services more open, accountable and welcoming of sustained, meaningful patient involvement. Co-production necessarily requires things to be done differently—not only at the individual level of patient and professional, but at a broader more systematic level if the more ambitious aims of efficiency, patient empowerment and accountability are to be delivered.

> This [co-production] is a fundamental and system-wide change in the relationship between health systems and the public, involving the doing with, rather than doing to and doing for, at all levels and in all areas of health system functioning. Such profound change involves [. . .] a significant re-imagining of traditional health system and practice trajectories.
> (Dunston et al., 2009, 41)

Co-Production and Expertise

A second potential limitation of co-production relates to the intersection of the expertise of professionals and the lay knowledge of patients. Traditional models of healthcare are based on a hierarchical understanding of expertise and relationships—patients are recipients of care or services, and the only valued source of expertise is that of the doctor or other medical professional. Promoting effective co-production, where patient and service user expertise and experiences are more valued, requires a shift in the culture of healthcare providers towards one where the relationship between patients and professionals is put on more equal footing (Hyde and Davies, 2004; NESTA, 2013). The move to a more consumerist approach to healthcare may be problematic in suggesting a passive role for the patient, rather than an empowered actor with a particular claim on expertise (Clarke et al, 2007). Speed's (2006) work on mental health services in the Republic of Ireland draws attention to tensions between the framings of patient, consumer and survivor.

Some scholars have argued that healthcare, which is characterised by a highly professionalised workforce, is therefore less conducive to co-production than other sectors, where service delivery professionals are not required to have many years of training (Parrado et al., 2013). Studies on the introduction of patient participation in healthcare have shown that medical professionals are, in some cases, resistant to these initiatives for fear of receiving criticism from patients and having their expertise undervalued or undermined (Vennik et al., 2015). Furthermore, even in cases where professionals may welcome more co-productive ways of working, this often requires a huge shift in practice and organisational culture and professionals may not necessarily have the skills or experience required to co-produce. More particularly, co-production has been linked to asset-based approaches, which emphasise patients' capabilities, whereas healthcare models have been more focused on their deficits and impairments (Kretzmann and McKnight, 1993).

The challenge for professionals in respecting patients as experts is particularly intense given the opportunities for patients to acquire knowledge which does not conform to evidence thresholds respected within medical science. So-called 'scientific citizenship' is becoming a patient-led alternative, whereby individuals take a dynamic role in enhancing their own scientific literacy (Elam and Bertilsson, 2003). This often involves the use of the media, and specifically the internet, which allows people to link up with support groups (Rose and Novas, 2004). Those who practice this 'scientific citizenship' use complex methods to challenge established forms of authoritative knowledge and to promote intuitive ways of knowing and knowledge sharing (Cheyney, 2008). In a health system that acknowledges patients as experts and may make them budget-holders, this creates a strong point of tension. Professional ambivalence towards this shift is exemplified in the title of a *British Medical Journal* editorial: 'Expert patient: dream or nightmare?' (Shaw and Baker, 2004). The introduction of personal health budgets into the NHS in England led to an article in *Pulse*—a magazine for General Practitioners—with the headline 'Revealed: NHS funding splashed on holidays, games consoles and summer houses'. The article went on: 'the scheme to give "patients more control over their care" has been used to buy many unevidenced treatments at the expense of long-established services which have been defunded' (Price, 2015). The article exemplifies a number of points of professional resistance to personal health budgets, including the way in which patients choose treatments which lack a conventional evidence base and the extent to which this is reducing funding for collectively provided services.

Co-Production and Legal Liability

Attention to the unevidenced nature of some patient choices also highlights the scope for co-productive health initiatives to raise issues of legal liability where citizens make choices that run counter to a traditional evidence base. Legal recourse by patients whose health has suffered due to apparent malpractice or negligence by the medical profession have been growing, particularly in the USA but also in other countries with a less litigious culture (Fenn et al., 2000). There are also potential issues relating to the release of confidential information—for example when using peer mentors in acute psychiatric settings, the amount of the patient's case history that should be revealed (Stone et al., 2010). For co-productive work in people's homes, there are question marks over the extent to which the people providing support and the people being supported have had appropriate police checks (Restall, 2009).

However it may be that the development of co-productive relationships within a health setting can have a positive impact on outcomes and reduce the likelihood of legal disputes. Palumbo's review of the literature on health and co-production highlights that active engagement by patients can lead to better outcomes, by reducing the perceived psychological and cultural distance between the healthcare professionals and the patients (Leone et al.,

2012, cited in Palumbo, 2016, 80). By listening to patients and working with them as partners, both the appropriateness and the effectiveness of care can be enhanced (Elg et al., 2012, cited in Palumbo, 2016, 81). Although issues of data sharing and personal safety continue to require careful attention, these can be addressed through proportional application of the protocols which already exist within health organisations.

Conclusions

Co-production is a way of reforming services to produce more collaborative working relationships between service users, community members and/ or patients and the professionals who deliver services for and to them. In healthcare, co-production is conceptualised as an important way to restructure hierarchies whereby the expertise of patients is overlooked in favour of the knowledge of professionals. Co-production, in contrast to the traditional model of healthcare, provides a forum in which patients may be seen as 'experts by experience'—both at the individual level in relation to their own care, but also at the group and collective level in helping to inform treatment programmes and strategic planning of healthcare budgets and hospital governance. Scholarship thus far on co-production in healthcare has highlighted the benefits that this can bring to improving the care that patients receive, as well as in increasing provider competitiveness and efficiency. In order to achieve these ends, however, challenges such as organisational culture and professional reluctance to co-produce will need to be addressed.

References

Alakeson, V. (2011). *Active Patient: The Case for Self-direction in Healthcare*. Birmingham: University of Birmingham/Centre for Welfare Reform.

Alakeson, V. (2014). *Delivering Personal Health Budgets—a Guide to Policy and Practice*. Bristol: Policy Press.

Alford, J. (2009). *Engaging Public Sector Clients: From Service-Delivery to Co-Production*. Basingstoke, UK: Palgrave Macmillan.

Batalden, M., Batalden, P., Margolis, P., Seid, M., Armstrong, G., Opipari-Arrigan, L. and Hartung, H. (2015). Coproduction of Healthcare Service. *BMJ Quality & Safety*, 1–9.

Bovaird, T. (2007). Beyond Engagement and Participation: User and Community Co-Production of Public Services. *Public Administration Review*, (67, 5), 846–860.

Boyle, D., Clark, S. and Burn, S. (2006). *Hidden Work: Co-Production by People Outside Paid Employment*. York: Joseph Rowntree Foundation.

Boyle, D. and Harris, M. (2009). *The Challenge of Co-Production: How Equal Partnerships Between Professionals and the Public Are Crucial to Improving Public Services*. London: New Economics Foundation.

Brudney, J. L. and England, R. E. (1983). Toward a Definition of the Coproduction Concept. *Public Administration Review*, (43, 1), 59–65.

Cheyney, M. (2008). Homebirth as Systems-Challenging Praxis: Knowledge, Power, and Intimacy in the Birthplace. *Qualitative Health Research*, (18, 2), 254–267.

Christensen, T. and Laegreid, P. (2007). *Transcending New Public Management.* Aldershot: Ashgate.

Clarke, J., Newman, J., Smith, N., Vidler, E. and Westmarland, L. (2007). *Creating Citizen-Consumers: Changing Publics and Changing Public Services.* Thousand Oaks: Pine Forge Press.

Cornwall, A. (2008). Unpacking "Participation": Models, Meanings and Practices. *Community Development Journal,* (43, 3), 269–283.

Daniels, N. (2000). Accountability for Reasonableness: Opening the Black Box of Reasonableness: Establishing a Fair Process for Priority Setting Is Easier Than Agreeing on Principles. *British Medical Journal,* (321, 7272), 1300–1301.

Department of Health (DH). (2005). *Self Care—a Real Choice.* London: Department of Health.

Department of Health (DH). (2006). *National Evaluation of the Pilot Phase of the Expert Patient Programme.* London: Department of Health.

Doyal, L. (1996). The Politics of Women's Health: Setting a Global Agenda. *International Journal of Health Services,* (26, 1), 47–65.

Dunston, R. (2014). Arrangement of Co-Production in Healthcare. In T. Fenwick and M. Nerland (eds.), *Reconceptualising Professional Learning: Sociomaterial Knowledges, Practices and Responsibilities,* 140–154. Abington: Routledge.

Dunston, R., Lee, A., Boud, D., Brodie, P. and Chiarella, M. (2009). Co-Production and Health System Reform—From Re-Imagining to Re-Making. *Australian Journal of Public Administration,* (68, 1), 39–52.

Elam, M. and Bertilsson, M. (2003). Consuming, Engaging and Confronting Science the Emerging Dimensions of Scientific Citizenship. *European Journal of Social Theory,* (6, 2), 233–251.

Elg, M., Engstrom, J., Witell, L. and Poksinska, B. (2012). Co-Creation and Learning in Health-Care Service Development. *Journal of Service Management,* (23, 3), 328–343.

Fenn, P., Diacon, S., Gray, A., Hodges, R. and Rickman, N. (2000). Current Cost of Medical Negligence in NHS Hospitals: Analysis of Claims Database. *BMJ,* (320, 7249), 1567–1571.

Gofen, A. and Needham, C. (2015). Service Personalization as a Response to Noncompliance with Routine Childhood Vaccination. *Governance,* (28, 3), 269–283.

Greenhalgh, T., Humphrey, C. and Woodward, F. (2011). *User Involvement in Health Care.* Oxford: Wiley-Blackwell/BMJ Books.

Grit, K. and de Bont, A. (2010). Tailor-Made Finance Versus Tailor-Made Care. Can the State Strengthen Consumer Choice in Healthcare by Reforming the Financial Structure of Long-term Care? *Journal of Medical Ethics,* (36, 2), 79–83.

Hyde, P. and Davies, H. T. (2004). Service Design, Culture and Performance: Collusion and Co-Production in Health Care. *Human Relations,* (57, 11), 1407–1426.

Kretzmann, J. and McKnight, J. (1993). *Building Communities from the Inside Out: A Path Towards Finding and Mobilising a Community's Assets.* Evanston, IL: Institute for Policy Research.

Leadbeater, C. (2004). *Personalisation Through Participation: A New Script for Public Services.* London: Demos.

Leone, R. P., Walker, C. A., Curry, L. C. and Agee, E. J. (2012). Application of a Marketing Concept to Patient-Centered Care: Co-Producing Health with Heart Failure Patients. *Online Journal of Issues in Nursing,* (17, 2).

Marmot, L. (2010). *Fair Society: Healthy Lives.* London: Institute of Health Equity.

McLean, A. (1995). Empowerment and the Psychiatric Consumer/Ex-Patient Movement in the United States: Contradictions, Crisis and Change. *Social Science & Medicine*, (40, 8), 1053–1071.

Needham, C. (2008). Realising the Potential of Co-Production: Negotiating Improvements in Public Services. *Social Policy & Society*, (7, 2), 221–231.

Needham, C. (2009). Interpreting Personalization in England's National Health Service. *Critical Policy Studies*, (3, 2), 204–220.

Needham, C. (2011). *Personalising Public Services: Understanding the Personalisation Narrative*. Bristol: The Policy Press.

NESTA. (2013). *People Powered Health: Health for People, by People and with People*. London: NESTA.

Palumbo, R. (2016). Contextualizing Co-Production of Health Care: A Systematic Literature Review. *International Journal of Public Sector Management*, (29, 1), 72–90.

Parrado, S., Van Ryzin, G. G., Bovaird, T. and Loeffler, E. (2013). Correlates of Co-Production: Evidence from a Five-Nation Survey of Citizens. *International Public Management Journal*, (16, 1), 85–112.

Pestoff, V. (2008). *A Democratic Architecture for the Welfare State*. London: Routledge.

Price, C. (2015). Revealed: NHS Funding Splashed on Holidays, Games Consoles and Summer Houses. *Pulse*, September.

Restall, M. (2009). Volunteering and Legal Issues. In R. Scott and S. Howlett (eds.), *Volunteers in Hospice and Palliative Care: A Resource for Voluntary Services Managers*, 99–108. Oxford: Oxford University Press.

Rose, N., and Novas, C. (2004). Biological Citizenship. In A. Ong and S. Collier (eds.), *Global Assemblages: Technology, Politics, and Ethics as Anthropological Problems*, 439–463. Oxford: Blackwell Publishing.

Shaw, J. and Baker, M. (2004). Expert Patient—Dream or Nightmare? The Concept of a Well Informed Patient Is Welcome, but a New Name Is Needed. *BMJ: British Medical Journal*, (328, 7442), 723.

Slay, J. and Stephens, L. (2013). *Co-Production in Mental Health: A Literature Review*. London: New Economics Foundation.

Social Care Institute for Excellence. (2013). Coproduction in Social Care: What It Is and How to Do It. *SCIE Guide* 51. London: SCIE.

Speed, E. (2006). Patients, Consumers and Survivors: A Case Study of Mental Health Service User Discourses. *Social Science & Medicine*, (62, 1), 28–38.

Stone, N., Warren, F. and Napier, C. (2010). Peer Support Workers' Experience of an Intentional Peer Support Scheme on an Acute Psychiatric Ward. *Mental Health and Learning Disabilities Research and Practice*, (7, 1), 93–102.

Taylor, M. (2003). *Public Policy in the Community*. Basingstoke: Palgrave Macmillan.

Thomson, S., and Dixon, A. (2006). Choices in Health Care: The European Experience. *Journal of Health Services Research & Policy*, (11, 3), 167–171.

van Eijk, C. and Steen, T. P. (2014). Why People Co-Produce: Analysing Citizens' Perceptions on Co-Planning Engagement in Health Care Services. *Public Management Review*, (16, 3), 358–382.

Vennik, F. D., van de Bovenkamp, H. M., Putters, K. and Grit, K. J. (2015). Co-Production in Healthcare: Rhetoric and Practice. *International Review of Administrative Sciences*, (0, 0), 1–19.

World Health Organization. (2015). *WHO Global Strategy on People-Centred and Integrated Health Services*. Geneva: World Health Organization.

12.1 Case Study—Co-Producing Recommendations to Reduce Diagnostic Error

Suyeon Jo and Tina Nabatchi

Introduction

While co-production can be applied to many public service areas, it has the potential to be particularly beneficial in health services, where outcomes are dependent not only on the attitudes and behaviors of providers, but also on those of patients. Indeed, positive health outcomes are more likely to be generated when patients feel a sense of empowerment over their personal physical and mental wellbeing (Street et al. 2009). This case study reports on a recent project that engaged healthcare consumers in the co-production of recommendations for reducing diagnostic error and improving diagnostic quality. Specifically, we report on two collective co-production processes with healthcare consumers, the first of which focused on the development of patient-centered recommendations for improving the diagnostic process, and the second of which tested the perceived quality of those recommendations. A central theme of the project is that errors can be mitigated and diagnostic quality improved if patients are empowered and engaged in their personal healthcare.

Background

Diagnostic error, or diagnoses that are wrong, missed, or delayed, is a serious issue in healthcare. It is the number one cause of medical malpractice claims in the United States, and is estimated to occur in 5–15% of cases, result in 40,000–80,000 deaths annually, and lead to 17% of adverse events in medical settings (Graber, 2013). Most proposals to reduce diagnostic error focus on physicians and healthcare systems; few interventions have sought to reduce diagnostic error by empowering patients in the diagnostic process. Thus, patients represent a large, untapped, and critically important resource for improving the quality of diagnosis. Simply put: the development of patient-centered strategies that empower healthcare consumers in the diagnostic process may be necessary to reduce errors, improve safety and healthcare delivery, and ultimately ensure better quality health outcomes.

To this end, a collaborative team of practitioners and scholars designed and implemented a large-scale project called *Using Public Deliberation to*

Define Patient Roles in Reducing Diagnostic Error, which was funded by the U.S. Agency for Healthcare Research and Quality (AHRQ).[1] The overarching aim of the project was to engage healthcare consumers in the collective co-production of patient-focused recommendations for improving diagnostic quality and reducing diagnostic error that others can use in the future to individually coproduce diagnoses with their healthcare providers.

Experiences

This project engaged two different groups of healthcare consumers in two different co-production processes. The first co-production process engaged about 20 participants over the course of two weekends. The group was diverse, with members from a wide range of socio-economic and demographic backgrounds. Among the participants was a recovering addict, a transgender person, and a retired business professor.

During the first weekend, the co-production group engaged in an information session about diagnostic error provided by health professionals. The group then engaged in about 18 hours of facilitated deliberation centered on: (1) the roles patients are willing and able to play in preventing, identifying, and reporting diagnostic error; (2) the strategies that should be used to enable patients to play those roles; and (3) the changes needed in systems and structures for patients to assume those roles. Based on their deliberations, the group produced a set of draft recommendations for improving diagnostic quality. During the second weekend, this group spent approximately 20 hours refining and finalizing their recommendations. In total, the group developed 16 recommendations, which are lumped into five overarching categories: (1) present symptoms clearly and completely; (2) assert yourself in the relationship; (3) coordinate your care; (4) ensure accurate records and tests; and (5) manage your care. At the heart of each set of recommendations is the notion that patients should be empowered not only in the diagnostic process, but more generally in their healthcare. Analyses of survey results show that the co-production participants experienced positive and statistically significant changes in several individual-level health-related indicators, including the Patient Activation Measure, which assesses the level of empowerment people feel in managing their own health (Nabatchi, Jo and Salas, 2016).

The second co-production process occurred over the course of a day and engaged approximately 100 healthcare consumers who were diverse along a number of socio-economic indicators. After presentations on diagnostic error and the recommendations, the participants engaged in small-group, facilitated discussions, and examined the applicability of the recommendations in various scenarios. In addition, the participants were asked to rate the overall quality of the recommendations. Survey results indicate that they judged the recommendations as being understandable, usable, and potentially impactful. Of particular importance is that between 75% and 95%

said they were likely or extremely likely to use the recommendations, and between 63% and 79% said that the recommendations would be easy or very easy to use (Nabatchi and Jo, 2016). This suggests that recommendations developed during a collective co-production process can be acceptable to broader members of the public.

The Society to Improve Diagnosis in Medicine, a national non-profit organization in the health field, plans to use the recommendations to develop strategic plans, policy statements, and research agendas, as well as to create a patient engagement "tool kit" that can be used in healthcare settings to help patients and providers coproduce during the diagnostic process. Overall, this project demonstrates that healthcare consumers have the capacity to engage in complex discussions and that the experience of co-production can have meaningful individual level effects. Moreover, the project demonstrates that consumers can develop recommendations that are acceptable to others and that have the potential to activate, engage, and empower patients in the diagnostic process.

Note

1 The project was made possible by grant number R21HS023562–01 from the Agency for Healthcare Research and Quality/DHHS. All findings and products are solely the responsibility of the authors and do not necessarily represent the official views of AHRQ.

References

Graber, M. L. (2013). The Incidence of Diagnostic Error. *BMJ Quality & Safety,* (22, Suppl 2), ii21–ii27.

Nabatchi, T. and Jo, S. (2016). *Initial Phases of a Randomized Study of Public Deliberation About Diagnostic Error: An Analysis of the 2016 Healthcare Consumer Event.* Syracuse, NY: PARCC.

Nabatchi, T., Jo, S. and Salas, A. (2016). *Initial Phases of a Randomized Study of Public Deliberation about Diagnostic Error: A Preliminary Analysis of Three Healthcare Consumer Events in 2015.* Syracuse, NY: PARCC.

Street, R. L., Makoul, G., Arora, N. K. and Epstein, R. M. (2009). How Does Communication Heal? Pathways Linking Clinician—Patient Communication to Health Outcomes. *Patient Education and Counseling,* (74, 3), 295–301.

12.2 Case Study—Co-Production of Secondary Health Services in Nigeria and Ghana

Mary Mangai, Michiel S. de Vries, and Johan A. M. de Kruijf

Introduction

Mainly due to the unresponsiveness of government, the standard of secondary health services in Nigeria and Ghana has fallen in recent times. Inadequate financial and human resources are driving health professionals to co-produce healthcare with citizens and unemployed health professionals in order to meet the health needs of the burgeoning population of these countries. Unemployed health professionals voluntarily provide core healthcare services mainly because of their inability to secure paid employment, while other collaborations between health professionals and citizens are organised because of the need to improve healthcare services.

This case study discusses the framework for the type of co-production that is occurring in government secondary hospitals in Nigeria and Ghana and how such co-production is helping to improve healthcare services in those countries.

Background

Government secondary hospitals are limited to one per urban area in Nigeria and Ghana. The government is responsible for funding these hospitals, but in reality, they suffer from severe underfunding. Although secondary hospitals act as referral centres for primary health centres (PHCs), they are invariably overstretched because of the obsolete nature of PHCs. Services provided in these hospitals range from surgical services, in- and out-patient services, dental services, maternal and child healthcare, physiotherapy, nutritional services, psychiatric services, and ear, nose and teeth (ENT) services. Although all these services are, in principle, available at all secondary hospitals, this is not always the case in reality. The health professionals whom we interviewed blamed the government for the inadequacy of the services provided.

In an earlier study, Mangai (2016) corroborated the opinion of the health professionals regarding government failures by reporting how the government was deterring effective public service delivery in various policy areas, including healthcare provision. Mangai's study shows that the government is failing to respond to inadequate service provision in Nigeria and Ghana. Such unresponsiveness and the resulting funding issues have resulted in a shortage of human resources, inadequate facilities, infrastructural deficiencies, obsolete equipment and low remuneration, as reported by health professionals. These problems and unemployment have been a driver for health professionals, some of whom are unemployed, to co-produce core healthcare services.

Experiences

According to the definition of co-production provided in Brandsen and Honingh in this volume (chapter 2), the type of co-production seen in Nigeria and Ghana is *co-production in the design and implementation of core services*. Citizens and unemployed health professionals are directly and actively involved in the production of the core health services mentioned. Co-production is institutionalised due to the financial and human resource gap and the problem of unemployment. Structural co-production is driven by political and socio-economic conditions, even though notable improvements in healthcare services are the result of such co-production processes.

On the side of the professionals, the positive inclination towards co-production is driven by inadequate funding and a shortage of positions for qualified health personnel. Inadequate funding has compelled health professionals to devise other means of securing funds to run their facilities. In Nigeria, health professionals have organised a forum called the *Hospital League of Friends*. According to health professionals, the forum is made up of societal elites, which enables it to mediate between health professionals and the government because it enjoys easy access to government circles. The results of the forum's contribution include: the construction of additional hospital buildings; the provision of power generation installations; the purchase of hospital consumables; and the construction of mechanised water facilities (boreholes). These inputs are examples of *co-creation of complementary services* (see Brandsen and Honingh in this volume, chapter 2). In Ghana, health professionals share the challenges faced by hospitals with societal elites and members of parliament in a so-called *durbar* meeting, which is organised by health professionals. The outcome of their interactions are similar to those achieved in Nigeria.

Another factor that inclines health professionals towards co-production is the shortage of official personnel. Due to the lack of official personnel, health managers use the services of unemployed health professionals who are willing to volunteer in hospitals in the hope of one day being officially employed by the government. There are limited work incentives for unemployed health professionals because they are considered as casual workers. Depending on the finances available to the hospital, casual workers are paid 10%-30% of the official monthly salary to keep them coming in to work.

Hospital managers have little control over these casual workers, however, because of the limited motivation they have to provide core healthcare services. In Nigeria, some units are staffed entirely by these so-called casual workers.

Despite the poor working conditions, the primary motivation of these casual workers for co-producing core health services is the prospect of unemployment. The unemployment rate is high in both Nigeria and Ghana. In the last quarter of 2016, the unemployment rate in Nigeria was 13.9%, and in Ghana, it was 8.7% (Ghana Statistical Service, n.d.; National Bureau of Statistics Nigeria, n.d.).

There is also an implicit motivation for casual workers to co-produce core health services. They co-produce in order to enhance and update their skills and knowledge while awaiting formal employment. While their explicit or implicit motivation to co-produce core health services is based on the expectation that they will one day be absorbed by the system, this expectation often remains unmet. We found that on average casual workers have put in seven years of non-contractual work experience before they have any hope at all of securing official employment status.

We conclude that co-production provides common ground for the health professionals and unemployed health professionals to solve their problems and, in this sense, it improves health services and outcomes. However, there is no guarantee about co-production in the future if, for instance, there are negative behavioural changes on the part of casual workers. Such changes could result in instability in the provision of core healthcare services.

Unless the abnormality in the system is put right, the system remains unfair to unemployed health professionals, who have invested their accumulated human capital into a profession that cannot provide them with enough to earn a living. The system exposes casual workers to an insecure future. Nonetheless, this type of co-production is expected to continue as long as the unemployment rate remains high and the government does not improve its per capita expenditure on healthcare.

References

Ghana Statistical Service. (n.d.). (online).

Mangai, M. S. (2016). The Dynamics of Failing Service Delivery in Nigeria and Ghana. *Developments in Administration Journal*, (1, 1), 85–116.

National Bureau of Statistics Nigeria. (n.d.). (online).

13 Parents as Co-Producers in Primary Education

Marlies Honingh, Elena Bondarouk and Taco Brandsen

Primary education is one of those services in which the co-producers are not (only) the clients themselves, but other individuals responsible for their well-being—in this case the parents. In schools and educational policies, there is a growing recognition of the importance of engaging parents,[1] families and communities in raising the quality of education (e.g. Harris and Goodall, 2008; Addi-Raccah and Arviv-Elyashiv, 2008; Baeck, 2010; Educational Council, 2010). Developmental, sociological and educational theories stress the potentially positive effects of strong connections between children's home and school environments (e.g. Coleman et al., 1996). Parents may play a vital role in promoting children's school success by contributing to educational quality and strengthening the schools' legitimacy (Higgins and Katsipataki, 2015). As active partners and co-producers in education, they could be involved not only indirectly through formal decision-making processes in parents' councils, but also directly in school and learning activities (e.g. Harris and Goodal, 2008).

Despite these hopes to engage parents more actively in primary education, the empirical evidence on the contribution parents actually make is far from complete. Many questions remain about what parents contribute exactly, under which conditions, what motives they have and whether there are other than SES related biases. In this chapter we will examine the different types of parental contributions and their potential effects on the parent-teacher relationship, as well as conclusions that can be drawn from existing research.

Types of Parental Contributions

As co-producers actively contribute to the work of the organization (see Brandsen and Honingh, 2016), we need to define first which are the core activities of primary education. This is not straightforward, because schools have multiple purposes (Hooge et al., 2011; Willemse et al., 2015). Schools serve two crucial purposes (comp. Biesta, 2014). The first one is qualification. This has to do with the acquisition of knowledge. The second purpose is socialization, or citizenship development, which has to do with the way in which, through education, pupils become part of existing traditions and ways of doing and being. The teachers' role is to support students to be active, responsible and socially engaged citizens.

Turning to the contributions parents can make to the school's work, different examples are possible, from offering help in the school garden, guiding pupils on excursions, to becoming a 'reading or math parent'. Over the last twenty years, several studies have been undertaken in educational sciences (especially in the US) to categorize the nature of parental involvement. Since the broad framework of parent-school partnership, first introduced by Epstein (1995), different categories of parental involvement have been identified (Bakker et al. 2013; Jeynes, 2012; Higgins and Katsipataki, 2015; Lusse, 2015).

Parental activities at school can be distinguished in terms of the parental involvement and presence at school. Even though a lot of empirical research has been conducted into the latter, Bakker et al. (2013) show that there is no direct effect of parental presence in school, for example parental volunteering to help in the garden, on the academic achievements of children. Simply being at school has little effect on individual attainment unless there are direct and explicit connections to learning and thus educational involvement (Ho Sui-Chu and Willms, 1996). Hence, even though for example helping in the garden involves co-operation between parents and school, such activity can only be regarded as complementary co-production, since it does not address the core purpose. Both of the cases on education in this book focus on such complementary activities. However, if one is to understand co-production in education, parental involvement in the school's core tasks should become more central in the research agenda.

Lusse (2015) defines four categories of parental involvement. First, activities parents undertake in school and the classroom. These are general involvement programs (see Jeynes, 2012, for more examples). Home involvement of parents in their children's education is a second category (Lusse, 2015), a typical example of which is a school-led encouragement of parents to read together with their children or to check every day whether their children have completed their homework (see Jeynes, 2012). A third category of activities constitutes a more direct form of collaboration between parents and teachers. Exemplary involvement programs concentrate on the communication and partnership of teachers and parents to develop common strategies, rules and guidelines that are thought necessary to help children to use their full potential (Jeynes, 2012). The final category of activities reflects the support parents receive to help their children. These involvement activities target the parents themselves. For example, there are programs to raise the language skills of parents, enabling them to effectively help their children with homework and realize higher levels of participation.

Evidence on Parental Contributions to School Activities

When it comes to the effect these different forms of involvement have on the academic achievements of pupils, different studies have confirmed the positive relationship between such school-initiated involvement programs and children's learning performance (Crosnoe et al., 2016; Jakobsen and Andersen, 2013; Jeynes, 2012). Second, specifying this effect per category of parental involvement, in his meta-analysis Jeynes (2012) found that home involvement programmes, which were directed at parents reading together with their children, yield the highest effect. The category of activities with the second largest effect size was that of programmes that emphasized partnership and helps parents and teachers to collaborate as equal partners, which is most important to co-production.

Despite the importance of this partnership between parents and teachers for the academic achievements of pupils, it has received little attention in research. This stands in stark contrast to the empirical knowledge on the *school-led* partnerships, in which schools are driving the parent-teacher partnership. The school-centered perspective has been dominant in the research in this area. In her influential work, Epstein (1987) developed a theory of overlapping spheres of influence of families and schools on students' learning and development and on family and school effectiveness. This approach asserts that students learn more and succeed at higher levels when home, school and community work together to support students' learning and development. In studies of school-based partnership programs, the model of overlapping spheres of influence has been used to explain how educators, families and communities may connect to support student learning and success in school. Recent research show that parental involvement (among other variables outside of the school, like socio-economic background, parents' educational attainment, family structure and ethnicity), is strongly connected to achievement and attainment (Harris and Goodall, 2008). These findings are highly informative against the background of co-production and recent governance attempts to offer service users a bigger role in the design and implementation of public services. However, research in this area mirrors the limitation of Epstein's work, which is that it is relatively school-centered and teacher-initiated. Parental engagement is seen solely from the perspective of the school, as part of its overall strategy.

There has also been relatively little attention for the inclusiveness of co-production initiatives. That active participation becomes possible does not imply that all potential participants will become active. Whether co-production can mobilize all parents and what the social consequences of unequal participation will be remains to be seen.

Parents' cultural and social capital may prove of great importance here, as an indicator of the resources parents have to co-produce and to develop productive relationships within schools. Many studies suggest that not all parents will be able to co-produce and that first they need to be educated to be fit for participation. For example, Higgins and Katsipataki (2015) identify specific family literacy interventions, and targeted interventions for families in particular need. In his categorization, Jeynes (2012) paid specific attention to the programs developed to raise the language skills of parents and to empower them to realize higher levels of participation. Generally, research on this area has focused on programmes for socio-economically disadvantaged families and ethnic minorities. It remains to be seen how co-production is different from other types of participation with respect to how it replicates patterns of social inequality.

The Relationship Between Teachers and Parents

When comparing the position and role of teachers in school organizations in the 1990s with today's context, we can observe some major differences. Due to changes in the school organization, new governance structures and a stronger control of professional work, teachers increasingly have to cope with an ongoing process of rationalization and formalization. Like professionals in other fields, they increasingly have to accommodate other actors, norms, rules and standards, including parents' wishes and preferences. Theoretically, this creates an institutional environment that is more open to co-production.

In practice, however, this is not always the case. Addi-Raccah and Arviv-Elyashiv (2008) have described how, despite organizational changes and a stronger focus on other actors, an increase in parental involvement in school still has the potential to lead to conflict, because a number of teachers regard this development as a threat to their positions. In response, they may attempt to distance themselves from parents through the insistence on professionalism, a strategy which tends to be applied especially in relation to well-educated parents (Baeck, 2010). Reactions such as this suggest that teachers may lack the required self-efficacy and managerial support. In much of the literature, there is therefore an explicit call for more training to teach the teachers how better to cope with parents and achieve a more balanced partnership (see Honingh et al., 2017 for an overview).

Of course this does not apply to all parents and teachers equally. Addi-Raccah and Arviv-Elyashiv (2008) found that teachers who do have sufficient confidence in their professional ability seem to be less concerned about their position. They display their mastery in teaching, apply an open style of communication with parents and try to gain the latter's support. This should be read less in terms of a power shift than in terms of a role shift.

Coleman and Tabin (1992) already stated that teachers should 'permit' teacher collaboration as their failure to do so prohibits important parental activities. Permitting parents to collaborate does not necessarily mean that teachers have to step back. For example, it allows them to provide parents with the knowledge of curriculum and methodology they need to help their child more effectively, or to encourage activities which parents and children can jointly engage in. In effect, this makes teachers instructional mediators between parents and their children. This does not imply that parents take over the teacher's role. Rather, it is a type of co-production that supports activities outside of, but relevant to, the core activities of the organization.

Unfortunately, we still lack systematic knowledge about parent-teacher relationships in co-production settings. Higgins and Maria Katsipataki (2015) note that, despite the accumulation of research evidence about the relationship between parental involvement and children's learning abilities at school, there is still little agreement about the practices that have the most influence on academic attainment and what the role of teachers is in supporting the development of these practices in collaboration with parents. The evidence does suggest that teachers feel most challenged in cases where parental involvement touches more directly upon their professional activities. An interesting example is that teachers are more eager to ask parents questions about behavioural or health issues than about the learning strategies children apply at home (e.g. when solving a puzzle [see Honingh et al., 2017]). At the same time, we notice a growing interest in preparing teachers for partnerships with parents. Conceptual papers offer different practice-oriented tips regarding how to communicate and team-up with parents in order to enrich educational impact (e.g. Larocque et al., 2011;.Kenney, 2011; Hynds, 2008)

As such, we can tentatively conclude that teachers' perceptions of parents' role are ambiguous. They do advocate parents' involvement in school and regard them as an essential resource for school improvement and functioning (Addi-Raccah and Arviv-Elyashiv, 2008). However, teachers appear to approve more of parental involvement the less it touches upon their professional work in the classroom. But again, more research is needed to substantiate this.

Conclusion

In this chapter we have argued that co-production in schools comes with substantial challenges for teachers and parents. However, we still lack solid empirical evidence about the way teachers and parents should shape co-production to contribute to the pupils' academic achievements. Research has identified different types of parental contributions and, to some extent, how these affect the parent-teacher relationship. However, the bulk of the research so far has concentrated on certain groups (especially those with special needs) in certain countries (especially the US), applying a school-centered perspective (Honingh, 2017). Next steps in research should be to broaden the scope of the research and allow more systematic comparisons between countries, approaches and types of students, to learn more about the institutional determinants of co-production. As is the case for all services discussed in this book, we need to get a better sense of the short- and long-term effects of co-production under different conditions, for different types of groups.

Note

1 The term 'parents' is used in this chapter to include adults who have the direct responsibility for the well-being of young people, regardless of their biological relationship.

References

Addi-Raccah, A. and Arviv-Elyashiv, R. (2008). Parent Empowerment and Teacher Professionalism Teachers' Perspective. *Urban Education*, (43, 3), 394–415.

Baeck, U-D. K. (2010). 'We are the professionals': A Study of Teachers' Views on Parental Involvement in Schools. *British Journal of Sociology of Education*, (31, 3), 323–335.

Bakker, J., Denssen, J., Denissen, E. and Oolbekkink-Marchand, H. (2013). *Leraren en ouderbetrokkenheid; een reviewstudie naar de effectiviteit van ouderbetrokkenheid en de rol die leraren daarbij kunnen vervullen.* Nijmegen: Radboud Universiteit Nijmegen: Behavioural Science Institute.

Biesta, G. (2014). *Het prachtige risico van onderwijs.* Culemborg: Uitgeverij Phronese.

Brandsen, T. and Honingh, M. (2016). Distinguishing Different Types of Coproduction: A Conceptual Analysis Based on the Classical Definitions. *Public Administration Review*, (76, 3), 427–435.

Coleman, P., Collinge, J. and Tabin, Y. (1996). Learning Together: The Student/Parent/Teacher Triad. *School Effectiveness and School Improvement: An International Journal of Research, Policy and Practice*, (7, 4), 361–382.

Coleman, P. and Tabin, Y. (1992). *The Good Teacher.* Paper presented at the Annual Meeting of the American Educational Research Association, San Francisco.

Crosnoe, R., Purtell, K. M., Davis-Kean, P., Ansari, A. and Benner, A. D. (2016). The Selection of Children from Low-Income Families into Preschool. *Developmental Psychology*, (52, 4), 599–612.

Educational Council. (2010). *Ouders als Partners.* The Hague: Onderwijsraad.

Epstein, J. L. (1987). Toward a Theory of Family-School Connections: Teacher Practices and Parent Involvement Across the School Years. In K. Hurrelman, F. Kaufmann, and F. Losel (eds.), *Social Intervention: Potential and Constraints*, 121–136. New York: de Gruyter.

Epstein, J. L. (1995). School, Family, and Community Partnerships: Caring for the Children We Share. *Phi Delta Kappan*, (76, 9), 701–712.

Harris, A. and Goodall, J. (2008). Do Parents Know They Matter? Engaging All Parents in Learning. *Educational Research*, (50, 3), 277–289.

Higgins, S. and Katsipataki, M. (2015). Evidence from Meta-Analysis About Parental Involvement in Education Which Supports Their Children's Learning. *Journal of Children's Services*, (10, 3), 1–11.

Ho Sui-Chu, E. and Willms, J. D. (1996). Effects of Parental Involvement on 8th-Grade Achievement. *Sociology of Education*, (69, 2), 126–141.

Honingh, M., Bondarouk, E. and Brandsen, T. (2017). *Co-Production in Primary Education: A Systematic Literature Review and Directions for Research.* Paper presented at the Public Management Research Conference 2017, Washington, DC.

Hooge, E. H., Honingh, M. E. and Langelaan, B. (2011). The Teaching Profession Against the Background of Educationalisation: An Exploratory Study. *European Journal of Teacher Education*, (24, 4), 297–315.

Hynds, A. (2008). Developing and Sustaining Open Communication in Action Research Initiatives: A Response to Kemmis (2006). *Educational Action Research*, (16, 2), 149–162.

Jakobsen, M. and Andersen, S. C. (2013). Coproduction and Equity in Public Service Delivery. *Public Administration Review*, (73, 5), 704–713.

Jeynes, W. (2012). A Meta-Analysis of the Efficacy of Different Types of Parental Involvement Programs for Urban Students. *Urban Education*, (47, 4), 706–742.

Kenney, S. H. (2011). School Music Goes Home. *General Music Today*, (25, 2), 41–43.

LaRocque, M., Kleiman, I. and Darling, S. M. (2011). Parental Involvement: The Missing Link in School Achievement. *Preventing School Failure: Alternative Education for Children and Youth*, (55, 3).

Lusse, M. (2015). *Van je ouders moet je het hebben*. Inaugural lecture, Rotterdam University of Applied Sciences.

Willemse, T. M., Ten Dam, G., Geijsel, F., Wessum, L. and Volman, M. (2015). Fostering Teachers' Professional Development for Citizenship Education. *Teaching and Teacher Education*, (49), 118–127.

13.1 Case Study—Partners for Possibility

Co-Production of Education

Dirk Brand and Marleen Rolland

Introduction

Due to the history of South Africa, the diversity of the citizens of the country and the continuous inequality and poverty, the South African education system is deemed as being in crisis. After more than twenty years of democracy in South Africa, the school education system is not yet producing the results it is expected to deliver. Only about 5,000 of 25,000 schools in the country are functioning properly and delivering the expected education outputs (Collins, 2015). With high enrolment rates but high early drop out and increasingly poor Grade 12 outputs, it is clear that a greater focus should fall on improving the quality of education. The latter is one of the key priorities in the National Development Plan: Vision 2030 (South African Government, n.d.). However, a main factor preventing students from receiving quality education is the lack of good leadership in schools, more specifically under-resourced schools.

Therefore, in 2010, Dr. Louise Van Rhyn, a business manager who wanted to do something to change the education system, met Mr. Ridwan Samodien, principal of Kannemeyer Primary School in Western Cape, one of the many underperforming schools in South Africa. He wanted to change his school to be a successful, winning school with an engaged parent community. Van Rhyn and Samodien started to engage the parents and the community surrounding the school, including the local businesses. The enthusiastic discussions that took place that day led to various initiatives that involved parents, businesses, alumni from the school and the Western Cape Education Department. A partnership was born to co-produce education at this school. This was the start of the Partners for Possibility program (Partners for Possibility, n.d.).

Background

Partners for Possibility is a co-production of education initiative that focuses on leadership development. It is based on a partnership between business leaders, who must each contribute R30,000 (about 2.000 euro) to the program, and school principals from under-resourced schools in South Africa. The two leaders work together in a structured program to make a difference in the school community and positively impact the quality of education at that school. Business leaders use this contribution as part of their corporate social responsibility initiatives, but this has not prevented companies in committing again for another period.

"Changing one school at a time" is the motto used by Partners for Possibility to move towards transforming the education landscape in South Africa. The Partners for Possibility program consists of the following:

- "A partnership program between a business leader and school principal from an under-resourced school for one year.
- The partners must complete a tailored leadership development course, which includes theoretical courses, experiential learning and action learning.
- Professional coaching by an experienced learning process facilitator.
- The partners are grouped into a Leadership Circle of 8–10 partnerships acting as solution incubators.
- The partners in each school design an improvement plan custom-made for their school and which addresses the specific challenges of that school using the tools they get from this program.
- The partners act together in engaging their respective communities to become actively involved in the execution of this plan". (Collins, 2015)

The program thus focuses on school leadership to change the performance of schools. The theory of change, as applied in schools, is based on the idea that school principals must lead the change process in their schools. Principals and business leaders co-operate to effect change in schools at four levels:

(i) The principal—building confident energetic principals to lead and manage their schools effectively;

(ii) The school management team—the expertise of business leaders is harnessed to develop the school management team into a cohesive unit aligned to the vision created through this initiative, for example, the school management team learns to adopt business strategies such as marketing their school properly, developing communication strategies and approaching the school management more strategically through businesses facilitating strategic planning sessions with the school management;

(iii) The community of teachers—principals and business leaders work together to re-energize and re-engage the teachers at the participating schools; for example, principals will facilitate strategic planning sessions with teachers to address challenges which the teachers face and approach these challenges together to ensure all inputs are generated.

Teachers now become a part of the problem-solving team, instead of just being informed of decisions by management;

(iv) The community of parents and other citizens around the schools— getting active support from the parents and other citizens in the local community, for example, increased parent-teacher meetings, hosting sport days where the parents can engage with the school and each other, involving parents in their children's education and keeping them updated on their children's progress. (Collins, 2015)

The underlying theory on which Partners for Possibility is based is rooted in complexity science. This understands the quality of outcomes or results to depend on the quality of the collective thinking, which in turn is influenced by the quality of relationships between the members of an organisation and its partners (Collins, 2015).

Experiences

The Partners for Possibility started in the Western Cape, South Africa with one small school in 2010. Six years later it has grown to encompass many aspects beyond leadership, assisting under-resourced schools through the contribution of resources by business leaders, but also through its various funding initiatives. It has moved beyond focusing mainly on principals and leadership towards incorporating education tools designed for the modern child. The Partners for Possibility initiative has led to change in under-performing under-resourced schools by equipping principals and school management committees with the necessary skills. The initiative continues to develop leadership, a capable state and active citizenship to ultimately ensure social cohesion.

Over 450 schools are involved across South Africa, including 321 business leaders from 255 organisations who are in partnership with South African school principals. The programme additionally resulted in creating a "Community of Committed Parents", which actively involves the parent community in all the school's activities. Other results include a new upgraded computer lab and a new library to a specific school in need of this; a crowdfunding initiative where 500 citizens pledge R200 for ten months to ensure R1 million unrestricted funding; and a positive school environment where learners receive good quality education and can achieve good results (Collins, 2015).

References

Collins, M. (2015). *Partners for Possibility*. Randburg, South Africa: Knowres Publishing.
Partners for Possibility. (n.d.). [Online].
South African Government. (n.d.). National Development Plan [Online].

13.2 Case Study—Co-Creating School Meals Services

Giuseppe Aquino and
Maddalena Sorrentino

Introduction

All children in Italy receive free, compulsory schooling and have all the rights to school and community education services, including school meals, according to constitutionally founded basic educational principles. The decentralised education model operated by the State assigns overall responsibility for preschool, primary and secondary education to the Ministry of Public Instruction (instructional guidelines, learning goals, exit exams, school curriculum and organisation) and the administrative and operational side to the local authorities (school year scheduling, school closures/openings, building maintenance, etc.). The latter are responsible also for the complementary services that enable the right to education, such as school transportation, special needs and school meals. In the eyes of Italian law, the right to education marches in lockstep with the children's right to health.

To operate a school meals service, the municipal authorities must set up an SMJC (School Meals Joint Committee) composed of the CEd (Councillor for Education), pupil-parent representatives, teachers and a council expert. Tasked with basic advisory duties, the SMJC can, however, assume greater responsibilities.

Mapping the experience of the School Meals Joint Committee set up in Abbiategrasso, a town in the Metropolitan City of Milan, Lombardy, northern Italy, identifies three interconnected drivers of co-production in a basic school and community education service:

- the significant influence of the citizens in shaping the process;
- the opening of direct communication channels to connect the key stakeholders (the parents of primary and secondary school-goers, the teachers, the town council and the school meals provider), including online access to meeting minutes, monitoring reports and the SMJC's recommendations;
- the diffusion of sustainability best practices.

The Abbiategrasso case informs how the SMJC successfully addressed essential co-production issues, such as accountability, equity and the relationship between the lay persons and the professional staff.

Background

The school meals service is mandated by the Italian State to the town councils. Around 80% of these hire external companies to deliver five meals per week to 53.4% of Italy's school-goers, with preschool accounting for 64.4%, primary 26.7% and lower secondary just 6.1% (Ministero della Salute, 2014).

The SMJC established in 2000 by the mid-size municipality of Abbiategrasso (pop. 32,000) brings together the users of three public schools and the external school meals provider to 'co-create' meals for around 2000 pre-, primary and lower secondary school day students aged between 3 and 13.

Headed by the CEd, the SMJC started out as a nine-member 'technical table' for the purpose of formal consultation with the stakeholders (parents, teachers, local authorities, school meals provider), but has since branched out in two additional directions: quality control, both independently and jointly with the council, and recommendatory, e.g., menu, service delivery, external provider contractual specifications.

The case study demonstrates that the organisation and the effectiveness of the school meals service have both benefited significantly from the readiness of the SMJC to develop its consultative role into a fully pro-active endeavour.

Under its guidance, new initiatives were launched, such as the 'zero-kilometre' organic food chain, for which it also helped to define the contractual specifications; the fight against food wastage; the reduction of waste; and the adoption of 'pupil-sized' tableware. The SMJC assisted in the definition of the special quality monitoring system procedures that involve the parent-representatives of all three school types in an average of three inspections per month, the results of which are posted on the Abbiategrasso council's website. It also gave the council the reach it needed to better identify and respond to the special needs and/or food ethics of pupils.

Hence, the SMJC has become a major enabling force in the school meals monitoring operations, allowing the council to take on education-related challenges that were previously beyond its limited capabilities.

Experiences

The Abbiategrasso school meals experience is a typical case of the co-creation and co-production of a complementary school and community education service. As a co-creator, the SMJC works closely with the council's technical and managerial staff to define the content, methods and contractual specifications of the school meals service, while the parents and the catering experts jointly define a healthy, balanced, tasty and appealing menu. As a co-producer, the SMJC acts both independently and in conjunction with the council staff to inspect the school meals provider's kitchen premises and equipment; the school cafeterias; the organisation of service and staff; the foodstuffs; and the quality/quantity of the portions.

The involvement of the SMJC members in the diverse stages of the decision-making process has created a new institutional arena in which the actors play a central role in shaping the school meals service.

Rated positive by all the key stakeholders, the Abbiategrasso initiative casts light on three interrelated and well-recognised co-production issues: accountability, equity and the relationship between the lay persons and the professional staff, otherwise known as the institutionalisation factors of success.

First, the dual accountability of the CEd to the parents and to the town council and his/her attendance of the SMJC open citizen meetings are clear indicators of the council's sharp focus on education policies.

Second, the SMJC acts as guarantor, working alongside the council and the provider to create menus that take account of the school-goers' ethnic, cultural and health needs. Taking meals at school is an inherently educational ritual that offers several advantages in that it teaches even the smallest kids to eat properly and promotes socialisation and inclusion among peers.

Third, the SMJC case study has shown that bringing on board the citizens generates valuable inputs that go a long way to optimising the efficacy of the public service mission. The parents and teachers all acknowledge that the ongoing interactions afforded by the online and offline communication channels set up since the SMJC's inception have led to an overall improvement in the quality of the school meals service. Based on the knowledge that 'we're all in it together', the lay persons (parents and teachers) and the professionals (council technicians, service provider experts) have built a relationship of trust conducive to the transparent addressing of issues that concern both the town council and the service provider.

Given that about 70% of Italian schools deliver a school meals service and that only 52% have a pro-active SMJC, the Abbiategrasso case evidences several meaningful points of interest on the practice of co-production in service design and implementation.

Reference

Ministero della Salute. (2014). *Indagine conoscitiva sulla ristorazione scolastica in Italia*. Relazione 2014. Roma: Ministero della Salute.

14 Co-Production and the Environment

Marco Ranzato and Luisa Moretto

The co-production of water, energy, and waste services, in which the recipient of a service also plays a fundamental role in managing the resources involved, has recently received considerable attention. In the context of citizen-government co-production, service recipients are thus more than consumers, and production alters their perceptions of and connections with a resource. However, the extent to which and circumstances under which the co-production of water, energy, and waste services could help to answer the urgent need for equitable access to common pool resources remains unclear. A meaningful understanding of the ecological impact of co-production is only possible through an interdisciplinary approach that takes into account environmental and social theories and instruments.

Co-Production of Water, Energy, and Waste Services

The work of the Nobel Prize winner Elinor Ostrom has focused on the concepts of service co-production (1996) and the accessibility and sustainable management of common pool resources (Ostrom et al., 1999). Such resources are defined as natural or man-made systems "sufficiently large as to make it costly (but not impossible) to exclude potential beneficiaries" from using them (Ostrom, 1990, 30). This body of literature, however, offers few insights into the specifics of co-producing such key common pool resources as water, energy, and waste services. We argue here that co-production of these services carries with it specific and unavoidable environmental implications relevant to the urgent need for equitable access to common pool resources. These services are examples of common pool resources that require both natural materials and human actions, mediated through technical devices, in order to be considered services. In other words, water, energy, and waste services create and discard materials that are themselves the human products of natural resources or, commonly, a mixture of such products.[1] The provision and/or disposal of water, energy, or waste thus creates a web of connections between production and consumption (for example, the conveyance of potable water from the point of extraction to the that of consumption).

Both social and natural perspectives are relevant here. Current research on service provision and co-production tends to emphasise one at the expense of the other, but the study of the supply and disposal of water, energy, and waste requires more comprehensive observations that combine the social and natural perspectives (see for instance Swyngedouw, 1999). This also applies to the co-production of water, energy, and waste services. In this respect, the claim that "institutional diversity may be as important as biological diversity for our long-term survival" (Ostrom et al., 1999, 278) can be understood as an attempt to bridge the sustainable management of natural resources with inputs—in terms of organisational capacities and infrastructure development—from diverse actors who together co-produce common pool resources. Approached this way, an exploration of the co-production of water, energy, and waste services can help to reveal the extent to which common pool resources are amenable to service co-production and, in turn, the potential benefits of water, energy, and waste service co-production for the environment.

Co-Production or Co-Creation

According to the distinction made by Brandsen and Honingh in this volume (chapter 2), common pool resources can be both co-produced and co-created. In effect, collaboration between users and service agents can take place at the strategic level of service planning as well as during service design and implementation. With respect to service planning, Allen et al. (2017), for instance, have asserted that the case of water supply schemes in Dar es Salaam, Tanzania, shows that there are "examples where there is significant collaboration between poor communities and the authorities [that has] led to the inclusion and representation of low-income dwellers in political processes and decision making." The handling of this resource in this way can be described in terms of the "co-creation of a core service" (Brandsen and Honingh, in this volume, chapter 2). The co-production of residential services in Medellin, Colombia—where residents are, for instance, mobilised to collect payments for service bills and maintenance costs (Duque Gomez and Jaglin, 2017)—can be assimilated to "co-production in the implementation of core services" (Brandsen and Honingh, in this volume, chapter 2). We similarly argue that, again in these researchers' terminology, "co-creation" generally leads to greater democratisation and re-politicisation of the service supply than does co-production, since the former takes place during the planning phase of the service provision process, as the case of Dar es Salaam just mentioned demonstrates. Nevertheless, in previous literature, cases in which common pool resources have been co-created seem quite few. For the sake of clarity and consistency, we use here only the term "co-production" without entering into further discussion regarding the distinction between this concept and that of co-creation.

The Unique Role of the Environment

The Relationship Between Users and Common Pool Resources

As defined by Ostrom (1996, 1079), co-production refers to "one way that synergy between what a government does and what citizens do can occur." From this perspective, in co-production, citizens, or the recipients of a service, are engaged, which is to say that they play meaningful roles and are proactive. In co-production, citizens exercise their agency beyond just consuming resources and/or releasing residuals. Users can instead co-produce conventional services (meaning those that are organised through a centralised network and are generally operated by a monopoly) and thereby alter their behaviour and have direct effects on the overall metabolic cycle—or the sum of processes—concerning the resource(s) being conveyed (Figure 14.1). An example of such co-production is the storage of potable water by citizens at the household level in response to unreliability in the water supply service. Studies show that, in these forms of co-production, users tend to become acquainted with common pool resources and come to understand both how resource systems operate and the effects that their own actions can have on them (Ostrom et al., 1999; Moretto and Ranzato, 2017).

The User-Resource Proximity

The synergy pointed out by Ostrom has, then, another important ecological implication. Whenever, in the co-production of water, energy, and waste

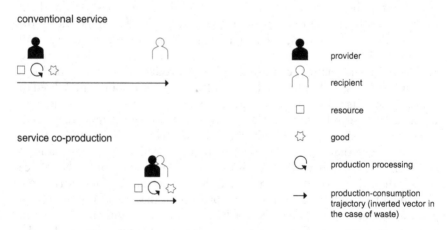

Figure 14.1 Production/Consumption of Natural Resources in Physical Relation to the User/Resource According to the Conventional Model for Water, Energy, and Waste Services and to Co-Production; the Shift is Both from the User's Resource Consumption to the Recipient's Resource Production and from Distance to Proximity with Regard to Resources and Recipients

services, the user, at some point beyond consumption, participates directly in the processing of a natural resource, co-production is a signifier of greater proximity between the user and the conveyed resource than would be the case for the conventional service model. As Coutard and Rutherford (2012) have observed, the ideal of modern infrastructure, that from the advent of the industrial city has been mastering the configurations of water, energy, and waste services, "is contested on the grounds of its incompatibility or unsustainability with regard to new financial arrangements, political and institutional functioning, individualised lifestyles" and also with respect to "increasing concern for environmental resource use and impact" (p. 7). According to the conventional model, water, energy, and waste are mediated by a standardised, centralised, and networked infrastructure. Not only do these large technical systems tend to exclude users from the production phases (Yu et al., 2011), but they also exploit ecosystems. Suppliers of natural resources and sinks for emissions are often located far beyond the urban bioregion as defined by natural features (for example, topography and biodiversity). Owing to this distance, these technical systems have been identified as "key catalysts of environmental problems like air, water, and soil pollution" (Monstadt, 2009, 1026). Instead, the proximity that would be found in the case of co-production could bring with it alternative—which is to say, decentralised or hybrid—technological systems that operate on a more local scale and could be associated with more favourable environmental outcomes.[2] Household retention of rainwater as a means to cope with discontinuity of water service is, as alluded to above, one example of the shorter circuits involved in the use of local resources (in this case, rainwater) mediated by a decentralised device (a rainwater tank) and associated with environmental implications (reduced water consumption).

Research on Co-Production of Common Pool Resources

Despite the existence of forms of co-production relating to water, energy, and waste services, theoretical research thus far has done little in the way of integrating environmental concerns into the co-production of conventional services. The conceptualisation of service co-production has rather concentrated primarily on such social services as education, health care, and policing. Co-production of these services has been analysed from a variety of public administration, management, and governance perspectives, and the organisation of service co-production and the institutional systems and normative frameworks favouring this provision option have been explored (e.g., Bovaird and Leoffler, 2012; Bovaird et al., 2016; Jakobsen, 2013; Osborne and Strokosh, 2013; Sicilia et al., 2016; Verschuere et al., 2012). Since education, policing, health care, and similar services do not rely directly on any given natural resource (though they can have environmental consequences), environmental considerations are not generally addressed in this branch of the literature.

At the same time, no mainstream study of transformation processes relating to water, energy, and waste has yet investigated, at least in any depth, co-production in terms of the sustainable management of common pool resources. Studies by nature scientists and industrial ecologists, on the other hand, have examined the circulation of flows in depth (see for instance, Baccini and Brunner, 1991; Girardet, 1992), though the socio-political implications are often disregarded in such studies (Wachsmuth, 2012). Only recently has urban political ecology produced historical-geographical accounts of the socio-natural production processes relating to water, energy, and waste resources (see for instance, Gandy, 2004; Swyngedouw, 2015). This branch of the literature does offer a solid understanding of the sum of the processes involving these resources, but without reference to co-production.

The Resource and Technological Dimensions

The scholarship on the co-production of common pool resources, then, is not very extensive. Among the studies that have been done, work by Yu et al. (2011, 2012) on decentralised storm water systems in Australia has investigated how co-production can influence the design of these systems' governance arrangements. These researchers proceeded from the hypothesis that co-production can involve end-users in the various phases of a water service cycle. The water sector has been undergoing far-reaching transformations, both in terms of the diversification of sources and infrastructure at various scales and with respect to the integration of various actors. Based on a wide-ranging survey of studies in public administration, public sector governance, and environmental sociology, these studies identified within co-production in the water sector the following four variables: the *providers* (i.e., traditional service delivery organisations and agents) and forms of provisions (including a blend of public and private entities and various levels of dependence on the government); *resources* (and their associated risks and opportunities); *technology* (covering the scale, complexity, and connectedness of systems used for service delivery and management); and *end-users* (i.e., clients, citizens, and neighbourhood associations). Two dimensions of the *resource* variable were identified, namely public health and the environment, and proper attention to the latter was presented as fundamental to understanding the options for co-production (Yu et al., 2011). As a matter of fact, and by way of example, alternative service delivery actually holds the potential to transform water nuisances (such as storm water) into resources, while potential risks related to the natural or physical environment tend to increase the centralisation of service delivery systems. This framework is particularly useful for integrating a resource variable and an environmental dimension explicitly into the understanding of the co-production of services that are based on natural resources. Further comparative investigation seems necessary, as some of the assumptions behind this work, such as the tendency to manage large environmental risks through service centralisation, have been called into question by other scholars (see for instance, Ranzato, 2017).

Including Spatial and Flow Dimensions

A reinterpretation of work by Tjallingii (1996) in the light of conventional service co-production was recently proposed (Moretto and Ranzato, 2017). Similar to approaches rooted in urban political ecology (see for example, Smith, 2006; Heynen et al., 2006), Tjallingii argued that the physical and social conditions of a given context have to be considered together from an ecological perspective and proposed an "ecological condition strategy" in which the dimensions of *actor, flow,* and *area* are stimulating factors for the planning process. This threefold conceptual framework has proved to be successful not only when it comes to informing planning processes but also in combining a public approach to management with a governance perspective in order to understand service co-production in terms of its environmental and spatial aspects relating to water, energy, and waste service. Accordingly, the *actor* dimension takes into account the typology of stakeholders involved in service co-production, including how and at what levels (Bovaird and Löffler, 2012) they collaborate in co-producing services and the nature of their institutional and political configurations (Osborne and Strokosh, 2013). The *flow* dimension relates to the organisation and management of the metabolic transformation processes of resources used in, or produced by, service delivery, while the *area* dimension focuses on the socio-spatial dynamics of service co-production, including the various technical devices used in the delivery process and the various scales of service delivery. This research has the merit of linking accessibility, environmental sustainability, and spatial considerations in the co-production of conventional services. Further work is needed, however, to unfold underlying logics and mechanisms in reference to these three dimensions and to integrate the technological issue.

Co-Production and Environment on the Ground

Making the Environment a Driver for Co-Production

The literature has only lately demonstrated the potential significance of co-produced water, energy, and waste services for both natural resources and the society. Recent scholarship has made available noteworthy observations on the renewed relationship and proximity between users and natural resources in the co-production of these services (see for instance Allen et al., 2017; Moretto and Ranzato, 2017; Button, 2017).

In India's East Kolkata Wetlands, for instance, wastewater generated by the city are reused and recycled through fisheries, effluence-irrigated paddy cultivation, and vegetable farming on garbage substrates located on the outskirts of the city, initiatives that are managed by cooperatives in agreement with local institutions (Allen et al., 2017). In Rio de Janeiro, Brazil, by contrast, household waste is separated by dwellers in the city's various *favelas* and collected at "Ecopoints" managed by local NGOs. This process provides discounts to citizens' electricity bills, thereby improving access to energy from one side and directly feeding into the chain for later recycling of waste products from the other (Pilo, 2017). In a further example, local community leaders in low-income settlements of the Metropolitan Area of Caracas, Venezuela, have the authority to close the drinking water pipes of the co-produced secondary network—which was built through collaboration between citizens and local authorities—should infrastructure damage occur, so as to reduce water losses and flooding (Moretto, 2014). These case studies show that co-producing services invites users to play significant roles in the circulatory processes of the flow by preserving, collecting, separating, purifying, reusing, or recycling the materials channelised by the service.

Scholars have also demonstrated that the co-production of water, energy, and waste services can lead to greater reliance on local resources and decreased dependence on ecosystems distant from an urban bioregion. Improved access to water service provisions in both Cochabamba, Bolivia, and Dar es Salam, Tanzania, for instance, is effected through co-produced local arrangements that rest on various local adaptations (such as secondary independent networks and boreholes) that extract groundwater onsite (Allen et al., 2017; Cabrera, 2015). In Sfax, Tunisia, an agreement between small local enterprises and the public waste management agency coordinates the collection and partial recycling of five different kinds of local urban waste, the so-called *ECO-filières* (Moretto and Azaitraoui, 2015). In Hamburg, Germany, a 10 MW solar co-production project enables local collection of solar energy, a renewable resource otherwise wasted (Becker et al., 2017). And in the community of Forest in Brussels, Belgium, local citizens' committees, non-profit organisations, and citizens themselves collaborated with representatives of the local municipality in the design and implementation of storm water source control operations as a step toward separated storm water service (see the case presented by Ranzato in this volume, chapter 14.1).

These examples confirm that the co-production of services, besides increasing the accessibility, quality, quantity, affordability, variety, and so on of service options, can also contribute to environmental sustainability (Moretto and Ranzato, 2017). In relying on local resources, these co-produced services are self-sufficient and thus accessible; they reduce negative externalities on the surrounding environment and support short, lasting circulatory processes that are more oriented to recycling and up-cycling of the resources.

Challenges of a Changed Recipient-Resource Relation

The "altered" recipient-resource relationship involving the co-production of water, energy, and waste services may carry with it significant environmental implications. Co-production per se does not necessarily mean implementing water, energy, and waste services that are in balance with the environment and that thus contribute to the careful use of resources. Increased proximity to a certain resource could, for example, result in its overuse owing to the perception that it is unlimited (Yu et al., 2011; Moretto and Ranzato, 2017). This being the case, a comprehensive and nuanced approach is required in order to unpack and explicate the ecological facets of co-production involving these services.

The primary challenge remains integrating an environmental emphasis into the socio-political domain, for this is the main characteristic of co-produced common pool resources. Tools and inquiry strategies from both the social and the natural sciences need to be combined in order to elucidate fully the various mutual positions of a resource and its end-users. Spatialising the co-production of water, energy, and waste services represents a step in this direction. It is necessary to map the recipient-resource relationship beyond the co-production governance structure if the geographical extension of the service is to be made clear. Another key issue is the effect of co-production on the resources mobilised by these services. The integration of analytical methods for quantifying the flows (as with material flow analysis; see for example, Baccini, 1997) could, in combination with historical-geographical accounts regarding their production processes, make it possible to situate the changes produced within the cycles of the resources and to determine the extent to which and circumstances under which co-production may or may not result in short production-consumption cycles.

Furthermore, recent studies (Yu et al., 2011; Moretto and Ranzato, 2017) seem to agree that technology plays a key role in making the co-production of water, energy, and waste services possible. The overriding technocratic regime has placed the management of natural resources in the hands of governments or, more recently, of private enterprises. Hybrid and/or decentralised systems could prove to be more accessible to citizens than large centralised and standardised ones (Yu et al., 2011). A crucial consideration here is the relationship between co-production and traditional—and mainly off-grid—grassroots socio-technological systems (see for example, Jaglin, 2012; Allen et al., 2017) and between co-production and the emergence of a hybrid infrastructure landscape consisting of "localized," "decentralized," "distributed," or "alternative" technologies (Coutard and Rutherford, 2012, 2015; Coutard et al., 2014). Relevant in this context are a variety of technical and design perspectives, including that of industrial design. Ultimately, it should thus be possible to frame the role of the user interface in the co-production of these services.

Finally, as Ostrom et al. (1999) stressed, users are likely to engage in self-organised processes for natural resource management when they perceive that they themselves benefit from doing so. The benefits for users are assessed through an "accurate knowledge" of the boundaries and attributes of a given resource and the predictability of its flow and, as a consequence, citizens may arrive at a greater awareness of "how the resource systems operate and how their actions affect each other and the resource" (Ostrom et al., 1999, 281). By extension, co-producing water, energy, and waste services has the potential both to expand users' awareness of natural resources and capacity to manage them and also to afford them a renewed role in the political and decision-making processes that guide the provision of services. The effort should accordingly be made to understand more fully the potential of service co-production, with a variety of alternative and hybrid service options, to contribute to a sustainable *commoning* approach[3] in terms of the mobilisation of natural resources and the development of new political imaginaries (Susser and Tonnelat, 2013; Becker et al., 2017). At the same time, the mechanisms through which co-production genuinely democratises and re-politicises conventional service provisions should be revealed.

Future research on the environmental implications of water, energy, and waste co-production have for the most part been disregarded. Moreover, future research on the matter should avoid the usual rhetoric on sustainable development, since it often conceals market interests (see for example, Kenis and Lievens, 2016). The urgent need for equitable access to natural resources—which is inseparable from the durable management of these resources (Robertson, 2012)—demands instead examination of the extent to which co-production of common pool resources can simultaneously bring about genuine participation, socio-spatial equity, and environmental sustainability.

Notes

1 There are evident interrelations—or a nexus—between these services and the resources conveyed. In some cases, the services are interdependent or one is the raison d'être of the other (for example, the supply of drinking water and disposal of sewage); in others, the resource conveyed by a service is needed to run another service (for instance, the energy required to supply or treat water).
2 According to Coutard et al. (2014, p. 91), "the liberalization of network industries, growing concerns for the use of environmental resources and impacts on these resources, new financial arrangements and the increasing individualization of lifestyles are all challenging the supremacy of centralized solutions and promoting the development of alternative technological systems at a more local scale."
3 Chatterton (2010, p. 626) defines the "practice of commoning" as "dynamic spatial practices . . . the common is complex, and relational—it is produced and reproduced through relations weaving together a rich tapestry of different times, spaces and struggles."

References

Allen, A., Hofmann, P., Mukherjee, J. and Walnycki, A. (2017). Water Trajectories Through Non-Networked Infrastructure: Insights from peri-urban Dar es Salaam, Cochabamba and Kolkata. *Urban Research & Practice*, (10, 1), 22–42.
Baccini, P. (1997). A City's Metabolism: Towards the Sustainable Development of Urban Systems. *Journal of Urban Technology*, (4, 2), 27–39.
Baccini, P. and Brunner, P. H. (1991). *Metabolism of the Anthroposphere*. Berlin: Springer-Verlag.

Becker, S., Naumann, M. and Moss, T. (2017). Between Coproduction and Commons: Understanding Initiatives to Reclaim Urban Energy Provision in Berlin and Hamburg. *Urban Research & Practice*, (10, 1), 63–85.

Bovaird, T. and Loeffler, E. (2012). From Engagement to Co-Production. How Users and Communities Contribute to Public Services. In V. Pestoff, T. Brandsen, and B. Verschuere (eds.), *New Public Governance, the Third Sector and Coproduction*, 35–60. New York and London: Routledge.

Bovaird, T., Stoker, G., Jones, T., Loeffler, E. and Roncancio, M. (2016). Activating Collective Co-Production of Public Services: Influencing Citizens to Participate in Complex Governance Mechanisms in the UK. *International Review of Administrative Sciences*, (82, 1), 47–68.

Button, C. (2017). The Co-Production of a Constant Water Supply in Mumbai's Middle-Class Apartments. *Urban Research & Practice*, (10, 1), 102–119.

Cabrera, J. E. (2015). *Fragmentation urbaine à travers les réseaux techniques. L'example de strategies locales de gestion de l'eau dans la Municipalité de Quillacollo du department de Cochabamba*. PhD thesis. Liège: Université de Liège.

Chatterton, P. (2010). Seeking the Urban Common: Furthering the Debate on Spatial Justice. *City*, (14, 6), 625–628.

Coutard, O. and Rutherford, J. (2012). From Networked to Post-Networked Urbanism : New Infrastructure Configurations and Urban Transitions. Paper presented at the International Roundtable Workshop, Université Paris-Est, 17–20 July 2012.

Coutard, O. and Rutherford, J. (eds.). (2015). *Beyond the Networked City: Infrastructure Reconfigurations and Urban Change in the North and South*. London: Routledge.

Coutard, O., Rutherford, J. and Florentin, D. (2014). Towards Hybrid Socio-Technical Solutions for Water and Energy Provision. In J. Y. Grosclaude, R. K. Pachauri and L. Tubiana (eds.), *Innovations for Sustainable Development*, 91–100. New Delhi: TERI Press.

Duque Gomez, C. and Jaglin, S. (2017). When Urban Modernization Entails Service Delivery Co-production: A Glance from Medellin. *Urban Research and Practice*, (10, 1), 43–62.

Gandy, M. (2004). Rethinking Urban Metabolism: Water, Space and the Modern City. *City*, (8, 3), 363–379.

Girardet, H. (1992). *The Gaia Atlas of Cities*. London: Gaia Books.

Heynen, N., Kaika, M. and Swyngedouw, E. (2006). Urban Political Ecology: Politicising the Production of Urban Natures. In N. Heynen, M. Kaika and E. Swyngedouw (eds.), *In the Nature of Cities Urban Political Ecology and the Politics of Urban Metabolism*, 1–19. London and New York: Routledge.

Jaglin, S. (2012). Services en Réseaux et Villes Africaines: L'universalité par D'autres Voies? *L'espace Geographique*, (41, 1), 51–67.

Jakobsen, M. (2013). Can Government Initiatives Increase Citizen Coproduction? Results of a Randomized Field Experiment. *Journal of Public Administration Research and Theory*, (23, 1), 27–54.

Kenis, A. and Lievens, M. (2016). Greening the Economy or Economizing the Green Project? When Environmental Concerns Are Turned into a Means to Save the Market. *Review of Radical Political Economics*, (48, 2), 217–234.

Monstadt, J. (2009). Conceptualizing the Political Ecology of Urban Infrastructures: Insights from Technology and Urban Studies. *Environment and Planning*, (41), 1924–1942.

Moretto, L. (2014). *Assessing Urban Governance: The Case of Water Service Co-Production in Venezuela*. Brussels: PIE Peter Lang.

Moretto, L. and Azaitraoui, M. (2015). La valorisation des déchets urbains à Sfax (Tunisie): entre reformes politiques et récupération informelle. In B. B. Florin and C. Cirelli (eds.), *Sociétés Urbaines et Déchets*, 336–396. Presses Universitaires François Rabelais, Tours.

Moretto, L. and Ranzato, M. (2017). A Socio-Natural Standpoint to Understand Coproduction of Water, Energy and Waste Services. *Urban Research & Practice*, (10), 1–21.

Osborne, S. P. and Strokosch, K. (2013). It Takes Two to Tango? Understanding the Co-Production of Public Services by Integrating the Services Management and Public Administration Perspectives. *British Journal of Management*, (24), 31–47.

Ostrom, E. (1990). *Governing the Commons. The Evolution of Institutions for Collective Action*. Cambridge, UK: Cambridge University Press.

Ostrom, E. (1996). Crossing the Great Divide : Co-Production, Synergy, and Development. *World Development*, (24, 6), 1073–1087.

Ostrom, E., Burger, J., Field, C. B., Norgaard, R. B. and Policansky, D. (1999). Revisiting the Commons: Local Lessons, Global Challenges. *Science*, (284, 5412), 278–282.

Pilo, F. (2017). Co-Producing Affordability to the Electricity Service. *Urban Research & Practice*, (10, 1), 86–101.

Ranzato, M. (2017). Landscape Elements as a Basis for Integrated Water Management. *Urban Water Journal*, (14, 7), 694–703.

Robertson, M. (2012). *Sustainable Cities*. Ottawa: Practical Action Publishing.

Sicilia, M., Guarini, E., Sancino, A., Andreani, M. and Ruffini, R. (2016). Public Services Management and Co-Production in Multi-Level Governance Settings. *International Review of Administrative Sciences*, (82, 1), 8–27.

Smith, N. (2006). Foreword. In N. Heynen, M. Kaika, and E. Swyngedouw (eds.), *In the Nature of Cities: Urban Political Ecology and the Politics of Urban Metabolism*, xii–xv. [Online]. London and New York: Routledge.

Susser, I. and Tonnelat, S. (2013). Transformative Cities: The Three Urban Commons. *Focaal—Journal of Global and Historical Anthropology*, (66), 105–132.

Swyngedouw, E. (1999). *Modernity and Hybridity: The Production of Nature: Water and Modernization in Spain*. Paper presented at the Water Issues Study Group, SOAS, University of London, 25 January 1999.

Swyngedouw, E. (2015). *Liquid Power: Contested Hydro-Modernities in Twentieth-Century Spain*. Cambridge, MA: MIT Press.

Tjallingii, S. P. (1996). *Ecological Conditions. Strategies and Structures in Environmental Planning*. Wageningen: Institute for Forestry and Nature Research.

Verschuere, B., Brandsen, T. and Pestoff, V. (2012). Co-Production: The State of the Art in Research and the Future Agenda. *Voluntas*, (23, 4), 1083–1101.

Wachsmuth, D. (2012). Three Ecologies: Urban Metabolism and the Society-Nature Opposition. *The Sociological Quarterly*, (53), 506–523.

Yu, C., Brown, R. and Morison, M. (2012). Co-Governing Decentralised Water Systems: An Analytical Framework. *Water Science and Technology*, (66, 12), 2731–2736.

Yu, C., Farrelly, M. A. and Brown, R. R. (2011). *Co-Production and the Governance of Decentralised Stormwater Systems*. Report, PROJECT 6: Society & Institutions, Centre for Water Sensitive Cities, School of Geography & Environmental Science, Faculty of Arts, Monash University, Australia.

14.1 Case Study—Balade Verte et Bleue and Ilôt d'eau

Co-Creation and Co-Production for the Environment

Marco Ranzato

Introduction

In Brussels, as in many other European urban areas, the separate management of storm water—and the related service—represents a major environmental challenge. In 2007, in the municipality of Forest, one of the nineteen municipalities in the Brussels Capital Region, citizens formed the Comité Stop Inondations Saint-Denis in an effort to focus on the ongoing threat that flood waters were posing to the lower part of the community (Ranzato and Bortolotti, 2015). These citizens sought to increase awareness on the part of both local institutions and the broader society in regard to the local water cycle, in particular the role of rainwater as a source. They were able to attract the attention of other citizens and associations and, relatively recently, to garner recognition from the relevant local authorities. Other such initiatives have also flourished, including two sets of participatory activities, the Balade Verte et Bleue ("Green and Blue Walk") and Ilôt d'Eau ("[Urban] Water Block/Island"), designed to formulate feasible environmental measures for the implementation of separate drainage service. Balade Verte et Bleue and Ilôt d'Eau are both part of the same process of democratization, accountability, and empowerment of citizens with respect to the management of water. Thus each of these initiatives combines a participatory design with social innovation, using co-design as a means of reinforcing the role that citizens play by contributing their local knowledge to the forging of environmental measures (see Manzini and Rizzo, 2011).

Background

Balade Verte et Bleue is a co-creation of environmental measures designed, as just mentioned, to facilitate the implementation of a separate drainage service. Citizens collaborate with a non-profit association, the Etats Generaux de l'Eau a Bruxelles (EGEB), a local architectural firm called Arkipel, existing citizens' committees (among them the Comité Stop Inondations Saint-Denis), and with the municipality in planning service strategies. Balade Verte et Bleue calls for a number of actions, including the following:

- During group walks called "promenades," citizens, designers, and experts explore a section of the urban landscape, discussing and taking notes regarding soil conditions, water springs, drainage trajectories, paving rates, traces of former streams, vegetation, and any other features that may influence the behaviour of storm water.
- Following each promenade, citizens and experts, with the guidance of a designer, engage in a participatory mapping session to record perceived problems and missed opportunities relating to storm water. Also during these sessions, possible future configurations of the infrastructure of a separate drainage service are envisioned, including such source control measures as trenches, porous structures, swales, ponds, and road ditches.
- The non-profit EGEB and the citizens' committees report their proposed solutions and negotiate the implementation of the separate service with the municipality, the regional department for the environment, and local real estate developers.

Ilôt d'Eau is another co-production of environmental measures designed to implement a separate drainage service. Citizens living in the same urban block collaborate with a non-profit platform for urban design and research called Latitude, two local architectural design schools, existing citizens' committees (again including the Comité Stop Inondations Saint-Denis), and with officials from the local municipality on the design of source control operations, which could be key components of the future separate storm water service. Ilôt d'Eau includes four main steps:

- For neighbourhood and urban block analysis and design, citizens inhabiting the same urban block join with architectural students and designers, civil servants, and various experts in a workshop designed to explore water-related interdependency between the urban block and the larger neighbourhood. Among the visions for the future that emerge from these workshops are source control solutions at the urban block level that are consistent with a separate drainage system and that take into account the diagnoses and solutions co-produced in the Balade Verte et Bleue.
- For the purpose of analysing households and designing household collectives, small groups of citizens who inhabit the same urban block and share the same source control solution(s) further elaborate their proposals in light of detailed analyses of inflows, outflows, and water usage at the household level.
- Next come the processes of negotiation and paperwork, as the household collectives, supported by the aforementioned Latitude, work

with the municipality to connect source control solutions of the urban block with the separated drainage system in the public space. The same solutions are framed within existing municipal and regional incentive schemes so that the citizens' collective can be in a position to receive financial support.

- Through a process of self-construction, citizens and architectural designers and students, supported by the local non-profit organization Casablanco, which specializes in works construction and rehabilitation into working life, join together to implement the source control solutions.

Experiences

As noted above, the Comité Stop Inondations Saint-Denis in the municipality of Forest was established in 2007. Since that time, the quest for a separate storm water drainage system as a means to confront problems caused by flooding has expanded to involve some 100 citizens, a dozen citizens' committees, a number of local non-profit associations, and various professionals and civil servants. In the process, the project's aims have moved beyond raising awareness and disseminating information to action-oriented and community-organized advocacy for social change.

Although the municipal institutions directly responsible for the combined drainage service have been only marginally involved, the citizens' committee and the EGEB found a way to engage them in public assemblies at which possible solutions to drainage problems are presented and discussed (Nalpas et al., 2015). Furthermore, the Brussels Capital Region, which is responsible for the surface drainage system (including ponds and existing open-air streams), and which would be in charge of the separate drainage service in the future, has shown a keen interest in this effort. Thus the Balade Verte et Bleue, which again was first established in various areas of the municipality of Forest, and Ilôt d'Eau, established in two urban blocks of the same municipality, are now to be implemented in other municipalities throughout the Brussels Capital Region with the support of regional funds for scientific research and innovation from the local research institute Innoviris.

The Balade Verte et Bleue and Ilôt d'Eau initiatives thus demonstrate that citizens are willing to engage with environmental issues. Concern for the management of water in the neighbourhood of Forest was certainly heightened by the area's history of damaging flood events. In addition to the desire to confront this shared problem, another key factor in the success of these initiatives was their capacity over time to attract the attention of local academics as well as other regional associations working on the same environmental matters. These alliances proved to be significant in the procurement of the municipal and regional funding needed to expand Balade Verte et Bleue and Ilôt d'Eau.

References

Manzini, E. and Rizzo, F. (2011). Small Projects/Large Changes: Participatory Design as an Open Participated Process. *CoDesign*, (7, 3–4), 199–215.

Nalpas, D., Debatty, F. and Bastin, M. (2015). Cahier 1. Introduction générale. In D. Nalpas and M. Bastin (eds.), *Actes d'une naissance annoncée. Versant solidaire de Forest*, 1–20. Belgium: EGEB, Brussels.

Ranzato, M. and Bortolotti, A. (2015). Towards Water Sensitive Co-Design in Brussels: The Forest Case Study. In K. Donyun, K. Sungah, T. Schuetze, S. Saehyung, T. Hendrik, C. Lorenzo, O. York, and W. Marc (eds.), *8th Conference of the International Forum on Urbanism (IFoU) True Smart & Green City?* International Forum on Urbanism, 22–24 June 2015, Incheon, Korea, pp. 1–15.

14.2 Case Study—Co-Producing Flood Risk Governance in England, the Netherlands and Flanders

Hannelore Mees

Introduction

The prevention of flood damage appears at first sight to be a classic example of a service to be delivered by the state; it would be inefficient for each citizen to provide his own protection and the benefits of collective protection infrastructure are independent of its number of users and non-excludable (Meijerink and Dicke, 2008; Geaves and Penning-Rowsell, 2016). This case chapter gives a short overview on how citizen co-production emerged in the discourse and practice of flood risk governance in England (UK), the Netherlands and Flanders (Belgium). A more detailed analysis can be found in Mees (2017).

Background

Both in England, the Netherlands and Flanders, policymakers advocate an increased citizen involvement in the implementation of flood risk measures, albeit in divergent forms and degrees. Mees et al. (2016) observed that the prevalent discourses on co-produced flood risk governance are founded on three main rationales:

1 Resilience. The projected consequences of climate change and inadequate spatial planning have increased awareness among authorities that floods can no longer be entirely prevented. Consequently, new strategies need to be adopted to make society more resilient to flooding, amongst others by pursuing individual or community-based flood risk measures. This rationale is particularly dominant in the Dutch flood risk governance, which remains strongly focused on public flood protection. Here, citizen co-production is considered to be part of contingency planning, as a back-up system in case the protective infrastructure would fail.

2 Efficiency. In recent decades, increasing emphasis in England and Flanders is put on the efficiency of flood risk governance. By including citizens in policy delivery, governments aim to reduce public spending on flood risk governance or to increase its return on investment.

3   Fairness. English and Flemish policymakers sometimes legitimise their discourse on co-production with the stance that the general taxpayer should not bear the full cost of human settlements in flood-prone zones. Instead, its inhabitants should contribute to prevent and reduce flood damage ("beneficiary pays" principle).

Experiences

The ways in which citizens can contribute to the delivery of flood risk governance vary substantially. Generally speaking, individual or community-based flood risk measures can be sorted out into two main categories. First, citizens can take property-level protection measures to make their property flood resistant or resilient, e.g. using waterproof interior materials, installing floodgates, flood resistant wall coatings, etc. By protecting their homes, citizens decrease the necessity for strongly developed protection or damage compensation mechanisms to be provided by the state. Second, citizens can prepare for a flood in an organisational way. For example, inhabitants can develop a neighbourhood flood emergency plan, which stipulates different tasks to be carried out by them in case of a flood event (e.g., monitor water levels, door-to-door warning systems, communication with crisis services, etc.). Moreover, citizens can assist official crisis services, e.g. by filling and distributing sandbags.

Practices of co-production can be observed both in England, Flanders and the Netherlands, but in varying ways and degrees (Mees, 2017). In all countries, coercive co-production is imposed by building regulations: designated floor heights, property-level water storage, etc. In addition, incentivised co-production also exists, whereby authorities encourage citizens to co-produce by providing incentives. Examples are subsidies for property-level protection measures by some Flemish municipalities and awareness-raising campaigns, such as *"Know your flood risk"* (England), *"Overstroom ik?"* (*"Am I flooding?"*, Netherlands) and *"Hoog water zonder kater"* (*"High water without a hangover"*, Flanders). These campaigns aim to increase citizens' knowledge of flood risks and potential individual actions. In England and Flanders, they also stress citizens' co-responsibility for flood risk action.

Both coercive and incentivised co-production are initiated by governmental bodies and include one-way interaction between these authorities and citizens. Co-produced flood risk governance can, however, also be established in deliberation between both actors. Examples hereof are the so-called *flood action groups* (FAGs) in England. These groups unite residents from flood-prone areas to collectively address flood risks through community-based actions, next to lobbying for flood protection towards the government. The activities performed by FAGs vary but the formation of *community flood action plans* is a common task. The action plans are drafted in deliberation with governmental bodies and include measures to be implemented by governments and citizens. Consequently, the FAGs both co-create and co-produce. In many cases, this form of co-creation and co-production has developed bottom-up, i.e. initiated by the local residents. FAGs can, however, also be established on the initiative of a government, i.e. top-down. In 2012, for instance, the English government launched the Flood Resilience Community Pathfinder scheme, whereby 13 pilot projects were funded to make communities more resilient to flooding (Defra, 2012). In several of these pilots, the creation of FAGs belonged to the project's deliverables.

In England, citizen co-production is far more developed than is the case in the Netherlands or Flanders. This conclusion relates both to coercive and incentivised co-production, combined co-creation and co-production, infrastructural and organisational measures, and individual and community-based co-production. An exception is formed by the countries' fire brigade systems, which include volunteering staff in Flanders and the Netherlands but not in England. Overall, co-produced flood risk governance is not a widespread phenomenon in the Netherlands and Flanders, although ever more local cases arise in which citizens are encouraged to take flood risk actions either through the provision of information and/or subsidies, or through a deliberative partnership between authorities and citizens.

References

Defra. (2012). *Flood Resilience Community Pathfinder Prospectus.* London: Department for Environment, Food and Rural Affairs.

Geaves, L. H., & Penning-Rowsell, E. C. (2016). Flood Risk Management as a Public or a Private Good, and the Implications for Stakeholder Engagement. *Environmental Science & Policy,* (55), 281–291.

Mees, H. (2017). *Co-Producing Flood Risk Governance Between Authorities and Citizens in Flanders and Abroad. How 'co' Can We Go?* Antwerp: University of Antwerp, Dissertation for the obtainment of a degree as Doctor in the Social Sciences.

Mees, H., Crabbé, A., Alexander, M., Kaufmann, M., Bruzzone, S., Lévy, L. and Lewandowski, J. (2016). Coproducing Flood Risk Management Through Citizen Involvement: Insights from Cross-Country Comparison in Europe. *Ecology and Society,* (21, 3), 7.

Meijerink, S. and Dicke, W. (2008). Shifts in the Public—Private Divide in Flood Management. *International Journal of Water Resources Development,* (24, 4), 499–512.

15 Co-Production in Community Development

Daphne Vanleene and Bram Verschuere

Introduction

Community development is a good case to assess how co-creation and co-production can have an impact on local neighbourhoods. One often-used illustration of the success of co-production in community development is the well-known case of Porto Alegre in Brazil. This project highlights the improvement of the local infrastructure, education, health and social care through the use of co-production, and finds its origin in co-productive community development (Ackerman, 2004; Bovaird, 2007).

This case shows that 'community development' can have a variety of intended outcomes, and is not as straightforward as it sounds. The aim of community development is more than simply improving the social bonding of a neighbourhood's community (i.e. developing community), as it also includes betterment of the citizens' socioeconomic position, by acquiring skills and knowledge, and the citizens' living environment, by improving the neighbourhood's image, through urban planning or community policing, where citizens aid in lowering crime rates.

Community Development Inherently is Co-Production

In 1955, The United Nations offered a first, relatively, clear definition of community development, which has been reused and re-established since: "*Community development can be tentatively defined as a process designed to create conditions of economic and social progress for the whole community with its active participation and the fullest possible reliance upon the community's initiative*" (United Nations, 1955, p.6). The whole aim of community development is to reduce societal and social issues that have an impact on most or even all residents of the community, like poor housing conditions, bad public infrastructure, high unemployment levels and poverty, high crime rates and so on. Community development principally aims at implementing solutions, via concrete and tangible actions, in a collective manner with necessary input from the residents themselves (Verschuere and Hermans, 2016). As such, it can be considered as a kind of community based 'movement for social change', in which two types of partners are active: professional community workers and the residents of the neighbourhood in which community development projects are implemented (Gilchrist and Taylor, 2016). As the social and societal issues in the neighbourhood are often complex and multi-dimensional, community development practices also require multidimensional, innovative and creative thinking and action, to boost effective positive outcomes (Gilchrist and Taylor, 2016; Phillips and Pittman, 2014).

Community development is also inherently 'co-productive' and 'co-creative' in nature. We consider community development in the general sense as *the collective and joint action of professionals and people in communities, in the fight for the betterment of their environment.* Therefore co-production in community development can be seen as the different strategies with which these paid employees and residents work together to improve the community's liveability or 'betterment' (Batten, 1974; Craig, Popple, and Shaw, 2008; SCDC, 2011). These strategies can be deployed in the design-phases (identifying social and societal issues, and identifying possible actions to reverse the issues) and the implementation phases (deployment of community development projects), making community development an example of both co-creation and co-production (see Brandsen and Honingh in this volume, chapter 2).

To substantiate this, we use the example in which community development workers (the professionals) and residents re-purpose a public space to create a green and healthy environment in their neighbourhood, with the purpose of increasing the neighbourhood's liveability (Vanleene, Voets and Verschuere, 2017) (see also the case study by Vanleene and Verschuere in this volume, chapter 18.2):

1   Citizens can *design*, by providing new ideas and feedback on the project and propose changes to the public space to their needs. For example, residents could request a playground, a bicycle repair shop or even a communal bread oven in their community garden.
2   Citizens are needed for the *implementation* of the community development services as well, as their participation is inherent to keep the project afloat. After all, without the citizens' support and input, there is no effective increased social cohesion, nor an increased sense of civic responsibility to keep the communal space, and neighbourhood, clear and safe. For example, citizens could be paramount to keep up the garden, safeguard the communal space and/or befriend one another.

In sum, co-production in community development may be different from co-production in other policy domains like health care, safety or education. First, co-production seems to be an inherent feature of community development, whereas in the other policy fields mentioned, services can be produced and created without any real input from citizens/consumers.

If people do not contribute, the community cannot develop in the 'right' direction. Secondly, the aim of community development can be very heterogeneous, and is always aimed at benefits for the whole community: improving living conditions, empowering people, fighting social and societal issues in the community. This makes the 'outcome' of community development not always tangible, or with consequences for individuals alone. This contrasts to a certain extent with the features and outcomes of co-production in other policy domains (e.g. co-production with the aim of becoming a healthy or educated person, or personal safety).

Co-Producers in Community Development

In the literature, citizens are often considered the experts who can best respond to the neighbourhood's opportunities and issues (Brandsen, Trommel and Verschuere, 2014; Durose, 2011; Gilchrist and Taylor, 2016). Hence the importance of taking residents on board of local community development projects.

Community development projects regularly take place in so-called derelict neighbourhoods with many different social issues. In such neighbourhoods, community development workers target hard-to-reach populations and vulnerable groups, to engage them in the participation processes. This highlights the first interesting feature of co-production projects in community development, as they specifically engage with residents of disadvantaged neighbourhoods, and also citizens with a low socioeconomic status (SES) (Craig et al., 2008; Jakobsen, 2013; Vanleene, Verschuere and Voets, 2015). We can again refer to the case of Porto Alegre, which first started off as participatory budgeting project, but eventually was extended to projects that led to improved infrastructure, education, health and social care.

This is interesting, given the often mentioned 'usual suspects syndrome' of citizen participation, meaning that participation projects are dominated by white, middle-aged, educated men (Goodlad, Burton and Croft, 2005; Jakobsen, 2013; Verba, Schlozman and Brady, 1995). Community development projects show that governments can indeed also engage with people that do not belong to this group.

This is not to say that engaging people in neighbourhoods that have a certain level of deprivation is easy. In their study, Ross, Mirowsky and Pribesh (2001) found that residents in a disadvantaged position are often more mistrusting, and may have a higher sense of powerlessness. Moreover, as Batten (1974) states, people cannot 'want what they don't know exists', which can be specifically true for those disadvantaged minorities. The role of the professionals that coordinate community development projects thus becomes essential for the success of the co-production project (see also Steen and Tuurnas in this volume, chapter 8).

Previous research already revealed the important role professionals play: they 'ask', 'enable' and 'respond' (de Graaf, van Hulst and Michels,

2015; Durose, 2011). Adapted from a political participation model, these researchers identified and applied a set of roles for the professionals who provide community development in disadvantaged neighbourhoods. These professionals identify the marginalised groups (ask), specifically encourage participation of those groups that are often excluded from society (enable) and respond to the needs and wishes of their target group. This shows that professionals are crucial in order for co-production in community development to work: they ensure that the target group is reached, that they can easily participate and that issues or questions from citizens can be heard and responded to (see also Verschuere, Vanleene, Steen and Brandsen in this volume). From this it is clear that the professional support may be very important to determine the motivations and incentives of citizens to participate in co-productive community development.

Furthermore, it is critical that the needs of residents are integrated in the community development projects, in order to motivate participation (Tuurnas, 2016; Verschuere, Brandsen and Pestoff, 2012). Community development needs to lead to real improvement in the eyes of the participants, in order to keep them engaged (Halvorsen, 2003). This implies that co-production needs to focus on what is salient (or interesting) for residents to engage in (Pestoff, 2012). Blakeley and Evans (2009), who researched co-producers' motives in an urban regeneration project in East Manchester, found that the majority of the respondents had experienced the decline of their neighbourhood, and were motivated because of their attachment to the physical neighbourhood and their neighbours. By participating, the majority of these residents felt they could contribute to the betterment of their neighbourhood. Likewise, Denters and Klok (2010) studied a co-creation project where hard-to-reach residents overcame their hesitation and lack of competence to participate in rebuilding their neighbourhood following an explosion of the nearby fireworks factory. Even though this case was extraordinary, as citizens were displaced and houses were destroyed, the attachment to the neighbourhood still provided the major incentive to participate. Furthermore, the presence of a committed professional—who could listen and mould the projects to the citizens' needs—had a significant impact that lowered the threshold for less competent citizens to engage (Denters and Klok, 2010).

Effects of Co-Produced Community Development

As already discussed above, with community development, a variety of outcomes, aimed at the betterment of the neighbourhood, can be intended. This 'betterment of the neighbourhood' refers to the creation of social cohesion (Van Dooren and Thijssen, 2015), but also to the improved physical appearance of a neighbourhood, e.g. through urban planning (Denters and Klok, 2010), and may even be used when attempting to lower crime rates and increase a sense of safety, e.g. through community policing (van Eijk, Steen and Verschuere, 2017; Verschuere and Carette, 2016). Co-productive strategies in community development can take on numerous shapes, for example city gardening (Vanleene et al., 2017), art workshops and cultural activities (Tuurnas, 2015), or urban redevelopment (Denters and Klok, 2010). Looking at potential effects, we can discern between different effects: direct results in terms of betterment of the neighbourhood and integration of people in their neighbourhood, or more indirect effects like empowerment of people, increased social capital and changed attitudes of people towards (local) government.

Direct Results: A Better Neighbourhood to Live In

Direct 'betterment' of the neighbourhood can come in many forms. For example through environmental change, e.g. the neighbourhood is physically improved, safer and/or cleaner (Batten, 1974). These direct cases of community development are often the basis for researchers to study the process of co-production and motives of co-producers. The studies done by Blakeley and Evans (2009) and Denters and Klok (2010) showcase these classical types of 'community development', as both projects where created with the aim of improving the physical neighbourhood. Vanleene et al. (2017) studied the case of a public garden which is used as a tool to enhance the citizens' sense of ownership of their neighbourhood and thus create a cleaner and safer neighbourhood through co-production. A similar tool in co-productive community development is community policing, which improves the citizens' sense of safety and thus their vision of the neighbourhood (van Eijk et al., 2017).

Another direct effect may be the integration of people in their neighbourhood. Due to its focus on derelict neighbourhoods, and the commonly accepted idea of the citizen expert, several authors have researched whether co-production in community development actually achieves the inclusion of people in their neighbourhood. This is what Strokosch and Osborne (2016) found when researching asylum seekers in Scotland. In their study it became apparent that involving these asylum seekers in co-production, therefore allowing them to act in an unofficial capacity as citizens, promotes further integration. Similarly, when Van Bouchaute, Depraetere, Oosterlynck, and Schuermans (2015) researched solidarity in a culturally diverse neighbourhood in Belgium, they discovered co-production's effect on integration. More specifically, they noted that co-productive community development projects, wherein vulnerable groups were engaged, positively affected the integration of these residents and even changed the stigma that surrounds the residents, portraying them as respectable citizens with respect for their environment (see also the case study by Vanleene and Verschuere in this volume, chapter 18.2).

By contrast, in a study on types of exclusion in a Danish urban regeneration program, the predictions regarding the case when it was set up—that it would have difficulty integrating certain segments of the population—turned out to be a self-fulfilling prophecy, as exclusion of these exact groups became apparent a decade later (Agger and Larsen, 2009). The reasons for exclusion were reflected in Lombard's (2013) study in Mexico, where the economic situation of residents as well as a lack of political focus and powerful opponents re-establish existing inequalities in the neighbourhood. However, in the study, Lombard (2013) also notes that citizen participation is not the cause of the exclusion, it simply inadvertently reproduces the pre-existing imbalance. These studies both indicate the lack of, and thus need for, professional support in co-productive community development if the aim is to ensure inclusion (de Graaf et al., 2015).

As is the case in Vanleene et al.'s (2017) study, the projects' clear and direct results, a garden, a clean neighbourhood, integration, are not always the sole purpose of the co-production venture. These tangible results could also lead to other, more indirect effects.

Indirect Effects: Competent, Empowered and Trusting Citizens

Co-productive community development can also lead to a series of indirect effects, such as the social and personal progress of the participants: the citizens' competence, empowerment and renewed trust in their government.

Planning theory, as presented by Van Dooren and Thijssen (2015), suggests that the direct effect of creating a physically 'better' neighbourhood, for example by creating a variation of functions in the neighbourhood (working, shopping, residing. . .), can strengthen and craft social networks which in turn will enhance active citizen participation. As stated above, it is assumed that minority groups are often excluded. And one cause often mentioned is their low competence, i.e., having the ability and resources to participate, which is largely based on income and education. But through co-productive community development, by providing new forms of participation and creating new ways of responding to these differences, that inequity can be overcome (John, 2009). Moreover, through development and training, co-production can actually strengthen the skills and knowledge of the co-producers (Simmons and Birchall, 2005; Vanleene, Verschuere and Voets, 2016). Meanwhile, once they crossed that threshold, citizens' skills and competence increases by participating, which in turn contributes to their positive feelings towards government, their community and democracy as a whole (de Graaf et al., 2015).

This leads to another indirect effect that is expected from co-production in community development, that is the changing view of citizens towards their government. As stated previously, it is often assumed that disadvantaged residents and minorities are more mistrusting and have a higher sense of powerlessness (Ross et al., 2001). Yet co-production is expected to reduce this democratic deficit and increase trust and transparency (Durose, 2011) (see also Fledderus in this volume, chapter 19).

Based on the idea of deliberative democracy, both Goodlad et al. (2005) and Bovaird, Stoker, Jones, Loeffler, and Pinilla Roncancio (2016) state that involving the community is a way to strengthen democratic practice from the bottom up. Gaventa and Barrett (2012), who compared a sample of a hundred research studies, but also Fung and Wright (2003) in their evaluation of five deliberative democracy experiments, concluded that engaging citizens in local community development strengthens their sense of citizenship, and thus empowers. These empowered citizens, and their renewed relationship with government, then create stronger alliances which in turn could contribute to a more responsive and accountable (local) government. Co-production in community development therefore leads to greater citizen satisfaction, and to less complaints and misunderstandings (Marschall, 2004). Particularly in developing countries, as stated by Ostrom (1996), co-production is crucial to achieving higher levels of welfare and combatting corruption.

Discussion

Community development offers an important and unique viewpoint on co-creation and co-production with vulnerable groups. As Goodlad et al. (2005) point out, neglected neighbourhoods can be particularly challenging locations for co-production because of their history, the high levels of distrust of institutions and typically low levels of activism by residents. With growing diversity and individualisation across the world, community development can offer an interesting site to research hard-to-reach populations (Aigner, Flora and Hernandez, 2001; Strokosch and Osborne, 2016; Wagenaar, 2007). Moreover, it allows for a more diverse population of co-producers which in turn overcomes the classic effect of the 'usual suspects' as mentioned by Verba et al. (1995) and Goodlad et al. (2005).

However, from this chapter we can derive some remaining questions that should be investigated in future studies. First and foremost, as stated above, community development has a very holistic goal: 'betterment for the neighbourhood'. As seen in the variety of cases mentioned and the broad subdivision in effects, this is incredibly non-specific and could lead us to question the importance of the field. For, if everything is betterment, then how does co-productive community development actually contribute? In this we echo the argument of Tuurnas (2016) that there is the risk that co-production becomes a trend, co-production for the sake of co-production. This is an issue that can become particularly prevalent in community development, which is inherently co-productive and co-creative in nature. Without a more clearly defined mission, output and/or outcomes, this is the perfect example of co-production for the sake of co-production. The inclusion, empowerment and equity of the citizen co-producers, as well as transparency and trustworthiness of the participating governments, are not always tangible results and can each be an unintended benefit resulting from co-productive community development with a different goal. For example, as citizens' skills and competence increase through co-production, so do their positive feelings towards government, their community and democracy as a whole (de Graaf et al., 2015). This is not particularly a negative consequence, but, for researchers to qualitatively evaluate, advise and support community development projects, its basis should be clarified. It could thus be a suggestion for future researchers to research different community development goals and the direct and indirect results and establish a systematic evaluation of the resulting effects of community development projects and its successes. As stated before, community development needs to lead to real improvement in the eyes of the participants, in order to keep them engaged (Halvorsen, 2003; Tuurnas, 2016; Verschuere et al., 2012).

Secondly, in community development, the element of 'place' or 'location' may be an important factor that influences the processes and conditions of co-production. The community of people taking part in the co-production process is directly linked to the neighbourhood where this community lives. In other words, there are spatial borders within which the co-producers participate, and within which the outcome of co-produced community development becomes visible (nicer neighbourhood), or is 'consumed' (consequences for the residents). This 'spatial dimension' is not only physical, in the sense of a delineated neighbourhood. 'Space' can also be conceptualised as the general socioeconomic conditions in the neighbourhood: for example, average levels of welfare, education, poverty and employment in the neighbourhood, or levels of cultural diversity. Such location-specific features may influence the dynamics of co-production, not only but certainly in co-produced community development, and future research should be well aware of these specific spatial features.

This leads us to a final issue, the impact of engaged employees. It may be the case in community development (but also in other policy domains) that professional support may be very important to determine the motivations and incentives of citizens to participate. And though de Graaf et al. (2015) and Durose (2011) offer a first idea as to the importance of community development workers, research on the role and impact of the employees within the co-productive community development effort is still underrepresented. For when, how and what can they do to encourage co-production in community development? And what should they not do? Moreover, what impact do they have on the subsequent effects of the community development project?

References

Ackerman, J. (2004). Co-Governance for Accountability: Beyond 'exit' and 'voice'. *World Development*, (32, 3), 447–463.

Agger, A. and Larsen, J. N. (2009). Exclusion in Area-Based Urban Policy Programmes. *European Planning Studies*, (17, 7), 1085–1099.

Aigner, S. M., Flora, C. B. and Hernandez, J. M. (2001). The Premise and Promise of Citizenship and Civil Society for Renewing Democracies and Empowering Sustainable Communities. *Sociological Inquiry*, (71, 4), 493–507.

Batten, T. R. (1974). The Major Issues and Future Direction of Community Development. *Community Development Journal*, (9, 2), 96–103.

Blakeley, G. and Evans, B. (2009). Who Participates, How and Why in Urban Regeneration Projects? The Case of the New 'City' of East Manchester. *Social Policy & Administration*, (43, 1), 15–32.

Bovaird, T. (2007). Beyond Engagement and Participation: User and Community Coproduction of Public Services. *Public Administration Review*, (67, 5), 846–860.

Bovaird, T., Stoker, G., Jones, T., Loeffler, E. and Pinilla Roncancio, M. (2016). Activating Collective Co-Production of Public Services: Influencing Citizens to Participate in Complex Governance Mechanisms in the UK. *International Review of Administrative Sciences*, (82, 1), 47–68.

Brandsen, T., Trommel, W. and Verschuere, B. (2014). *Manufactured Civil Society: Practices, Principles and Effects*. London: Palgrave Macmillan.

Craig, G., Popple, K. and Shaw, M. (2008). *Community Development in Theory and Practice: An International Reader*. Nottingham: *Spokesman*.

de Graaf, L., van Hulst, M. and Michels, A. (2015). Enhancing Participation in Disadvantaged Urban Neighbourhoods. *Local Government Studies*, (41, 1), 44–62.

Denters, B. and Klok, P.-J. (2010). Rebuilding Roombeek: Patterns of Citizen Participation in Urban Governance. *Urban Affairs Review*, (45, 5), 583–607.

Durose, C. (2011). Revisiting Lipsky: Front-Line Work in UK Local Governance. *Political Studies*, (59, 4), 978–995.

Fung, A. and Wright, E. O. (2003). Deepening Democracy: Institutional Innovations in Empowered Participatory Governance. *Politics & Society*, (29, 1), 5–41.

Gaventa, J. and Barrett, G. (2012). Mapping the Outcomes of Citizen Engagement. *World Development*, (40, 12), 2399–2410.

Gilchrist, A. and Taylor, M. (2016). *The Short Guide to Community Development*. Bristol: Policy Press.

Goodlad, R., Burton, P. and Croft, J. (2005). Effectiveness at What? The Processes and Impact of Community Involvement in Area-Based Initiatives. *Environment and Planning C-Government and Policy*, (23, 6), 923–938.

Halvorsen, K. E. (2003). Assessing the Effects of Public Participation. *Public Administration Review*, (63, 5), 535–543.

Jakobsen, M. (2013). Can Government Initiatives Increase Citizen Coproduction? Results of a Randomized Field Experiment. *Journal of Public Administration Research and Theory*, (23, 1), 27–54.

John, P. (2009). Can Citizen Governance Redress the Representative Bias of Political Participation? *Public Administration Review*, (69, 3), 494–503.

Lombard, M. (2013). Citizen Participation in Urban Governance in the Context of Democratization: Evidence from Low-Income Neighbourhoods in Mexico. *International Journal of Urban and Regional Research*, (37, 1), 135–150.

Marschall, M. J. (2004). Citizen Participation and the Neighborhood Context: A New Look at the Coproduction of Local Public Goods. *Political Research Quarterly*, (57, 2), 231–244.

Ostrom, E. (1996). Crossing the Great Divide: Coproduction, Synergy, and Development. *World Development*, (24, 6), 1073–1087.

Pestoff, V. (2012). Co-Production and Third Sector Social Services in Europe: Some Concepts and Evidence. *Voluntas*, (23, 4), 1102–1118.

Phillips, R. and Pittman, R. (2014). *An Introduction to Community Development, Second Edition*. Milton Park: Routledge.

Ross, C. E., Mirowsky, J. and Pribesh, S. (2001). Powerlessness and the Amplification of Threat: Neighborhood Disadvantage, Disorder, and Mistrust. *American Sociological Review*, 568–591.

SCDC. (2011). *Community Development and Co-Production. Issues for Policy and Practice*. SCDC Discussion Paper, Scottish Community Development Centre.

Simmons, R. and Birchall, J. (2005). A Joined-Up Approach to User Participation in Public Services: Strengthening the 'participation chain'. *Social Policy & Administration*, (39, 3), 260–283.

Strokosch, K. and Osborne, S. (2016). Asylum Seekers and the Co-Production of Public Services. *Journal of Social Policy*, (45, 4), 673–690.

Tuurnas, S. (2015). Learning to Co-Produce? The Perspective of Public Service Professionals. *International Journal of Public Sector Management*, (28, 7), 583–598.

Tuurnas, S. (2016). Looking Beyond the Simplistic Ideals of Participatory Projects: Fostering Effective Co-Production? *International Journal of Public Administration*, (39, 13), 1077–1087.

United Nations. (1955). *Social Progress Through Community Development*. New York: United Nations.

Van Bouchaute, B., Depraetere, A., Oosterlynck, S. and Schuermans, N. (2015). Solidariteit in superdiversiteit: het transformatief potentieel van een complementaire munt in een superdiverse wijk. www.solidariteitdiversiteit.be/publicaties.php (consulted November 2017)

Van Dooren, W., & Thijssen, P. (2015). Who You Are/Where You Live. Do Neighbourhood Characteristics Explain Coproduction. *International Review of Administrative Sciences*, (81, 2).

van Eijk, C., Steen, T. and Verschuere, B. (2017). Co-Producing Safety in the Local Community: A Q-Methodology Study on the Incentives of Belgian and Dutch Members of Neighbourhood Watch Schemes. *Local Government Studies*, (43, 3), 323–343.

Vanleene, D., Verschuere, B. and Voets, J. (2015). *Co-Producing a Nicer Neighbourhood: Why Do People Participate in Community Development Projects?* Paper presented at the IIAS Workshop on Coproduction, Proceedings, Nijmegen, The Netherlands.

Vanleene, D., Verschuere, B. and Voets, J. (2016). *The Democratic Quality of Co-Production in Community Development: A Pilot Study in the Rabot Neighbourhood in Ghent, Belgium*. Paper presented at the EGPA Permanent Study Group VIII: Civil Society, Citizens and Government, Utrecht, The Netherlands.

Vanleene, D., Voets, J. and Verschuere, B. (2017). Co-Producing a Nicer Neighbourhood: Why Do People Participate in Local Community Development Projects? *Lex Localis-Journal of Local Self-Government*, (15, 1), 111–132.

Verba, S., Schlozman, K. L. and Brady, H. E. (1995). *Voice and Equality: Civic Voluntarism in American Politics*. Cambridge, MA: Harvard University Press.

Verschuere, B., Brandsen, T. and Pestoff, V. (2012). Co-Production: The State of the Art in Research and the Future Agenda. *Voluntas*, (23, 4), 1083–1101.

Verschuere, B. and Carette, P. (2016). Coproductie van veiligheid in buurtinformatienetwerken: een analyse van gepercipieerde meerwaarde. *Vlaams Tijdschrift voor Overheidsmanagement*, (3), 61–69.

Verschuere, B. and Hermans, K. (2016). *Welzijn in Vlaanderen: beleid, bestuurlijke organisatie en uitdagingen*. Brugge: Die Keure.

Wagenaar, H. (2007). Governance, Complexity, and Democratic Participation—How Citizens and Public Officials Harness the Complexities of Neighborhood Decline. *American Review of Public Administration*, (37, 1), 17–50.

15.1 Case Study—Co-Production and Community Development in France

Caitlin McMullin

Introduction

Across France, associations called *'centres sociaux'*, which roughly translates to social centres in English (*social* as in social services, rather than social club), provide a range of services and activities to promote community development. These associations are based on the ideals of the settlement movement that originated in the United States and England, which aimed to bridge the gap between rich and poor by advocating middle class volunteers working alongside the poor in locally based settlement houses to provide services such as education, training, childcare and healthcare (Durand, 1996). Social centres continue this tradition by acting as community development organisations and community centres, promoting activities to support active citizenship and social cohesion. There are now over 2,000 such social centres across France.

Social centres are unique in promoting a distinct approach of co-creation and co-production, in the sense that they mainstream the notion of collaboration between citizens and professionals through their very definition and founding values. Despite this approach, the word 'co-production' itself is little used in France, with a preference for terms such as 'co-construction' and simply 'participation' being used to describe these activities. Co-production takes place between professionals and local residents at the stage of planning and defining organisational strategy, as well as in delivering services and projects. This case study chapter focuses in particular on five social centres located in Lyon and the ways in which co-production has developed and takes place.

Background

The idea of 'community development' is one that is to an extent difficult to reconcile with French political traditions, which equate the notion of 'community' with communitarianism and thus a splintering of groups that refuse to adhere to the ideal of French Republicanism. Nevertheless, social centres arguably can be considered to promote community development, whereby individual citizens come together to take collective action to solve common problems in an area. To be deemed a social centre, an association must sign the Federal Charter of French Social Centres, which defines a social centre as the following:

> The social and socio-cultural centre aims to be a centre of initiatives brought by associated residents, supported by professionals, who are able to define and implement a social development project for the entire population of a local area.
>
> (Charte Fédérale des Centres Sociaux et Socio-Culturels de France, 2000)

Signing this charter also means that an organisation agrees to adhere to three founding values—human dignity, solidarity and democracy.

- *Human dignity* refers to the importance of respecting each individual's liberty and individuality, and *laïcité* (the particularly French concept of secularity which insists on a strict separation between religion and public life).
- *Solidarity* refers to the importance of social cohesion through supporting active citizenship, links between neighbours and associative engagement.
- Finally, *democracy* is key for social centres in order to promote an 'open society, open to debate and the sharing of power' (Charte Fédérale des Centres Sociaux et Socio-Culturels de France, 2000).

The idea of co-production—despite the term itself not being used—is actually thus enshrined in the very definition of social centres as organisations. In signing the charter, an organisation explicitly commits to promoting citizen participation and social solidarity. Involving local people in developing and delivering projects is framed as being about supporting active citizenship and social cohesion, and advancing the values outlined by the National Federation of Social Centres.

Experiences

In Lyon, there are 16 social centres, most of which were founded when there was considerable government investment in the social sector in the 1970s and 1980s. Social centres are primarily funded by local and national government grants, which are allocated by and large to support the broad aims of social cohesion and active citizenship promoted by the social centre movement. In practice, co-production in the Lyon social centres takes place in two main areas—the creation of organisational strategies and plans, and the promotion and support of citizen-led projects.

Co-creation takes place by social centres in the development of strategic organisational plans. One of the requirements of being designated a social centre is that an association must develop a multi-year 'social plan' in conjunction with local inhabitants, which specifies the association's priorities and the ways in which the organisation will put these into action in partnership with local people and other local associations. Co-planning or co-prioritisation is undertaken with local residents in a variety of ways by the five social centres in Lyon. Whilst some social centres rely on traditional consultation methods to engage with local residents, others have developed innovative methods of co-planning and co-design between professionals and residents. For example, the social plan of one social centre was developed through collaboration with local residents through a project of writing aims and wishes on paper light bulbs that were hung throughout the community centre. Other social centres hold events so that local residents and paid professionals can collaborate to determine the direction of the organisation.

Secondly, social centres undertake co-production in promoting projects that are citizen-led and supported by paid professionals. At one social centre, a local resident suggested the idea of a weekly community picnic during August when the social centre building was closed. Paid staff at the social centre supported the resident by designing and distributing flyers, and organising necessary permits for the picnics, whilst the local residents recruited volunteers and brought food, drinks and activities to the picnics. Another social centre highlighted the importance of co-production in their activities for local young people. Teenagers at the social centre's youth club expressed the desire to develop a volunteering and fundraising project to build an orphanage in Africa, which was then supported by staff at the organisation, helping them to develop the necessary skills, and find funding and resources. These two examples highlight the ways in which social centres prioritise citizen empowerment (or '*pouvoir d'agir*' in French) through co-production.

References

Charte Fédérale des Centres Sociaux et Socio-Culturels de France. (2000). Texte adopté par l'Assemblée générale d'Angers, 17–18, 2000. [Online].
Durand, R. (1996). *Histoire des centres sociaux: du voisinage à la citoyenneté*. Paris: La Découverte.

16 Providing Public Safety and Public Order Through Co-Production

Elke Loeffler

This chapter discusses key conceptual issues of co-production in public safety and public order. It provides quantitative data on the extent of co-production in public safety, with a comparison across European countries. This is followed by qualitative research, based on international case studies, to explore which co-production approaches are currently in place to improve public safety and public order. Finally, the chapter provides a critical assessment of the benefits, risks, barriers and limits to co-production in public safety and public order.

Conceptual Issues of Co-Production in Public Safety and Public Order

From a public management perspective, there is a natural tendency to look exclusively to law enforcement for solutions to problems of crime and anti-social behaviour (Sabet, 2014, 245). Since Thomas Hobbes and John Locke, the protection of citizens from the state, as well as the protection of citizens from each other by the state, have been considered as core tasks of the modern state.

The prevention and protection of citizens from dangers affecting public safety involves a broad range of government responsibilities, which have evolved over time. While this initially focused on policing and criminal justice, the modern welfare state also provides victim support and probation services. Another sub-set of the wider public and community safety field includes community engagement to reduce or prevent anti-social behaviour. Recently, public safety programmes at different levels of government have focused on issues such as domestic violence, sexual exploitation and cybercrime.

Public safety and public order cannot be "produced" by the state alone and simply be "consumed" by citizens. Instead, it is necessary for citizens to contribute to the delivery of a desirable level of public safety and law and order. As Sabet (2014, 246) points out, despite the common perception promoted by television shows that crimes are solved by brilliant detective work of one key investigator, research clearly shows that the vast majority of cases are resolved because the victim, witnesses or accomplices come forward with information. In other words, "because the police cannot be on every street corner, law enforcement agencies cannot be effective without the support of citizens" (Sabet, 2014, 246).

Percy (1978) provided an early analysis of the wide range of actions through which citizens co-produce public safety and public order with public enforcement agencies. Elinor Ostrom (1978, 102) considered citizens to be positive co-producers in regard to policing when they engaged in activities such as the following:

- "Call upon police when they see something suspicious in the neighbourhood;
- Call the police immediately upon discovery of a victimization;
- Ask their neighbours to watch their home when they are away;
- Mark their property with an engraving pen;
- Purchase lights, locks, fences, dogs, or weapons for their own defence;
- Patrol in their neighbourhood;
- Participate in community organisations that focus on problems of law enforcement".

Building on this, we can distinguish between different intensities of individual or collective forms of co-production to improve public safety and public order, which may be citizen- or user-led.

Co-production of public safety at an individual level may entail preventive measures, such as putting locks on doors, but it also means reporting crime, providing information to the police and serving as witnesses. At the same time, the criminal justice system relies on offenders and victims as "service users" complying with the court process. Public service providers also expect offenders to change their behaviour in a positive sense as a result of their prison sentence or community service. Similar distinctions can be made in relation to collective co-production (Table 16.1).

As early as the 1980s, the research of Elinor Ostrom and her colleagues (Parks et al., 1981) on policing in Chicago pointed out the impact of co-production of public safety: crime rates went up when the city's police officers retreated from the street and lost access to the knowledge and networks of local communities. This showed the police needed the community as much as the community needed the police to improve public safety. As Kappeler and Gaines (2015) point out, community policing is a philosophy and organizational strategy that expands the traditional police mandate of fighting crime to include forming partnerships with citizenry that endorse mutual support and participation.

Clearly, the conceptualization of the "protective state" has evolved in public law over time, and the role of citizens in policing has altered significantly. Kelling and Moore (1988, 5), writing about the USA, suggest that "the proper role of citizens in crime control" in the period up to the

Table 16.1 Intensities of Citizen- and User-Led Co-Production in Public Safety and Public Order

INTENSITY	Individual co-production (citizen-led)	Individual co-production (user-led)	Collective co-production (citizen-led)	Collective co-production (user-led)
Low	Putting locks on doors	Cooperating with court process	Members of neighbourhood watch groups	Attendance at probation meetings
Medium	Reporting crime	Peer training by offenders for young people at risk (see Pawelke, 2011)	Participatory budgeting for police service	Prison councils (see Hine-Hughes, 2011)
High	Witness in court	Changing behaviour to integrate with society	Street watch groups (Meyer and Grosser, 2014)	Peer support groups of probationers

1970s was to be "relatively passive recipients of professional crime control services", whose actions to defend themselves or their communities were regarded as inappropriate, smacking of vigilantism. However, more recently, the rise of community policing has relied on an intimate relationship between police and citizens, e.g. through programmes that emphasize familiarity between citizens and police, using consultations, crime control meetings for police and citizens, assignment to officers of "caseloads" of households with ongoing problems, etc. (Kelling and Moore, 1988, 12). A similar process has been observed in the criminal justice system. O'Brien and Robson (2016, 25) suggest that:

Broadly speaking, between the late 18th century and the mid-to-late 20th century, the system in England and Wales shifted from one based on treating prisoners as rightless objects, to treating people as largely passive subjects with needs and limited rights, and then—to some extent—to a model that recognises prisoners as citizens, with values and capabilities that could and should be nourished.

Furthermore, the legal and social acceptance as to how far co-production in public safety and law and order can go differs between countries. In particular, in administrative law countries, public safety and public order tend to be seen as a core or so-called "sovereign task" of the state. This means that co-production approaches such as community speedwatch schemes are often considered to be against the "law" in Spain or German states, whereas many police forces in the UK actively promote such schemes. More research is needed regarding how these different legal traditions and frameworks impact on the way citizens and public services co-produce public safety and public order.

Finally, the coercive nature of some public interventions in public safety and public order raise the controversial issue as to whether forced collaboration (e.g. an arrested criminal providing the police with information about other criminals) can still be considered as a form of co-production. Brudney and England (1983) and Whitaker (1980) share the view that co-production only involves voluntary, cooperative action in public service delivery—so, if citizens follow laws and regulations because they fear reprisals for their refusal or because they have become habituated to that set of behaviours, they do not see this as co-production. Sharp (1980), however, argues that compliance is included in the meaning of co-production. According to her, co-production is one means by which citizens help to set the "service conditions"—the social and physical environment of service delivery. Alternatively, following the definition of Brandsen and Honingh (this volume, chapter 2), compliance of citizens with laws and regulations can be interpreted as falling in the category "co-production in the implementation of core services". This occurs when citizens are actively engaged in the implementation, but not the design, of an individual service that is at the core of the organization. However, this suggests that "compliance with legal requirements" can indeed be a form of "co-production". Of course, the co-production of better outcomes in public safety or public order does not always require a public service—when parents teach their children to cross roads only when the traffic light is green, so complying with the law and traffic regulations, the contribution of parents and children is likely to improve road safety but in most cases, there is no public "service" involved.

However, individual and collective citizen or user-led co-production to maintain public order is not just about compliance with laws but involves people behaving sensibly and rationally in public spaces, and respecting others. At the same time, public safety is more than the absence of crime—it also involves subjectively perceived safety. It therefore includes crime prevention, crime reporting, support to the victims of crime and restorative justice, all of which require varying contributions from citizens and service users.

The Extent of Co-Production in Public Safety— A Comparison Between Countries

This section briefly explores the role of co-production in the policy field of public safety from an international comparative perspective. It draws on quantitative evidence from a five-country co-production survey undertaken in 2008 (Loeffler et al., 2008) as well as on qualitative evidence from focus groups with public service professionals as part of the 2008 study and a German co-production study commissioned by the Bertelsmann Foundation in 2015 (Loeffler at al., 2015).

This European survey demonstrated significant differences in the extent of co-production between public safety and other public policies and, moreover, across five EU countries (Germany, France, the UK, Denmark and Czech Republic). In particular, it revealed that the level of co-production in public safety is relatively low. This study focused in particular on citizens' contributions to preventative activities in environmental improvement, community safety and health. A co-production index was created to compare the intensity of co-production across the three sectors—it was considerably lower for prevention of crime and even lower for reporting crime to the police/personally intervening to stop anti-social behaviour.

These findings reveal a dilemma: Although the pathbreaking work by Ostrom and colleagues (e.g. Parks et al., 1981) shows the importance of co-production in reducing crime rates, the actual level of co-production in public safety and public order appears relatively low. This requires further research into incentives for co-production, in particular the key question remains how urban residents can be mobilized to participate in collective efforts for a neighbourhood (Sharp, 1978). A study by Sundeen and Siegel (1987) explores the relationship between community and police department characteristics and the intensity of use of citizen auxiliary police officers. Data was obtained from 18 cities in Los Angeles County for comparison. The analysis shows that more extensive volunteering is found in smaller, predominately white communities and that larger, lower income, heterogeneous communities have been less able to activate volunteers. One recent survey of citizens in neighbourhood watch groups in Belgium and the Netherlands suggests that in many cases, the engagement of people to co-produce is triggered by a combination of factors, including personal attributes, individual capabilities (in terms of mastered skills) and self-interest (van Eijk et al., 2017) and that different people may be driven differently to co-produce community safety. Another study by Thijssen and Van Dooren (2016) suggests that co-production activities at a neighbourhood level are not only explained by individual variables but also by neighbourhood characteristics.

The extent to which citizens participate in groups or organizations to improve public safety in their neighbourhood was quite low in all five countries in the European study, but with significant differences between countries (Loeffler et al., 2008): In the UK, 12% of citizens often participate in such activities, and 15% do it sometimes. In Denmark, by contrast, only 7% of citizens do so sometimes and merely 2% do it often. This finding illustrates the influence on co-production of political and social values—there are more than 10 million members in UK neighbourhood watch groups and the police in the UK actively promote co-production by communities. In Denmark the focus group participants shared the view that most Danish citizens expect the welfare state to deal with and solve social issues, as the quotes of two participants at a focus group session in Copenhagen suggest: "... *Danish society is a bit different. Somehow we gave all social affairs to the public sector and people do not want to get involved* ...". "... *as x*

*said, we don't take part in voluntary initiatives as citizens, because the pub-
lic sector is taking care of that . . . it is not like in other countries in which
the involvement of the state is not high . . ."* (Loeffler et al., 2008, 25). Of
course, this was only partly supported by the survey responses of Danish
citizens, many of whom DID co-produce.

Co-Production Approaches to Improving Public Safety and Public Order

In this section, we explore which co-production approaches are currently in
place to improve public safety and law and order, including co-commissioning,
co-design, co-delivery and co-assessment (Loeffler, 2016a, 331–332), and
illustrate these approaches with revealing examples. This concept of co-
production acknowledges that citizens may not only be involved "in the
implementation, but also in the design and initiation of a service" (Brandsen
and Honingh, 2016, 5).

Co-Commissioning of Priority Outcomes in Public Safety and Law and Order

This co-production approach engages service users and/or local communities in the commissioning process to help identify the outcomes which are
important, the priorities between different services and different groups of
service users, and the appropriate choice between service provider models
and providers. While involving service users in commissioning processes
in public safety or law and order is quite exceptional, particularly in
community-based criminal justice services (Weaver and McCulloch, 2012, 10),
there is an increasing number of commissioning initiatives working with
deprived communities, with a focus on improving public safety, such as the
"Listening Events" with local communities in North West Kilmarnock in
Scotland (Bone, 2012).

Co-Design of Improved Pathways to Outcomes in Public Safety and Public Order

Co-design is typically more targeted at improving public services than at
shaping community strategies. It generally involves service providers harnessing creative ideas of service users and/or communities to develop and
test new solutions to achieve better outcomes. While design thinking and
methods are getting increasingly popular in public services, harnessing "user
experience" to improve services in public safety or public order is still not
very common. The UK-based charity User Voice (2016) is majority staffed
and led by people who have experienced the same problems the charity is
seeking to solve. Through service user councils, service users of probation
services can co-design service improvements. Moreover, "community confer-
encing" in restorative justice in many European Countries, the US, Canada

and Australia typically involves offenders, volunteer community representatives and public services co-designing solutions to repair relationships with local people who have been impacted by illegal and inappropriate behaviour.

Co-Delivery of Pathways to Better Outcomes
in Public Safety and Public Order

Co-delivery includes a wide range of approaches of service providers working (directly or indirectly) with service users and/or communities as asset- and skills-holders, role models, success factors and legitimators to achieve improved outcomes. In the policy fields of public safety and law and order, co-delivery is widely used as a co-production approach to promote:

- prevention of crime;
- elevated levels of public order (for example, Kelling and Wilson (1982) demonstrate that community policing may not be able to reduce crime but elevate the level of public order);
- behaviour change of risk groups (e.g. reduction of re-offending, speeding or substance abuse);
- rehabilitation of victims of crime;
- compliance with regulations and desired forms of behaviour.

This often involves community-led forms of co-production such as the co-operation of the police with local Neighbourhood Watch groups in the UK—the largest voluntary movement in England and Wales with around 173,000 coordinators covering 3.8 million households (Neighbourhood Watch, 2017). Other co-delivery schemes involve user-led co-production, such as the peer training of learner drivers by offenders in Austria (Pawelke, 2011).

In the information age, the internet and social media provide the police with new opportunities to engage with the public. For example, a recent study on the use of Twitter by the Canadian police (O'Connor, 2015) suggests Twitter was used to help manage the image of the police and build community. In the Netherlands, the police have been developing and scaling up a new system for engaging citizens in intervening police work called Burgernet (Meijer, 2012, 199–201). Citizens may sign up to the system and provide information about their home or work address which enables the police to contact citizens in a targeted way in real time after a crime has happened. This means that the participating citizens may receive a message from the police asking for help or reassuring them when an issue has been solved. Finally, the promotion of compliance with regulations and desired forms of behaviour may also involve the use of "nudges" (Thaler and Sunstein, 2008). However, Avineri (2014, 36–37) cautions that it may be difficult to achieve sustainable behavioural change just by designing measures based on the nudge approach. Without promoting behaviour change through values and attitudes, the effects of nudges are likely to be cancelled out.

Co-Assessing to what Extent Outcomes have been Improved in Public Safety and Public Order and How Well Stakeholders have Collaborated in Terms of Public Governance Principles

Co-assessment gives service users and/or communities a voice in the assessment of outcomes achieved and evaluation of the quality of co-production between citizens and public services and partnership working between organizations. This is particularly relevant in public safety and public order, as objective performance information (e.g. crime figures) does not necessarily reflect citizens' subjective perception of public safety.

Increasingly, police forces are using social media to engage with citizens, as in the West Midlands Police (Hine-Hughes, 2013). As a result, social media are becoming much more important as a "soft" co-assessment tool, which complements formal complaints mechanisms.

Benefits, Risks, Barriers and Limits to Co-Production In Public Safety

The existing research evidence indicates a range of benefits of co-production in public safety and public order. Given its emphasis on public service evaluation, the most extensive evidence comes from the UK, but some other international studies are relevant.

- *Improved outcomes*: Performance data from the Wiltshire Community Speedwatch Scheme in the UK (Milton, 2011) shows that in December 2015, there were 140 Volunteer Teams active across Wiltshire and Swindon Counties with 765 volunteers carrying out regular speed checks on local roads. The whole ethos of this co-production approach is to educate drivers and to avoid fines, red tape and the need for volunteers to appear in court as witnesses. By 2014 fatal and serious injuries associated with road traffic accidents in Wiltshire had reduced by 35%, compared to the average between 2005–2009; the average reduction for Great Britain during the same period was 22% (Loeffler, 2016b).
- *Behaviour change*: In Surrey County Council, restorative justice approaches have been a key element of working with young people and the victims of their crimes for a number of years. Surrey Youth Support Service is committed to reducing the offending of young people whilst also ensuring high levels of victim satisfaction in the process. Consequently, the Youth Restorative Intervention assists young people to try to repair the harm caused by their actions. An external evaluation published in 2015 revealed that this co-production scheme had led to an 18% reduction in re-offending by young people in Surrey (Surrey County Council, 2015).
- *Improved public services:* In the UK the SOS Gangs Project of the St Giles Trust trains and employs reformed ex-offenders as caseworkers, who provide practical and psychological support to their clients—primarily

other ex-offenders, but also those at risk of offending—to help them to avoid offending and reintegrate themselves into society. This intensive, tailor-made support by ex-offenders with lived experience of the issues facing their clients has been highlighted as a key strength of the project. In interviews with a sample of the SOS Project's current and former clients and partner organization, 87% of client interviewees said that engaging with the SOS Project had changed their attitude to offending and 73% said that it was important that their caseworkers were ex-offenders themselves, as they could relate to them and felt inspired that they too could turn their lives around (Social Innovation Partnership, 2013, 8).

- *Improved public governance:* The governance assessment of a housing estate in Cornwall, undertaken by *Governance International*, involved qualitative assessments by focus groups of local different stakeholders of both key outcomes and governance principles. Many respondents, particularly young parents, felt disturbed or unsafe because of the anti-social behaviour of some troublemakers in their immediate neighbourhood. The feeling of safety was clearly better on those estates where there was a neighbourhood watch scheme, a community worker or a tenants' association (Bovaird and Loeffler, 2007).

At the same time, the perception of risks associated with co-production in public safety varies between countries. For example, in the German co-production study commissioned by the Bertelsmann Foundation (Loeffler et al., 2015), a number of focus group participants—staff working in a range of public services related to public safety—suggested that not all aspects of public safety are suitable for co-production with citizens. One participant thought that "Citizens can only play a subordinate role in police actions to provide security for the population" (Loeffler et al., 2015, 32). Another participant saw the risk that volunteers might behave as "substitute police officers", which could itself disrupt social harmony in the area.

Whereas community speedwatch schemes are very exceptional in Germany, they are actively promoted by the police across the UK, as are a range of other roles for volunteers (www.police.uk/volunteering/). This suggests that the perceptions of risks and barriers to co-production in public safety and public order are strongly linked to different legal frameworks and administrative traditions. Williams et al. (2016) show that a further barrier to co-production in public order is perceived power asymmetry between professionals and citizens, in this case between undergraduate students and campus police, so that professionals and citizens may both undermine each other's contribution to outcomes.

These examples show that the way in which governments assure and provide public safety and public order is changing. More multi-disciplinary research is therefore needed, both at theoretical and empirical levels: social scientists need to engage in a positive and normative debate with public safety and law enforcement agencies to identify the legal implications of co-production between citizens and public services. However, co-production of public safety and public order must also have clearly defined limits in modern states, as the state has the monopoly on the use of physical force (within the limits of the rule of law).

Co-production in public safety may be ineffective or even produce adverse effects when these limits are not recognized. The case study of an American citizen volunteer, who was active in a neighbourhood watch group and shot a "suspicious looking" teenager, highlights multiple public value failures and offers important insights into the often hidden, yet embedded aspect of the "dark side" of co-production (Williams et al., 2015).

At the same time, more empirical research is required on effective pathways to outcomes. In public law and public order, we often deal with complex knowledge domains where it appears unlikely that specific pathways to outcomes will ever be predictable, although the effect of specific co-production approaches in limiting a set of undesirable outcomes or increasing the likelihood of a set of favourable outcomes may be predictable (Bovaird and Loeffler, 2016, 400).

References

Avineri, E. (2014). *Nudging Safe Road Behaviours*. Research Report funded by the Ran Naor Foundation.

Bone, T. (2012). *Reducing Crime and Improving Health in NW Kilmarnock Using Community Assets*. Birmingham: Governance International.

Bovaird, T. and Loeffler, E. (2007). Assessing the Quality of Local Governance: A Case Study of Public Services in Carrick UK. *Public Money & Management*, (7, 2), 293–300.

Bovaird, T. and Loeffler, E. (2016). Public Management and Governance: The Future? In Tony Bovaird and Elke Loeffler (eds.), *Public Management and Governance*, 395–409. Third edition. London: Routledge.

Brudney, J. L. and England, R. F. (1983). Toward a Definition of the Coproduction Concept. *Public Administration Review*, (43, 1), 59–65.

Hine-Hughes, F. (2011). *User Voice's Council Model: Only Offenders Can Stop Re-Offending*. Birmingham: Governance International.

Hine-Hughes, F. (2013). *Follow @wmpolice—How West Midlands Police Engages with Communities*. Birmingham: Governance International.

Kappeler, V. E. and Gaines, L. K. (2015). *Community Policing. A Contemporary Perspective*. Seventh edition. London: Routledge.

Kelling, G. and Moore, M. H. (1988). *The Evolving Strategy of Policing*. Perspectives on Policing Bulletin (No. 4). Washington, DC: U.S. Department of Justice, National Institute of Justice.

Kelling, G. and Wilson, J. Q. (1982). The Police and Neighbourhood Safety: Broken Windows. *The Atlantic Monthly*, (249, 3), 29–38.

Loeffler, E. (2016a). Co-Production of Public Services. In Tony Bovaird and Elke Loeffler (eds.), *Public Management and Governance*, 319–336. Third edition. London: Routledge.

Loeffler, E. (2016b). *Citizen Powered Cities: Co-Producing Better Public Services with Citizens*. Blog for the OECD Observatory for Public Sector Innovation, Paris.

Loeffler, E., Bovaird, T., Parrado, S. and Van Ryzin, G. (2008). "If you want to go fast, walk alone. If you want to go far, walk together": Citizens and the Co-Production of Public Services. Report to the EU Presidency, Paris.

Loeffler, E., Timm-Arnold, P., Bovaird, T. and Van Ryzin, G. (2015). *Koproduktion in Deutschland*. Studie zur aktuellen Lage und den Potenzialen einer partnerschaftlichen Zusammenarbeit zwischen Kommunen und Bürgerinnen und Bürgern. Gütersloh: Bertelsmann Stiftung.

Meijer, A. (2012). Co-Production in an Information Age. In Victor Pestoff, Taco Bransden and Bram Verschuere (eds.), *New Public Governance, the Third Sector and Co-Production*, 192–208. London: Routledge.

Meyer, G. and Grosser, M. (2014). *Streetwatchers Reclaim the Streets of Weyhe*. Birmingham: Governance International.

Milton, S. (2011). *Community Speedwatch Scheme in Wiltshire to Reduce Speeding and Empower Residents*. Birmingham: Governance International.

Neighbourhood Watch. (2017). Knowledge Base. Wigston: Neighbourhood and Home Watch Network.

O'Brien, R. and Robson, J. (2016). *A Matter of Conviction: A Blueprint for Community-Based Rehabilitative Prisons*. London: RSA.

O'Connor, C. D. (2015). The Police on Twitter: Image Management, Community Building, and Implications for Policing in Canada. *Policing and Society*, 1–14.

Ostrom, E. (1978). Citizen Participation and Policing: What Do We Know? *Journal of Voluntary Action Research*, (7, 1–2), 102–108.

Parks, R. B., Baker, P. C., Kiser, L., Oakerson, R., Ostrom, E., Ostron, V., Percy, S. L., Vandivort, M. B., Whitaker, G. P., and Wilson, R. (1981). Consumers as Coproducers of Public Services: Some Economic and Institutional Considerations. *Policy Studies Journal*, (9, 7), 1001–1011.

Pawelke, A. (2011). Peer Training of Learner Drivers by Offenders in Austria, Governance International Case Study.

Percy, S. L. (1978). Conceptualizing and Measuring Citizen Co-Production of Community Safety. *Policy Studies Journal*, (7, s1), 486–493.

Sabet, D. M. (2014). Co-Production and Oversight: Citizens and Their Police. Washington DC: Wilson Center

Sharp, E. B. (1978). Citizen Organizations in Policing Issues and Crime Prevention: Incentives for Participation. *Journal of Voluntary Action Research*, (7, 1–2), 45–58.

Sharp, E. B. (1980). Toward a New Understanding of Urban Services and Citizen Participation: The Coproduction Concept. *Midwest Review of Public Administration*, (14), 105–118.

The Social Innovation Partnership. (2013). *An Evaluation of the St. Giles Trust's SOS Project*, December 2013.

Sundeen, R. A. and Siegel, G. B. (1987). The Community and Departmental Contexts of Volunteer Use by Police. *Journal of Voluntary Action Research*, (16, 3), 43–53.

Surrey County Council. (2015). *How Surrey Is Leading the Way*. https://www.surreycc. gov.uk/people-and-community/restorative-practice/restorative-justice-in-surrey/ how-surrey-is-leading-the-way

Thaler, R. H. and Sunstein, C. R. (2008). *Nudge: Improving Decisions about Health, Wealth and Happiness*. New Haven, CT: Yale University Press.

Thijssen, P. and Van Dooren, W. (2016). Who You Are/Where You Live: Do Neighbourhood Characteristics Explain Co-Production? *International Review of Administrative Sciences*, (82, 1), 88–109.

User Voice. (2016). User Voice Establishes New Service User Councils with the Help of Sodexo. Blog at service.org (28 November 2016).

van Eijk, C., Steen, T. and Verschuere, B. (2017). Co-Producing Safety in the Local Community: A Q-Methodology Study on the Incentives of Belgian and Dutch Members of Neighbourhood Watch Schemes, *Local Government Studies*, (43, 3), 323–343.

Weaver, B. and McCulloch, T. (2012). Co-Producing Criminal Justice: Executive Summary, Scottish Government Social Research Report No. 5, October 2012.

Whitaker, G. P. (1980). Co-Production: Citizen Participation in Service Delivery. *Public Administration Review*, (40), 240–246.

Williams, B. N., Kang, S-C. and Johnson, J. (2015). (Co)-Contamination as the Dark Side of Co-Production: Public Value Failures in Co-Production Processes. *Public Management Review*, (18, 5), 692–717.

Williams, B. N., LePere-Schloop, M., Silk, P. D. and Hebdon, A. (2016). The Co-Production of Campus Safety and Security: A Case Study of the University of Georgia. *International Review of Administrative Sciences*, Special issue: Co-Production of Public Service, (82, 1), 110–130.

16.1 Case Study—The Blue and You Police-Community Forum

Co-Production of a Community Conversation

Brian N. Williams, Dan Silk, Hadley Nobles and JaiNiecya Harper

Introduction

Recent Gallup and Pew opinion poll data in the United States paint a contrasting picture in "black" and "white." This public portrait highlights that police-community relations in the United States are in a precarious state. Notable interactions between citizens and police officers have resulted in deaths of unarmed citizens. These local interactions have been captured and transmitted nationally and globally by the technology of our information society, negatively impacting public trust and confidence.

In minority and historically marginalized communities within the US, these incidents remind residents of the desolate and discriminatory days of old, and can serve to stigmatize all police officers. These perceptual realities are counterproductive for efforts to utilize the public as partners in co-creating and co-producing public safety and public order. As a consequence, the historical narrative of the coercive *power-over* approach to public safety and public order seems to be the modus operandi and contradicts the co-creative and co-productive or *power-with* approach to citizen engagement and community well-being that the American public now expects.

To take advantage at the local level of the national conversation surrounding use of force issues during interactions between citizens and police, the Blue & You Police-Community Forum was individually conceived, but collaboratively designed and implemented.

Background

The Blue & You Forum is a co-production of a community conversation initiative that focuses on improving police-community relations within Athens-Clarke County (A-CC), Georgia—a unified city-county jurisdiction located in northeast Georgia and home to the University of Georgia. With an estimated population of 120,938, A-CC has a median age of 26.2, a median household wage of $33,060 with 37.8% of the population below the poverty level, and is racially diverse with Whites, Blacks, Hispanics/

Latinos and Asians representing 65%, 28%, 11% and 4.5% of the population, respectively (Athens-Clarke County Unified Government, n.d.).

The Forum reflects co-production in the design and implementation of a core service as an initiative to enhance the effectiveness of complementary co-production in service implementation where residents are more likely to assist local law enforcement in public safety and public order efforts like the "see something, say something" civic engagement campaign. Dr. Brian N. Williams, of the University of Georgia, initially conceived of the idea and envisioned an asset-based approach to community development to identify and leverage local individuals, public institutions and non-profit organizations that could serve as co-creators and co-producers of the Forum. Dr. Williams identified, recruited and secured commitments from local assets and served as a liaison to begin the process of bringing together citizens, the local police and representatives from the University of Georgia (UGA).

Key assets included the Boys & Girls Club of Athens, Chess and Community, Flanigan's Portrait Studio, UGA's J. W. Fanning Institute for Leadership Development, the Clarke County Sheriff's Office, A-CC Police Department, Clarke County Schools Police Department and the University of Georgia Police Department. These institutions were engaged in both the design and the delivery of the Forum.

As active participants in the design phase, these individuals deliberated and agreed to develop and embrace a strategy that utilized a pro-active— or getting ahead of a negative situation—instead of a reactive approach to enhance police-community relations. Consensus was reached in terms of four goals: to enhance understanding, to improve communications, to encourage a better working relationship between youth and local law enforcement agencies and to target "purposeful populations" as essential participants in the community conversation.

Consensus was also reached to recruit and train a total of 25 youth, teens and college students to serve as moderators and to utilize *reflective structured dialogue* as the approach to facilitate a meaningful community conversation. This relationship-centered approach to build, sustain and/or restore trust enables participants to share their experiences and explore clarifying questions regarding their perspectives and the perspectives of those with whom they are in conflict.

Experiences

On Saturday, April 9, 2016, the Boys & Girls Club of Athens hosted the Blue &You Police-Community Forum. More than 175 people participated in this community conversation, far exceeding an anticipated crowd of 60. Since that date, additional co-created programmatic activities have been organized. Activities include panel discussions in the community and on local radio stations on how to bridge the police-community divide, community conversations on "Police Use of Force" and a "Back to School" event co-created by youth development organizations, the school district, UGA and the law enforcement community. Most recently, a three-panel mural was co-designed and collaboratively painted by teens, UGA students, police officers and community members to serve as a visible reminder of how the past impacts the present but provides an opportunity for a brighter future in terms of police-community relations. Currently, anecdotal evidence of the success of this initiative abounds, but quantifiable data are not available regarding the effects of this type of co-creation and co-production. Anticipated outcomes do include better communication, enhanced public trust and confidence and a more effective partnership in the co-production of public safety and public order.

Reference

Athens-Clarke County Unified Government. (n.d.). *Athens-Clarke County by the Numbers*. https://www.athensclarkecounty.com/DocumentCenter/Home/View/535

16.2 Case Study—Dutch and Belgian Citizens' Motivations to Engage in Neighbourhood Watch Schemes

Carola van Eijk, Trui Steen and Bram Verschuere

Introduction

In this case, we discuss citizens' co-production activities in the domain of safety, more specifically neighbourhood watch schemes in the Netherlands and Belgium. Members of neighbourhood watch schemes keep an eye on their neighbourhoods. Often, they gather information via citizen patrols on the streets and report their findings to the police and the municipal organisation. They alert the authorities regarding issues such as streetlamps not functioning, broken pavements, or youth gangs hanging around on streets and causing trouble. Furthermore, neighbourhood watch schemes draw their fellow neighbours' attention to windows or back doors not being closed, making it possible for burglars to sneak in. Through the neighbourhood watch schemes, local governments and the police thus collaborate with citizens to increase social control, tackle antisocial behaviour, stimulate prevention, and increase safety and liveability in the neighbourhood.

Background

Citizens are inherently connected with the safety and liveability of their own property and the neighbourhood where they reside, and for many decades they have undertaken several activities. Examples of these activities include not only neighbourhood watch schemes, but also installing alarm equipment, or police-citizen councils. One would recognise that only some of the activities citizens perform fit the definition of co-production as used in this volume. In neighbourhood watch schemes the co-production element is prominent, as information gathered during the patrols is actively shared with the police, who in turn support the citizens. The idea of citizens patrolling the streets originated in the US, where it became popular in the late 1960s. Thereafter, it rapidly spread out to the other Anglo-Saxon countries, yet in continental Europe it only got foothold more recently.

Actively involving citizens in the co-production of safety and liveability issues has advantages, but also entails important risks. One of the advantages is that neighbourhood watch schemes are expected to decrease opportunities for crime, due to extra surveillance, increased home security measures, and increased social control. Furthermore, neighbourhood watch schemes can increase citizens' feelings of safety; because other residents know the neighbourhood watch scheme keeps an additional eye on their neighbourhood, they feel safer. Yet, at the same time the opposite argument can be made. Because the neighbourhood watch scheme is operational, more attention is focused on safety issues and disturbances in the neighbourhood, increasing citizens' awareness as well as their anxiety about safety issues. Situations they were not aware of before are now labelled as 'unsafe', therefore negatively impacting on safety perceptions. Another potential risk of neighbourhood watch schemes refers to the backgrounds of its members: often the members are not representative of the entire population of residents, for example in terms of age or ethnic background, potentially causing tensions with other residents. Furthermore, since the members are not trained professionals, it may lead to a detrimental outcome when they (unintentionally) enter violent situations. Finally, neighbourhood watch schemes might pave the way for individuals to take the law into their own hands, especially when roles/responsibilities between the police and the neighbourhood watch scheme are blurred, or when 'cowboys' driven by feelings of excitement become part of the team.

Experiences

In the Netherlands and Belgium, several citizens are involved in the co-production of community safety through neighbourhood watch schemes. We analysed the opinions of Dutch and Belgian members of neighbourhood watch schemes regarding their motivations to become engaged in neighbourhood watch schemes, and found these are quite diverse (see van Eijk, Steen and Verschuere, 2017). To illustrate, in Belgium we identified a group of co-producers which we named 'protective rationalists'. They joined the neighbourhood watch scheme to increase their own personal safety or the safety of their neighbourhood, but they also weigh the rewards (in terms of safety) and costs (in terms of time and effort). In the Netherlands, to give another example, we found co-producers (labelled 'normative partners') who are convinced that their investments help protect the common interest. Although they do not want to overestimate their efforts, they believe that simply walking around the neighbourhood leads to several important results. Furthermore, they value partnerships with the police highly: they do not want to take over the tasks of the police but argue that they also cannot function without police involvement.

Thus, among the citizens involved in the co-production of safety through neighbourhood watch schemes, different groups of co-producers can be identified, each of these reflecting a different combination of motivations and ideas. The engagement of citizens to co-produce seems to be triggered by a combination of factors, including, for instance, self-interest and community focus, and individual characteristics in terms of mastered skills. Local governments that want to stimulate citizen co-production need to be aware of citizens' motivations to co-produce safety. Their policies and communication strategies need to allow for diversity. For example, people who co-produce from a normative perspective might feel underappreciated when compulsory elements are integrated, while people who perceive their engagement as a professional task might be motivated by the provision of extensive feedback.

Furthermore, van Eijk (2017) found that for both citizens and public professionals (e.g., police officers and civil servants from the municipal organisation), feelings of appreciation are very important to keep actors engaged in the co-production of community safety over time. Professionals who assess that little useful output is provided by the neighbourhood watch scheme might perceive they have to put too much effort into the collaboration; while citizens who get the impression their efforts are not valued by the professional partners might feel disappointed and dissatisfied, and as such feel less inspired to continue their activities. Co-production means that both citizens and professionals have to invest efforts in the collaboration over time. When new neighbourhood watch schemes are initiated, professionals, for instance, need to actively contribute and collaborate in order to prevent the new initiatives from being stillborn. Moreover, once the neighbourhood watch scheme is operational, the connection between professionals and citizens can only be loosened to a certain degree: even though some citizens highly value a more autonomous position from the police, they are not police officers and are continuously in need of professional guidance and support.

References

van Eijk, C. J. A. (2017). Helping Dutch Neighborhood Watch Schemes to Survive the Rainy Season: Studying Mutual Perceptions on Citizens' and Professionals' Engagement in the Co-Production of Community Safety. *VOLUNTAS*, online first publication, 1–25.

van Eijk, C., Steen, T. and Verschuere, B. (2017). Co-Producing Safety in the Local Community: A Q-Methodology Study on the Incentives of Belgian and Dutch Members of Neighbourhood Watch Schemes. *Local Government Studies*, (43, 3), 323–343.

Part 4

The Effects of Co-Production and Co-Creation

17 Co-Production, Co-Creation, and Citizen Empowerment

Suyeon Jo and Tina Nabatchi

Introduction

Advocates claim that in comparison to traditional models of service delivery, co-production can have many benefits for citizens (e.g., Levine and Fisher, 1984; Needham, 2008). This chapter explores those claims, and focuses specifically on the potential empowerment effects of co-production for citizens. The basic argument is that when citizens play proactive roles through co-production, services become more closely aligned with their interests and needs (Whitaker, 1980; Brudney and England, 1983; Levine and Fisher, 1984; Pestoff, 2006; Thomas, 2013), which leads to greater satisfaction with services (Pestoff, 2006; Voorberg, Bekkers and Tummers, 2015). Moreover, the process of exercising voice, control, and influence (which is generally absent in traditional service delivery) generates a sense of empowerment among citizens (Needham, 2008). To unpack this argument, we begin with a brief discussion about co-production and its application at the individual, group, and collective levels. We then introduce a theory of empowerment and draw connections to each level of co-production. Finally, we review the literature, concentrating on empirical studies that examine empowerment.

Types of Co-Production

Scholars have used diverse criteria to delimit and categorize various types of co-production, such as its objectives, and the relationships, roles, and interactions of professionals and users (Bovaird, 2007; Brudney and England, 1983; Voorberg, Bekkers and Tummers, 2015). A recent typology by Nabatchi, Sancino, and Sicilia (2017) defines three levels of co-production. First, *individual co-production* occurs when a state actor works directly with a single lay actor (typically a client or customer). This is probably the most common form of co-production. Second, *group co-production* occurs when one or more state actors work directly and simultaneously with a number of lay actors in a specific population category (e.g., users of a specific service, residents of a specific neighborhood, or patients with a specific disease). This form of co-production begins to take on some of the characteristics associated with traditional notions of public participation. Finally, *collective co-production* occurs when one or more state actors (from one or more organizations) work directly and simultaneously with several lay actors who are diverse members of the community. This form of co-production most closely resembles public participation. Each of these forms of co-production can take place during any of the four phases of the service cycle: commissioning, design, delivery, and assessment.

The degree and nature of the actors' involvement and interactions differ across the levels of co-production, which in turn means that each type of co-production is likely to have different empowerment effects on participants. Specifically, individual co-production may generate empowerment at the individual level; group co-production may generate empowerment at both the group and individual levels; and collective co-production may generate empowerment at the community, group, and individual levels. The following section explores these claims by drawing on a theory of empowerment.

A Theory of Empowerment and Co-Production

The concept of empowerment has been widely used in many disciplines, making it an important buzzword with no clear definition (Pitts, 2005). For the purposes of this chapter, we rely on a theory that regards empowerment as both a process and an outcome (Zimmerman, 2000). Empowerment as a process refers to "the development and implementation of mechanisms to enable individuals or groups to gain control, develop skills and test knowledge," and empowerment as an outcome refers to "an affective state in which the individual or group feels that they have increased control, greater understanding and are involved and active" (Harrison and Waite, 2015, 503). Simply stated, this theory centers on "empowering" processes and "empowered" outcomes (Zimmerman, 2000).

The theory also holds that empowerment can be generated at multiple levels; therefore, both empowering processes and empowered outcomes should be analyzed at the individual, group, and community levels (Perkins and Zimmerman, 1995; Zimmerman, 2000). Although empowerment occurs when individuals, groups, or communities gain "mastery over their lives" (Zimmerman, 2000, 44), the specific factors that contribute to empowering processes and empowered outcomes vary across the three levels, as shown in Table 17.1.

With this theory in mind, it is fairly easy to articulate how co-production could lead to both empowering processes and empowered outcomes. Empowerment in co-production is related to "the ability of individual service users to control their experience of a public service and contribute to their own desired outcomes" (Osborne and Strokosch, 2013, S38). Specifically, through co-production, lay actors are provided the opportunity to convey their interests and directly participate in the commissioning, design, delivery, and assessment of public services. These opportunities involve

Table 17.1 Empowering Processes and Empowered Outcomes Across Levels of Analysis (Zimmerman, 2000)

Level of Analysis	"Empowering" Processes	"Empowered" Outcomes
Individual	Learning decision-making skills Managing resources Working with others	Sense of control Critical awareness Participatory behaviors
Group	Opportunities to participate in decision-making Shared responsibilities Shared leadership	Effectively compete for resources Networking with other organizations Policy influence
Community	Access to resources Open government structure Tolerance for diversity	Organizational coalitions Pluralistic leadership Residents' participatory skills

making meaningful contributions and maintaining substantive control over the experience, both of which are core elements in the theory of empowerment. Moreover, these opportunities may engender the process and outcome elements of empowerment listed in Table 17.1. That is, each type of co-production—individual, group, and collective—can be linked with the factors related both to empowering processes and to empowered outcomes.

First, individual co-production may generate individual-level empowerment. During the process of individual co-production, the lay actor controls (1) inputs, for example through requests or applications, (2) outputs, which are created through interactions with state actors, and (3) impacts, by engaging in follow up or follow through, for example by job seeking after vocational training or making dietary changes after a physician visit (Wirth, 1991). These activities implicitly involve the factors associated with an empowering process: lay actors learn decision-making skills, for example, by choosing whether and how to engage; manage resources by controlling inputs and outputs; and work with others to develop shared understanding of the problem and solutions. These activities may also lead to empowered outcomes: lay actors are provided with a sense of control, develop critical awareness about the issues, and engage in participatory behaviors throughout the co-production process.

Second, group co-production may generate empowerment at both the group and individual levels. Group co-production involves multiple lay actors who share common problems or goals and who seek to obtain benefits not only for the group, but also for themselves (Brudney and England, 1983; Nabatchi et al., 2017). The use of group co-production requires at least a modest degree of formal coordination (Brudney and England, 1983, 64), and may involve the factors associated with an empowering process: lay actors are provided the opportunity for shared responsibilities and leadership in group decision-making by providing inputs, determining outcomes, and taking actions that have impacts. Furthermore, group co-production may yield empowered outcomes: through the process of co-production, the group negotiates for resources and networks with others to influence policy. These characteristics of empowering processes and empowered outcomes are likely to operate not only at the group level, but also at the individual level (Zimmerman, 2000).

Finally, collective co-production may generate empowerment at the community, group, and individual levels. "Unlike group co-production, which targets a specific segment of the population and is aimed at producing benefits for the group members, collective co-production targets diverse members of the community and is aimed at producing 'goods whose benefits may be enjoyed by the entire community'" (Nabatchi et al., 2017, citing Brudney and England, 1983, 64). This form of co-production requires a great deal of formal coordination, but also implicitly involves the factors of an empowering process. In collective co-production, the community is able to access resources through an open government structure, and the interactions among heterogeneous community members can generate tolerance for and appreciation of diversity. Moreover, collective co-production may have empowered outcomes: through their engagement, lay actors can build organizational coalitions, learn to appreciate the value of pluralistic leadership that incorporates diverse interests, and develop stronger participatory skills. Once again, these characteristics of an empowering process and empowered outcomes are likely to operate not only at the community level, but also at the group and individual levels (Zimmerman, 2000).

In sum, the theory of empowerment suggests that co-production may generate empowering processes and empowered outcomes at the individual, group, and community levels. Moreover, it provides theoretical support for the claim that group and collective co-production are more beneficial than individual co-production, because they are more likely to generate greater cumulative impacts (e.g., Brudney and England, 1983; Bovaird et al., 2015; Needham, 2008). Unfortunately, the empirical research on co-production and empowerment has a long way to go to test this theory.

Empirical Research on Co-Production and Empowerment

Given that most studies employ exploratory, single case methods, the evidence base to support the theorized benefits of co-production—including empowerment—is relatively weak (Bovaird and Loeffler, 2016; Jo and Nabatchi, 2016b). A recent systematic literature review found that most co-production studies did not aim to assess outcomes, impacts, or benefits, but rather sought to identify drivers or create typologies (Voorberg, Bekkers and Tummers, 2015). Our review of the literature suggests that this claim holds when examining the connections between co-production and empowerment.

A handful of studies have used empirical methods to examine the role of empowerment (or related constructs such as self-efficacy, political efficacy, self-esteem, and ownership) as a driver of individual, group, and collective co-production. For example, a study of five European Union countries found that citizens' sense of self-efficacy (the belief that they can make a difference with regard to a problem) is significantly associated with the likelihood of participating in individual and collective co-production (Bovaird et al., 2015; see also Bovaird and Loeffler, 2016). Similarly, an analysis of four cases in the Netherlands and Belgium found that participants' sense of internal efficacy (the belief that they can understand and participate in co-production) and external efficacy (the belief that professionals will make room for participation and be responsive to input) were important drivers for active participation in group and collective co-production (van Eijk and Steen, 2015). Another study found that neighbourhood levels of social capital, measured as the activity of neighbourhood associations and considered to be a proxy for perceptions about control over one's life, had a strong and positive effect on the likelihood of participating in collective co-production (Thijssen and Van Dooren, 2016).

Others have examined the role of service providers in fostering an empowering process and the consequent impacts on other outcomes. For example, a case study about individual co-production found that a communication strategy led by health professionals and aimed at empowering patients enabled patients to be more effective co-producers of recuperation after surgery. Specifically, patients who were empowered through this communication strategy saw reduced hospital stays, lower incidence of problems, and faster transfer to less intensive care levels, and gave higher ratings to the quality of care provided by doctors and nurses (Trummer et al., 2006). Similarly, a systematic literature review of co-production in healthcare suggests that the creation of empowering processes, for example through the establishment of multi-disciplinary healthcare teams, the improvement of patient-provider communication, and the enhancement of the use of ICTs can foster greater patient engagement (Palumbo, 2016). Another exploratory case study about the group co-production of care services for autistic children in Italy found that user empowerment was an important managerial tool. Specifically, when professionals focused on fostering user empowerment, service delivery was improved (Sicilia et al., 2016). This handful of studies suggests that co-production is often conceived of and implemented as a process intended to generate empowerment, but with the goal of leading to other kinds of outcomes. Accordingly, these and other studies describe the co-production process as being "empowering," but forgo empowerment measures in favor of other outcome measures.

It is also worthwhile to look at the public participation literature, given the commonalities between participation and collective and group co-production. Once again, much of this literature addresses theoretical connections between (good) participation processes and citizens' normative beliefs or desired outcomes. These include, for example, improved perceptions about the responsiveness of public agencies (Halvorsen, 2003) and procedural fairness (Herian et al., 2012; Webler and Tuler, 2000), greater tolerance for diverse opinions (Halvorsen, 2003), and stronger social connectedness and engagement of disadvantaged communities (de Graaf, van Hulst and Michels, 2015).

Only a few studies in public administration explicitly focus on the link between empowerment and participation. Buckwalter (2014) draws on cases in Kentucky, Utah, and Pennsylvania to suggest that the perceived legitimacy of participatory processes strengthens the connections between citizens and administrators, and results in citizen empowerment. While this study does not test the impact of participation on empowerment, it does offer testable propositions. In a review of the deliberative participation literature, Pincock (2012) cites several studies that examine elements of citizen empowerment, such as self-efficacy and political-efficacy.

We found only two attempts to specifically test the impacts of co-production on empowerment. One set of studies examines the impacts of collective co-production on several individual-level outcomes, including empowerment (Jo and Nabatchi, 2016a; Nabatchi and Jo, 2016; Nabatchi, Jo and Salas, 2016). Specifically, as part of a larger project on developing recommendations for reducing diagnostic error in healthcare (see the case study on healthcare, chapter 12.1 in this volume), researchers found that participants in two different collective co-production groups experienced significant gains in their patient activation measure (PAM), a 13-item index that uses a Guttman scale to assess individuals' "knowledge, skills and confidence for managing their own health" (Hibbard et al., 2004). However, the intensity of the effects on empowerment varied between the two groups, suggesting that the overall design and purpose of co-production affect outcomes.

A second study sheds light on the connections between design and outcomes. Specifically, a study involving 727 participants investigated the effects of internet-based, virtual co-creation on consumer empowerment, and found that levels of perceived empowerment varied depending on the design of the process (Füller et al., 2009). Participants experienced empowered outcomes when they were provided with appropriate tools that increased their understanding and enjoyment, and were given specific tasks for the activity that enabled them to share responsibilities. In turn, these elements contributed to an increased sense of empowerment. The results of this study suggest that to achieve empowered outcomes in virtual co-production, elements of an empowering process should be used, including immediate feedback, intuitive user interfaces, unrestricted solution spaces, and maximum user decision-making control.

In short, few studies have empirically tested the empowerment effects of individual, group, and collective co-production. This is perhaps not surprising as scholars have struggled to understand the theoretical connections between co-production and empowerment, a challenge we have tried to address in this chapter. Beyond using the theory of empowerment presented here, co-production scholars might also benefit from looking at the research on public deliberation (a category of participatory processes that typically shares many common characteristics with group and collective co-production), where ample studies investigate and find numerous empowerment and other individual-level effects (for a review of this research, see Pincock, 2012). That said, future research on both co-production and public deliberation needs to work to better specify and measure empowerment effects at the individual, group, and community levels.

Conclusion

Although many advocates have claimed that co-production can have numerous benefits for participants, "the actual and potential impact of co-production on citizen outcomes is as yet only sketchily researched" (Bovaird and Loeffler, 2016, 1013). The result is scant empirical evidence about the relationship between co-production and empowerment, which makes it difficult to judge the strengths of claims (cf. Voorberg, Bekkers and Tummers, 2015). Perhaps one challenge that underlies the lack of empirical research is that little attention has been paid to developing the theoretical basis for the connections between co-production and empowerment.

To address that issue, this chapter introduced a theory of empowerment that disaggregates the concept into empowering processes and empowered outcomes at the individual, group, and community levels. Further application of this theory (and perhaps other theories) could enable scholars to articulate the mechanisms by which different forms of co-production generate empowerment. Moreover, a retrospective analysis of the few studies that have explored the relationship between co-production and empowerment might be able to tie those effects to the theory presented here. Nevertheless, more empirical and explanatory studies are needed, and scholars would be well served by stronger theoretical grounding. Such efforts would not only increase our understanding about the effects of co-production on empowerment, but would also advance the study and practice of co-production as a whole.

References

Bovaird, T. (2007). Beyond Engagement and Participation: User and Community Co-Production of Public Services. *Public Administration Review*, (67, 5), 846–860.

Bovaird, T. and Loeffler, E. (2016). User and Community Co-Production of Public Services: What Does the Evidence Tell Us? *International Journal of Public Administration*, (39, 13), 1006–1019.

Bovaird, T., Van Ryzin, G. G., Loeffler, E. and Parrado, S. (2015). Activating Citizens to Participate in Collective Co-Production of Public Services. *Journal of Social Policy*, (44, 1), 1–23.

Brudney, J. L. and England, R. E. (1983). Toward a Definition of the Co-Production Concept. *Public Administration Review*, (43, 1), 59–65.

Buckwalter, N. D. (2014). The Potential for Public Empowerment Through Government-organized Participation. *Public Administration Review*, (74, 5), 573–584.

De Graaf, L., Van Hulst, M. and Michels, A. (2015). Enhancing Participation in Disadvantaged Urban Neighbourhoods. *Local Government Studies*, (41, 1), 44–62.

Füller, J., Mühlbacher, H., Matzler, K. and Jawecki, G. (2009). Consumer Empowerment Through Internet-Based Co-Creation. *Journal of Management Information Systems*, (26, 3), 71–102.

Halvorsen, K. E. (2003). Assessing the Effects of Public Participation. *Public Administration Review*, (63, 5), 535–543.

Harrison, T., and Waite, K. (2015). Impact of Co-Production on Consumer Perceptions of Empowerment. *The Service Industries Journal*, (35, 10), 502–520.

Herian, M. N., Hamm, J. A., Tomkins, A. J. and Zillig, L. M. P. (2012). Public Participation, Procedural Fairness, and Evaluations of Local Governance: The Moderating Role of Uncertainty. *Journal of Public Administration Research and Theory*, (22, 4), 815–840.

Hibbard, J. H., Stockard, J., Mahoney, E. R. and Tusler, M. (2004). Development of the Patient Activation Measure (PAM): Conceptualizing and Measuring Activation in Patients and Consumers. *Health Service Research*, (39, 4), 1005–1026.

Jo, S. and Nabatchi, T. (2016a). *Coproducing Public Health: Patient Engagement in the Diagnostic Process*. Paper presented at the Public Management Research Conference, Aarhus, Denmark.

Jo, S. and Nabatchi, T. (2016b). Getting Back to Basics: Advancing the Study and Practice of Co-production. *International Journal of Public Administration*, (39, 13), 1101–1108.

Levine, C. H. and Fisher, G. (1984). Citizenship and Service Delivery: The Promise of Co-Production. *Public Administration Review*, (44), special issue, 178–189.

Nabatchi, T. and Jo, S. (2016). *Initial Phases of a Randomized Study of Public Deliberation about Diagnostic Error: An Analysis of the 2016 Healthcare Consumer Event*. Syracuse, NY: PARCC. (Report on file with authors).

Nabatchi, T., Jo, S. and Salas, A. (2016). *Initial Phases of a Randomized Study of Public Deliberation about Diagnostic Error: A Preliminary Analysis of Three Healthcare Consumer Events in 2015*. Syracuse, NY: PARCC. (Report on file with authors).

Nabatchi, T., Sancino, A. and Sicilia, M. (2017). Varieties of Participation in Public Services: The Who, When, and What Co-Production. *Public Administration Review*, (77, 5), 766–776.

Needham, C. (2008). Realising the Potential of Co-Production: Negotiating Improvements in Public Services. *Social Policy and Society*, (7, 2), 221–231.

Osborne, S. P. and Strokosch, K. (2013). It Takes Two to Tango? Understanding the Co-Production of Public Services by Integrating the Services Management and Public Administration Perspectives. *British Journal of Management*, (24, S1), S31–S47.

Palumbo, R. (2016). Contextualizing Co-Production of Health Care: A Systematic Literature Review. *International Journal of Public Sector Management*, (29, 1), 72–90.

Perkins, D. D. and Zimmerman, M. A. (1995). Empowerment Theory, Research, and Application. *American Journal of Community Psychology*, (23, 5), 569–579.

Pestoff, V. (2006). Citizens and Co-Production of Welfare Services: Childcare in Eight European Countries. *Public Management Review*, (8, 4), 503–519.

Pincock, H. (2012). Does Deliberation Make Better Citizens? In T. Nabatchi, J. Gastil, G. M. Weiksner, and M. Leighninger, (eds.), *Democracy in Motion: Evaluating* the Practice and Impact of Deliberative Civic Engagement, 135–162. New York, NY: Oxford University Press.

Pitts, D. W. (2005). Leadership, Empowerment, and Public Organizations. *Review of Public Personnel Administration*, (25, 1), 5–28.

Sicilia, M., Guarini, E., Sancino, A., Andreani, M. and Ruffini, R. (2016). Public Services Management and Co-Production in Multi-Level Governance Settings. *International Review of Administrative Sciences*, (82, 1), 8–27.

Thijssen, P. and Van Dooren, W. (2016). Who You Are/Where You Live: Do Neighbourhood Characteristics Explain Co-Production? *International Review of Administrative Sciences*, (82, 1), 88–109.

Thomas, J. C. (2013). Citizen, Customer, Partner: Rethinking the Place of the Public in Public Management. *Public Administration Review*, (73, 6), 786–796.

Trummer, U. F., Mueller, U. O., Nowak, P., Stidl, T. and Pelikan, J. M. (2006). Does Physician—Patient Communication that Aims at Empowering Patients Improve Clinical Outcome? A Case Study. *Patient Education & Counseling*, (61, 2), 299–306.

van Eijk, C. and Steen, T. (2015). Why Engage in Co-Production of Public Services? Mixing Theory and Empirical Evidence. *International Review of Administrative Sciences*, (82, 1), 28–46.

Voorberg, W. H., Bekkers, V. J. and Tummers, L. G. (2015). A Systematic Review of Co-Creation and Co-Production: Embarking on the Social Innovation Journey. *Public Management Review*, (17, 9), 1333–1357.

Webler, T. and Tuler, S. (2000). Fairness and Competence in Citizen Participation: Theoretical Reflections from a Case Study. *Administration & Society*, (32, 5), 566–595.

Whitaker, G. P. (1980). Co-Production: Citizen Participation in Service Delivery. *Public Administration Review*, (40, 3), 240–246.

Wirth, W. (1991). Responding to Citizens' Needs: From Bureaucratic Accountability to Individual Co-Production in the Public Sector. In F. Kaufmann (ed.), *The Public Sector: Challenge for Coordination and Learning*, 69–88. Berlin: De Gruyter.

Zimmerman, M. A. (2000). Empowerment Theory. In J. Rappaport and E. Seidman (eds.), *Handbook of Community Psychology*, 43–63. New York: Kluwer Academic/Plenum Publishers.

17.1 Case Study—Co-Creation and Empowerment

The Case of DR Congo in Agricultural and Rural Sector

Peter Ngala Ntumba

Introduction

Like other countries, the Democratic Republic of Congo (DR Congo) is experimenting with co-creation tools in its various sectors of activity. In the agricultural and rural sector in particular, an approach called in French "Conseil Agricole Rural de Gestion" (CARG, Agricultural Rural Management Council) was set up, bringing together public and private actors (commercial enterprise and civil society in the broad sense, including voluntary organizations and individual citizens). The approach creates spaces for discussion, guidance and provision of agricultural and rural services to local communities.

In the context of this approach, individual citizens are grouped according to the themes of activities that make up the CARG and make their respective contributions, materially or financially, to support the functioning of this framework. Our case thus illustrates an example of co-creation. So, *how does this co-production initiative in DR Congo support citizen empowerment? What are the drivers or barriers for increasing citizen empowerment?*

Background

Since the DR Congo became independent in 1960, several policies have been put in place to promote development in the agricultural and rural sector (Ngalamulume, 2011). Failures have been recorded and these policies have not achieved the expected objectives. According to the diagnostic analyses of the Government of the Republic, these failures are the result of several reasons, including the approaches which have been followed (Makala, 2015). All policies have implemented the "top-down" scheme and considered the peasant not as an actor in his development, but rather as a "beneficiary" of development services (Makala, 2015; Ngalamulume, 2011).

Since this diagnosis has been posed, the Ministry of Agriculture and its partners considered that it was necessary to focus the Ministry restructuring on decentralization and the creation of decentralized management structures where the State local agents would work in close cooperation with the private and voluntary sectors (Coopman, 2009). Indeed, for more than five years, a so-called "Conseil Agricole Rural de Gestion" (CARG)—which is a "Public-Private partnership" mechanism—has been experimented with in the agricultural and rural field, throughout the Republic. Thus, the reform promotes the co-production of goods and services by both the public and the private sector in order to achieve the empowerment of local communities.

The CARG is a consultative mechanism and advisory support, based on rural sociology in DR Congo. Three pillars support the concept: community dynamics, local know-how or peasant knowledge and self-management. According to Makala (2015, 83), "these pillars, which have a secular nature, have always facilitated solidarity, voluntary work, environmental control and above all, accountability for productive activities in rural areas, individual practices or collective practices".

The CARG approach is based on the main idea that the group and the community continue and will continue to play the leading role in the socio-cultural and economic activities of the rural and even the urban context, despite the modernity achievements (Makala, 2015). In order to promote self-care, each CARG ought to be composed of one-third of representatives of the public authorities and two-thirds of representatives of civil society.

In summary, the CARG approach makes it possible to implement platforms in local entities. These are the spaces dedicated to check out solutions to local problems as observed and formulated by all the actors involved in solutions searching; their finality remains individual and collective self-management. The approach tends to empower each farmer by giving him/her the necessary and even practical advice for his/her self-care.

Experiences

Nowadays the Ministry of Agriculture has succeeded in establishing the "CARG" platforms in more than 135 of the 145 territories of the DR Congo. The coordination of these platforms is mostly managed by the main delegates of the civil society, most of whom are elected by their peers which are usually local groups of citizens. What's important is that this arrangement offers the delegates of the public authorities and the civil society the opportunity to gather, to discuss some important issues of their communities and to propose resolutions rather than expecting everything from the public power authorities, higher authorities or foreign partners, and to develop together the Development Plans of their own entities and self-management strategies, particularly through exchanges of experience with the facts occurring in the society. After all, the CARG is committed to a good distribution of agricultural inputs and production tools to the peasants concerned.

However, in spite of its theoretical advantages and these few cumulative benefits, the CARG approach encounters, in practice, several challenges, especially:

1) The lack of a common and shared vision of the CARG approach by the actors of the agricultural and rural sector in DR Congo.

One of the designers of the CARG approach states: "*Designed as a platform for dialogue at the territory and sector level,*[. . .] *the operationalization of the CARG approach is immediately thwarted by divergent speeches*" (Makala, 2015, 17). It is true that the actors in the field do not have the same perception of the CARG. As a platform, CARG is presented as a consultative framework, as a decision-making body or as an executive body of the local entity. Therefore, it is not possible for local actors to appropriate the tool.

2) The lack of political will to comply with the reform that promotes cocreation and is based on the empowerment of local actors.

During our field surveys, an international expert said the following: "*Even with one-third of the members representing the State and sometimes defectors, 'ghosts' in the Civil Society,* [. . .] *the State takes control of this*". In other words, "*we do not want change, and we want a status quo. So we take control of this consultation platform that was established*" (Interview, 2015). The hierarchical authorities interfere in the organization and functioning of local CARGs, the monopoly of public authorities in the Steering Committee, the absence of adequate and clearly defined mechanisms for support, coordination and operational monitoring of the CARGs are possible evils to fight at this level. All these challenges require appropriate remedies in order to effectively achieve the empowerment of local communities targeted by the CARG approach. In general, the actors concerned must define and respect the rules of the game together.

References

Coopman, P. (2009). Décentralisation et code agricole: pour une gestion réaliste du monde rural congolais. (Interview d'Alain Huart). In *Eco Congo*: La plateforme numérique de la République démocratique du Congo. www.ecocongo.cd/fr/sys tem/files/f-pc-e2-p1-s1.5-1.pdf

Makala, N. P. (2015). *Le conseil agricole rural de gestion et développement à la base en RDC*. Paris: L'Harmattan.

Ngalamulume, T. G. (2011). *Projets de développement agricole, dynamiques paysannes et sécurité alimentaire. Essai d'analyse transversale et systémique de la rencontre entre les actions globales et les initiatives locales au Kasaï-Oriental (RD Congo)*. Thèse de l'Université Catholique de Louvain, Faculté des Sciences économiques, sociales, politiques et communication. Louvain: Presses universitaires de Louvain.

18 Democratic Co-Production
Concepts and Determinants

Bram Verschuere, Daphne Vanleene,
Trui Steen and Taco Brandsen

Introduction

Even with the growing academic and practitioner interest, co-production research still lacks in certain areas. More specifically, there is still little research done on the effects and added value of co-production (Verschuere, Brandsen, and Pestoff, 2012). One of the areas in co-production research that deserves further attention is whether co-production is 'democratic' in nature. It is clear that when one talks about citizen participation (of which co-production or co-creation are examples), an underlying connection with 'democracy' is always presumed (Bakker, 2015). Citizen participation is thus often considered as a virtue in itself (Voorberg, Bekkers, and Tummers, 2014). However, whether this connection is justifiable is often discussed (Jawando, 2015; Teasdale, 2008; Vermeij, 2015). Do such participation projects truly reach all citizens, or only the middle class participants, those with the least need for it (Michels, 2015)? Are citizens with a lower socioeconomic status able to participate (Jakobsen and Andersen, 2013)? Can governments actively entice their citizens to participate (Bakker, 2015; Jakobsen, 2013)? Are the benefits from this participation fairly distributed among citizens (Cuthill, 2010)?

If co-production is considered as a solution to give more people fair and equal access to basic services like education, safety or healthcare, then these assumptions cannot remain untested. And, if it is true that there are still large groups in society excluded from or underrepresented in public service delivery, one should test the assumed benefits of participation and co-production in this respect (Fung, 2004 Denters and Klok, 2010, Jakobsen and Andersen, 2013 Michels, 2011).

The review of the literature presented in this chapter shows that most knowledge is available on the democratic quality of citizen participation in general. Based on this literature, we first try to conceptualize 'democratic quality' of participation and co-production. Secondly, we focus on the current knowledge about the (possible) determinants of democratic participation and co-production.

Democratic Quality of Co-Production

If we want address the question whether co-production leads to policy-making or service delivery of better democratic quality, we need to explain what we mean with this very ambiguous and multi-faceted concept. From a co-production and participation point of view, 'democratic quality' is often conceptualized as the extent to which people from different societal groups or backgrounds are included in co-production or participation. In fact, the participation of citizens is directly connected to the idea of democracy. This view originated from Rousseau, who believed that the participation of each citizen is vitally important for the state to function well. Since then, modern theorists have expanded on this theory, adding that this participation should stretch even further, into workplaces and local communities (Michels, 2011). Looking at the literature, democratic quality of participation can be made more specific by looking at concepts like equity, inclusion (or exclusion), (lack of) impact while participating or co-producing, and empowerment of participants or co-producers.

Equity and Inclusion

Inclusion refers to the possibility for everyone that is affected by, or depends on, the co-produced service delivery to participate to co-production projects. This concept also relates to Halvorsen's (2003) concept of 'accessibility', or the ability to attract people of a variety of viewpoints with the aim to achieve a fair representation of citizens in co-production or participation projects. It is, after all, important, and a matter of legitimacy, that those who are affected by co-produced services or by participatory decision-making are also included in the process, and have an actual influence on the outcome (Young, 2000). When concluding an international comparison on the effects of citizen participation, Michels (2011) found that there are still large groups excluded or underrepresented in participatory projects such as participatory policy-making and referendums. These lower levels of inclusion seem to show that many citizens may still have doubts about the benefits of participation.

This should raise concern about the actual democratic quality of participatory policy-making and public service delivery, and questions the assumption made by Rousseau, but since then Robert Putnam as well, that simply letting citizens participate already leads to more inclusion, as a matter of democratic quality (Michels, 2011). This democratic quality, obviously, will be hampered if large groups in society are restrained in their opportunities to participate. And this participation-gap becomes even larger if other, more affluent groups (Agger and Larsen, 2009) are over-represented. An example of such structural inequalities can be found in the case study of Lombard (2013) on participation at the neighbourhood level in Mexico. She found that inequalities in levels of inclusion are sometimes institutionalized:

the legal framework on which the public participation projects are based is written in such a way that it reinforces existing social segregation based on the citizens' status, thus already excluding certain citizens before they can even consider participation. Agger and Larsen (2009) and Verba et al. (2000) also point out the possibility of 'structural exclusion', in which citizens with fewer resources, networks or skills are simply less likely to participate. For, as Batten (1974) explains, people cannot 'want what they don't know exists'.

Resulting from this observation that participation-levels might differ between different groups in society, the benefits of participation and co-production are not always evenly and fairly distributed as well. If certain groups are excluded from, or simply have no access to participation or co-production projects, then the chances that these citizens benefit from participation will most likely decrease. After all, in designing and processing co-productive service delivery, co-producers have the opportunity to define the nature, the quality and the quantity of the services of interest to them. Non-participants are deprived from this opportunity. Here comes the concept of 'inequity', which Jakobsen and Andersen (2013) define as limitations on the input of certain service-users because of lack of knowledge and other resources, and as an uneven distribution of benefits resulting from the co-productive project. There might thus be a real risk attached to the crowding-out of people from co-production or participation in terms of benefits or other outcomes of co-production and participation (see e.g. Brandsen and Helderman, 2012; Irvin and Stansbury, 2004). But even when all societal groups are evenly included, there might be a risk of inequity, which occurs when the most powerful members of a collaborative group push selfish decisions, implying that those that already hold a strong position in their community will gain even more (Van Dooren and Thijssen, 2015). In sum: typically in co-production or participation, equity would mean getting equal opportunities, being equally free of risks and dangers and having equal access to resources (Fung, 2004).

Impact and Empowerment

Another feature of 'democratic quality' of co-production is rather process-based. People need to feel that they have impact on the decisions made, and this requires a certain level of empowerment: having the chances to influence the nature, quality and quantity of the services they produce together with professionals. It comes down to the necessary condition that co-producers perceive a real ability to actively participate. Empowerment then comes through having the feeling that one is able to express their viewpoint and influence the discussion, and that one feels to be treated with respect while the professional counterpart is transparent and trustworthy (Herian, Hamm, Tomkins, and Zillig, 2012; Webler and Tuler, 2000). Although we can consider empowerment and impact of co-producers as a necessary ingredient of co-production that is 'democratic', we will not further elaborate on this in this chapter. For a more comprehensive discussion, we refer to the chapter of Suyeon Jo and Tina Nabatchi in this volume (chapter 17).

Determinants of Democratic Co-Production

The democratic quality of co-production can thus depend on the extent to which the project leads to equity, inclusion, crowding-in of the greatest variety of people and societal groups involved, and on the extent to which the project allows for real impact and empowerment of people. The literature on participation in general provides us with some answers to the question under which circumstances co-production is democratic in nature or not. First, there seems to be a need for a sufficient and truthful *professional support*, from professionals in public or non-profit organizations. Second, there is the need for a minimal level of *competency* of co-producing citizens, which is established through knowledge and resources, but also in their self-confidence and belief in their own competence ('efficacy', see e.g. van Eijk and Steen, 2014). Third, there is the *salience* of the task or service provided, more specifically, the importance of the content, the goals and (in)direct results of the project for the co-producing citizens, or at least the intended citizen co-producers.

Professional Support

According to Fung (2004), there are five reasons for non-participation: the lack of incentive (Pestoff, 2006), the lack of knowledge and skill (Jakobsen and Andersen, 2013), the lack of personal resources (Jakobsen, 2013), the lack of social capital and the presence of a dominant political culture (Weinberger and Jutting, 2001). Each of these issues could potentially be resolved through professional support (see also Steen and Tuurnas in this volume, chapter 8). In co-production research, the role of the professional is encased in a larger concept, namely the 'ease of involvement'. Here the focus lies on whether information about the project is easily available to citizens, and how far the professional service provider is from the citizens. This distance can be measured both in a literal sense, if there are offices and professionals in the neighbourhood, and figuratively, if the professionals are easy to approach (Verschuere et al., 2012).

There is already some evidence that professional support may bring people over the threshold of participation and co-production. By engaging with those groups who are excluded, who (believe they) lack the competence to participate, professional support can aid in strengthening the skills, knowledge and capacity needed to participate (Durose, 2011; Vanleene, Voets, and Verschuere, 2017). Hence, quite some literature suggests that by enabling citizens, that is, by teaching them or providing the correct knowledge and resources, they will be more able to participate (Wagenaar, 2007; Jakobsen, 2013; Jakobsen and Andersen, 2013). For example, Jakobsen (2013) and

Jakobsen and Andersen (2013) showed that with professional support and the provision of specific tools, restrictions for co-produced education by minority groups could be reduced. The increased professional input, focussing on the target group, resulted in larger participation.

Next to that, besides providing resources and tools, professionals also mobilize via direct invitation, and not simply by providing the option without any further action on their part. Getting citizens to participate requires more personal ways to approach and entice them (de Graaf, van Hulst, and Michels, 2015; Frieling, Lindenberg, and Stokman, 2014). Durose (2011) refers to this as 'reaching', and notes the importance of identifying the excluded groups and focusing on their integration in the community. The importance of 'being asked' in the process of mobilization of participants is reiterated by Simmons and Birchall (2005), who point out that the person who asks needs to be a well-considered choice and, preferably, a professional who is known in the neighbourhood and thus easily approachable. Professionals need to know and understand the potential participants, as they need to reinterpret the formal governmental rules to fit the situation and the people involved, thereby enhancing willingness and participation (de Graaf et al., 2015; Durose, 2011).

Also, professionals need to show the co-producers the positive results of their participation. Without evidence of their influence, citizens will get disheartened and lose interest in the project (de Graaf et al., 2015). Buckwalter (2014) notes that direct and frequent interactions with professionals could lead to a sense of empowerment for the citizens. However, having the option or venue to participate does not guarantee a voice. Thus, he agrees with the statement of de Graaf et al. (2015) that citizens need to be informed and made aware of their impact on the project (Buckwalter, 2014). Halvorsen (2003) supports this view, claiming that when the government offers the option of participation, but then disregards the citizens' input, the effects could be worse than when there is no option for participation at all.

Lastly, one more important note to make here is the potential negative influence of professional support. This is mentioned as 'discursive exclusion' by Agger and Larsen (2009), in their study of a Danish urban regeneration project. In many instances, the power of the decision lies in the hands of the planners (the professionals). More specific, the planners can select which issues to undertake. They are also more likely to direct themselves towards those areas where it is easier to achieve results, i.e. they focus on those participants with whom it will be easier to reach an agreement (Agger and Larsen, 2009).

Competence

As already mentioned above, citizens need to have the resources and knowledge to participate. This is considered one of the main reasons behind inequity in citizen participation, and this even more so when the project relies heavily on the input of the service user, as in co-production (Jakobsen and Andersen, 2013). Competence is also an influence mentioned in the study of de Graaf et al. (2015), explaining that those excluded citizens often lack the resources (and interest) to participate. This inequity is largely based on income and education, but by providing new forms of participation and as stated above, by creating new ways of responding to these differences, inequity can be overcome (John, 2009). It should also be taken into account that it is not only the citizens' competence that needs to be ensured. After all, the perception of their competences, efficacy, plays a major role in their willingness to participate (Blakeley and Evans, 2009; van Eijk and Steen, 2014). In their study of a deprived neighbourhood, Denters and Klok (2010) uncovered the importance of this, when their results showing the citizens' lack of confidence in their own personal skills. There are two ways to consider the citizens' competence and their influence on their sense of equity. Firstly, there is the (experienced) competence before co-producing. Here, the study done by Webler and Tuler (2000) can provide a definition. In their research on public involvement in the Northern Forest Land Council, they divided the concept into two requirements: 'access to information and its interpretations and use of the best available procedures for knowledge selection' (Webler and Tuler, 2000, p. 571). This way the concept can be linked back to professional support, as to gain access to information is the view from the citizens' side, whereas professionals need to provide that access and the information. Similarly, Simmons and Birchall (2005) point to the need for development, training and schemes that helps build citizens' skills and confidence, which would in turn strengthen both their competence and their efficacy, thus potentially attracting more participants.

Secondly, once they crossed that threshold and start co-producing, there is the possibility that citizens' skills and competence increase by participating, which in turn contributes to their positive feelings towards government, their community and democracy as a whole (de Graaf et al., 2015).

Lastly, Fung (2004) notes that the option of 'power' can convince those disadvantaged citizens who would be considered less competent to participate when there is an urgent issue. This leads to the consideration of the 'salience' of the project as another important factor.

Salience

Pestoff (2012) provides the clearest explanation for the concept of 'salience'. As he clarifies, citizens will consider the importance of the service for them, their family and friends, as well as its effect on their lives and life chances. So, if people need to be included in participation or co-production projects, the salience of the project for them needs to be proven. For example in deprived neighbourhoods, where citizen competence is perhaps lower, the salience of the project can be considered even more important. After all, high levels of deprivation may motivate residents to participate, counteracting the issue of competence (Denters and Klok, 2010; Fung, 2004). This influence is also noted by Denters and Klok (2010) in the discussion of their successful participation project. The rebuilding project they researched was a highly salient issue for the residents, and the success in acquiring representative participation could be directly linked with this. People who are satisfied with their living conditions will feel less need to change their environment. To the contrary, changing the living environment will be of more importance or salient to people that are less satisfied. Perhaps this might trigger people more easily to participate or co-produce in projects focussed on altering the living environment (Simmons and Birchall, 2005).

Conclusion

The main lesson from this chapter is that we are in need of research that focuses on the democratic quality of co-production and co-creation. This is important, both from an academic and practitioner point of view, and could enable us to find empirical support (or not) for the commonly held assumption that co-production is inherently democratic.

We can find some inspiration for this in the broader participation literature, on which we relied for this chapter. This literature provides some initial ways to refine a rather general concept like 'democratic quality': equity, inclusion, empowerment and impact. The literature also provides us with some first assumptions on potential drivers for democratic co-production: professional support, a sense of competency and salience may be important to lift target groups over the threshold.

Care is needed, however, in translating knowledge from the broader participation literature to more specific co-production and co-creation research, as there may be empirical differences between general citizen participation and specific co-production, in terms of 'who's in', and what 'representativeness' means. Think about the stereotypical white highly educated male participating in participatory budgeting in the neighbourhood, versus the unemployed and uneducated lady co-producing care as a volunteer in the local hospital. Or think about the participatory budgeting in which representativeness means all groups in society, versus co-production of education by minority groups with the goal of language skill improvement where representativeness is more about attracting a specific target group.

References

Agger, A. and Larsen, J. N. (2009). Exclusion in Area-Based Urban Policy Programmes. *European Planning Studies*, (17, 7), 1085–1099. doi:10.1080/096543 10902949646

Bakker, H. (2015). Burgerinitiatieven kunnen niet zonder de representatieve democratie. *Socialevraagstukken.nl.*

Batten, T. R. (1974). The Major Issues and Future Direction of Community Development. *Community Development Journal*, (9, 2), 96–103. doi:10.1093/cdj/9.2.96

Blakeley, G. and Evans, B. (2009). Who Participates, How and Why in Urban Regeneration Projects? The Case of the New 'City' of East Manchester. *Social Policy & Administration*, (43, 1), 15–32. doi:10.1111/j.1467–9515.2008.00643.x

Buckwalter, N. D. (2014). The Potential for Public Empowerment Through Government-Organized Participation. *Public Administration Review*, (74, 5), 573–584. doi:10.1111/puar.12217

Cuthill, M. (2010). Strengthening the 'Social' in Sustainable Development: Developing a Conceptual Framework for Social Sustainability in a Rapid Urban Growth Region in Australia. *Sustainable Development*, (18, 6), 362–373. doi:10.1002/sd.397

de Graaf, L., van Hulst, M., & Michels, A. (2015). Enhancing Participation in Disadvantaged Urban Neighbourhoods. *Local Government Studies*, (41, 1), 44–62. doi:10.1080/03003930.2014.908771

Denters, B. and Klok, P.-J. (2010). Rebuilding Roombeek: Patterns of Citizen Participation in Urban Governance. *Urban Affairs Review*, (45, 5), 583–607. doi:10.1177/1078087409356756

Durose, C. (2011). Revisiting Lipsky: Front-Line Work in UK Local Governance. *Political Studies*, (59, 4), 978–995. doi:10.1111/j.1467–9248.2011.00886.x

Frieling, M. A., Lindenberg, S. M. and Stokman, F. N. (2014). Collaborative Communities Through Coproduction: Two Case Studies. *American Review of Public Administration*, (44, 1), 35–58. doi:10.1177/0275074012456897

Fung, A. (2004). *Empowered Participation: Reinventing Urban Democracy*. Princeton: Princeton University Press.

Halvorsen, K. E. (2003). Assessing the Effects of Public Participation. *Public Administration Review*, (63, 5), 535–543. doi:10.1111/1540–6210.00317

Herian, M. N., Hamm, J. A., Tomkins, A. J. and Zillig, L. M. P. (2012). Public Participation, Procedural Fairness, and Evaluations of Local Governance: The Moderating Role of Uncertainty. *Journal of Public Administration Research and Theory*, (22, 4), 815–840. doi:10.1093/jopart/mur064

Irvin, R. A. and Stansbury, J. (2004). Citizen Participation in Decision Making: Is It Worth the Effort? *Public Administration Review*, (64, 1), 55–65. doi:10.1111/j.1540-6210.2004.00346.x

Jakobsen, M. (2013). Can Government Initiatives Increase Citizen Coproduction? Results of a Randomized Field Experiment. *Journal of Public Administration Research and Theory*, (23, 1), 27–54. doi:10.1093/jopart/mus036

Jakobsen, M. and Andersen, S. C. (2013). Coproduction and Equity in Public Service Delivery. *Public Administration Review*, (73, 5), 704–713. doi:10.1111/puar.12094

Jawando, M. (2015). Citizens United at Five: Money Undermines Meaningful Participation. *Huffington Post.*

John, P. (2009). Can Citizen Governance Redress the Representative Bias of Political Participation? *Public Administration Review*, (69, 3), 494–503. doi:10.1111/j.1540-6210.2009.01994.x

Lombard, M. (2013). Citizen Participation in Urban Governance in the Context of Democratization: Evidence from Low-Income Neighbourhoods in Mexico.

International Journal of Urban and Regional Research, (37, 1), 135–150. doi:10. 1111/j.1468-2427.2012.01175.x

Michels, A. (2011). Innovations in Democratic Governance: How Does Citizen Participation Contribute to a Better Democracy? *International Review of Administrative Sciences*, (77, 2), 275–293. doi:10.1177/0020852311399851

Michels, A. (2015). Hoe we uit het ideologische doe-democratie-debat kunnen komen. *Samenlevingsvraagstukken.nl.*

Pestoff, V. (2006). Citizens and Co-Production of Welfare Services. *Public Management Review*, (8, 4), 503–519. doi:10.1080/14719030601022882

Pestoff, V. (2012). Co-Production and Third Sector Social Services in Europe: Some Concepts and Evidence. *Voluntas*, (23, 4), 1102–1118. doi:10.1007/s11266-012-9308-7

Simmons, R. and Birchall, J. (2005). A Joined-Up Approach to User Participation in Public Services: Strengthening the "participation chain". *Social Policy & Administration*, (39, 3), 260–283. doi:10.1111/j.1467-9515.2005.00439.x

Teasdale, S. (2008). Reaching Out to Volunteers. *The Guardian.*

Van Dooren, W. and Thijssen, P. (2015). Who You Are/Where You Live. Do Neighbourhood Characteristics Explain Coproduction. *International Review of Administrative Sciences*, (81, 2).

van Eijk, C. and Steen, T. (2014). Why People Co-Produce: Analysing Citizens' Perceptions on Co-Planning Engagement in Health Care Services. *Public Management Review*, (16, 3), 358–382. doi:10.1080/14719037.2013.841458

Vanleene, V. and Verschuere, B. (2017, published online). The Co-Production of a Community: Engaging Citizens in Derelict Neighbourhoods. *Voluntas.* doi:10.1007/s11266-017-9903-8

Vermeij, L. K. and Kullberg, J. (2015). Wordt de stad een exclusief feestje voor kansrijke stedelingen? *Socialevraagstukken.nl.*

Verschuere, B., Brandsen, T. and Pestoff, V. (2012). Co-Production: The State of the Art in Research and the Future Agenda. *Voluntas*, (23, 4), 1083–1101. doi:10.1007/s11266-012-9307-8

Voorberg, W. H., Bekkers, V. J. J. M. and Tummers, L. G. (2014). A Systematic Review of Co-Creation and Co-Production: Embarking on the Social Innovation Journey. *Public Management Review*, (17), 1–25. doi:10.1080/14719037.2014.930505

Webler, T. and Tuler, S. (2000). Fairness and Competence in Citizen Participation—Theoretical Reflections from a Case Study. *Administration & Society*, (32, 5), 566–595. doi:10.1177/00953990022019588

Weinberger, K. and Jutting, J. P. (2001). Women's Participation in Local Organizations: Conditions and Constraints. *World Development*, (29, 8), 1391–1404. doi:10.1016/s0305-750x(01)00049-3

Young, I. (2000). *Inclusion and Democracy.* New York: Oxford University Press.

18.1 Case Study—Co-Production of New Immigrant Services in Hong Kong

Facilitating the Integration of New Immigrants into Community

Xuan Tu

Introduction

As the number of immigrants from Mainland China has been increasing, the integration of new immigrants becomes a key challenge of the government in public service delivery. To respond to a flow of new immigrants, the Hong Kong government, non-profit organisations and new immigrants have been engaged in co-production for the betterment of residents' life. An example of such a non-profit organisation is the Hong Kong New Immigrant Service Association (HKNISA), which engages new immigrants in co-producing services that include a Food Bank programme and a series of education and training programmes for women, children and senior residents.

Background

It is not surprising to find that co-production occurs in new immigrant services because new immigrants are in need of assistance and care that drives them to join service programmes such as job seeking workshops, language training courses and beauty salons. The focus of the case is on the Food Bank programme which engages the government, HKNISA and new immigrants in co-producing services. The goal is to cultivate the talents of new immigrants, to improve their living conditions and to eventually facilitate their long-term life security.

Below is an example that illustrates how new immigrants are engaged in the co-production process.

Ms. L came to Hong Kong in 2010 with two young kids and did not have a stable job to support her family. Through a friend she got connected to the New Immigrant Service Association hoping to get some help. Like thousands of new immigrants, Ms. L became one of the service recipients and was assisted with daily food provided by the Association to cook at home. Her daughter also benefited from tutorials provided by the Association, on top of her lessons at school. Gradually Ms. L's daughter improved in her main subjects and made some new friends. Instead of simply assisting these immigrants, HKISA and the government established a partnership that enabled them with access to information and workshops on language, job and housing. Ms. L got inspired and started doing volunteer work in her community. For example, she was active in reaching out to other new immigrants who needed help and in helping seniors do cleaning in the neighbourhood. By doing these, Ms. L got motivated and became an active co-producer of several service programmes.

Rather than asking new immigrants how the Association could help, new immigrants were encouraged to co-create programmes and to co-produce them. During one of the visits, new immigrants were happy to share how they prepare and carry out a food activity. This activity was financially supported by the Social Welfare Department and the Association prepared the venue for cooking where new immigrants could gather. The new immigrants designed the menu themselves and it created opportunities where new immigrants engaged in conversations about jobs and life. Programmes like food activities enabled new immigrants to build social networks and friendship. Through face-to-face communication, these immigrants could easily exchange thoughts and information, which enabled them to get connected to a wider community.

From being helped to helping others, it reflected an important element of co-production: a reciprocal process of service delivery. The role of co-producers was recognised through a relationship established with contribution to service delivery. In other words, each group involved in this process had a role to play. They chose to co-produce hoping that a service could be available for their future use. In this case, the government was not directly involved in delivering immigrant services; it provided a platform in which non-profit organisations play a major role in connecting new immigrants. Through a co-production approach, foods were delivered directly to the hands of the needy. To ensure a long-term service delivery, co-production was needed to realise the needs and demands of different groups.

Experiences

What's reflected from the case is that, first, new immigrants had more choices when the platform of participation was accessible. In this sense, co-production may be an effective approach that could facilitate the active role of service users. Second, service users had some decision-making power in carrying out service programmes in the process of delivery. As indicated by previous studies, co-production may transfer some power from professionals to users. It means that each party has the potential to make a substantial contribution to long-term service delivery through regular participation in community services and activities. One of the immigrants interviewed said: "to me, participating is more than a self-beneficiary process; but a way of building my confidence toward life and I feel I'm part of the community". Third, the non-profit organisation had played a mediating role in co-production of immigrant services. It connected government organisations and service users through a partnership which enabled the non-profit organisation to amplify the voices of service users for the advancement of their lives. A programme leader interviewed shared her experiences of working with those immigrants and government agencies: "we engage them from design to participation. We often have face-to-face communication during co-delivering services, for instance language training workshops. This enabled us to know what immigrants really need so that we can co-design some programmes to address their expressed needs". The case showed that co-production could be implemented as a strategy to improve service outcomes. For new immigrants, the care and support from the community was an important part of their integration.

18.2 Case Study—The Rabot Neighbourhood

Co-Production in Community Development

Daphne Vanleene and Bram Verschuere

Introduction

The Rabot neighbourhood is one of the poorest in Ghent: it has more people receiving benefits, more low incomes, more unemployment and more single-parent families compared to the rest of the city's districts (Staes, 2012). Rabot is also known as an arrival district, where there is a general rotation of 10% of the residents every year. In the diverse neighbourhood, 29.6% of residents are foreign nationals (District Monitor Ghent, 2015) and 68.5% percent of residents are of foreign descent (District Monitor Ghent, 2013). In this neighbourhood, community development workers assist citizens to become active and organise themselves to respond to issues and opportunities that can help both the neighbourhood and their own personal development. They do this through a variety of activities that can be considered as co-production in core public services (see Brandsen and Honingh in this volume).

Background

Within the neighbourhood different co-production projects can be found, organised by the city as well as by non-profit organisations, all aimed at reversing neighbourhood decline, counteracting crime rates and/or social exclusion, and increasing liveability. There are also several partners working in this neighbourhood:

(i) the City of Ghent, mainly represented by a district director and a project leader, which steers, funds and helps to create the community development projects in the neighbourhood.

(ii) The city delegates most of the day-to-day and fieldwork to a local non-profit: Community Development Ghent. This non-profit has four field workers employed in this neighbourhood, aided in their task by a policy worker and several citizens in a work program.

(iii) The citizen co-producers are the human capital behind the co-productive community development. Contrarily to the typical community development projects where the target group is only local residents, these projects also aim to reach the hard-to-reach citizens who do or will not permanently live in the neighbourhood. This implies that the community also includes renters living in poor housing conditions, asylum seekers passing through and homeless with a network of friends in the neighbourhood.

(iv) A fourth partner can be found in the many local shopkeepers and entrepreneurs who participate in the community projects, specifically by allowing payment with the complementary community currency. Here the aim is to stimulate the local economy. The system of a complementary currency aims to attract citizens to co-produce. The currency can be earned by residents (e.g. for keeping their street clean and/or putting flowers on the windowsill) but is also used in the co-production initiatives as a mini compensation, 25 Torekes/hour (=2.5 euro), with which co-producers can then rent a city garden or shop at local shops and restaurants.

There are several ongoing projects in the neighbourhood. The Site is one of the first and largest projects in the neighbourhood. Created in 2007, the old concrete, city-owned, factory floor included a 3000 m² city field, 160 mini-gardens, a multipurpose sports field, a playground, two conservatories, storage containers and even a citizen-initiated sharing shop. By working in the gardens co-producers get the opportunity to broaden and diversify their social networks. The Site aims to increase new residents' integration and break through their social isolation, as well as promote the empowerment of vulnerable groups.

Other projects include a Social Grocery which is run by co-producers and offers residents affordable items such as diapers, eggs, bread and locally grown (at the Site) fruit and vegetables, or Rabot on Your Plate, where citizen co-producers create new products such as yam, soups and hummus from the unsold fruit or vegetables grown in the community gardens. Finally we also mention the social restaurant 'Toreke' in the neighbourhood, where locally grown crops are used. Here citizens can have lunch and dinner at affordable prices (and even pay with the complementary currency) and on Thursday evenings this restaurant turns into a local café 'Barabot'.

Experiences

This case of community development in the Rabot neighbourhood has been studied in several research projects (e.g. Vanleene et al., 2017, Van Bouchaute et al., 2015). Two major findings are:

(i) Although these co-production projects are based on a rewards-system (the complementary currency), it was found that though the complementary currency might lower the threshold for co-production and participation, the citizens are also motivated to co-produce because of solidarity, altruism. It appears that these community development projects offer an informal space to build solidarity in a diverse neighbourhood and help in dealing with the differences between its residents. It speaks to the projects' success that many of the co-producers who take part in the projects also come from those vulnerable groups.

(ii) The importance of paid employees (professionals) in the process is a second main finding. The increase in solidarity between neighbours did not just appear 'bottom up', but was created by the efforts from the city and the non-profit organisation 'Community Development Ghent'. Thus, the professionals' influence on the co-producers and the co-production process cannot be disregarded.

References

District Monitor Ghent (n.d.). https://gent.buurtmonitor.be/

Staes, B. (2012). Rabot is de armste Gentse wijk, Drongen de rijkste. *het Nieuwsblad*. October 12.

Van Bouchaute, B., Depraetere, A., Oosterlynck, S. and Schuermans, N. (2015). *Solidariteit in superdiversiteit: het transformatief potentieel van een complementaire munt in een superdiverse wijk*. www.solidariteitdiversiteit.be/publicaties.php (consulted November 2017)

Vanleene, D., Voets, J. and Verschuere, B. (2017). Co-Producing a Nicer Neighbourhood: Why Do People Participate in Local Community Development Projects? *Lex Localis—Journal of Local Self-Government*, (15, 1), 111–132.

19 The Effects of Co-Production on Trust

Joost Fledderus

Introduction

Co-production is associated with positive effects on the trust relation between citizens and public institutions, and on trust in society in general (Fledderus, 2016). However, Levine (1984) already explicitly warned the public sector that 'if the use of citizens in service delivery is treated as a marginal activity by public agencies, then we should not expect co-production to be a very effective instrument for improving the competence or commitment of citizens' (Levine, 1984, 185). One may indeed wonder whether governments use co-production as a way to reduce costs or as a way to genuinely integrate service users into design and delivery procedures. The classic 'ladder of participation' of Sherry Arnstein comes into mind: when citizens are asked to participate, but virtually lack the power to influence any decision-making, participation comes close to nonparticipation and manipulation in the worst case (Arnstein, 1969).

The attractiveness of the concept of co-production appears to have won the battle against these early warnings. Thinktanks inform policy makers about the high potential of co-production and help to implement new, co-productive forms of service delivery. Here too, the expectation that co-production will be able to increase trust and social cohesion is frequently addressed (Boyle and Harris, 2009; Löffler et al., 2012). Meanwhile, academic research has been picking up and analyzing local, innovative examples of co-production that seem to confirm this thesis (Bovaird and Löffler, 2012; Needham and Carr, 2009). Still, recent research has also shed more light on factors that could obstruct trust-building in co-produced services. This research provides insights on the mechanisms and conditions that could explain if and why there is a relation between co-production and trust (Fledderus, 2016). In this chapter, I will discuss these insights.

What we Know from Previous Scholarship on the Effects of Co-Production on Trust

Why Co-Production Affects Trust

Trust can be defined as 'the belief that others, through their action or inaction, will contribute to my/our well-being and refrain from inflicting damage upon me/us' (Offe, 1999, 47). There could be very different reasons for people to trust others—it could be based on previous experiences, on reputation, on dispositions, et cetera (Rousseau et al., 1998). When it comes to the relation between co-production and trust, there is an underlying assumption that experiences of service delivery have an effect on trust attitudes.

A first idea is that co-production improves the outcomes of services, leading to a better evaluation of governments and institutions responsible for those services. In his dissertation, Van de Walle (2004) concludes that we should actually abandon this 'micro-performance' hypothesis. He presents a number of arguments for this conviction. For instance, people have opinions about government and institutions even if they had no bureaucratic encounters. It is more likely that the image of public institutions, for a large part formed by media, influences people's attitudes. Also, the experiences people do have do not necessarily have a causal relation with people's assessment of government and institutions. People might have a predisposition that is either positive or more negative towards public institutions (Kampen et al., 2006), which might be better explained by social-historical context than by actual experiences with public services. Does it then make sense to expect that co-production has any effect on trust?

Recent work on the relation between the process of service delivery and trust seems to indicate that it does make sense. Van Ryzin (2007, 532) states that 'traditional performance measures do not necessarily capture the dimensions or features of service quality that matters most to citizens'. In his subsequent work, Van Ryzin (2011, 2015) argues that (perceived) performance might actually have little influence on trust. To the contrary, *processes* might be much more important for citizens' trust in public institutions than actual outcomes. Specifically, beneficial aspects of process, such as fairness, participation, equity, respect and honesty might matter to people as much as outcomes. Empirical research does indeed show support for this thesis (Van Ryzin, 2011, 2015).

Thus, in order to assess the impact of co-production on trust, it is necessary to focus on how co-production changes the process of service delivery, instead of (solely) focusing on whether the outcome is influenced by co-production. However, for a complete picture of the relation between co-production and trust, research shows that the initial stage of service delivery should also not be dismissed. This leads to three stages of service delivery that play a role: the initial stage, the process stage and the outcome stage (Fledderus, Brandsen and Honingh, 2014). These stages will be discussed in more detail.

Three Stages of Service Delivery

Initial Stage

In the initial stage of service delivery, it is determined *who* is involved in co-production. Research shows that co-producers are more likely to trust government and fellow citizens than non-co-producers (Fledderus and Honingh, 2016). This can be explained by the fact that trust is recognised as one of the key conditions for collaboration (Yamagishi and Cook, 1993). People with low levels of trust in (local) government and/or the service provider are likely to be less convinced by the benefits of co-production than individuals who have high levels of trust. This refers to the perception of external efficacy: 'is the service able to help me?' (Calzada and Del Pino, 2008). Research has shown that efficacy is an important determinant of co-productive efforts, especially of collective co-production (Bovaird et al., 2015; Parrado et al., 2013). Moreover, when co-production involves collective co-production, having trust in fellow citizens is also more likely to be an important precondition. Furthermore, research shows that intrinsic motivation is an important predictor for involvement in co-production, and highly motivated co-producers tend to have more trust in public institutions as well (Fledderus and Honingh, 2016, van Eijk and Steen, 2014).

The importance of trust, efficacy and motivation as conditional factors for citizens to co-produce can be seen as a form of self-selection, resulting in a typical group of co-producers. But there can also be selection on the part of the public service organisation. Research shows that public service organisations, partially because of performance indicators and targets, tend to select the most qualified citizens for programmes that demand active user involvement (such as activation programmes; Van Berkel, 2010). These 'qualified' citizens often appear to be highly educated and trusting citizens.

Organisational selection, leading to a bias in favour of high trusting citizens, may also occur for other reasons. For instance, there could be clear reasons to involve a particular group of residents in a neighbourhood watch programme. As volunteers might be exposed to confrontations with suspects, selection on certain criteria might be necessary. It is likely and understandable that those who are responsible for selecting participants (e.g. police officers, public officials) will pick out willing, intrinsically motivated and cooperative citizens to join the neighbourhood watch (considering they might be confronted with violence). Likewise, in the case of health care, it is not unlikely that doctors differentiate in the room they provide for patients to get involved in the treatment, depending on the mental and physical state of the patient. In these cases, selection might actually improve the outcome (safety, health) for disadvantaged individuals too. Furthermore, selection might be crucial for collective forms of co-production. The success of collective co-production is dependent on the willingness of users to cooperate. In order to increase the likeliness of this cooperation to happen, organisations could use 'recruitment and selection processes designed to bring into the system individuals whose values are congruent with those of current organisational members' (Robertson and Tang, 1995, 71). Yet, this again may lead to a biased composition of users. For instance, parental cooperatives in Sweden attract mainly highly educated parents with a concern about the quality of child care (Vamstad, 2012). Although such a selection might have positive outcomes for the people involved in co-production, it could also lead to rather closed communities and the exclusion of other citizens (Brandsen and Helderman, 2012).

Process Stage

Whereas the initial stage of service delivery determines trust levels at the beginning of co-production, the process stage has the potential to further build trust. When users co-produce, the expectation is that they will develop a sense of control over the service (Fledderus, Brandsen and Honingh, 2014). This sense of control is particularly fostered through face-to-face interaction with professional staff, which allows users to negotiate experience and outcomes with personnel, gaining influence over service delivery in turn. An increase in perceived control relates to a perception of professional support and responsiveness, being beneficial for trust in the service provider. Yet, there is not much evidence to confirm this hypothesis. Studies on private services and health care do seem to confirm the idea. For instance, Rajah et al. (2008) find that co-production increases the buyer-seller relationship through frequent interactions and higher levels of customisation and personalisation. Teichert and Rost (2003) maintain that customers reduce the experience of risk through high involvement, which has a positive effect on their trust. In health care, it appears that encouraging patient involvement indeed increases patients' sense of control over their illness condition, builds effective relationships with physicians and improves the perception of patients of professional support, which all positively affect trust in the physician (MacStravic, 2000; Ouschan et al., 2006; Pontes and Pontes, 1997). A study on co-production of public services and effects on perceived control did not show any effect, which was (partly) explained by the lack of participatory structures (Fledderus, 2015a, see also the case by Fledderus in this volume, chapter 19.1).

Outcome Stage

Only few studies systematically investigated the impact of *outcomes* of co-production on trust levels. Fledderus (2015b) used vignettes to compare co-produced with non-co-produced public services, varying the outcomes of those services. It appears that in the case of successful outcomes, users of non-co-produced services have higher trust in the service organisation/professional compared to co-produced services. This can be explained by the mechanism of the *self-serving bias*, which refers to 'a person's tendency to claim more responsibility than a partner for success and less responsibility for failure in a situation in which an outcome is produced jointly' (Bendapudi and Leone, 2003, 15). Hence, when co-production leads to outcomes worse than expected, the service provider is blamed rather than the client him- or herself. Yet, when the outcome of co-production is successful, users might attribute this success partly to themselves, resulting in less satisfaction with the service provider compared to a situation without co-production. This leads to the counterintuitive expectation that whatever the outcome may be, co-production would at best reach the same and at worst poorer satisfaction levels as compared to 'regular' service delivery. An important finding of the study was that the self-serving bias was especially present when the service provider was physically less involved in the co-production (Fledderus, 2015b). Visibility of the involved professionals was highly appreciated. The absence of the service provider (e.g. when the service provider only provided materials to ensure co-production) gives users the feeling that they are left alone, taking all the credit for success.

Main Questions for Research

Research shows that the actual impact of co-production on trust is dependent on conditions and mechanisms in three consecutive stages of service delivery. Important to notice is that there is an interplay between these three stages. Current research often neglects this interaction and mostly focuses on a single stage of the service delivery chain. Particularly, there seems to be much attention for the initial phase, in terms of questions on motivation (Bovaird et al., 2015; van Eijk and Steen, 2014) and distributional biases (Clark et al., 2013; Jakobsen and Andersen, 2013). Other research has focused on the process of co-production (Bovaird and Löffler, 2012; Cepiku and Giordano, 2013; Isett and Miranda, 2015; Meijer, 2011). Finally, only little research revolves around the outcomes and outputs of co-production (Marks, 2009; Vamstad, 2012). A specific issue that is under little scrutiny is the relation between co-production and accountability: to what extent can users and/or the public service organisation be held responsible for outcomes? What happens when the outcomes of the co-produced service are not successful? Research suggests that transparency over and discussion about the potential risks of co-production can prevent users to blame the public service organisation for negative outcomes (Fledderus, Brandsen and Honingh, 2015; Fledderus, 2015b).

Research on co-production and trust would also benefit from integrating the coexisting mechanisms that take place at different levels: the individual, the organisational and institutional levels (Fledderus, Brandsen and Honingh, 2015). For example, research on the initial phase mostly focuses at the individual level (the motivations of users, the distribution bias of users), but only exceptions mention the selecting role that public service organisations may have at this point (Alford, 2009). Scholars working on the process stage of co-production either put emphasis on the individual experiences (Pestoff, 2006), or on the organisational level, such as the effects on the behaviour of professional staff (Cepiku and Giordano, 2013; Tuurnas, 2015). The institutional level of co-production is only rarely addressed (Joshi and Moore, 2004; Tuurnas et al., 2015. Processes that play a role on this level could affect trust-building. For instance, laws, rules or contracts could decrease the discretionary space of professionals. This space is essential for professionals to adapt and shape the service in accordance with the input users deliver when they co-produce (Fledderus, Brandsen and Honingh, 2015).

Including several stages and multiple levels of analysis in research on co-production and trust will require a multidisciplinary framework, using social-psychological, organisational and institutional theories. Moreover, the different nature of the questions related to the different stages and levels also demand methodological diversity. Although the methodological variety in studies on co-production has been vastly improved over the past couple of years, including Q-methodology (van Eijk and Steen, 2014), large-N surveys (Parrado et al., 2013) and longitudinal designs (Fledderus, 2015a), there are still promising avenues, including the use of experiments (Jakobsen, 2013; Fledderus, 2015b).

References

Alford, J. (2009). *Engaging Public Sector Clients: From Service-Delivery to Co-Production*. Hampshire and New York: Palgrave Macmillan.

Arnstein, S. R. (1969). A Ladder of Citizen Participation. *Journal of the American Institute of Planners*, (35, 4), 216–224.

Bendapudi, N. and Leone, R. P. (2003). Psychological Implications of Customer Participation in Co-Production. *Journal of Marketing*, (67, 1), 14–28.

Bovaird, T. and Loeffler, E. (2012). From Engagement to Co-Production. How Users and Communities Contribute to Public Services. In V. Pestoff, T. Brandsen, and B. Verschuere (eds.), *New Public Governance, the Third Sector and Co-Production*, 35–60. New York and London: Routledge.

Bovaird, T., Van Ryzin, G. G., Loeffler, E. and Parrado, S. (2015). Activating Citizens to Participate in Collective Co-Production of Public Services. *Journal of Social Policy*, (44, 1), 1–23.

Boyle, D. and Harris, M. (2009). *The Challenge of Co-Production. How Equal Partnerships Between Professionals and the Public Are Crucial to Improving Public Services*. London: NESTA.

Brandsen, T. and Helderman, J.-K. (2012). The Trade-Off Between Capital and Community: The Conditions for Successful Co-production in Housing. *Voluntas*, (23, 4), 1139–1155.

Calzada, I. and Del Pino, E. (2008). Perceived Efficacy and Citizens' Attitudes Toward Welfare State Reform. *International Review of Administrative Sciences*, (74, 4), 555–574.

Cepiku, D. and Giordano, F. (2013). Co-Production in Developing Countries: Insights from the Community Health Workers Experience. *Public Management Review*, (16, 3), 317–340.

Clark, B. Y., Brudney, J. L. and Jang, S-G. (2013). Co-Production of Government Services and the New Information Technology: Investigating the Distributional Biases. *Public Administration Review*, (73, 5), 687–701.

Fledderus, J. (2015a). Building Trust Through Public Service Co-Production. *International Journal of Public Sector Management*, (28, 7), 550–565.

Fledderus, J. (2015b). Does User Co-Production of Public Service Delivery Increase Satisfaction and Trust? Evidence from a Vignette Experiment. *International Journal of Public Administration*, (38, 9), 642–653.

Fledderus, J. (2016). User Co-Production of Public Service Delivery: Effects on Trust.

Fledderus, J., Brandsen, T. and Honingh, M. E. (2014). Restoring Trust Through the Co-Production of Public Services: A Theoretical Elaboration. *Public Management Review*, (16, 3), 424–443.

Fledderus, J., Brandsen, T. and Honingh, M. E. (2015). User Co-Production of Public Service Delivery: An Uncertainty Approach. *Public Policy and Administration*, (30, 2), 145–164.

Fledderus, J., and Honingh, M. (2016). Why People Co-Produce Within Activation Services: The Necessity of Motivation and Trust—an Investigation of Selection Biases in a Municipal Activation Programme in the Netherlands. *International Review of Administrative Sciences*, (82, 1), 69–87.

Isett, K. R. and Miranda, J. (2015). Watching Sausage Being Made: Lessons Learned from the Co-Production of Governance in a Behavioural Health System. *Public Management Review*, (17, 1), 35–56.

Jakobsen, M. (2013). Can Government Initiatives Increase Citizen Co-production? Results of a Randomized Field Experiment. *Journal of Public Administration Research and Theory*, (23, 1), 27–54.

Jakobsen, M. and Andersen, S. C. (2013). Co-Production and Equity in Public Service Delivery. *Public Administration Review*, (73, 5), 704–713.

Joshi, A. and Moore, M. (2004). Institutionalised Co-Production: Unorthodox Public Service Delivery in Challenging Environments. *Journal of Development Studies*, (40, 4), 31–49.

Kampen, J. K., Van de Walle, S. and Bouckaert, G. (2006). Assessing the Relation Between Satisfaction with Public Service Delivery and Trust in Government. *Public Performance & Management Review*, (29, 4), 387–404.

Levine, C. H. (1984). Citizenship and Service Delivery—the Promise of Co-Production. *Public Administration Review*, (44), Special Issue: Citizenship and Public Administration, 178–189.

Löffler, E., Parrado, S., Bovaird, T. and Van Ryzin, G. (2012). 'If you want to go fast, walk alone. If you want to go far, walk together': Citizens and the Co-Production of Public Services. Birmingham: Governance International.

MacStravic, S. (2000). The Downside of Patient Empowerment. *Health Forum Journal*, (43, 1), 30–31.

Marks, M. B. (2009). *A Theoretical and Empirical Investigation of Co-Production Interventions for Involuntary Youth in the Child Welfare and Juvenile Justice Systems*. Albany, NY: State University of New York, Doctoral Thesis.

Meijer, A. J. (2011). Networked Co-Production of Public Services in Virtual Communities: From a Government-Centric to a Community Approach to Public Service Support. *Public Administration Review*, (71, 4), 598–607.

Needham, C. and Carr, S. (2009). *Co-Production: An Emerging Evidence Base for Adult Social Care Transformation*. London: Social Care Institute for Excellence.

Offe, C. (1999). How Can We Trust Our Fellow Citizens? In M. E. Warren (ed.), *Democracy & Trust*, 42–87. Cambridge: Cambridge University Press.

Ouschan, R., Sweeney, J. and Johnson, L. (2006). Customer Empowerment and Relationship Outcomes in Healthcare Consultations. *European Journal of Marketing*, (40, 9/10), 1068–1086.

Parrado, S., Van Ryzin, G. G., Bovaird, T. and Loffler, E. (2013). Correlates of Co-Production: Evidence from a Five-Nation Survey of Citizens. *International Public Management Journal*, (16, 1), 85–112.

Pestoff, V. (2006). Citizens and Co-Production of Welfare Services—Childcare in Eight European Countries. *Public Management Review*, (8, 4), 503–519.

Pontes, M. and Pontes, N. (1997). Variables that Influence Consumers' Inferences About Physician Ability and Accountability. *Health Care Management Review* Spring 1997, (22, 2), 7–20.

Rajah, E., Marshall, R. and Nam, I. (2008). Relationship Glue: Customers and Marketers Co-Creating a Purchase Experience. *Advances in Consumer Research*, (35), 367–373.

Robertson, P. J. and Tang, S-Y. (1995). The Role of Commitment in Collective Action: Comparing the Organizational Behavior and Rational Choice Perspectives. *Public Administration Review*, (55, 1), 67–80.

Rousseau, D. M., Sitkin, S. B., Burt, R. S., et al. (1998). Not So Different After All: A Cross-Discipline View of Trust. *Academy of Management Review*, (23, 3), 393–404.

Teichert, T. and Rost, K. (2003). Trust, Involvement Profile and Customer Retention—Modelling, Effects and Implications. *International Journal of Technology Management*, (5–6), 621–639.

Tuurnas, S. (2015). Learning to Co-Produce? The Perspective of Public Service Professionals. *International Journal of Public Sector Management*, (28, 7), 583–598.

Tuurnas, S. P., Stenvall, J., Rannisto, P-H., Harisalo, R. and Hakari, K. (2015). Coordinating Co-Production in Complex Network Settings. *European Journal of Social Work*, (18, 3), 370–382.

Vamstad, J. (2012). Co-Production and Service Quality: The Case of Cooperative Childcare in Sweden. *Voluntas*, (23, 4), 1173–1188.

Van Berkel, R. (2010). The Provision of Income Protection and Activation Services for the Unemployed in 'Active' Welfare States. An International Comparison. *Journal of Social Policy*, (39, 1), 17–34.

Van de Walle, S. (2004). *Perceptions of Administrative Performance: The Key to Trust in Government?* Leuven: KU Leuven, Doctoral Thesis.

van Eijk, C. J. A., and Steen, T. P. S. (2014). Why People Co-Produce: Analysing Citizens' Perceptions on Co-Planning Engagement in Health Care Services. *Public Management Review*, (16, 3), 358–382.

Van Ryzin, G. G. (2007). Pieces of a Puzzle: Linking Government Performance, Citizen Satisfaction, and Trust. *Public Performance & Management Review*, (30, 4), 521–535.

Van Ryzin, G. G. (2011). Outcomes, Process, and Trust of Civil Servants. *Journal of Public Administration Research and Theory*, (21, 4), 745–760.

Van Ryzin, G. G. (2015). Service Quality, Administrative Process, and Citizens' Evaluation of Local Government in the US. *Public Management Review*, (17, 3), 425–442.

Yamagishi, T. and Cook, K. S. (1993). Generalized Exchange and Social Dilemmas. *Social Psychology Quarterly*, (56, 4), 235–248.

19.1 Case Study—Building Trust in Work Corporations

Joost Fledderus

Introduction

Welfare states develop active labour market policies to encourage labour market participation. Increasingly, these policies aim to involve various service delivery actors (i.e. public/private, for-profit/non-profit) and are characterised by a greater emphasis on the co-production of services in close collaboration with users. In the municipality of Nijmegen, such co-produced re-employment services were developed in the summer of 2011. So-called 'work corporations' aimed at re-employing social assistance recipients by offering work, guidance and education and were entirely run by the beneficiaries under the supervision of and with the support of professionals. These work corporations provide an interesting case of co-production, particularly in relation to trust. Firstly, this is because they entail a mandatory element, whereas generally co-production is considered to be a voluntary or intrinsically motivated act. By the use of (the threat of) sanctions, clients were compelled to collaborate and take up particular activities. As a result, the work corporations may actually reach citizens who are generally unmotivated and have low levels of trust in public institutions. Secondly, they provide the opportunity to track changes in (trust) attitudes, as the work corporation programmes typically have a duration of several months. Thirdly, co-producers within work corporations have to deal with several actors, such as fellow users, the professional service organisation and (local) government. This makes it possible to investigate how the experience of co-production affect trust on different levels.

Background

In the summer of 2011, several work corporations started operating in the municipality of Nijmegen, a middle-sized city in the Netherlands (Fledderus, Broersma, and Brandsen, 2014). The municipality took care of recruiting participants, this is, determining who is eligible to join. It also provided required facilities for the reemployment programme and monitored the output target (in terms of outflow of clients). Beneficiaries could enter a work corporation either voluntarily through applying for vacancies, or they could have been obliged to join a so-called job market, where they visit stands of different work corporations in order to apply at one of them (facing sanctions when they do not partake).

Most of the work corporations had their origins in delivering publicly funded non-profit services. For example, in one work corporation participants cooked and served food in a restaurant in combination with lower secondary vocational education; another guided participants who do maintenance in neighbourhoods; and a third work corporation was a furniture and decoration shop where people learned to work as a vendor.

The next section describes the experiences of participants, relying on several sources of data, such as repeated questionnaires, interviews with participants, project leaders and policy makers (Fledderus, 2015).

Experiences

Despite the mandatory elements of the programme, participants of work corporations appeared to be generally highly motivated. These high levels of motivation go hand in hand with relatively high levels of trust, particularly when it comes to trust in other people ('generalised trust') and trust in local government. Interestingly, such selection effects are not found on 'traditional' background characteristics such as gender, ethnicity and health. This indicates that it may be more fruitful to regard trust as an important precondition for participation in co-production, rather than a result of co-production.

The programme suffered from high levels of drop-out—after a half year, one-third of the participants had left the work corporation. It appeared that the drop-outs have lower levels of trust—in local government, the work corporation and national government—than those who stayed in the programme. This points at 'self-selection', resulting in exclusion of individuals who have a negative disposition towards government. 'Organisational' selection on part of the municipality and work corporations played a role too. Factors such as a focus on output (the percentage of participants finding a paid job) and the pursuit of self-sufficiency resulted in an (informal, and sometimes unconscious) selection procedure, selecting highly motivated, trusting and more skilled individuals.

Participation in work corporations did not lead to increased trust. Negative changes were found for trust in the work corporation, generalised trust and trust in fellow participants. A relation was found between a decrease in general motivation and a decrease in trust in fellow participants and in the work corporation. Several conditions may explain the inability of the programme to increase trust. A first condition relates to the participants' perceptions of 'support' from the environment during their programme. This support can take on different forms: showing interest in participants as a manager of a municipal worker; provision of an official educational programme; adaptation of work hours for personal circumstances; or simply giving support to daily work activities by providing work clothing or tools. A second conditional factor for trust-building was the ability of the work corporation to build a sense of 'commitment'. Participants with high commitment cared about their tasks and the quality of their work and were prepared to take on more responsibilities. Furthermore, these participants disapproved the lack of commitment and free-riding behaviour of other group members.

Finally, co-production was found to be more likely to foster affection-based trust than cognition-based trust (Fledderus, 2016). This means that participants' judgements on the trustworthiness of the project leaders and fellow participants were more often based on aspects of benevolence (the belief someone genuinely cares for you, a key characteristic of affection) than on characteristics such as competence or integrity (i.e. the cognitive dimension). This could be explained by the key role of the process within co-production (working together, building mutual commitment). Still, in order to build affective trust through co-production, issues such as self-selection and organisational selection, and conditions such as enduring motivation, support and commitment must be effectively managed.

References

Fledderus, J. (2015). Building Trust Through Public Service Co-Production. *International Journal of Public Sector Management*, (28, 7), 550–565.

Fledderus, J. (2016). *Co-Production and Trust: Cognition or Affection?* Paper Presented at the NIG Annual Work Conference, Antwerp, 24–25 November.

Fledderus J, Broersma F. and Brandsen T. (2014). The Netherlands - Nijmegen. In Evers A., Ewert B. and Brandsen T. (eds.), *Social Innovations for Social Cohesion*. WILCO Publication. http://www.wilcoproject.eu/downloads/WILCO-project-eReader.pdf

20 Assessing the Effect of Co-Production on Outcomes, Service Quality and Efficiency

Elke Loeffler and Tony Bovaird

Introduction

In this chapter a conceptual model is developed in order to distinguish the impacts of co-production.

The chapter then summarises the current state of evidence on how co-production policies, projects and initiatives have performed in terms of improvements to outcomes, service quality, efficiency, social capital and governance principles. While the evidence is still sparse, there are indications that the potential of co-production is sufficient to justify wider experimentation in public policy and practice and deeper research into the mechanisms causing the impacts.

A Conceptual Model of Role of Co-Production in Service Quality, Efficiency and Effectiveness

In this section, we will explore how co-production can bring about different kinds of benefits and costs to public service organisations and communities. Brandsen and Honingh (this volume, chapter 2) distinguish six categories of citizen input which constitute co-production and co-creation. We explore how the impacts of these can be evaluated, by examining the different ways in which professionals and citizens make better use of each other's assets, resources and contributions to achieve better outcomes or improved efficiency, considering the separate impacts of co-commissioning, co-design, co-delivery and co-assessment of services and of public outcomes.

In Figure 20.1, we show a range of different pathways which link inputs to outcomes. In highly professionalised provision, with low levels of user/community involvement, the link to service outputs and service quality is clear, but it is often less clear how these services impact on outcomes. At the other extreme, individuals or groups can achieve some outcomes for themselves through 'self-help', and not directly through the use of public services (although public services may be providing indirect or 'background' support whose contribution is invisible to them but would become more obvious if it were withdrawn).

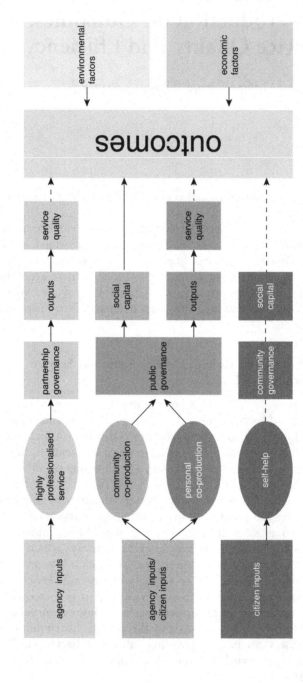

Figure 20.1 Pathways Linking Co-Production Activity to Public Services and Publicly Desired Outcomes

Co-production lies between these two extremes. It may involve service users or communities making increased contributions to public services so that public service organisations can decrease their inputs (for example public sector-led volunteering schemes). This is 'substitutive co-production' from a public sector point of view (Loeffler and Timm-Arnold, 2016), and is distinguished from 'additive co-production', where the public sector increases its inputs to complement those of citizens, for example by supporting care-givers to have respite breaks, which makes their contribution more sustainable in the long-term.

However, co-production does not always involve a public service. A key distinguishing characteristic of co-production as against highly professionalised provision is that, just like self-help, it may be able to make use of the citizen's potential for creating a strong direct impact on outcomes, for example through preventing problems arising in the first place or through behaviour change so that problems are reduced. At least in the short-term, this may require additional resource input of the public sector—for example, to build capacity of service users to co-produce or to undertake other interventions to support behaviour change ('additive co-production' of the public sector). However this means that, in the medium- and long-term, the need for public services may reduce.

Figure 20.1 makes the important distinction between user-led and community-led forms of co-production, showing that their outcome pathways may be rather different. Community-led forms of co-production can be expected to have more impact than individual co-production on collectively experienced pay-offs, such as pride in the local community. They are also more likely to increase the level of social capital, defined here to mean the capacity of a social group or area to act together to achieve an agreed outcome.

While community co-production may be more effective in increasing social capital, it may be more challenging for public service organisations. Specifically, public agencies are likely to have to invest more inputs (staff time, financial resources, facilities) in order to build connections and trust between citizens themselves and also between citizens and public service organisations to undertake effective co-production in groups. Although there is the possibility that individuals who are more involved in user-led co-production may more easily be encouraged to join in community co-production, there is little research on this.

Figure 20.1 also shows that *governance processes* are needed in all pathways, even though the forms of governance may vary. In the case of highly professionalised service provision, 'effective partnership working' is a key issue—this is shown as 'partnership governance'. In the case of both community and user-led co-production, 'public governance' will be needed—in particular, there will be issues around power relationships and accountability which need to be agreed upon. Furthermore, there may be conflicts between personal and publicly desired outcomes, which requires elected politicians to broker interests between multiple stakeholders. In the case of self-help, citizens have to negotiate between themselves who does what in order to achieve the aspired outcomes—we label this 'community governance'.

Evaluating the Effects of Co-Production

We now focus on the effects of co-production on the key variables high-lighted in Figure 20.1. Throughout this analysis, we have to recognise that what is seen as a benefit or a cost of co-production may differ between stakeholders. For example, if increased levels of volunteering in local com-munities enable a local council to reduce the budget for social care while increasing the level of care provided (volunteers may be more flexible than paid staff), this may be welcomed by the politicians but be less popular with care-givers, who are already stretched, and not at all welcomed by front-line staff who have lost their jobs. Therefore, any analysis of costs and benefits of co-production needs to be stakeholder specific.

Increased Outcomes Arising from Co-Production

Public outcomes refer to the achievement of the highest level objectives of public agencies. The outcomes in Figure 20.1 include both the impact from co-produced activities on the personal well-being of individuals or groups of citizens (for example the quality of life of people with disabili-ties) and on more collective outcomes (for example the long-term sustain-ability of the natural environment). Politicians need to balance priorities between these, which is likely to bring them into conflict with some interest groups. Outcomes which are less tangible to citizens, including many collec-tive outcomes, are typically more difficult to measure (especially when they are longer-term) and often harder to link causally to co-produced activities (Bovaird, 2012).

The most dramatic case of increased outcomes, achieved partly (although not solely) through co-production is perhaps the recommissioning of ser-vices for young people by Surrey County Council in 2012. In spite of a 25% budget cut, the number of disadvantaged young people ('NEETs'—people not in employment, education or training) fell by 60% and the number of young people becoming known to the criminal justice system fell by 90% (Tisdall, 2014).

In some cases, the outcome improvements can be given a monetary value, in line with cost-benefit analysis and the social return on invest-ment approach—for example the Speedwatch initiative in Wiltshire County Council involved 765 local residents in 140 volunteer teams in rural areas monitoring motorists' speed with a laser speedgun (with built-in camera) and sending photos of offending cars and speed readings to those driving above the speed limit (Milton, 2011). This resulted in a 35% reduction of fatal and serious injuries from traffic accidents (in Wiltshire compared to a national fall of 22% during this period). Using the values for road accidents saved suggested in HM Treasury (2014), this had a monetary value of £15m. This economic calculus can be taken even further, to estimate the monetary value of quality-adjusted extra years of life ('quality life years' or QALYs) saved by a co-production intervention. The Manchester Community Health Trainers programme in the UK was based on the concept of getting help from neighbours, who have been trained in the skills which can help make a difference to a person's health (Lawson, 2014). A value for money assessment was undertaken in 2011/12 for over 500 clients who progressed through the programme and achieved various lifestyle goals. The assessment tool (the Portsmough Ready Reckoner) indicated that the net cost of the programme was £4784 per QALY, well under the £10,000 threshold which is considered good value for money in behaviour change programmes.

Increased Service Quality from User/Community Involvement

As service users and communities bring in resources, such as expertise and information, not available from professionals, service quality can be improved. Moreover, active involvement of citizens in the service delivery process may change their subjective perceptions of quality. Measuring these perceptual benefits from co-production may require client surveys or in-depth exploration through interviews.

It might therefore be expected that greater user satisfaction would result from co-production (Vamstad, 2012, 310). However, this may only be so when the customer has the expertise necessary to co-create a good or service to his or her liking (Lusch, Brown, and Brunswick, 1992). Indeed, some simple measures of satisfaction may actually decrease where service users are given more responsibility or have to engage with a service in new ways (Horne and Shirley, 2009, 68).

In the context of co-production of private sector goods and services, Haumann et al. (2015), drawing on a large field experiment with customers engaging in actual co-production processes, demonstrate that co-production intensity reduces customers' satisfaction with the co-production process. Further, Bendapudi and Leone (2003, 26) demonstrated in experiments that a customer who participates in production is subject to a self-serving bias (attributing successful outcomes more to his/her inputs and unsuccessful outcomes to other actors or the context). Fledderus (2015) demonstrated a similar effect in experimental research on public services with students. Bendapudi and Leone (2003, 26) also show, however, that this tendency is reduced when a customer can choose whether to participate in production. Thus co-production may reduce satisfaction with a service provider but less markedly when the co-production is freely chosen by the service user.

Furthermore, a service user who believes he or she has the expertise and chooses to co-produce may be more likely to attribute success and failure to his/her own efforts, rather than to the service provider, whereas a service user lacking expertise but feeling forced to co-produce (for example because appropriate advice is not available from service personnel) may be more negative about the effects of co-production on service quality (Bendapudi and Leone, 2003, 26). Finally, service users who can co-create service recovery, where it has failed, may be more satisfied with that recovery (Dong et al., 2008, 132). However, these results have not yet been researched in a public service context.

Increased Service Efficiency Resulting from Reduced Organisational Inputs or Increased Organisational Outputs

In the UK, since the severe austerity policy from 2010, a key criterion for all public sector policies has been cost savings through reduction of agency inputs. One example where this has been achieved is in Stockport Council, where a significant reduction of over £300,000 was achieved in staff costs as a result of an improved website, which was co-designed by service users (Wells, 2010), with costs of just £75,000 (from building an online calculator, providing search functionality for services, undertaking the research with customers and providing staff time).

However, such calculations are often flawed in practice. Typically, only direct costs appearing in agency budgets are recorded accurately and reductions in uncosted agency inputs, for example the time of unpaid Board members, are often ignored. Moreover, most public service organisations do not record how staff time is used and how it is affected by co-production.

Greater efficiency can also be achieved by increasing outputs at little extra cost. For example, the National Library of Finland (NLF) needed to convert millions of pages of old written archive material into digital format for its website. However, optical character recognition software made lots of mistakes which had to be corrected by people, since the human brain beats machines at transcribing hard-to-read text. Using full-time staff for this would be very expensive, so the NLF developed *Digitalkoot*, working with a crowdsourcing company *Microtask*, which used online volunteers to fix the mistakes. In the first 18 months, more than 100,000 volunteers donated over 400,000 minutes and corrected over 7.5m mistakes in the online historical newspaper archive (Miettinen, 2012).

A further reduction in agency inputs, which is given significant weight in the UK evaluation approach, is the reduction in social security benefits which occurs. Similarly, extra income accruing to public agencies is also given significant weight, for example through increases in tax payments or user fees and charges. This is, for example, a critically important benefit from the reduction of NEETs in Surrey County Council. However, these savings in social security benefits and increases in tax payments mainly have the effect of reducing central government expenditure, they are not savings experienced by the local authority. This reduces the incentive to the local authority to seek such savings, since it does not share in all the benefits achieved.

Increased public agency income can arise in other ways, too—for example, where co-production initiatives improve an area so much that house prices and the rents paid to social landlords rise. Social landlords in the area can use the resulting higher rental income for activities which benefit the residents. In two low income neighbourhoods of Birmingham which have pioneered co-production approaches, this 'neighbourhood equity premium' was calculated as nearly £38,000 per property in Balsall Heath and nearly £10,000 per house in Castle Vale (Slatter, 2010, 72).

Reduction in Service User Inputs

Service users also want their time and other resources to be used efficiently. In some cases, therefore, public service providers may increase their inputs in order to make self-help initiatives more efficient, for example, through professionals providing information, training or other support to help caregivers be more efficient and effective. Such cases also need to be evaluated.

An example is given by the town of Arnsberg in Germany, where the Volunteering Agency coordinates respite care by volunteers to support hard-pressed care-givers (Stadt Arnsberg, 2016, 18). Similarly, the Shared Lives project of Age UK is a national alternative to homecare and care home arrangements, where a person with dementia can spend time in the home of another care-giver, so their own care-giver gets a break. Although these are probably examples where the total citizen time involved remains essentially constant, it does mean that the time having to be spent by the priority citizen group, the hard-pressed care-giver, has been reduced by public sector action.

Improvements to Governance Arising from Co-Production

It is important to explore how co-production affects the achievement of key public governance principles, as outcomes are not enough in themselves—'the ends do not justify the means'. Moreover, the 'dark side' of co-roduction could involve dumping on service users, carers and other citizens some of the most difficult tasks of the state, and punishing them where they do not perform as expected (see also Steen, Brandsen and Verschuere in this volume, chapter 21). Although clearly a key area for establishing the impact of co-production, little research has so far been undertaken on this. However, the public governance effects of co-production, including transparency, partnership working, sustainability and honest and fair behaviour, were explored in detail with a range of stakeholders on the Beacon housing estate in Carrick UK (Bovaird and Loeffler, 2007). This study, like most research so far into public governance principles, has been qualitative, as this area does not lend itself easily to quantification.

Increases in Social Capital Arising from Co-Production

Social capital is both a pre-requisite for effective co-production in a community and a well-attested outcome of co-production. This makes it tricky to separate out the effects of co-production activities on the level of social capital. Nevertheless, Slay and Stephens (2013, 10), in a review of the literature on co-production and mental health, concluded that the strongest evidence on outcomes related to improved social networks and inclusion, including stronger relationships with peers, family and friends; a reduced sense of stigma associated with mental health conditions; and a greater sense of belonging to local groups, communities of interests and networks. Evaluations showed that in one project in London (supporting people with stress, anxiety and depression to stay in or get back into work), 90% of participants reported reduced isolation, while 28% of participants in the national Expert Patients Programme made or sustained new friendships.

Identifying the Costs of Co-Production

The costs of co-production are clearly an important offset to its potential benefits. However, this has so far been little researched. The main costs involved for public service organisations include:

- *Increased front-line staff inputs*—both to encourage service users or communities to contribute their time and effort to co-production and to support them in their co-production activities, including time for staff training and 'learning by doing' on how to work effectively with non-professionals (Angelova-Mladenova, 2016). These costs are easier to calculate for those co-production initiatives which are 'add-ons' to existing services, but it is necessary to calculate them also when intensive levels of co-production are embedded within a service.
- *Increased managerial inputs* to embed co-production in the commissioning, procurement and contracting of public services, but also to create a management framework encouraging and supporting co-production (for example agreement of risk management framework, human resources competencies framework with 'co-production friendly forms of staff behaviour', outcomes-based performance management system), and to oversee the operation of more intensified co-production practices. These increased managerial costs may be especially high where increased citizen involvement raises the level of contention of a public sector intervention (Bartenberger and Sześciło, 2015).

- *Increased inputs of local councillors* to engage with local communities in their roles as 'community mobilisers' and 'guardians of public governance'. Although councillors' time is often not costed in public policy evaluations, it has an opportunity cost and should not be ignored.
- *Increased investments in ICT-enabled forms of co-production* (for example assistive technologies, online platforms, databases for time-banking and other social networking). In the nature of ICT solutions, these costs are often front-loaded as one-off capital investment in systems with near zero marginal costs thereafter, as seen in the US Open Government Directive which has seen the launch of health.data.gov and the creation of a new health 2.0 industry (Linders, 2012, 449).
- *Increased investment in public and infrastructure* to allow citizens to make a greater contribution (for example, public and social transport to support the mobility of co-producing citizens who interact with each other, community centres which act as meeting places and 'clearing houses' to match the needs of some citizens with the co-production offers of other citizens) (OECD, 2011; Andrews and Erickson, 2012).

Clearly, evaluations should also explore the costs imposed on service users and communities by co-production, although these have often been ignored:

- *Increased inputs to learn about co-production opportunities* (for example searching for volunteering opportunities, reading newsletters of public service providers, turning up at meetings arranged by public service commissioners and providers) (Batalden et al., 2016).
- *Increased inputs for preparatory and training activities* (for example training citizens who are potential co-producers in risk assessment, in health and safety procedures and in complying with safeguarding procedures for children and older people with whom they may come in contact during the co-production activity) (Asquer, 2014).
- *Increased operational inputs* resulting from more intensive co-production (for example the time which co-producing citizens have to sacrifice or any extra monetary costs which they incur for travel to meetings or food and refreshments during their co-production activities) (Alford, 2002).
- *Increased monetary donations* made by co-producing citizens (for example donations made to crowdfunded initiatives, or donations to nonprofit-organisations which are sponsoring co-production projects) (Davies, 2014; Wessel, 2016).
- *Increased 'psychic' costs* (Etgar, 2008) where co-producing citizens have to make changes to their lifestyle (for example to modify their behaviour and discourse when helping people from different ethnic or religious groups) or build new social relationships (for example when

working with police officers or strangers, in whose company they do not naturally feel comfortable).

However, there are few case studies where these costs have been systematically assessed, so that the overall cost-benefit evaluation for specific co-production initiatives seems to be still very much a seat-of-the-pants judgement, rather than a rational calculation.

Putting it all Together—Pathways to Outcomes

Evaluating all these elements allows us to check if indeed there is an evidence-based pathway to outcomes through co-production activities. Simply checking that increases in co-production activity are correlated with increases in outcomes, or indeed to any of these other effects, does not demonstrate that co-production was the cause of the improvements (Bovaird, 2012). This even applies in double blind randomised placebo controlled trials—if there is no plausible causal chain linking co-production to the benefits achieved, then even such 'gold standard' research results must be regarded with great caution.

The construction and testing of pathways to outcomes is still relatively rare in co-production activities. One very strong example is given by Surrey County Council, which undertook an extensive and participative exercise in developing and testing new pathways for outcomes which would reduce the number of NEETs in Surrey—these pathways allowed the risks involved in this major transformation of the service to be better understood and more carefully managed (Tisdall, 2014).

Conclusion: Issues for Research

Some important conclusions for researchers emerge from this chapter. First, most co-production initiatives have only a fragmentary evidence base—researchers could valuably provide templates for evidence collection in respect of the different types of co-production which they are researching, which would, in return, help to enrich the evidence base for future research.

Second, while the evidence is still sparse, it suggests the potential of co-production is sufficient to justify wider experimentation in public policy and practice. To boost the evidence base, research on co-production should seek to highlight the hypothesised causal chain linking inputs to outputs, service quality, governance principles and outcomes—not only is each of these important in its own right for some key stakeholders but together they make up the overall theory of change. Moreover, research is needed into how the priorities between these benefits are established in the political process and how this might best be influenced by citizens themselves.

Third, evaluation of co-production initiatives should not only compare 'input/outcome' ratios, which are generally unreliable—the hypothesised pathways to outcomes must also be tested to enable learning about WHY some co-production approaches work better than others and to throw light on the risks involved and how they can best be managed by the multiple stakeholders involved.

References

Alford J. (2002). Defining the Client in the Public Sector: A Social-Exchange Perspective. *Public Administration Review*, (62, 3), 337–346.

Andrews, N. O. and Erickson, D. J. (2012). *Investing in What Works for America's Communities*. San Francisco: Federal Reserve Bank of San Francisco.

Angelova-Mladenova, L. (2016). *Study of Co-Production in Services for People with Disabilities*. European Platform for Rehabilitation. http://www.epr.eu/images/EPR/documents/Studies/Co-production_Study_2016/EPR_Co-production_study_2016.pdf

Asquer, A. (2014). The Co-Production of What? Consumption Goods, Investment Goods, and the Delivery of Public Services. https://ssrn.com/abstract=2429435

Bartenberger, M. and Sześciło, D. (2015). The Benefits and Risks of Experimental Co-Production: The Case of Urban Redesign in Vienna. *Public Administration*, (94, 2), 509–525.

Batalden, M., Batalden, P., Margolis, P., Seid, M., Armstrong, G., Opipari-Arrigan, L. and Hartung, H. (2016). Coproduction of Healthcare Service. *BMJ Quality and Safety*, (25, 7), 509–517.

Bendapudi, N. and Leone, R. P. (2003). Psychological Implications of Customer Participation in Co-Production. *Journal of Marketing*, (67), 14–28.

Bovaird, T. (2012). Attributing Outcomes to Social Policy Interventions—'gold standard' or 'fool's gold' in Public Policy and Management? *Social Policy and Administration*, (48, 1), 1–23.

Bovaird, T. and Loeffler, E. (2007). Assessing the Quality of Local Governance: A Case Study of Public Services in Carrick, UK. *Public Money and Management*, (27, 4), 293–300.

Davies, R. (2014). *Civic Crowdfunding: Participatory Communities, Entrepreneurs and the Political Economy of Place*. Cambridge, MA: MIT Press.

Dong, B., Evans, K. R. and Zou, S. (2008). The Effects of Customer Participation in Co-Created Service Recovery. *Journal of the Academy of Marketing Science*, (36), 123–137.

Etgar, M. (2008). A Descriptive Model of the Consumer Co-Production Process. *Journal of the Academy of Marketing Science*, (36, 1), 97–108.

Fledderus, J. (2015). Does User Co-Production of Public Service Delivery Increase Satisfaction and Trust? Evidence from Vignette Experiment. *International Journal of Public Administration*, (38, 9).

Haumann, T., Güntürkün, P., Marie Schons, L. and Wieseke, J. (2015). Engaging Customers in Coproduction Processes: How Value-Enhancing and Intensity-Reducing Communication Strategies Mitigate the Negative Effects of Coproduction Intensity. *Journal of Marketing*, (79, 6), 17–33.

HM Treasury. (2014). *Supporting Public Service Transformation: Cost Benefit Analysis Guidance for Local Partnerships*. London: HM Treasury, Public Service Transformation Network and New Economy.

Horne, M. and Shirley, T. (2009). *Co-Production in Public Services: A New Partnership with Citizens*. London: Cabinet Office.

Lawson, D. (2014). *How Community Health Trainers in Manchester Enable Positive Lifestyle Changes*. Birmingham: Governance International.

Linders, D. (2012). From E-Government to We-Government: Defining a Typology for Citizen Coproduction in the Age of Social Media. *Government Information Quarterly*, (29), 446–454.

Loeffler, E. and Timm-Arnold, P. (2016). Nachhaltige kommunale Haushaltssicherung durch die Koproduktion öffentlicher Wirkungen mit Bürgerinnen und Bürgern? *Management und Verwaltung*, (22, 12), 306–314.

Lusch, R. F., Brown, S. W. and Brunswick, G. (1992) A General Framework for Explaining Internal Versus External Exchange. *Journal of the Academy of Marketing Science*, (20, 2), 119–134.

Miettinen, V. (2012). *Digitising Finnish History Using Crowdsourced Volunteers*. Birmingham: Governance International.

Milton, S. (2011). *Community Speedwatch Scheme in Wiltshire to Reduce Speeding and Empower Residents*. Birmingham: Governance International.

OECD. (2011). *Together for Better Public Services: Partnering with Citizens and Civil Society*. Paris: OECD.

Slatter, P. (2010). *Looking Sideways: A Community Asset Approach to Coproduction of Neighbourhoods and Neighbourhood Services in Birmingham*. Birmingham: Chamberlain Forum and Birmingham City Council.

Slay, J. and Stephens, L. (2013). *Co-Production in Mental Health: A Literature Review*. London: New Economics Foundation.

Stadt Arnsberg. (2016). *Geschäftsstelle Engagement Förderung Arnsberg Eigene Potentiale erkennen und nutzen*. Arnsberg: Stadt Arnsberg.

Tisdall, C. (2014). *The Transformation of Services for Young People in Surrey County Council*. Birmingham: Governance International.

Vamstad, J. (2012). Co-Production and Service Quality: A New Perspective for the Swedish Welfare State. In V. Pestoff, T. Brandsen and B. Verschuere (eds.), *New Public Governance, the Third Sector and Co-Production*. New York: Routledge.

Wells, J. (2010). *Stockport Council's New Adult Social Care Website 'My Care, My Choice': A Business Case for Service Co-Design*. Birmingham: Governance International.

Wessel, F. (2016). Citizen Financial Participation Schemes as Part of New Public Governance. *Zeitschrift für öffentliche und gemeinwirtschaftliche Unternehmen*, (39, 1–2), 53–64.

20.1 Case Study—Amadiba Adventures
Co-Creating Community-Based Tourism

Ntuthuko Mchunu and Francois Theron

Introduction

Even though the South African Government has identified tourism as a key economic sector, due to its potential to contribute to poverty alleviation, employment, growth and equity, the tourism industry has not yielded meaningful benefits for rural communities. Considering that the direct contribution of South Africa's travel and tourism industry to gross domestic product (GDP) in 2015 was 113.4 billion Rand or 3%, while the direct and indirect contribution combined was 357.0 billion Rand or 9.4% (World Travel and Tourism Council Report, 2016), there should be a concern that tourism benefits are more widely distributed. Rural communities should ideally benefit from and participate in the tourism industry, but lack tourism awareness and skills. As a result, established tourism operators and investors have captured the industry and deplete communities' natural and cultural resources without any benefits accruing to the communities themselves. Therefore, there is a need for community beneficiation as a tool that can help alleviate poverty and create jobs.

A member of the Pondo Community Resources Optimisation Programme (PondoCROP), which is a Non-Governmental Organisation (NGO), identified the tourism potential of the Amadiba area. The Amadiba area has assets such as the coastline and houses which can be used for tourists' accommodation. He observed that tourists liked the area, a rural village located on South Africa's Wild Coast in the Eastern Cape Province, which boasts landmarks with scenic beauty, which have beautiful hills, caves, rivers and streams and has its traditions and culture intact (Ntshona and Lahiff, 2003). Based on this experience, he approached PondoCROP with the idea of initiating a community-based tourism project in the area where the community will collectively use their assets to create a unique tourism experience. He wanted to change the livelihoods of the underprivileged Amadiba community by increasing their participation and benefits in tourism. PondoCROP began discussions with the local community, the tribal authority, Reconstruction and Development Programme (RDP) committees and local government officials together with a government small business funding entity.

The discussions led to the formation of a partnership to co-create and co-produce a community-based tourism venture called Amadiba Adventures (Ntshona and Lahiff, 2003).

Background

Amadiba Adventures is a community-based tourism venture that empowers previously disadvantaged communities to play a meaningful role in tourism. It is based on a partnership between the Amadiba community, RDP committees, PondoCROP, Government and a funding entity. In this partnership, each partner contributes to create a unique tourism venture that emphasises local culture and uses it to attract tourists that are interested in learning about their culture and meeting local people. The venture provides scope for the local community to actively participate in planning, implementation, operation and management, thus raising the public value of tourism in the area.

To achieve this partnership, firstly, partners are mobilised to support the venture. This includes explaining the potential benefits that can be derived from the venture and ensuring that community members and the RDP committee agree to invest their resources and assets in the venture, as well as allaying fears of the loss of these assets. Secondly, partners undergo a training programme that specifically focuses on tourism, business management and accounting. Thirdly, partners appoint a Management Committee comprised of members from all partners. This committee is responsible for day to day management, developing policies and ensuring that the venture is locally controlled (Ntshona and Lahiff, 2003).

The venture is created around a variety of community tourism initiatives: a hiking trail, horse riding, that is also used to transport tourists from one bush campsite to the other, accommodation in the form of lodges, organised visits to a traditional healer, canoeing trips, traditional food, cultural dance and storytelling. These initiatives are used to foster community participation and to improve the livelihoods of the poor. The following co-production process is followed:

- The Amadiba local community as individuals or collectively contribute their local knowledge, social capital, labour and provide their assets, i.e. homes, land and horses, to declare a stake in the project and provide tourists with an authentic "African bush experience".
- The NGO acts as an interface between the local community, donors and training providers and coordinates technical support and capacity building.
- The Management Committee ensures the smooth running, allocates responsibilities to partners and ensures local control of the venture.
- A Government's small business funding entity provides funding for operations and training of the local community.
- The tribal authority authorises land usage, approves venture committees and ensures that benefits accrue to the community.

- The public officials advise on legislative frameworks, mobilise private sector funding and investments together with the partners, but the role is limited to that of a facilitator.

In this partnership, the marginalised community is empowered to become skilled and active participants. This enables them to safeguard their interests and use them to transform their livelihoods, thus becoming self-reliant. The venture also ensures that benefits do not only accrue to asset holders but to the wider communities and partners.

Experiences

In the two years of operation, Amadiba Adventures was adopted as a pilot project for the Wild Coast Community Tourism Initiative (WCCTI), a programme that fosters participation of local communities in all aspects of tourism in the north-eastern region of the Eastern Cape. The venture started in one village in which its success attracted funding from the European Union which made it necessary for its replication to the whole Wild Coast region. The European Union made 84 million Rand available to areas around the Wild Coast. A total of 300 community tourism ventures were started and 1,470 jobs were created in the area (Ntshona and Lahiff, 2003).

The venture was identified by the International Union for the Conservation of Nature (IUCN), Fair Trade in Tourism Initiative, as one of the role models for the region, embodying their principles of fair sharing, transparency, sustainability and reliability. In an audit conducted by the South African Department of Environment Affairs and Tourism, Amadiba Adventures was judged the most significant operating community tourism project in South Africa. Amadiba Adventures also won the Community Public Private Partnership, State Presidential award (Ntshona and Lahiff, 2003).

The venture not only added public value by providing employment opportunities and income benefits to asset holders and for the local people but also contributed to community infrastructural projects. A daycare centre (crèche) was built to serve children in the area. The community had one traditional church; however, the project enabled the community to build a new church. Local youths benefited from an innovative asset-based youth empowerment programme created and run by the Friends Uniting for Nature (FUN) Society (Ntshona and Lahiff, 2003).

References

Ntshona, Z. and Lahiff, E. (2003). *Community-Based Eco-Tourism on the Wild Coast, South Africa: The Case of the Amadiba Trail.* Sustainable Livelihoods in Southern Africa Research Paper 7, Brighton: Institute of Development Studies.
World Travel and Tourism Council Report. (2016). *2016 Travel & Tourism Economic Impact-South Africa* [Online], 1. London: World Travel and Tourism Council Report.

21 The Dark Side of Co-Creation and Co-Production

Seven Evils

Trui Steen, Taco Brandsen and Bram Verschuere

Introduction

Co-production could go horribly wrong. Patients could die because of self-administered treatments. Self-appointed vigilantes could "co-produce" public safety by attacking strangers. In co-creating the developments of their neighbourhoods, the highly educated and wealthy may further press their already considerable advantages.

Whether all this will happen is an empirical question. Several literature reviews (e.g. Verschuere et al., 2012; Voorberg, Bekkers and Tummers, 2015) and several chapters in this volume have pointed out that research on effects is the least developed part of research in this area. Nonetheless, the overall literature on co-creation and co-production of public services is optimistic with respect to its presumed effects. Proponents claim that close collaboration between regular service providers and citizens provides opportunities for improving efficiency and quality of public service delivery, and for enhancing democratization and trust in government. Indeed, the terms themselves are skewed towards optimism. "Creation" and "production" are the glittering objectives of economic discourse.

The normative tendency towards optimism tends to mask a number of potential pitfalls. It is this dark side of co-creation and co-production that we address in this chapter. We will address seven potential evils: the deliberate rejection of responsibility, failing accountability, rising transaction costs, loss of democracy, reinforced inequalities, implicit demands and co-destruction. We argue that scholars should fully open up to these possibilities and make them part of the research agenda, because otherwise they risk damaging their own academic credibility.

The Deliberate Rejection of Responsibility

User engagement and calling upon the responsibilities of citizens can be regarded as a means for government to enhance collective action and, as such, address its dependency on citizens in dealing with societal challenges such as demographic change or climate change (Pollitt, 2014). Yet it can also be a cover for minimizing governments' responsibilities and accountability in a context of scarcity of financial resources in the public sector in general, and in social and health care services most specifically. Indeed, financial concerns and pressures for a smaller and more efficient government are assessed as driving forces behind the interest in engaging citizens in the production of public services in the UK's "big society" and "community right to challenge" initiatives (cf. Ishkanian and Szreter, 2012), the Dutch "participatory society" debate (cf. Nederhand and Van Meerbeek, this volume) and similar initiatives in other countries.

Failing Accountability

In addition to deliberate efforts to shed responsibility, co-production and co-creation may inadvertently lead to a lack of clear responsibilities. As the boundaries between public, private and voluntary sectors become blurred (Bovaird, 2007; Joshi and Moore, 2004), there is concern about ensuring supervision of and accountability for quality of public services in the context of co-creation and co-production. The need for clearly outlined roles and responsibilities of the different actors involved in co-creation and co-production of public services is illustrated through the example of sports clubs taking over the management of local sport facilities. Such an initiative may provide opportunity for new services to be initiated—as illustrated by the swimming hours for persons with dementia being organized in a Dutch community. However, it also calls for concern on issues such as delineating the specific responsibilities of government and co-producers, establishing financial processes and accountability and ensuring continuity of service delivery. Brandsen et al. (2016) find that social innovations often remain local and temporary. And while the authors assert that the positive effect of small, temporary initiatives should not be disregarded, this points out the precarious nature also of many co-creation and co-production initiatives. What are the implications, for example, if constant seeking for common aims among the co-producing partners, or a need to continually meet difficulties in the collaboration leads to "partnership fatigue" (cf. Huxham and Vangen, 2005) and makes one of the co-producing partners decide to decrease their engagement?

A similar problem may arise at the individual level. If clients co-design and co-produce a service, and the service subsequently fails, it is less clear who is ultimately responsible. For instance, if patients carry out part of their own treatment, are they solely responsible for failures? Or do doctors retain responsibility, despite the fact that they have less influence on the outcome? Blurred responsibilities may make it harder to litigate against failing professionals. Alternatively, the threat of litigation may make professionals wary of engaging patients in co-production.

Rising Transaction Costs

There are hidden costs associated with involving citizens. A wider objection against collaborative governance is that it comes with high transaction costs, including process costs related to the information asymmetries between actors, information seeking and sharing; *implementation costs* related to changed response capacity to others' concerns and needs; and *costs associated with participant behaviour* including, for example, accounting for non-participants or dealing with different viewpoints of actors, adverse reactions and delays (Agranoff, 2016, 94, based on Weber, 1998). Of course, this also applies to co-creation and co-production. Meetings and consultations without added value may seem like victimless crimes, but they draw resources from service provision that can only be compensated for by significant improvement in the quality of the services.

Loss of Democracy

Co-production is usually seen as a tool to reinvigorate democracy. Yet there are also grounds for seeing it as a potential threat to democracy. According to Bovaird (2007, 856), the redistribution of power among stakeholders that comes along with co-production "calls into question the balance of representative democracy, participative democracy, and professional expertise". Leach (2006) presents a normative framework consisting of seven democratic ideals to assess collaborations: (1) inclusiveness, or openness to all who wish to participate; (2) representativeness, ensuring that the interests of all stakeholders are effectively advocated; (3) impartiality, or all parties being treated equally; (4) transparency, or clear and public rules governing the process; (5) deliberativeness, allowing participants to brainstorm, critically examine each other's arguments, identify common interests and build a base of shared knowledge and social capital; (6) lawfulness, upholding all existing statutes and regulations and (7) empowerment, enabling participants to influence policy outcomes. His empirical assessment of the democratic merits of collaborative watershed management as practiced in two US states shows diverging results across these indicators, with strong deliberativeness but weak representativeness of the partnerships studied. Yet, he acknowledges that by judging collaborative processes against a set of abstract democratic ideals, he arguably "holds collaborative management to a higher standard than is typically applied to traditional forms of public administration (. . .). Neither this study nor many others that I know of can confirm whether collaborative public management is generally more or less democratic than its alternatives" (Leach, 2006, 108). In order words, holding high expectations of the democratic level of service delivery through co-production might imply that we tend to be overly critical, especially when compared to the expectations held of non–co-produced forms of public service delivery. However, the reverse is also possible: institutionalizing involvement of users paradoxically may prevent them from taking a critical stance (cf. Salamon, 2002; Ishkanian, 2014).

Reinforced Inequalities

Co-creation and co-production challenge the relative power positions of government, civil society and citizens. The usual assumption is that this will help to level power imbalances and make co-producers equal partners in the co-production process. However, in practice, unequal power positions—in terms of formal position, knowledge, expertise, resources or ability to set the rules of the co-production game—will pose barriers for partnership and affect the collaboration. It may indeed allow stronger parties to exercise power over or increase the dependency of weaker parties (cf. Agranoff, 2016). While at first sight, co-creation and co-production strengthen the role of non-government actors, they may do the opposite. Ishkanian (2014, 335), for example, argues that due to diminished funding availability and challenged working conditions, they might instead be "creating a situation where the independence and ability of civil society organizations to engage in progressive policy making is weakened".

The same may occur at the individual level. Some studies have argued that co-production lowers the bar for citizens to participate and that it encourages a representative mix of participants (Clark, Brudney and Jang, 2013; Alford and Yates, 2016; Bovaird and Loeffler, 2015). Yet wealthy and highly educated citizens may come to dominate such processes, as is often the case with classical types of participation, because of their superior social and cultural capital. Research focused on motivations of citizens to co-produce (e.g. van Eijk and Steen, 2014; van Eijk, Steen and Verschuere, 2017) shows that not only willingness, but also feeling capable to co-produce, explains engagement in co-production. Dodge (2012) finds that public organizations tend to increase requirements regarding expertise and technical knowledge needed in order to be allowed to participate. This kind of "professionalization" is a threat to the democratic character of user co-production.

This raises the questions how equal access to services and equal treatment are ensured, and how the interests of service users, their families, people living in the neighbourhood and other stakeholders are protected. Since (individual) co-production tends to personalize services, it runs the danger of preventing more collective approaches and increasing existing inequalities. Hastings (2009), for example, found that residents of better off neighbourhoods tend to benefit more from co-production than residents of deprived neighbourhoods, further increasing their socio-economic inequality. Brandsen and Helderman (2012) discuss the case of German housing cooperatives who on paper are welcoming anyone to join at a relatively low cost, while in reality they are rather closed systems that are built around existing groups. Such insider/outsider dynamics may result in co-produced services accessible to specific social groups only. This issue of inclusiveness of the participative process implies a need for investment on the part of (local) government in co-production, and proactivity of public officials to ensure an equitable co-production process. An example is provided by Vanleene and Verschuere (case study in this volume, chapter 18.2), who discuss a co-production initiative in the Rabot neighbourhood in the city of Ghent. Here citizens with a diverse background collaborate in running a social restaurant or keeping community gardens, but continuous efforts are needed from community building professionals in motivating and supporting these actors.

No matter what the public organization involved might set as its mission and regulations, individual professionals at street level will need to cope with pressures and uncertainties, and will be influenced by actual needs of individual co-producers, resulting in diverging on-the-ground implementation of public policies (e.g., Maynard-Moody and Musheno, 2000). There is a clear paradox here, as "the professional has to be prepared to trust the decisions and behaviors of service users (. . .) rather than dictate them" (Bovaird, 2007, 856), yet in practice "outcomes of self-organising processes around co-production are not always socially desirable" (Bovaird, 2007, 857). Even if no explicit misuse by co-producers for their personal benefit is at hand, the potential tension between private and public value means that professionals cannot simply use co-producers' opinion as an indication of what is preferred by all clients of the delivered services (De Vries, 2010) nor of the community at large.

Implicit Demands

Depending on the service concerned and in contrast to engagement in deliberative democracy, it might not be the better-off members of the community but rather the less well-off who in fact collaborate in the production of public services. Birchall and Simmons (2004, 2), for example, found that user participation in housing and social care was mainly by persons on low incomes, who often were motivated to participate "through a concern about certain issues, such as poor quality of service, or 'putting something back in' for the service they have received". Non-take up literature argues that feelings of indebtedness towards the helper may inhibit people from help-seeking. Co-production can then can be a valuable way to ensure equality and feelings of reciprocity in the relation between the helper and the service recipient (Reijnders et al., 2016). Recently in Flanders (Belgium), a food bank closed because clients were found to be "too picky and ungrateful". Comprehending people's psychological needs such as need for reciprocity and self-determination helps us to understand the dynamics at hand, and shows that community led social groceries may have a more promising future. In contrast to food banks where pre-prepared food packages are provided for free, in social groceries people in a vulnerable situation (for example poverty, homelessness) pay small fees for products they can pick out themselves, and additionally they can also contribute by acting as volunteer.

Yet at the same time, McMullin and Needham (this volume) point out that a "pay back" principle might put pressure on vulnerable service users to participate in order for them to be able to claim service provision and quality. Thus not only who is included and who is excluded in co-production, but also why citizens should have to participate (Bovaird, 2007, 856) are of concern, especially as Western welfare systems seem to shift from supporting collective solidarity towards focusing on individual responsibility (see also Nederhand and Van Meerbeek, this volume).

Co-Destruction of Public Value

Based on a review of literature on co-creation and co-production of public services, Voorberg et al. (2015, 1345–1346) conclude that while little research systematically studies the outcomes of co-creation or co-production, the research on this topic that is available focuses mainly on effectiveness. As it shows mixed results, they state that "we cannot definitely conclude whether co-creation/co-production can be considered as beneficial" (2015, 1346). Co-creation and co-production are often referred to as central in addressing current societal challenges. Yet, as pointed out by Larsson and Brandsen (2016, 299), who discuss the dark side of social innovations, wicked problems do not have easy solutions. Thus common sense should prevail as to the potential of such innovations, including also closer collaboration with service users. Moreover, while Osborne, Strokosch and Radnor (in this volume, chapter 3) focus on the relationship between co-production and the creation of value through public service delivery, they point out that interaction between regular service providers and service users "has the potential to lead to the co-destruction of value as much as to its co-creation". Williams, Kang and Johnson (2016) use the concept of "co-contamination" to denote such co-destruction. They refer to the example of a healthy public housing project where inequitable partnerships and low trust between professionals and residents lead to missed opportunities to improve living conditions.

The same authors point out that co-destruction of value may go beyond mere missed opportunities. Co-producers may go as far as to misuse their role, as shown in the example of a neighbourhood watchman shooting an unarmed teenager in a gated community (Williams, Kang and Johnson, 2016). Similarly, Brandsen et al. (2016, 307) point out a risk for value destruction: social innovations may "represent cultural, economic and social aims and practices that are highly controversial or even seen by many as threatening rather than promising". Apps and social media generate personal information that may allow (self-)control of health and performance, for example enabling elderly persons to co-produce their health and social care, allowing them to (longer) live at home. However, this also risks government or private actors abusing data for their own purposes (cf. Brandsen et al., 2016). Scholars such as Bouchard (2016) or Bherer (2010), studying citizen deliberation, in turn refer to the potential misuse or manipulation of user input by government officials for their own ends, for example by manufacturing support for their own policy agenda. They call for "more critical assessments of participative exercises to deepen our understanding of when and why they may be manipulated for less democratic ends" (Bouchard, 2016, 516).

Also, if co-creation and co-production processes fail to meet inflated expectations, they risk increasing rather than diminishing distrust (cf. Fledderus, 2015). Scholars themselves may be responsible for creating these inflated expectations.

Conclusion: Avoiding Evils by Looking them in the Eye

Few have explicitly addressed these potential evils of co-creation and co-production. Not only are co-creation and co-production seen as instrumental tools for enhancing the quality and democratic quality of public service delivery, they are often regarded as a virtue in themselves. This implies that even if outcomes such as increased efficiency or effectiveness of public services are lacking or remain unproven, co-creation and co-production are still seen as holding a positive value in themselves (cf. Voorberg et al., 2015, 1346). This is dangerous. If research is or comes to be seen as biased, it will lose its credibility among academic colleagues and mislead the professionals and policymakers who are willing to experiment with these new approaches. As noted in the introductory chapter, the agenda-setting phase of co-production research, with its emphasis on best practices, is over.

Fortunately, recent research has started to address potential paradoxes related to co-production. This is illustrated not only in this chapter, but throughout this volume where different authors address "the dark side" of co-creation and co-production initiatives. Examples of things going bad referred to in this volume include co-creation and co-production being co-opted by government to limit the scope for collective approaches (McMullin and Needham in this volume, chapter 12) and to push forwards its financial cutback agenda (Nederhand and Van Meerkerk in this volume, chapter 4.1). Mangai, De Vries and De Kruif's example (this volume) of co-production inducing substitution of paid professional work by unpaid labour in the health care sector in developing countries must raise questions of exploitation. Other concerns relate to outcomes of co-production, such as parental involvement in education potentially enhancing cultural and social reproduction (Honingh and Brandsen in this volume, chapter 13).

Delving further into potential pitfalls of co-creation and co-production is needed. At present, when empirical data is available on the dark side of co-creation and co-production, this data tends to pertain to the study of specific cases of co-production, limiting the generalizability of findings. Yet gaining insight into the dark side of co-creation and co-production may help us learn from failure. As our discussion already shows, in order to avoid pitfalls, co-creation and co-production need real investment of time and money by government, but also an openness to comprehend the concerns of different actors involved. In sum, assessing the dark side forces us to pose more critical questions when looking into the practice of co-creation and co-production, including questions such as:

- Who is in, and who is out?;
- Who benefits, and who loses?;
- How is power redistributed?;
- What were stakeholders' goals, was there consensus over these goals, have goals been met and, if so, whose goals?;
- Which services are scaled up, and which are slimmed down?; and
- Who can service users or other stakeholders keep accountable for lacking or inadequate services?

References

Agranoff, R. (2016). The Other Side of Managing in Networks. In R. D. Margerum and C. J. Robinson (eds.), *The Challenges of Collaboration in Environmental Governance*, 81–107. Cheltenham: Edward Elgar.

Alford, J. and Yates, S. (2016). Co-Production of Public Services in Australia: The Roles of Government Organisations and Co-Producers. *Australian Journal of Public Administration*, (75, 2), 159–175.

Bherer, L. (2010). Successful and Unsuccessful Participatory Arrangements: Why Is There a Participatory Movement at the Local Level? *Journal of Urban Affairs*, (32, 3), 287–303.

Birchall, J. and Simmons, R. (2004). User Power: The Participation of Users in Public Services. Report prepared for the National Consumer Council. https://dspace.stir.ac.uk/bitstream/1893/3261/1/NCC071ft_user_power.pdf

Bouchard, N. (2016) The Dark Side of Public Participation: Participative Processes that Legitimize Elected Officials' Values. *Canadian Public Administration*, (59, 4), 516–537.

Bovaird, T. (2007). Beyond Engagement and Participation: User and Community Coproduction of Public Services. *Public Administration Review*, (67, 5), 846–860.

Bovaird, T., Van Ryzin, G. G., Loeffler, E. and Parrado, S. (2015). Activating Citizens to Participate in Collective Co-Production of Public Services. *Journal of Social Policy*, (44), 1–23.

Brandsen, T., Evers, A., Cattacin, S. and Zimmer, A. (2016). The Good, the Bad and the Ugly in Social Innovation. In T. Brandsen, S. Cattacin, A. Evers, A. Zimmer (eds.), *Social Innovations in the Urban Context*, 303–310. New York, Dordrecht, London: Springer Cham Heidelberg.

Brandsen, T. and Helderman, J.-K. (2012). The Trade-Off Between Capital and Community: The Conditions for Successful Co-production in Housing. *Voluntas*, (23, 4), 1139–1155.

Clark, B., Brudney, J. and Jang, S-G. (2013). Coproduction of Government Services and the New Information Technology: Investigating the Distributional Biases. *Public Administration review*, (73, 5), 687–701.

De Vries, P. (2010). *Handboek Ouders in de School*. Amersfoort: CPS.

Dodge, J. (2012). Addressing Democratic and Citizenship Deficits: Lessons from Civil Society? *Public Administration Review*, (73, 1), 203–206.

Fledderus, J. (2015). *User Co-Production of Public Service Delivery*. Nijmegen: Radboud University.

Hastings, A. (2009). Neighbourhood Environmental Services and Neighbourhood 'Effects'. *Housing Studies*, (24, 4), 503–524.

Huxham, C. and Vangen, S. (2005). *Managing to Collaborate: The Theory and Practice of Collaborative Advantage*. London: Routledge.

Ishkanian, A. (2014). Neoliberalism and Violence: The Big Society and the Changing Politics of Domestic Violence in England. *Critical Social Policy*, (34, 3), 333–353.

Ishkanian, A. and Szreter, S. (eds.). (2012). *The Big Society Debate. A New Agenda for Social Welfare?* Cheltenham: Edward Elgar Publishing Limited.

Joshi, A. and Moore, M. (2004). Institutionalised Co-Production: Unorthodox Public Service Delivery in Challenging Environments. *Journal of Development Studies*, (40, 4), 31–49.

Larsson, O. S. and Brandsen, T. (2016). The Implicit Normative Assumptions of Social innovation research: Embracing the Dark Side. In T. Brandsen, S. Cattacin, A. Evers, and A. Zimmer (eds.), *Social Innovations in the Urban Context*, 293–302. Springer.

Leach, W. (2006). Collaborative Public Management and Democracy: Evidence from Western Watershed Partnerships. *Public Administration Review*, (66, s1), 100–110.

Maynard-Moody, S. and Musheno, M. (2000). State Agent or Citizen Agent: Two Narratives of Discretion. *Journal of Public Administration Research and Theory*, (10, 2), 329–358.

Pollitt, C. (2014). *Future Trends in European Public Administration and Management*. COCOPS.

Reijnders, M., Schalk, J. and Steen, T. (2016). *Services Wanted? Understanding the Non-Take-Up of Informal Support at the Local Level*. Paper for the EGPA Conference, Utrecht.

Salamon, L. M. (2002). The New Governance and the Tools of Public Action: An Introduction. In L. M. Salamon (ed.), *The Tools of Government. A Guide to the New Governance*, 1–47. Oxford and New York: Oxford University Press.

van Eijk, C. and Steen, T. (2014). Why People Co-Produce: Analyzing Citizens' Perceptions on Co-Planning Engagement in Health Care Services. *Public Management Review*, (16), 358–382.

van Eijk, C., Steen, T. and Verschuere, B. (2017). Co-Producing Safety in the Local Community: A Q-Methodology Study on the Incentives of Belgian and Dutch Members of Neighbourhood Watch Schemes. *Local Government Studies*, (43, 3), 323–343.

Verschuere, B., Brandsen, T. and Pestoff, V. (2012). Co-Production: The State of the Art in Research and the Future Agenda. *Voluntas*, (23, 4), 1–19.

Voorberg, W., Bekkers, V. and Tummers, L. (2015). A Systemic Review of Co-Creation and Co-Production: Embarking on the Social Innovation Journey. *Public Management Review*, (17, 9), 1333–1357.

Weber, E. P. (1998). *Pluralism by the Rules: Conflict and Cooperation in Environmental Regulation*. Washington, DC: Georgetown University Press.

Williams, B. N., Kang, S-C. and Johnson, J. (2016). (Co)-Contamination as the Dark Side of Co-Production: Public Value Failures in Co-Production Processes. *Public Management Review*, (18, 5), 692–717.

21.1 Case Study—Experts-by-Experience in Finnish Social Welfare

Taina Meriluoto

Introduction

Finland—a Nordic welfare state with a history of strong public service provision and tight collaborative ties with the public and the third sector—adopted a strong participatory emphasis in its public governance outlines when entering the 21st century (see Salminen and Wilhelmsson, 2013). The co-governance ethos was presented as an answer to both the increasing political apathy and the consequent 'legitimacy crisis' of the state, as well as the rising costs of the public services. Tighter collaboration between the citizens, the third, and the public sectors was thought to create both more active citizens, as well as more efficient services.

Resulting from this participatory norm, public and third sector social welfare organisations were tasked with finding 'new and innovative ways' to include citizens in the design and production of social services. One of the most popular innovations was a new concept of *expertise-by-experience*. Drawing on examples from the UK and Denmark, mental health NGOs started to recruit former service users as new 'experts', performing varying co-creation and co-production tasks in social services. The concept and practice was fast disseminated to other areas of social welfare and health care, and to both public sector organisations and NGOs (see Rissanen, 2015). As it stands, the incorporation of expertise-by-experience has become somewhat of a marker for adhering to the norm of participatory governance in social welfare and health care. However, its effects remain ambiguous, with service users also reporting experiences of co-optation over true possibilities of influence in co-creating and co-producing services.

Background

Expertise-by-experience is a practice that has been employed and developed in projects carried out by both NGOs and public sector organisations. The projects have advanced co-production on two levels: they have sought to co-create and co-produce the organisations' own activities, transforming the organisations' own culture to become more 'inclusive and participatory', and to create a 'bank' of experience-based experts who can be used by other organisations in their efforts of co-production and co-creation.

The projects have varying expectations towards co-production. Expertise-by-experience is presented as a means towards cheaper and better-functioning services, more legitimate governance as well as 'empowered' participants. Depending on which goal is emphasised, different interpretations of co-production and co-creation are translated into practice. The type of activities in the initiatives can be categorised (applying the typology of Brandsen and Honingh in this volume, chapter 2), as follows:

1) *Co-creation of the organisation's core services.* Experts-by-experience partaking in service design workshops to develop the organisation's everyday work.
2) *Co-production of the organisation's core services.* Experts-by-experience producing services alongside trained professionals, e.g. in peer support groups, or having their own appointment hours in health clinics.
3) *Co-creation of other organisations' core services.* Experts-by-experience 'ordered' from projects that train experts-by-experience to provide local knowledge to service development committees elsewhere, e.g. an NGO-trained expert-by-experience included as a service user representative in public service development.
4) *Co-production of other organisations' core services.* Experts-by-experience invited to train social welfare practitioners to 'develop' their working methods, or to assess public services through various means of 'service user research' and feedback committees.

Experiences

The plethora of possible forms and aims of co-production and co-creation, placed under the title of expertise-by-experience, has caused heated debate concerning what 'the correct form' of expertise-by-experience is. Particularly strong views have been presented regarding who should be allowed to participate as an expert-by-experience, whether or not they should be trained, and furthermore, paid for their efforts. The proponents of training—and hence of selecting the experts-by-experience—argue that the professionals have the responsibility to evaluate when an expert-by-experience is 'ready' for their tasks of co-production and co-creation. The critique, in turn, suggests that such evaluation could result in cherry picking from the organisations' point of view, and in only including those voices that comply with the organisations' pre-existing views.

Furthermore, the ambiguity and inexplicit nature of the projects' goals has resulted in disappointment among some experts-by-experience. It appears that the service users, the practitioners, and the administration quite frequently have different, or even contradicting expectations for co-production. While the service users often get involved in order to gain recognition for the experiences they have experienced as harmful, and to present criticism and 'contrasting points of view' to service development, they feel their criticism is often silenced through strict conditions set for their participation. For example, emotion-filled speech is often deemed a sign of instability, and consequently labelled as unfitting for a setting of co-production, set to be carried out in partnership among neutral experts (see Meriluoto, 2017). The administration's definitions for 'usable knowledge' prioritise technocratic expertise and, contrarily to the inclusive rhetoric, can be used to devalue individual points of view.

The experiences of experts-by-experience show how co-production schemes have a potential to select their participants by delineating what kind of contributions are 'useful', and what type of knowledge is 'credible'. These initiatives tend to depart from the administration's objectives, and value co-production practices first of all because of their outputs, rather than as the participants' right to be included. The output-focused approach can be used to derail some service users' critical voices. ·It can also de-politicise social disputes, as the issues tackled are presented in the realm of technocratic governance, where best decisions are reached not through opinion-based debate but through information-based management.

References

Meriluoto, T. (2017). Turning Experience into Expertise: Technologies of the Self in Finnish Participatory Social Policy. *Critical Policy Studies*, [online first]. doi:10. 1080/19460171.2017.1310051.

Rissanen, P. (2015). *Toivoton tapaus? Autoetnografia sairastumisesta ja kuntoutumisesta. [A Hopeless Case? An Autoethnography of Getting Mentally Ill and Rehabilitation of It]*. Helsinki: Kuntoutussäätiö.

Salminen, O. and Wilhelmsson, N. (2013). *Valtioneuvoston demokratiapolitiikka 2002–2013. Katsaus ministeriön demokratiapolitiikan toteutuksiin* [The Democracy Policy of the Finnish Government 2002–2013. An Overview on the Implementation of Democracy Policy]. Oikeusministeriö: Selvityksiä ja ohjeita 52/2013.

Part 5
Concluding Chapter

22 How to Encourage Co-Creation and Co-Production

Some Recommendations

Taco Brandsen, Trui Steen
and Bram Verschuere

This book has given the most comprehensive review of co-production research to date. Here, in this final chapter, we would like to share practical recommendations that emerge from this overview of the state of the art. The chapter was compiled with the help of all authors in the volume, for which we are grateful.

The Potential of Co-Production and Co-Creation Appears Sufficient to Justify Wider Experimentation in Public Policy and Practice

On the one hand, there is insufficient evidence to make hard claims of any sort on these approaches. On the other hand, the existing research does suggest a range of potential benefits of co-production and co-creation, for which some evidence is beginning to build. The most extensive evidence comes from a small range of countries like the UK, where there is regular public service evaluation, but there is now a broader range of international studies available. This also concerns the dark side of co-production—for instance, when citizens as co-producers of safety fail to respect that the state has the monopoly on the use of physical force. Since legal frameworks and traditions of citizen participation and the level of citizens' initiatives vary between countries, the policy opportunities for co-production and co-creation also vary. Policy experimentation is crucial to achieve a better understanding of the pathways to outcomes, and by implication which co-production and co-creation initiatives are likely to work, and which not.

Experiments in Co-Production and Co-Creation Should have Clearly Limited and Explicitly Defined Expectations

The evidence from different fields suggests that, when experimenting, it is important to manage expectations carefully. For a start, there is the risk of pinning too many hopes on the concept. Theoretically there is much that co-production initiatives could help attain: reach better outcomes, outputs, service quality, greater efficiency, inclusiveness and empowerment. However, attempts to achieve all of these simultaneously undermine strategic focus. In that respect, policymakers need to clearly identify their strategic priorities.

Differences in the Public Administration Regime Should be Taken into Account when Defining Expectations

Co-creation and co-production take place in different public administration regimes, varying by country and domain. This not only changes how co-production and co-creation function in practice, but changes their very meaning. This is most evident in views on the role played by the citizens receiving or benefitting from such services, as well as the professionals or paid staff in guaranteeing the quality of public services. Citizens can be considered beneficiaries of services, consumers, co-producers or service providers; professionals as supervisors, competitors, collaborators or back-up agents. Careful calibration of policy expectations will help avoid unrealistic or unattainable goals in public policy; by contrast, less consideration of fundamental differences in user and professional behaviour in different contexts will often result in failure to enlist sufficient citizen participation. It also means that performance measurement should focus on dimensions of chosen values, rather than (just) simple outputs or outcomes.

Policymakers Must be Pro-Active in Developing the Potential for Digital Co-Production

Increasing digitization of society, computing power and data analytical capabilities provide the public sector with new opportunities for digital co-production. However, instead of simply reacting to external technological changes, the public sector needs to proactively develop a new set of technological capacities to explore, develop and/or adapt new technological solutions in designing and producing public services. For that to happen, governments should not only employ more people with digital and community involvement skills, but they should also create room for experimentation, debate and learning across the sectors.

In this, policymakers need to find a good balance between top-down and bottom-up approaches to digital co-production. Applying top-down technological solutions may enable more efficient co-production, yet it also structures and constrains active participation of citizens and increasingly creates algorithmic 'black-boxes' with limited control left for citizens over the decision-making rules. Policymakers should, thus, whenever possible aim at using truly co-creative practices in developing and applying digital technologies in co-production.

Service Providers and Citizens Should be Involved in the Process of Designing Experiments

More generally, co-creating experiments is likely to improve their effectiveness. Policy experiments should be based on an understanding of public services as 'services' and translated into policy that recognises the true nature of the delivery process, rather than try to force them into inappropriate product-dominant forms. In other words, they should recognise co-production and co-creation for what they are and put citizens at the heart of the delivery process. This is best done by involving service providers and citizens from the start, for instance, through a co-commissioning process. For instance, schools and parents should be encouraged to reflect jointly on the idea of parental co-production and in particular on the question of how the role of parents (in and around schools) is related to the school's didactic model. Patients in hospitals could be involved as 'experts by experience'—both at the individual level in relation to their own care, but also at the group and collective level, in helping to inform treatment programmes and strategic planning of healthcare budgets and hospital governance.

The Potential Benefits of Co-Creation and Co-Production Should be Clearly Communicated to Citizens

Users of services are more likely to engage when they can see the advantage of doing so. Policies that elicit the co-production or co-creation of public services will not automatically foster trust of citizens in service delivery and in (local) government. When designing and implementing co-production, attention can be paid to trust-building conditions, such as considering the motivations and capabilities of users to co-produce. This way, incentives that match motivations can be designed, possible risks can be discussed and mitigated, and the discretionary space of professionals and users can be specified. For instance, it could be shown how co-producing energy, water and waste services may improve the management of common pool resources. Alternatively, personal attention and the physical presence of public service staff, though often costly, may be most effective in encouraging citizens to engage.

Incentives Should be Tailored to Specific Types or Groups of Citizens

Influencing citizens' personal motivations is a complex task, due to their often highly individual nature. Co-producers are no unitary group. As a result, the design of the co-production process should be 'customised' to different groups of co-producers and should take into account the specific context where co-creation and co-production take place. For instance, in working with patients in healthcare, it is recommended to take an asset-based approach, rather than one that highlights deficits and impairments. Likewise, for each type of group, a tailored approach will work best.

However, such targeting should not lead to overemphasis on any particular group at the exclusion of others. For instance, programmes in support of parental co-production in primary education tend to be aimed only at specific types of families and especially at children who underperform in schools. This underplays the potential benefits of co-production as a general approach, as a change of attitude towards all families.

Co-Production Experiments Should be Accompanied by Tailored Training Strategies for Professionals

The support of professionals is essential for achieving effective results, especially in co-production. Their motivation to co-produce with citizens can be enhanced by creating incentives, supporting performance management and overall organisational support. They may need new skills to be able to navigate between the different values and views, and to integrate the different viewpoints in the best possible way for creating public value. However, the needs for training and development to encourage co-production will differ per domain. The rationalities underpinning performance management, accountability, leadership and strategy are sometimes more conducive to fostering collaboration with citizens than in others. It is impossible to recommend one catch-all strategy. That is why the need for training should be explicitly included in the initial design.

Index

Printed in the United States
by Baker & Taylor Publisher Services